TRANSITIONAL ECONOMIC SYSTEMS

The Polish-Czech Example

INTERNATIONAL LIBRARY OF SOCIOLOGY AND SOCIAL RECONSTRUCTION

Founded by Karl Mannheim

Editor: W. J. H. Sprott

A catalogue of the books available in the INTERNATIONAL LIBRARY OF SOCIOLOGY AND SOCIAL RECONSTRUCTION, and new books in preparation for the Library will be found at the end of this volume.

TRANSITIONAL ECONOMIC SYSTEMS

The Polish-Czech Example

by

DOROTHY W. DOUGLAS

ROUTLEDGE & KEGAN PAUL LTD
Broadway House, 68–74 Carter Lane
London

First published in 1953
by Routledge & Kegan Paul Ltd.
Broadway House, 68–74 Carter Lane
London E.C.4
Printed in Great Britain
by Latimer, Trend & Co. Ltd.
Plymouth

CONTENTS

INTRODUCTION *page* 1

I. U.S.S.R. INFLUENCES 5

Part I. Bases of Change: Poland 13

II. WAR AND PRE-WAR HERITAGE 15
1. The Pre-War Economy 15
2. War Heritage 22
3. The Western Territories 33

III. EARLY RECONSTRUCTION 44
1. Political Beginnings 44
2. Land Reform and Nationalization. The Early 'Three Sectors' View 49
3. The Three-Year Plan 57

Part II. Bases of Change: Czechoslovakia 69

IV. INDUSTRIALIZED CZECHOSLOVAKIA 71

V. REFORMS AND REVOLUTIONS 80
1. Land Reform and Nationalization, First and Second Stages 80
2. Nationality Question: Slovakia 90

VI. TWO- AND FIVE-YEAR PLANS: CHANGING OBJECTIVES 100

Part III. The Common Pattern 113

VII. PLANNING METHODS AND THE GROWTH OF CONTROL 115
1. Polish Experience: The Area of Control 115
2. Czechoslovakia: Coalition Planning? 119
3. Later Developments in Planning 127

VIII. SOCIALIST BANKING, SERVANT OF THE PLAN 143

IX. THE STRUCTURE OF NATIONALIZED INDUSTRY *page* 154

X. A CASE STUDY IN NATIONALIZED INDUSTRY: THE BAT'A-SVIT CONCERN 176

XI. LABOUR AND PRODUCTION 197
1. The Trade Union Movements 197
2. Wage and Output Problems 207
3. The Labour Market 225

XII. LABOUR AND SOCIAL SECURITY 235
1. Labour Amenities 237
2. Social Insurance Systems 253

XIII. THE REORGANIZATION OF AGRICULTURE 257

XIV. INTER-STATE ECONOMIC RELATIONS 290

Part IV. 'Transition to . . . Socialism' 315

XV. DISSOLVING THE PRIVATE SECTOR 317
1. Industry and Handicraft 324
2. Growth of Socialized Trade 328
3. The Co-operative Movement in Transition 332

XVI. 'SOCIALIST INDUSTRIALIZATION' 358

INDEX 369

INTRODUCTION

With the ending of the war in eastern Europe a series of new governments came to power calling themselves 'Popular Democracies'. They differed from the Soviet Union, in the wake of whose Red Army they had sprung up, in including at first a wide range of political parties, only the pre-war rightists being excluded, and in permitting small private enterprise. And they differed far more sharply from such countries as Sweden, and Britain while under the Labour Government, in the sweep of their nationalization and land reform practices and the scope and authority of their planning. This difference is characteristic and unmistakable from the outset. For some time, however, it was not clear how rapid their march to further socialization would be. There was much talk in Western circles of the hope of their reversing their trend. There is also considerable evidence that within the countries the leadership of the left-most elements at that time, the Communist parties, exerted a restraining influence upon their members and others to hold back from exploiting the revolutionary possibilities of the situation. Their argument was that an unprecedentedly peaceful and exceedingly gradual transition to socialism was now possible, owing to changed world conditions.

The new picture was held to be rational because of the changed relations of power internationally as well as nationally, with these countries safely within the orbit of the Soviet Union. Germany was defeated, and a new era of tolerance and possible co-operation between the Soviet Union and the Western powers had begun. Hence native small business groups, with their big leaders gone, might adapt themselves to the new régime, once it was clear they had no powerful outside help to look to. Similarly with the larger farmers. Now that the actual landed estates were gone, differences in interest between them and the new receivers of small holdings could be managed. Ultimately, of course, the small farmer would see the need of co-operative forms of agriculture, but that problem could be left to the future. Meanwhile an indefinitely long era of small-scale private farming was looked forward to, with the government doing its utmost to make it productive.

During 1948 these policies changed radically, in conformity with the worsening international situation. The Communist parties now moved to the forefront of a radical programme in each country. Previous leaders who had been the most marked in their expounding of the peaceful absorption of former opposition classes were now discredited. Changes were not ascribed in so many words to the deterioration in the international picture, but emphasis was laid upon what was called the sabotage of the private business groups and their parties within the various countries who, obviously, had been given hopes of their own by it. All capitalist elements were to be mistrusted and to be eliminated from all branches of the economy by economic pressure as rapidly as adequate technical substitutes for their work could be set up. Finally, after the Tito-Cominform split, all the Communist parties changed their peasant policy: the uneconomic nature of small-scale production was no longer to be glossed over, co-operative farming was to be systematically encouraged and prepared for, and meanwhile the larger farmer was to be treated as a potential exploiter and the smaller farmer was to be armed economically in every possible way against him.

Thus baldly to state the important changes taking place within the 'Popular Democracy'[1] countries, however, should not blind the observer to the even more fundamental constant elements. The initial shift of political power away from major capitalist groups, the initial degrees of socialization, the commitment of the economy to full-scale planning, these characteristics, unless blocked by positive counter-action, tend to have an inner logic of their own. Subsequent changes of economic policy could be viewed

[1] Once the Tito-Cominform split had taken full effect, all the remaining Cominform countries drew together much more closely than before, and, conversely, Yugoslavia sought to distinguish itself as clearly as possible from them. The present book deals with comparisons and contrasts among the Cominform countries only, and then only in so far as they relate to Poland and Czechoslovakia. The term 'Popular Democracy' is accordingly used here in a restricted and European sense, to refer to the countries of the Cominform group only, other than the Soviet Union. Yugoslavia is excluded, and so, for geographic reasons, is China. The term 'planned economy' is used similarly, except that of course it includes the Soviet Union.

as an outgrowth quite as much as a shift away from the earlier steps already taken. In any case, the student interested in seeing at first hand how an important social process of our time has been operating, can do no better than to watch one or another of these novel régimes.

The present book deals with the evolution towards socialism of the Communist type on the part of the two major countries in the European 'Popular Democracy' group: the largest of these countries, Poland, and the most advanced, Czechoslovakia. The author had the opportunity to study the two countries at first hand for several months each during the crucial period of their change to a full socialization programme, and subsequently more briefly when the fruits of the second stage of their development could begin to be assessed. Since then it is evident that the processes begun have been working out to their logical conclusion.

Differences between the two countries have seemed sufficiently striking to require giving separate attention to the historical backgrounds of each, particularly since to the Poles and Czechoslovaks[1] their recent past appeared very important. The bulk of the book, however, devotes itself concretely to the common pattern of the most recent years, with individual variations brought out to suggest in some degree the range of the materials.

The emphasis of the study throughout is economic and social. The author was interested in seeing, in the simplest possible terms, what kind of economic transformations took place in countries that thus decisively marched towards full-scale economic planning and socialization. Once the Communist ideology was adopted, and even on the way to that adoption, what was the nature of these countries' attempts regarding industry and agriculture, domestic development and foreign economic relations? What kind of economic measures were taken against obstacles, technical and social? To what extent did they follow Soviet example? What new inventions had to be made, as institutions taken over from the past were adapted or replaced to serve new ends?

[1] Throughout this book the term 'Czech' will often be used as an abbreviation for 'Czechoslovak'. Cf. the book's sub-title, 'THE POLISH-CZECH EXAMPLE'.

CHAPTER I

U.S.S.R. INFLUENCES

From the outset of their post-war life Poland and Czechoslovakia have been within the Soviet orbit, not only geographically but in economic and social terms as well. Before the war these countries' borders with the Soviet Union for long periods had been virtually 'blind, borders,[1] and ideologically their separation from the Soviet Union had been great.

In intent and direction now the two countries are socialist countries in the Communist pattern. When they first took shape the U.S.S.R. was the only example of this economic form. Moreover it was a huge and powerful neighbour and by so much bore the weight of great prestige; its new institutions by this time were fixed; and its interest in these countries was made the more intense by its past historical relations with them. It is futile to speculate as to what might have been the course of these two countries if the Soviet Union had never existed. To abstract from history in this manner assumes too much else that never happened. It is enough to realize that the effect of the Soviet Union upon the direction these countries took subsequent to the War has without question been enormous. The existence of that setting must at all times be allowed for as we consider developments in the post-war years.

Origins

As we shall see later, the period of occupation by the Germans and partisan resistance brought about powerful left parties, both Communist and Socialist in Poland, and Communist especially in Czechoslovakia, many of whose leaders had even spent a great deal of time as refugees in the Soviet Union. In the case of Poland the very government that subsequently established itself, namely the Lublin Committee, so-called, had taken form from the Union of Polish Patriots formed in the Soviet Union during the war. Con-

[1] Less than 1 per cent of Czechoslovak trade had been with the Soviet Union, and in 1938, less than ½ per cent of Polish.

versely, the more conservative parties, the natural strongholds of anti-Soviet sentiment, had lost prestige at home, again because of their war record.

When it came to drawing up instruments and principles of settled government, it was the Communists whose programme in the main got adopted. And it was the Communists first and foremost who formulated the main features of the basic land reform and nationalization programmes, moderate though these were by any standards of ultimate socialization. Doubtless the principle of these programmes, going thus far and no further, had been widely discussed beforehand in leading Communist circles, inside as well as outside the Soviet Union. Certainly U.S.S.R. publications praised the new measures unreservedly and expounded them to their readers at home.

In a very direct way the Soviet Union helped determine the physical configuration of the new Poland and Czechoslovakia, in boundaries and in terms of resources. In the case of Czechoslovakia the changes were not fundamental. The country lost to the Soviet Union Ruthenia, originally carved from Russia after the first World War. It was also the Soviet Union that supported Czechoslovakia in the matter of expulsion of the large number of German and Hungarian nationals. The new Czechoslovakia's smaller and much more homogeneous population was thus a direct result of Soviet policy.

In the case of Poland the changes encompassed were altogether of a different order. In the east the country gave up to the Soviet Union almost a half of its pre-war territory, inhabited in major part by Ukrainians and Byelorussians; and it received in the west smaller but more valuable territories from Germany, containing much industrial potential and a valuable coastline. Over the new border with the Soviet Union populations were exchanged; and from all the newly acquired western regions the Germans were expelled. For the first time Poland became a highly homogeneous nation with greatly increased industrial possibilities.

Foreign Relations

Looking back over the road that the two countries have traversed since their beginning, one can say that here, too, Soviet influence has been pivotal. In basic matters of foreign affairs both countries, unlike Yugoslovakia, have remained close within the Soviet orbit. Even while still under Beneš's presidency, in the critical summer and autumn of 1947, Czechoslovakia refused to enter the Marshall Plan, after having first given it apparent approval. The actions of Tito were condemned by Poland and Czechoslovakia as roundly as by all the rest of the Cominform countries, and his supporters within their own régimes were soon displaced. Indeed the general tightening up of political and economic policy in both countries in the course of 1948 followed hard upon the worsening of East–West relations as a whole.

Institutions

As to the basic character of the social institutions developing over the years, the influence of Soviet example must undoubtedly have been immense. The extreme emphasis during the early years—an emphasis common to all parties although voiced most strongly by the more conservative—upon everything in the new patterns that could possibly call itself Czech or Polish, should not blind us to this likelihood.

Thus the characteristically overall type of planning introduced so early in the 'People's Democracies', had been developed painfully and over a considerable historical period in the first instance in the Soviet Union. To say that something of the sort would undoubtedly have been developed in any society determined to take a decided course away from capitalism, does not cancel out the fact of the prior existence and prestige of the Soviet type of planning and planning organs.

Or take individual institutions such, for example, as the trade unions. It was the trade unions of the U.S.S.R. that first put their main emphasis upon production. And it was in the U.S.S.R. that output competitions and kindred movements on a wide scale first took their rise. Now these patterns are being followed in Poland and Czechoslovakia and elsewhere; in fact during the latest period even details of Soviet methods in such matters have been widely publicized there. Brief reflection, to be sure, upon the nature of economic incentives would suggest that any economy attempting full employment together with the absence of a capitalist owner would be bound to develop new incentives for its workers. The fact remains however that precisely these forms of institutions were first developed in the Soviet Union, and the other economies have followed suit.

Similarly with such a matter as the economic role of women and young people. The 'equal pay for equal work' principle, nationally adopted and heavily implemented in the U.S.S.R., is now adopted in Poland and Czechoslovakia as well. At the same time, various forms of mother and child protection enhance the costs of women's work to the employing agency. Here, too, not only ideological considerations common to the whole history of socialist thought, but reflection upon the nature of costing under overall socialism (the total versus marginal productivity question) might suggest that something of the sort would be tried. Nevertheless, what was innovation in the Soviet Union is no longer innovation here.

Or take the lately much discussed question of co-operatives. It was in the Soviet Union that the forms and functions of co-operatives, consumers', marketing and producers', were first altered to fit into a nationally formulated plan and to work in conjunction with nationalized industry. And it was here that they took on the function, in addition to protecting their own membership, of actively ousting capitalist elements. The Czechoslovak, Polish, and other co-operatives have similarly changed their orientation. Here, again, it is impossible to say how much was due to the felt necessities of a similar situation and how much to Soviet example.

Contrasts

Certain obvious differences of situation and history have made for a very different sequence of institutions, and to some extent of institutional content, in the Soviet Union from that of the 'People's Democracies' thus far. Broadly speaking, political revolution in the Soviet case came early and completely. Economic controls over that vast country, let alone major economic development, came late.

The Soviet Union was a huge land mass with a great complexity of ethnic and language groups. Only a huge country, presumably, could have withstood the shocks, external and internal, to which it was subject in its early years.

The Soviet Union at the outset was far less advanced than Czechoslovakia or even Poland. To say this, indeed, is a great understatement. So late as the eve of World War II, after twenty years of Soviet rule and enormous efforts at industrialization, the proportion of industrial to agricultural population in the Soviet Union was less than it is in Poland to-day and much less than it is in Czechoslovakia.[1]

[1] Cf. United Nations, Economic Commission for Europe, *Economic Survey of Europe in 1949*, Geneva, May 1950, p. 17, footnote:

The various parts of the Soviet Union, moreover, began at most uneven levels of development, with economic backwardness accentuated by nationality problems. Even the securing of literacy in the native tongues for the unschooled population of a large part of the country was a major and costly task.

The Soviet's career began with the complete social revolution of 1917, following a devastating war, and itself followed shortly by a prolonged civil war combined with foreign intervention. For three years there was so-called 'War Communism' within the country, emergency measures of requisitioning and rationing, with money almost out of circulation. Once the intervention was substantially over, and with economic life at a low ebb, there followed N.E.P., the New Economic Policy of 1921–7, permitting free trade in grain for the peasants and a limited amount of capitalist trade and small industry in the towns, until the country should have recuperated. It was not until 1927, ten years after the original revolution, that industrial production was back to the 1913 level. It was only then accounted possible to begin planning for a period of years on a national scale.

The first Five-Year Plan, occupying the period of the end of the 1920's and the beginning of the 1930's, contained the real industrial revolution and agricultural revolution of the Soviet Union. Large scale undertakings were now rushed along, at great sacrifice, with the construction of heavy industry coming first. (Previous industrial revolutions had always begun with light industry, which is less costly and more rewarding in its early stages.) At the same time, during the period of construction rather than operation of large scale industry, a policy of rapid collectivization of agriculture was undertaken, again at great cost.

'In this country [the Soviet Union] between 1926 and 1939, there seems to have been a three-fold increase in the working population in industry. . . . As a result of this development, the proportion of the population occupied in agriculture . . . had in 1939 declined to about 55 per cent from a level of about 75 per cent in 1926. Development in the Soviet Union thus started from a more extreme agrarian structure of the economy in the middle of the 1920's than that which, in 1950, forms the starting point for the Eastern European development in the next decade. At the present time Eastern Europe as a whole has largely the same occupational structure as the Soviet Union attained at the end of the inter-war period. The three selected countries (Czechoslovakia, Hungary, Poland) are even more urbanized, with about 50 per cent of the population in agriculture . . . in Hungary and Poland, and only 30 per cent in Czechoslovakia.'

In Poland and Czechoslovakia there was no physical social revolution to begin with. The enemy, Nazi Germany, had cleared the ground for social change. Hence land was never nationalized, the distribution of land to peasant holders had time to be orderly, and the nationalization of key industry was carried out under the 'principle of compensation'.[1] In spite of increasingly harsh administrative measures in recent years, these forms have continued to hold.

In the Soviet Union, at the end of twenty years, as set forth in the Constitution of 1936, the country could call itself fully socialist, with all productive property state or co-operatively owned, with the exception of property so small as to employ only the owner and his immediate family. No hiring of others for profit, no trade in the products of other people's labour, was any longer permitted. To this point the 'People's Democracies' have by no means as yet arrived, but they are heading actively towards it.

Czechoslovakia and even Poland, in spite of wartime destruction, started their new life at a much higher level of industrial and agricultural techniques than the Soviet Union had. They were also small, compact, and incomparably more homogeneous. They were able to launch nation-wide planning by 1946. Their industrial production went up rapidly, with increasing and painful effort, to be sure, devoted to heavy industry, but without the Soviet Union's separate period of enormous primary construction. And their attempt to change over from individual to co-operative and ultimately collective farming, was made much more gradually and with a much longer period for the preparation of a technical base.

Economic Influences

The direct economic influence of the Soviet Union upon these countries through the medium of trade and technology has undoubtedly been very great. And again it would be difficult to say how much of this has been intrinsic to, or inevitable because of,

[1] The Polish Minister of Industry, Mr. Minc, stated in 1946, in introducing the nationalization law: 'The confiscation of industrial property without compensation would mean embarking on the road to social revolution. This is not our road.' (Preface to *The Nationalization of Industry in Poland* . . . , Warsaw, 1946, p. 26.) The Minister went on to say that the country had, however, in common with the French Revolution, carried out an agrarian revolution; hence, in the land reform, they were giving, not pro rata compensation but only a social pension payment to the former owners.

the socialist and near-socialist structure of the two sets of economies, and how much to the very acute historical circumstances of the moment.

The circumstances were two: first of all, the post-war condition of destruction and great need of restoration of the new economies; and secondly, the increasing reluctance of the West to furnish them capital goods, especially following these countries' refusal of the Marshall Plan. In this situation, the Soviet Union rather than the West became the great supplier of their most sorely felt needs.

Of course the Soviet Union had suffered war damage itself on an unprecedented scale, and could have used all possible production now for its own needs. But here the factor of size enters in: an industry so very large as the Soviet Union's could, out of a manageable percentage of its products, supply a much larger proportion of its smaller neighbours' needs. And this is precisely what the Soviet Union did.

'The Soviet Union . . . supplied capital equipment such as tractors and machinery . . . also raw materials such as cotton, iron ore, manganese, and chemicals. . . . Poland (in 1948) was granted a credit . . . to finance the supply of a complete steel plant. . . .'[1]

The contrast between this sort of trade treatment and that received from Germany before the war was made much of in Polish and Czechoslovak publicity. Poland did not propose to remain 'a semi-colonial bread-basket nation', and the Soviet Union was not asking them to. The Soviet Union was said to be living up to its true Marxist doctrine: that a high level of industrial-agricultural output was a prerequisite for successful socialism, and that it was attainable for all nationalities without exception.

Much was also made of the alleged stabilizing effect of U.S.S.R. trade. As itself an 'economy without crises' and operating under long-term plans for continuous growth, the Soviet Union was said to be able to offer detailed, specific, and stably guaranteed terms of purchase and delivery, thus enabling its trade partners to make their own plans ahead with safety. The same reasoning was applied to the trade of the smaller planned economies with one another.

It was obvious nevertheless that the felt need of trade with all the rest of the world remained acute, and so late as 1950 the two

[1] United Nations, Economic Commission for Europe, *Economic Survey of Europe in 1948*, Geneva, 1949, pp. 146–7.

countries had managed to maintain enough western trade of one sort or another to make up about half of their increased total turnover. The Soviet Union supplied about a quarter and the other planned economies another quarter.

Along with the influences of trade have gone in the most recent years very strong concrete influences in the shape of technology. The Soviet Union has given a very great amount of technical and general economic information to Poland and Czechoslovakia, supplied by organized interchange of technicians, scientists, managers, and so on. This is over and above the question of ideological influences.

All told, it would probably be no exaggeration to say to-day that the channels for all forms of influence from the Soviet Union to Czechoslovakia and Poland are wide open, and that many of them have been abundantly used. If anything, the existence of these influences should lend added interest to the institutions now developing in these newer and smaller economies.

I

BASES OF CHANGE
POLAND

CHAPTER II

WAR AND PRE-WAR HERITAGE

I. THE PRE-WAR ECONOMY

THE Republic of Poland began its independent life after World War I as a backward, predominantly agrarian country. Some three-quarters of its population of around thirty million lived on the land. In the provinces east of the Curzon Line, comprising nearly half the territory of that time and inhabited by about a third of the population, the proportion living on the land was much larger: it ran to over five-sixths. Here also the living standards were lowest. The greater part of the inhabitants in these regions were Byelorussians and Ukrainians, while estate owners were chiefly Poles. A difficult minority problem was thus added to a difficult social situation.[1]

Polish land was for the most part of mediocre quality, better suited, it was held at that time, to rye and potatoes than to wheat. Forests were not very abundant and were chiefly to the east. Foodstuffs constituted over 40 per cent of all Polish exports between the wars—witness the fame of Polish bacon—but domestic consumption was grossly inadequate. 'The diet consisted largely of bread and potatoes.'[2] Timber was also important as an article of export, but cutting was wasteful: over half the timber felled was used for fuel, and this in a country exceedingly rich in coal. Less than 10 per cent of the timber output was put to industrial use.

Coal, by far Poland's greatest resource, came chiefly from the rich seams of the Silesian coal basin, none of it from the eastern regions. About a third of it was exported, and upon the remainder was based such industrial development as the larger Polish cities attained.

The land system, inherited from three empires, was the crux

[1] Taking the country as a whole, Poles constituted 68·9 per cent of the population and national minorities 31·1 per cent.

[2] United Nations Relief and Rehabilitation Administration, *Economic Recovery in the Countries Assisted by UNRRA*, Sept., 1946, p. 76.

of Poland's economic problem. Methods of tillage were antiquated and wasteful of man-power; production per acre was low. In many regions the strip system prevailed. Dwarf farms alongside large estates, rural overpopulation and the scarcity and high price of land continued throughout the period between the two wars.

So early as 1919, under pressure of the revolutionary wave that was sweeping Europe at the time, agrarian reform legislation had been passed in principle, to provide for the breaking up of large estates and the creation of peasant holdings of liveable size. But implementation remained far behind profession. In the census of 1931, two-thirds of rural holdings were below 12½ acres in size and a quarter were below 5 acres. The partition and sale programme had ended up, as is so often the case in agrarian reform programmes, in the hands of the estate owners themselves. Hence an excessively slow rate of division, high maximum sizes for the residual estates, numerous legal exemptions and exceptions, and still more illegal evasions. Also as usual in such cases, there remained a high purchase price for the land and no adequate provision for cheap credit. As a result, while the proportion of giant estates was greatly reduced, the greater part of the land sold from them had gone to build up smaller estates and large rather than small new farms. The total number of holdings of more than 250 acres each had been reduced by only 25 per cent. The small peasant had found land prices so high that when he did purchase, as many thousands did in their land hunger, his successive payments left him nothing for equipment and improvements. Rural standards of living, already wretched, declined rather than rose in many regions, and the burden of rural indebtedness increased. Subdivision of land among children made matters worse. Industry meanwhile was not developing rapidly enough to enable the cities to absorb the rural surplus population, estimated at some 5,000,000 out of a total of 20,000,000 dependent upon agriculture. Emigration, moreover, had been largely cut off, and increasing tariff barriers had been erected against agricultural products by the major industrial powers. The result was a vicious circle of impoverishment, inadequate domestic market for the products of industry, continued low industrialization and high urban unemployment, further damming back of the rural surplus on the land.

All these difficulties had been heightened by the depression of the early 1930's, which lowered agricultural prices disproportionately to industrial ones; but the disparity was not improved as depression began to recede in the face of rearmament. It is small wonder, therefore, that the years immediately before the second war saw acute peasant restlessness culminating in some regions in local outbreaks.

Industry in independent Poland developed slowly in the period between the two wars. Recovery from the devastations of World War I took a long time,[1] communications had to be improved and altered, and the whole economy had to reorient itself upon a unified instead of a centrifugal basis east, west, and south. The older industries and industrial centres found it hard to readjust, while newer businesses did better. Capital was scarce and inclined to be timid. The slowness of business growth is indicated by the census of 1931. Urbanization in ten years had increased but 3 per cent; mining and industry together employed but 15 per cent of the gainfully occupied, and in industry there were nearly half as many employers and self-employed workers as there were wage-earners—in other words, a great deal of so-called industry was still in the handicraft stage. The total number of industrial wage-earners was about a million and a half.

Over a large part of Polish industrial concerns foreign capital remained dominant. Thus in 1937 in mining and foundries, concerns predominantly foreign-owned controlled about 85 per cent of the total investment; in chemicals, 80 per cent; in electrical manufacturing, 90 per cent; even in textiles, 40 per cent.[2] Where employers were foreign, the government apparently treated them with great circumspection, and tension between workers and employers was quickly translated into tension with the government as well. Public suspicion of foreign firms was directed especially against the French in the case of the textile industry which had long needed renovation and was said to be being 'milked' by its owners in the search for quick profits, and against the Germans—by the 1930's the Nazis—who were concentrated in the all-important defence industry sector, particularly mines and iron and steel works, but also in chemicals and electrical manufacturing.

Poland's foreign trade, amounting to about 10 per cent of her

[1] By 1926 the level of Poland's manufacturing output was still less than 60 per cent of 1913.

[2] It was maintained subsequently that foreign-controlled firms had been able to withstand the strain of the great depression better than other firms because 'they could rely on the support of powerful holding groups'. Cf. Ferdinand Zweig, *Poland Between Two Wars*, London, 1944, p. 121.

total production, remained that of a predominantly agrarian country. Over half her exports consisted of foodstuffs and timber, 15 to 20 per cent of coal, while she imported manufactured goods. Germany was in a key position geographically to control the country's trade and used it to restrict rather than to further industrialization. The carrying trade was a serious problem. Transit across Germany to the west had been hampered by a prolonged tariff war. Subsequently the port of Gdynia was built by the Polish government on the narrow strip of coast furnished by the Polish Corridor, and considerable overseas trade, especially with England, developed. However, 90 per cent of the shipments from Gdynia were carried by foreign vessels. After the accession of Hitler, German trade policies became openly dominating. Purchasing foodstuffs and raw materials under terms increasingly severe for the seller, Germany, here as elsewhere in eastern Europe, sought in return the acceptance of manufactured goods on a scale necessitating large clearing balances.

Polish industry was highly organized. Employers' associations of different industries, many of them publishing their own technical and public relations literature, combined in the powerful Central Union of Polish Industry in Warsaw. The cartel movement was also highly developed in Poland.[1] By the beginning of the depression it controlled some 40 per cent of Polish industry, by its end, virtually all basic industry and much that was not basic, especially in the export trades. Internal cartelization, in turn, enabled Polish industry to participate in international cartels.

Government cartel policy apparently resembled that of the Weimar Republic: that is, it varied, but the cartels flourished, particularly the larger ones. There was the same disparity between the 'cartelized' and the 'free' prices that was so noticeable in Germany in the 1920's, with results that were even more disastrous

[1] See Zweig, op. cit., pp. 102–6: 'There was a powerful coal cartel, a zinc syndicate, a union of cotton producers, the sugar cartel, the cartel of timber producers, a syndicate of the petroleum industry . . . a cement cartel, a cartel of the mining industry, etc.' (p. 103).

Zweig cites as factors making for cartelization in Poland the high concentration of ownership, especially in the predominantly foreign concerns, Poland's high protective tariffs, the sharp differences in production costs in different industrial districts, which would have put some centres out of production altogether in case of a price war, the lack of effective competition from outsiders for lack of investment funds, and government restrictive regulation, especially import and export quotas.

because of the predominance and poverty in Poland of agriculture with its entirely 'free' price system. With the arrival of the depression, the price 'scissors' opened ever wider and never closed again. On the other hand, in spite of public clamour, the government found the cartels more than convenient. They served to support the government's two-price policy, of high internal prices and low export prices, secured in many cases by government export bounties; they tied in well with the system of state-owned enterprises of which we shall speak in a moment, and they were a source of serious political support.

The labour policy of Polish employers also apparently resembled somewhat that of the German industrialists of the 1920's.[1] There was a strong movement for rationalization, with marked results in some fields. It was claimed that an increase of almost 30 per cent in average labour productivity in large and medium industry had taken place between 1928 and 1937. The figures for productivity in coal mining are striking. The increase here between 1928 and 1937 had been 43 per cent, and absolute tonnage production at the latter date per man per day was said to be the highest in Europe.

Wages in Polish industry and mining were low in comparison with the more advanced industrial nations, but high in relation to Poland's farm wages and income. Accompanying rationalization and persisting unabated after the depression was over, went a very high unemployment rate. It was particularly serious in mining.

Social legislation in the new Poland began at an advanced level. In November 1918 a forty-six-hour week had been decreed, and in spite of various weakening provisions introduced later, the basic standard was not abandoned until 1933, when hours were lengthened to forty-eight. Paid vacations, introduced in 1922 on a high level, also continued, although sharply modified in 1933. The various forms of social insurance legislation were introduced early and remained. Here modifications took the familiar form of contracting the scope of the insurance, cutting its amounts, and shifting the cost incidence more heavily upon the employee. There were also administrative changes, removing from the machinery of administration the insured themselves and the trade unions.

Trade unions in Poland were highly organized and active for a country with so little large industry. They were split along both political and sectional lines. The Socialist federation of unions was

[1] Cf. R. Brady, *The Rationalization Movement in German Industry*, Berkeley, 1933.

the largest. Legally enforceable collective agreements prevailed over a large portion of industry, and the government sought to stabilize wages and prevent strikes by an elaborate system of compulsory arbitration boards. Serious waves of strikes under organized union leadership nevertheless took place.

Political parties were exceedingly numerous, an inheritance from Partition, a series of different labour parties, peasant parties, etc., duplicating one another from different sections of the country. While parliamentary rule lasted, they operated in rather large, heterogeneous combinations. After Pilsudski's *coup d'état* in 1926, Parliament became unimportant, and just before his death in 1935 the Constitution of 1921, which had based all power upon Parliament, was formally abrogated in favour of an authoritarian Constitution centralizing power in the hands of the President.

Interrelation between government and business interests was exceedingly strong, and one interesting form of it was the characteristic Polish *étatism*—a development of State-operated public and/or mixed ownership concerns. Lack of native capital in a new political setting was undoubtedly one of the initial reasons for this development, but a number of other factors are cited by Dr. Zweig.[1] The first of these was the inheritance by the new State of old State monopolies. 'The Polish State inherited from the Partition Powers large State-owned factories, railways, forests, mines, banks, and fiscal monopolies. The rule applied in these cases was that monopolies of this kind operating in one part of Poland were extended to cover the whole. . . .'[2]

Another reason was the pressure to begin installations of national importance for defence and communications. Large State munitions factories, the port of Gdynia, new railways, a large new chemical factory, were built by the State during the 1920's. In the latter 1930's a whole new regional industrial development, known as the Central Industrial District, was begun by the State for defence purposes.

In certain instances, large foreign undertakings were taken over by agreement with the shareholders. The most important of these was a great Upper Silesian complex of foundries, mines, and steel works, that had been entirely controlled by a German.

Again, with the advent of the depression, the Government felt itself constrained to take over, either directly or through its posi-

[1] Op. cit., pp. 106–10.

[2] Op. cit., p. 106.

tion as friendly creditor, various concerns of importance that were failing. 'Thus began a very peaceful process of what was called "cold socialization", i.e. the socialization of losses.'[1]

The net result of all this was a very considerable proportion of State ownership. Including government buildings, railways, forests, the fiscal monopolies and the shares in banking and industry, the total by 1927 ran to nearly 12 per cent of the national wealth.

'In industry the State controlled 70 per cent of the iron production, 30 per cent of . . . coal . . . 50 per cent of the metal industry . . . and the larger part of the chemical industry. . . .'[2]

Many concerns were mixed in character, with the State sharing ownership with private business. Again, State-owned enterprises often participated in the private cartels. To the foreign reader later on it was sometimes difficult to tell which was ivy and which was tree.

Polish foreign policy during the twenty years between the wars was closely bound up with the nature of the domestic régime. Of the three former empires out of which the new State was carved, it was the Russian against which it was most consistently oriented. Thence came the largest part of its territories, thence overwhelmingly the largest part of its minority populations. Moreover a considerable part of this territory and of these populations had been won by Polish force of arms in the Polish-Soviet campaign of 1919–20, following the Russian Revolution.

The Soviet border thereafter became almost a 'blind' border in terms of trade. Less than 1 per cent of Polish foreign trade flowed across it during the next 20 years, as compared to 40 and more per cent trade with Germany until Germany's tariff war cut the figure.

Polish armament efforts were extreme throughout the period of her independent existence. One-third of the national budget went regularly for defence; less than 2 per cent for education.

Trade and other relations with Czechoslovakia were strained. Industrial imports from there were kept down by Poland, while Czechoslovakia tried to keep out agricultural products. Relations with Hungary and Rumania were not developed and nothing came of an original project to canalize the waters of the Vistula and connect them with the Danube. Altogether, many of the

[1] Ibid., p. 108.
[2] Ibid., p. 109.

characteristics of an eighteenth-century mercantilist State may be seen flowering belatedly in new Poland.

With the approach of war from Germany after Munich, national policy, while glad of French and British assurances, found it impossible to choose common defence with the Soviet, involving Soviet troops on Polish soil, and when the Germans marched in, the country attempted to resist single-handed. After three weeks of fighting, marked by a heroic defence of Warsaw, led by its mayor, the Polish armies were defeated; and their commander, Colonel Beck, and the Chief of State, President Smigly-Rydz, fled the country. Within a day after they had escaped across the Rumanian frontier, the Russians marched into the country from the east and occupied it up to the point of the German advance. There the line of demarcation remained until the German attack upon the Soviet Union in June 1941, at which time these territories, too, fell under German domination.

2. WAR HERITAGE

The bulk of the lands lost to Poland in the east in the early days of the war, constituting nearly half of pre-war territory, never returned to her. At the end of the war the Polish-Russian frontier was fixed at approximately the 1919 Curzon line, with arrangement for interchange of populations. Figures of post-war Poland's material war damages therefore refer to damages sustained on territory west of this border. The direct damages were estimated to have amounted to no less than 30 per cent of all Poland's pre-war property, or five times the country's pre-war annual income. In the case of population losses, the figures referred to losses from the whole native Polish part of the 1939 population, including the five million-odd nationals east of the line, almost a million of them Jews, who would have been eligible subsequently for repatriation. Losses from the large Ukrainian and Byelorussian population formerly living under Polish rule in the eastern territories were not included. The total pre-war population of Polish nationals reckoned in this way amounted to 27,000,000 (out of a grand total of 35,000,000). Losses by death from this number amounted to no less than 22 per cent.

Such enormous destruction and loss of life, the Poles pointed out, was not accidental. Only a minor part of it occurred in the course of direct military action. Poland was fought over for a month in

September 1939; again, more protractedly, in 1944 and 1945 as the Germans retreated; there was also the period of the Warsaw rising in August–September 1944. All these actions together cost the native Polish population losses of some 600,000 killed, 500,000 of them civilians. But the war and occupation as a whole cost the Polish population losses ten times as heavy—6,200,000 dead in all, more than 5,500,000 of them killed by deliberate occupation policies. These policies were specially designed for eastern Europe.

The general pattern of German occupation in western Europe will be familiar to the reader. There was looting, official and unofficial. There was absorption of the native economy into the Nazi financial and war machine, there was the export of slave labour to Germany, there were varying degrees of subjection of native labour and of the native cultural leadership, to produce the most for Germany at the least cost and to stamp out hope of national resistance, and there was quite special treatment of the Jews. All these features were to be found also in Poland, though to a more extreme degree. But added to them was the special '*Lebensraum*' policy for eastern Europe, involving planned biological extermination. An increasing proportion of the native population was to be physically eliminated, to make way for German settlers, those alive at any given time serving as slave labour on the spot. Such slave labour might be used wastefully, underfed and used up, since a decrease in the total was desirable in any case.

Poland's geographic situation was doubly unfortunate. The Occupation here resembled western Europe's in extent, all of the country's territory being occupied; and it resembled the Soviet Union's in intensity, the Nazis seeking to vent upon Polish as upon Soviet soil not only their full economic but their full *Lebensraum* programme.

Two conflicting tendencies accordingly, alternately or in combination, were said to have characterized the German administration of Poland. One set of regulations appeared to concentrate upon maximum exploitation of the country and its population as a war base, another upon biological destruction, with whatever this might entail of immediate destruction of productive facilities.

Administration methods also differed from region to region and between different nationality groups. At the outset Upper Silesia was directly incorporated into the Reich, and other northern and western regions, reaching almost to Warsaw, were incorporated indirectly as a new German province, the *Neu-Reich*. In these regions Poles were declared to be not wanted and were to be subject to mass evictions, while in the rest of the country, the so-called 'General Government', they were at first promised tolerance. In the *Neu-Reich* marriage of Poles was forbidden, and the more extreme measures of suppression later extended to the other territories were begun here at once.

By the middle of 1940 expropriation here was complete, including all personal and household effects. Expulsions amounted to over a million, the most able-bodied of the population being sent to Germany proper as slave labour, the rest to the General Government for resettlement. There, stripped of all possessions and without adequate food, they were left for considerable periods of time in transit camps; thence the survivors were sent, some to concentration camps, the majority to assigned localities for permanent settlement. The residual Polish population in the incorporated regions remained in a state of extreme subjection, deprived of property rights, cleared out of the more habitable dwellings, forbidden education, and not allowed to practise skilled trades and professions. Only manual labour was permitted them. Half rations and special low wage scales were introduced for Poles, and longer hours of work were required of them than of Germans. A special penal code for Poles was introduced.

In the General Government conditions were at first much better. Poles, to be sure, were eliminated from the local administrations, but they were given to understand that they were supposed to continue at their daily business. It was only gradually that the full programme of destruction unfolded itself here.

One special section of the General Government, however, was singled out early for treatment comparable to that of the *Neu-Reich*. This was the region around Zamosc in the extreme south-east of the country, where a German colonization scheme was afoot. The idea was evidently, after beginning here, to extend a wide area of colonization northward all along the Polish-Soviet frontier, to create a protective belt, so to say, inhabited by Germans. Mass evictions were carried on here from late 1941 on, but were stopped after the German defeat on the eastern front in 1943.[1]

[1] From a telegram of the S.S. official in charge of the region, it appears that 140,000 Poles were scheduled for eviction here; 35,000 children under ten years of age were to be placed in children's camps (the desirable among them later to be sent to the Reich, the rest annihilated); 29,000 persons were to be

Typically, it was reported, evictions took place unannounced. A village would be surrounded, the inhabitants given a quarter-hour to pack up twenty to forty pounds of food and belongings each and to group up in the square; they would then journey to a transit camp where the racial selections, children's selections, etc., took place, and ultimately they would be sent to their respective destinations. Appalling sanitary conditions prevailed both in the camps and in the freight cars in transit. Undernourishment and disease caused a very high death-rate.

An important part of German administration policy was differential treatment for the different nationality groups on Polish soil. The 'Aryan' Poles found themselves midway in treatment between the Jews and the *Volksdeutsche* or 'racial' Germans. The *Volksdeutsche*, as the future instruments of German policy in Poland, were removed from the native ranks and given, wherever possible, local administrative posts. They had conspicuous security, special wages, lodging, and food. The Jews were removed from the native ranks at the other end. They were declared without rights, were the first to be plundered and evacuated from their homes, and had the securing of food made difficult for them; presently they were forbidden to exercise their trades, were subjected to unpaid labour, and were shut up in ghettoes. Finally the ghettoes were closed and their inhabitants ended in the extermination camps.

Yet further and finer distinctions between population groups prevailed, however. Ukrainians, Russians, and Byelorussians (subsequently subjected to extreme cruelty when the invaders reached their own land) were set apart as a class for more favoured treatment so long as they dwelt on Polish soil. They were given better wages and living conditions.[1] An imaginary, different, and superior nationality group was even created to serve the process of distinction-making, in the shape of the so-called 'Mountaineers', Poles who were supposed to represent independent, super-Slav elements. All the distinctions were maintained with great thoroughness, and every effort was made to have each group despise the group below it.

sent to concentration camps, 21,000 persons without families, to work; while 7,000 persons were found fit for Germanization. Actually some 110,000 persons from 297 rural localities here, including over 30,000 children suffered the fate scheduled for them. (*Information on Poland*, Warsaw, 1948, pp. 6–7 u.a.)

[1] It was noted, on the other hand, that no less than 500,000 Russian prisoners of war died at the hands of the Germans in camps on Polish soil.

From the first days of the Occcupation a serious effort was made to stamp out Polish national culture, and indeed culture of any kind for Poles. But the programme was not at first announced in so many words. The University of Cracow, Poland's oldest—and very conservative—centre of learning, assumed it had the right to open in the autumn of 1939; but it was promptly closed and its faculty sent for some months to the Sachsenhausen concentration camp, where a number of them died. No university was allowed to function during the Occupation. All general secondary schools were closed. Only low-grade primary and vocational schools were permitted, and the majority of these were said to 'vegetate', with inadequate programme and staffing. In some localities even primary schools were closed for long periods of time. History, geography, and other 'humanistic' subjects were forbidden. Poles, it turned out, were to be confined to strictly manual labour, and for this the three R's and some manual training should suffice. In the words of Hans Franck, the Governor-General, 'The Poles should be given only such possibilities of education as will prove the hopelessness of their national existence. . . . No Pole can occupy a higher post than that of foreman, no Pole will be allowed to receive a higher education in State schools.'[1]

Later, when war shortages made some skilled Polish personnel necessary, certain technical schools were allowed to open, and under cover of these, secret higher instruction, some of it of university level, was given by courageous teachers. Small groups of university and high school students also met in professors' homes, and very large numbers of younger children attended secret primary classes in Polish language and history. The writer subsequently conversed with some of these professors and teachers. The general effect of the Occupation upon the educational level of the country was nevertheless appalling, and at its end there was a six years' arrears not only of pupils but of teacher-training and of young professionals of all kinds.

Existing professionals, artists, and scientists, in proportion to their eminence, were singled out for maltreatment. They perished in larger numbers than the rest of the population. Some 700 university professors and research workers, 1,000 high school and technical school teachers and about 4,000 elementary school teachers perished during the Occupation.

Material objects of culture were systematically confiscated,

[1] Nuremberg War Trials document, op. cit., p. Ual.

looted, or destroyed. Confiscation and shipment to Germany of works of art, libraries, and scientific equipment, it was pointed out, occupied a very large staff of Germans for years. Private looting, by Germans of all ranks, was said to have accompanied this on an extraordinary scale, but especially striking was the amount of deliberate destruction. Buildings and monuments were destroyed with care, books in quantity were sent to paper mills to be ground up, precious Polish glass-ware was smashed, as were concert recordings; entire libraries and archives were burned. Altogether by these combined means Poland lost the great majority of her public and private art collections, her libraries, archives, and scientific institutes. Even ordinary equipment in schools, museums, and libraries was often destroyed or carried away. For instance, the losses in scientific equipment and books from higher schools was estimated at 70 to 80 per cent.

The economic policy of the Occupation, as indicated, had followed two different tendencies. One was the attempt to incorporate Polish production into the German war machine. In so far as this was followed, it meant great and one-sided expansion of some parts of industry, but permitted dismantling, looting, abandonment, and even actual destruction of premises not required for military purposes, however necessary their product might be for ordinary civilian life. Liquidation of the Bank of Poland and creation of a new Bank of Emission with new paper Occupation currency facilitated this process, as did the forms of German price control. In the towns low prices were fixed for industrial articles bought chiefly by Germans. Financial assets, public and private, social insurance funds, as well as great quantities of physical equipment were shipped out of the country. Often bank safes were simply looted and bank deposits confiscated.

The other tendency, that of 'pure' destruction, strangely enough appears to have alternated with and sometimes contradicted even war-time production needs. Often the two were combined in a purposely rapid using up of manpower and ravaging of resources even while production was going on. The burning and razing of all possible property during the retreat of 1944–5 only put the capstone on this process.

Urban losses were particularly heavy. Some 19,600 out of a total of 30,000 mining and industrial establishments were destroyed, over 35 per cent of all industrial buildings, over half of all power installations and four-fifths of all transport. In addition about 200,000 commercial and 85,000 handicraft worshops were completely destroyed. Finally there was the partial or total destruction of many whole cities, culminating in the house by house destruction of Warsaw where a million and a half people had lived.

Rural losses were less spectacular, but were to take even longer to replace. Forest destruction was estimated at 28 per cent; cattle at 60 per cent. Moreover, 350,000 farm buildings, about a quarter of the country's total, were destroyed or seriously damaged, thus leaving many stretches of land incapable of cultivation. Taking country and city dwellings, industrial establishments and public buildings together, total losses in building properties were estimated at 35 per cent.

In addition to losses in productive equipment and dwelling space, the systematic looting of the population's personal possessions created a serious economic problem for the immediate post-war. This was, of course, at its worst in the case of the millions evicted from their homes.

German biological policy, 'to break down the biological strength of the Polish nation by all means leading to this end',[1] operated in a number of ways. Toward the intelligentsia, as indicated above, the policy was, where possible, annihilation. Towards the Jews it was strictly annihilation. Towards the population at large it was whatever would cause the greatest excess of deaths over births, plus some sporadic annihilation.

The means employed for the Polish population at large were simple enough: excessive under-nourishment; overwork; overcrowding; destruction of sanitary facilities; mass evictions with accompanying high death-rate and breaking up of families; concentration and other camps with incredibly high death-rates, plus gas chambers chiefly for the Jews; and finally, mass executions, as reprisals or as clearing operations.

In the matter of food deprivation, very high compulsory levies in kind were imposed on farmers, impoverishing the countryside. Whole districts were spoken of in German documents as being weakened by starvation and subject to epidemics. Polish rations applied commonly only to Poles working directly for the Germans. The destruction and dismantling of sanitary facilities included hospitals, tuberculosis sanatoria, maternity

[1] From a letter of the Inspector of the Security Police and S.D. at Poznan (No. 4192/41), op. cit., p. 2 u.n.

and child care centres, clinics and laboratories.[1]

A special role in the biological policy field was played by the concentration camps. These were of three kinds. The first were labour camps, with three sub-types: ordinary labour camps, penal camps, and labour camps for Jews. The ordinary camps served simply to exploit manpower: to them were sent persons temporarily out of work. The penal camps were a cross between ordinary labour and concentration camps proper, with insufficient food rations and constant beatings entailing a high death-rate. They differed from concentration camps in that their inmates were committed for a certain period of time, whereas in the true concentration camps the length of stay was indefinite. Labour camps to which highly skilled Jewish craftsmen were sent were of a particularly exhausting character, with starvation, great overwork, and excessively brutal treatment. After being worked out, the Jewish workers were to be killed.

The concentration camps proper received inmates not only for specified offences, but often as a result of street or entire district or village round-ups. Their chief function appeared to be to accelerate death by natural causes, i.e. by food inadequate to sustain life for more than a few weeks or months, by exposure, overcrowding, and hence disease. Sometimes, but not always, overwork and beatings also played a part. Direct killings here were chiefly reserved for Jews. The extermination camps (*Vernichtungslager*) were operated almost exclusively for Jews. Usually Jewish sections were set apart in the larger concentration camps, with the victims killed in very large batches in gas chambers, either immediately upon arrival from a transport (this applied particularly to mothers and children) or after having been worked and starved into uselessness. (This applied more to able-bodied men and women and to seasons when the camp was not too full.)[2]

[1] The War Indemnities Office listed 352 hospitals, 29 tuberculosis sanatoria, 24 health resorts, 773 dispensaries, etc.

[2] The procedure was normally that the victims were told they were going to have a mass bath preparatory to being sent elsewhere on transport. They were given a piece of imitation soap (subsequently retrieved and handed to the next batch of victims) to heighten the impression, entered a disrobing room where each folded his things away under his own name, then were crammed standing into the sealed "bath" room, with vents in the ceiling resembling showers. From these presently there sprinkled the Cyclon gas, killing its victims in great agony within about ten minutes. (Coal gas, used in some camps, was introduced from near the floor and took half an hour.)

The largest of these camps, Oswiecim, actually processed 2,500,000 human beings. Its furnaces could accommodate 24,000 corpses a day when necessary, and it received Jews from all over Europe as well as from its native land. A number of railroad sidings received the many transports daily and despatched the possessions of the dead to Germany.[1]

The size of the business end of all this procedure and the number of Germans at home who must have knowingly engaged in it, appeared to impress the Poles most of all. Since nearly a million Poles in the post-war years, or about three out of every hundred living in Poland, are themselves survivors of concentration camp life, the feeling about the German danger was surely something that any investigation of Poland's post-war structure and policies would have to bear strictly in mind.

A hint at future biological policy for Poland in case the Nazis had not lost the war, was given by two features of the concentration camps. In several of them, medical experiments had been carried on on mass methods of sterilization of women by X-rays. So far the women experimented on had died, but if successful, the methods, it was pointed out, would have proved extraordinarily quick and inexpensive. The other feature was the enormous extension in size planned for the Oswiecim camp. Great tracts of land were still to be seen that had been in process of being prepared, and during the concluding months of the camp's life new buildings sufficient to fill street after street had been ready to be assembled.

The last of the German policies causing loss of life was group executions among the population at large. Usually these occurred

[1] The collection of passports, hand luggage, toilet articles, cooking utensils, school books, games, and children's garments remaining over after the sortings, is unbelievably great. There is a room with half a million shoes, and another with hair to be made into mattresses, from the heads of many thousands of women. The enormous business conducted here by the occupationists is recorded in finely printed German forms, listing every conceivable garment, and every kind of personal possession, from 'pencils-ordinary' and 'pencils-mechanical' to belts, garters and different kinds of collar buttons. Some of the furnaces themselves and their specially designed equipment could still be seen here in 1948, and also in the smaller Maidanek camp in eastern Poland, with the makers' names on them, as could hundreds of cans of 'Cyclon' gas, each can sufficient for 300 people and labelled in German 'Poison', to which was added on the Maidanek cans, 'Must be used within three months'. In the larger part of the Oswiecim camp (*Birkenau*), four great storage tanks, the size of large houses, still stand; these used to receive the human fat from the crematoria before it was processed into soap and fertilizer.

as a form of blanket reprisal for murder or injury done some German, sometimes for no assignable reason other than terror and the biological one. The victims themselves were commonly rounded up on the street. In any case, their ages, sexes, and numbers, and the manner of their deaths, followed no logical pattern.[1]

The most clearly marked succession of practices was to be seen in the territories already referred to, incorporated directly by the Germans into the Reich. In the city of Lodz, a textile centre with many thousands of Jewish inhabitants, the stage-by-stage development of German policy and the pattern connecting the fate of Jews and Gentiles were recounted to the writer by a survivor[2] approximately as follows. In the 'Old City', largely inhabited by Jews, the Germans made a ghetto, gathering together all the 70 or 80,000 Jews of Lodz, and adding to them gradually Jews from the surrounding area. This was the first stage. At first they could come and go to work, then the area was sealed off by a ditch around it and no one was allowed in or out.

Next the Poles were dispossessed. All Poles had to leave all the best streets and leave behind all their belongings except what they could carry. The Germans, said my informant, did this everywhere in the region within the first three months of their Occupation. This was stage two. In every park, café, tramcar now appeared the sign, 'For Germans Only'. Children from the age of twelve had to go to work, at street construction, at building labour, in factories.

Stage three consisted of the liquidation of the ghetto. Its inhabitants, their numbers greatly swollen by new arrivals, were driven away to extermination camps. The buildings were looted and then sold individually for destruction.

Now came stage four in what my informant called the 'conveyor system', with the Poles in their turn becoming 'raw material' for extermination. There were man-hunts (*lapanka*, the Poles called them), with no idea of selection of individuals on a logical basis.

[1] For example, there were 77 cases of mass burnings alive, 47 of them including children. At Lodz, a great textile centre not far from Warsaw, a burned-out factory could still be seen set in a barbed-wire stockade with observation turrets at the corners. Here some 3,000 Polish civilian prisoners, many of them simply rounded up on the street, were burned to death on 14 January, 1945, one day before the Russians liberated the city. Those who jumped from the windows were shot. A graveyard opposite now holds their memorials, together with that of the Jews of Lodz.

[2] June 1948.

Trucks would come and collect young people for work for the Germans. Or if a German had been found murdered or had been struck by a Pole, a *lapanka* would round up and kill great numbers of Poles on the street. Then they would put up a notice, a red one with black letters on it, saying, '100 × 1', signed by an S.S. leader.

The net biological effect of German Occupation policy and combat losses was calculated by the Poles as follows.[1] Out of a pre-war population of 27,000,000, total loss of life was estimated at something over 6,000,000. This figure included the killing in ghettoes and concentration camps of 3,200,000 Polish Jews; but it did not include the concentration camp killing on Polish soil of 1,500,000 Jews imported for that purpose from other countries in Europe.

Of these total losses, 644,000 or only something over 10 per cent, resulted from direct war operations. This included both civilian and military dead, and included such operations as the Warsaw rising. The remaining 90 per cent, nearly 5,400,000 persons, died from Occupation policy. A further breakdown of figures indicated over 3,500,000 murdered outright in extermination camps, ghettoes, so-called pacification processes, and executions. Something over 1,250,000 died in prisons, concentration camps and other places of detention from epidemics, starvation, bad treatment, etc. And something over 500,000 died outside of camps from under-nourishment, beatings, overwork, and so forth.

Very striking was the disproportionate loss of life among the urban population. In absolute figures it was almost four times as great, in terms of rate of loss, nearly ten times as great as that of the rural areas. These figures of course included the Jewish dead, almost all of whom were city dwellers. The rate of losses among intellectuals was also disproportionately high, although no total estimates were given. So was the loss among children. As to the balance between the sexes, the first post-war census taken in 1946, indicated a ratio among adults of 140 females per 100 males.[2]

Sickness caused by the Occupation can only be guessed at, but the Poles estimated an increase in tuberculosis cases above expectance of over a million. The crippled and otherwise disabled were reckoned at 600,000, five-sixths of them civilians.

[1] See tables in War Indemnities Office, 'Statement on War Losses and Damages of Poland in 1939–1945', Warsaw, 1947.

[2] The pre-war ratio had been 118 per 100.

In addition, nearly a million of the surviving population had suffered detention in concentration camps or prisons and nearly 2,500,000 had suffered transportation abroad for forced labour.

3. THE WESTERN TERRITORIES

Along with their treatment by Germany during the war, the Poles stressed the effect upon their future, of the lands now taken from Germany. The great shift westward of their centre of gravity, which they insisted was permanent, they held to be industrially as well as militarily of the greatest importance. They had both lost extensive territories in the east and gained more important ones in the west. They noted that the Yalta statement of Churchill, Roosevelt, and Stalin in February 1945 had read: 'The three heads of Government consider that the eastern frontier of Poland should follow the Curzon line with digressions from it in some regions of 5 to 8 kilometres in favour of Poland. They recognize that Poland must receive substantial accessions of territory in the north and west. They feel that the opinion of the new Polish Provisional Government of National Unity should be sought in due course on the extent of these accessions and that the final delimitation of the western frontier of Poland should thereafter await the Peace Conference.'

The Poles held that this statement and even that of Potsdam six months later had indicated merely a formal delay in the details of their western border demarcation, and not a postponement of the whole issue of their life in the new lands there.

The Potsdam declaration of Stalin, Truman, and Attlee in August 1945 had stated:

Poland

'The three heads of Government agree that, pending the final determination of Poland's western frontier, the former German territories east of a line running from the Baltic Sea immediately west of Swinemuende, and thence along the Oder River to the confluence of the western Neisse River and along the western Neisse to the Czechoslovak frontier, including that portion of East Prussia not placed under the administration of the U.S.S.R.

. . . and including . . . Danzig, shall be under the administration of the Polish State. . . .'[1]

In any case, the Poles had already ceded their eastern lands to the border republics of the U.S.S.R.; and they subsequently arranged by treaty with eastern Germany (the German Democratic Federated Republic) so soon as the latter was constituted, to make the new Oder–Neisse lines permanent. Meanwhile their great population and industrial shift had been accomplished.

The losses and gains envisaged in this shift were tremendous. About 46 per cent of Poland's pre-war territory was lost on the east and the equivalent of about 26 per cent was to be added on the west. The net effect was as if the Polish State, reduced about a fifth in size, had been picked up bodily and moved westward hun-

[1] Delineation of the Curzon and Oder-Neisse lines as definitive had been suggested in two earlier statements of Prime Minister Churchill in Parliament, in February and December 1944:

'. . . We did not approve the Polish occupation of Vilna in 1920. . . . The British view in 1919 stands expressed in the so-called Curzon line. . . . Marshal Stalin and I also . . . agreed upon the need for Poland to obtain compensation at the expense of Germany both in the North and in the West.' (397 *H.C. Debs.*, 5, Hansard, col. 698, 22 Feb. 1944.)

'Poland will gain in the North the whole of East Prussia west and south of Königsberg, including the great city and port of Danzig. . . . Instead of the threatened and artificial corridor which was built so laboriously after the last war, Poland will stretch broadly across the Baltic on a front of over two hundred miles . . . they gain in the west and north territories more important and highly developed than they lose in the east . . . expulsion of the Germans—because that is what is proposed, the total expulsion of the Germans . . . is the method . . . which will be the most satisfactory and lasting. . . . There will be no mixture of populations to cause endless trouble as in Alsace-Lorraine. A clean sweep will be made.' (406 *H.C. Debs.*, 5s, cols. 1483–4, 15 Dec. 1944.)

Similarly Sir Alexander Cadogan of the British Foreign Office in a letter to the foreign minister of the London Polish government-in-exile, 2 November 1944:

'You asked me in the first place whether, even in the event of the United States Government finding themselves unable to agree to the changes in the western frontier of Poland . . . , His Majesty's Government would still advocate these changes at the Peace Settlement. The answer of His Majesty's Government to this question is in the affirmative.

'Secondly, you inquired whether His Majesty's Government were definitely in favour of advancing the Polish frontier up to the line of the Oder, to include the port of Stettin. The answer is that His Majesty's Government do consider that Poland should have the right to extend her territory to this extent.' (Quoted in P. M. Raup, 'The Agricultural Significance of German Boundary Problems', *Land Economics*, University of Wisconsin, Madison, Wisconsin, May, 1950, p. 104.)

dreds of kilometres. A third of present-day Poland now consisted of the new western territories. The new location and resources were of the very greatest strategic and economic importance.

As over against a possibly resurgent Germany, the new Poland was now a compact, well rounded land mass. The frontier with Germany itself had become a short straight line on the west only, instead of a widely curved crescent. Poland's own coastline now stretched 550 kilometres across the entire northern end of the country, with three good harbours instead of one pinched one. A mountain border formed the south-west portion of the frontier. Sea and mountains together in fact now formed half of Poland's total borders.

The territories taken from Germany moreover had been the centre of Germany's most expansionist social groups: the Prussian Junkers and military caste, the Pomeranian landlords, the Silesian landlords and coal and steel operators. The break-up of these particular groups and the removal of this particular war potential were therefore very important in Polish eyes.

Economically the effects of the new position were even more striking. Acquisition of the Oder–Neisse river line shifted the whole centre of gravity of the country from the agricultural east to the agricultural-industrial-commercial west. Poland now had two great river basins at its command, the Vistula with unimpeded port facilities and the broad Oder basin draining the central and western part of the country. The greater part, some 70 per cent, of the Oder tributaries flow in from the Polish side. In the future, moreover, canalization could connect the Oder with the waters of the Danube, and a project to this effect was subsequently initiated, as will be seen later. Such a waterway would give direct passage from the Baltic to the Black Sea. Lateral rail connections were also improved by the move, with logical rail centres for the exchange of industrial and agricultural products now within Polish borders.

In agricultural resources the shift in location meant the loss of much low grade and poorly developed arable land, but also of great stretches of pasture, meadow, and forests. These latter were a real loss, as the western territories had only about half as much forests and but little natural meadows. In grain crops the difference was not so marked, as the western territories had been better farmed. In potatoes the western territories produced slightly more. In technical crops, particularly sugar beet, the gain was all on the side of the western territories: the sugar beet ratio west–east was

5 to 1. In terms of agricultural population, however, a far smaller number of farmers would be needed to farm the western lands than the eastern.

In industrial resources the change was tremendous. On the east were lost what were at that time Poland's only oil-fields, with a production of about 600,000 tons annually, considerable calcium salts and basalts, and a small, newly discovered coal-field. But that was about all; the eastern territories had had no other mineral wealth. On the west, on the other hand, were gained very large coal deposits, both bituminous and anthracite, with nearly 50,000,000 tons pre-war annual output, besides substantial amounts of zinc, lead, and minerals.

Industrial installations were incomparably more developed in the west. Electrical energy production was twelve times that of the east, railroad trackage was twice as long and three and a half times as dense. Altogether, the combination of the more industrially developed western half of the original territories with the additional coal and industrial riches of Silesia made possible a heavy industry base for the country that was altogether new. In terms of 1939 production, the addition of the western to the central territories meant a virtual doubling of industrial output and of national income. By the same token it meant a very considerable increase in urbanization. In the central territories in 1939 the proportion of urban to rural dwellers had been but little over 1 to 4; in what was now the western it was virtually 1 to 1; combining the two would give almost 1 to 2.[1] Destruction throughout the northern and western portions of the new territories—i.e. everywhere but Upper Silesia—had of course been exceedingly heavy, since the Germans made their last stand in these regions, and the weight of this destruction fell especially upon the cities. However, the urban and industrial foundations remained and could be rebuilt.

In population also the fortunes of war and the new boundaries made great changes. Absolute losses through death, as indicated in the previous section, totalled over 6,000,000. Among the dead

[1] The precise figures as given in charts at the Wrocław Exposition of 1948 were:

	Central Territories	*Recovered Territories*	*Combined*
	%	%	%
Urban	22	47	31
Rural	78	53	69

were some 3,500,000 Jews, virtually the entire pre-war Jewish population of Poland. In addition a number of million Ukrainians, Byelorussians, and others remained behind east of the Curzon line when the eastern territories were ceded to the Soviet Union. Poles from this region, on the other hand, to the number of nearly 2,000,000, could and largely did opt to return to their motherland, as did some 200,000 Polish war refugees in the Soviet Union. The great majority of these settlers were transferred clear across Poland to the western territories. From the western territories meanwhile a tremendous exodus of the entire German population had taken place, at first a flight, then a regulated expulsion with the refugees received in the Soviet and British zones of Germany. Together with them went whatever remained of the war-time German colonists and a scattering of earlier German inhabitants from within central Poland. Over a million 'autochthonous' Poles remained behind in the western territories and thus rejoined their motherland. These were Poles who had perhaps for centuries lived under German rule but had preserved the tradition of their original language and nationality. Some population exchanges also took place across the Czech border, and some long absent Polish repatriates arrived from France and overseas.

Altogether these population changes made Poland for the first time a strikingly homogeneous nation. Gone were the formerly oppressed minorities and gone were the Germans. The country now had only 24,000,000 inhabitants instead of 35,000,000, and conditions were exceedingly difficult, but the task of rebuilding began with a strong fund of common patriotism.

The Poles, it should be noted, at the outset called the new western territories the 'Recovered Territories'. They pointed to the remains of Polish culture in the architecture and arts of the region and to the old Polish substratum of inhabitants still dwelling there. A thousand years ago, they maintained, the Oder–Neisse region had been a centre of Polish rule, then in successive waves the Germans overran it and pushed the Poles eastward.

Whatever may be thought of this claim, it is clear that in recent centuries the German population had vastly predominated in the 'recovered' territories and that it was they who had built up the industry and agriculture of the region. However, agricultural conditions of the region had been such that for a number of decades there had been a large-scale outflow from here of Germans to western Germany—the so-called *Ostflucht* or *Landflucht*, very embarrassing to the German political objectives of *Drang nach Osten*. It was for this reason that such large numbers of Polish seasonal labourers were brought into the region, amounting in some years to three-quarters of a million men.

One difficulty with the region's agriculture between the two world wars, the Poles maintained, in addition to its semi-feudal structure, had been its disadvantageous relation to peace-time markets. For Germany these regions, particularly East Prussia, had been peripheral: in most inter-war years agricultural supplies for western Germany could be got more cheaply from Brandenburg and Saxony, or even from overseas. Agricultural surpluses hence had a tendency to back up and find an outlet only at uneconomic prices. But strategically, the Poles pointed out, the region had been too important for the Germans to let it run down: it remained therefore a deficit area, continually receiving financial assistance. In the event of another eastern war it could—and did—prove of the greatest value. For Poland and central Europe generally, on the other hand, these territories were not peripheral but central for normal market transactions.[1]

In industry the coal production of Silesia was second only to Germany's Ruhr, and again for the purposes of an eastern war it

[1] Cf. Philip M. Raup, 'The Agricultural Significance of German Boundary Problems', *Land Economics*, University of Wisconsin, Madison, Wisconsin, May, 1950, pp. 101–114.

'It was a region in which big farms, dependent on large labor forces and frequently on migratory labor, set the agricultural tone. . . . The pre-war labor supply consisted of a large percentage of German youth, impressed into labor battalions, plus foreign or migratory farm workers, largely Polish' (pp. 106, 113).

The foods sent to the rest of Germany from there were primarily grains and sugar, both heavily subsidized and both 'the very foodstuffs that Western Germany can to-day import to best advantage' (p. 108). 'These subsidies were held justified by Nazi Germany, in its preparation for war' (p. 112). Moreover, 'The eastern rail transport system had required continuous subsidy from the rest of Germany. Military considerations, and the eastern colonization policies of successive German governments had dictated a system of rail rate differentials' (p. 114).

After all the effort, 'In the pre-war period Germany, as presently bounded, received . . . 10 per cent of its flour and cereals . . . 18 per cent of its sugar . . . 6 per cent of its potatoes from east of the Oder-Neisse line. On the other hand, it received only 8 per cent of its meat, only 2·3 per cent of its fat, 0·9 per cent of its whole milk . . . 3 per cent of its eggs . . . If value comparisons could be made, it is clear that [the eastern region] . . . excelled in . . . foods having a . . . low value-ratio' (pp. 109, 110).

was invaluable. The foundries and metal industries were also important, but proportionately much less so for Germany than for Poland. Altogether, the Poles pointed out, the loss to Germany of these territories had meant a loss of 9 per cent of their 1939 income, while the gain for Poland (excluding the lost eastern territories) meant a gain of 94 per cent. Similarly in the number of industrial workers, the loss for Germany equalled 8·3 per cent and the gain for Poland 82 per cent.

To the outsider it seemed as if a parallel might be drawn between the condition of the rural portion of these territories under inter-war German rule and the eastern territories under inter-war Polish rule—in both a governing class of estate owners sharply to be distinguished from the working population, in both a somewhat serious market problem largely due to political boundaries, and in both a lagging behind of the social level of the country-side below that of the more central rural areas.

That the Poles had managed to take advantage of their new territories in the midst of difficulties was apparent even in 1948. The turmoil of population change in itself would have seemed enough to prevent recovery, but it had not done so. Absorption of the new arrivals had gone on at greatest speed. The pre-war population of the region, according to Polish figures, had been about 8,500,000, 80 per cent of them Germans. By 1948 some 7,000,000 Germans had moved out and 4,500,000 new Polish settlers had moved in. Added to the remaining million and a quarter Poles native to the region, the 'autochthones', this made a new, all-Polish population of approximately 6,000,000. Further accessions were expected from the crowded central agricultural regions of the old territories.

The expulsion of the Germans had apparently gone smoothly. An unknown number of Germans had fled in the wake of the retreating Nazi armies and others followed or were expelled in the succeeding months. By the decision of the Potsdam Conference the process had been regularized internationally, and the 3,500,000 remaining Germans were subsequently apportioned by the Allied Control Council to the Soviet and British zones of Germany.[1]

[1] The Potsdam Conference had stated:

TRANSFERS OF GERMAN POPULATION

'The conference reached the following agreement on the removal of Germans from Poland, Czechoslovakia, Hungary:

'The three Governments . . . recognize that the transfer to Germany of

The incoming Polish population had been of the most varied backgrounds. Diverse social groups, differing traditions, customs, and living standards, met here. The largest group, chiefly rural, had come from the eastern territories beyond the Curzon line. Then there were about a million and a half from central Poland, some leaving rural poverty, many originally from Warsaw and other destroyed cities. Over 1,000,000 were displaced persons from western Europe, and some were Poles who had gone abroad in pre-war years to better their condition and were now returning home. And besides the new-comers there was the local Polish population which had managed to hold on in spite of German dominaion.

It was this assorted population, bare for the most part of possessions, which had to and did, meet the difficulties of a destroyed country-side and industry. The results by 1948 were surprising. First combat bombing, then burning and mining by the retreating Germans had made skeletons of former cities. Industrial installations had been smashed or carried off. Farmland had been ruined. (In the first year and a half of recovery, over 6,000,000 mines and 20,000,000 bombs were destroyed or deloaded.) Horses and cattle had been carried off, agricultural implements dumped into rivers. The writer in 1948 saw the salvaged farm and industrial equipment in use once more, restored with great patience and ingenuity, the buildings going up with enormous use of hand labour, new heavy machinery of Polish manufacture beginning to fill the half-rebuilt factories, and industrial products emerging at the other end. By 1948 the year's production plan called for the following output by the Western Territories: Share of total industrial output of the country, 22 per cent; coal, 33 per cent; electric power, 38 per cent; freight cars, 73 per cent; sugar, 33 per cent.[1]

German populations, or elements thereof, remaining in Poland, Czechoslovakia, and Hungary, will have to be undertaken . . . they consider that the Allied Control Council in Germany should in the first instance examine the problem with special regard to the equitable distribution of these Germans among the several zones of occupation . . . and submit an estimate of the time and rate at which further transfers could be carried out. . . .'

The Allied Control Council decision of 20 November 1945 applied to 'the entire German population of 3,500,000 persons', 2,000,000 of them to be admitted to the Soviet zone of occupation and 1,500,000 to the British.

[1] Appended are some notes from a visit by the writer to two factories in Wrocław (Breslau). They are illustrative of Polish management attitudes in the Western Territories and of the type of difficulties surmounted.

'PAFAWAG' FACTORY, WROCLAW. JULY 1948

This factory was formerly the German 'Link & Kofmann' concern. It manufactured railroad cars. During the war it built parts for V-2s. It was said to be the largest car factory in Europe. Before the war, stated the director, the Germans had 6,000 workers here; during the war, it was not known how many: they used slave labour. Now there were 5,000 workers. The workers here, he stated, were a conglomeration, repatriates from all over the world. The whole factory had been destroyed—there were no machines, the glass was destroyed 100 per cent, buildings 40 per cent, no technical equipment was left. Now the factory was 80 per cent rebuilt, the remaining buildings were not very important.

In July 1945 the Poles had taken over the place from the Russians. Production began at the end of that September. The director had arrived in August. He had been for 18 years director of a factory in Warsaw until the Germans came. He had been incarcerated for a year at Mauthausen Concentration Camp. Upon being freed from Mauthausen he had two months' vacation, then came straight here. He arrived penniless, though he had formerly been wealthy.

By September 1945 came the first group of technicians and workers from a car factory in Warsaw which had been 100 per cent destroyed. Then a second group brought additional unskilled workers. 'We gave them practice making coal cars, of which a certain amount of parts had been left,' i.e. the Germans had left parts of 2,200 cars. By 26 January 1946, they had produced their first 100 cars of this German type and had a celebration to mark the event.

At first they began to repair the buildings. 'We had to do all these things at once: build cars, plus build buildings, plus build houses for workers. Daily new people came whom we trained—we set up quick schools for them.' By 1 May 1946, they had produced all the 2,200 cars. By this time there were no German skilled workers left (at first they had kept a few).

Now in May 1946 they began to produce new Polish cars of Polish type. Up to 1 June 1948 they built 13,000 cars. In addition, they built new passenger cars, tenders, and mail cars. They also repair all types of cars. They also make all the parts necessary for their production.

'All our raw materials we get from inside the country, none from abroad. (We got some machines, about two hundred, from reparations from the Russian and English zones of Germany.) To indicate how great the destruction was: up to 1946 we shipped out 2,000 car loads of debris.'

At the end of last February they celebrated their 10,000th car. They now (1948) produce monthly 700 freight cars, in addition to some passenger cars, tenders, and mail cars. They also repair cars and make street cars for Warsaw.

'It is the ambition, the spirit of the Polish people—Warsaw people. If it rained, a worker would cover his head and keep on working.'

RAYON SPINNING PLANT, WROCLAW. JULY 1948

Here the machines had been destroyed by the Germans. Machine parts were very difficult to secure. The few Polish engineers and experienced workers who were imported from two central Polish towns, had the task of reconstruction.

The strength of Polish public opinion concerning the western territories was unquestionably very great indeed. Economic need, strategic considerations, and the universal sense of loss at the hands of the Germans were everywhere referred to. The writer was even shown a published letter on the subject from a high church dignitary. In June 1948 the Pope had sent a message to the bishops of Germany which appeared to commiserate with them over Germany's lost territory. A week later the Primate of Poland wrote a message to the Polish settlers in the western territories in the name of the Church. His letter, published in the Catholic paper, *Djes y Jutro* of 20 June 1948, as read aloud to the writer, stated: '. . . Do not have any doubts concerning taking root and living out in freedom your Polish and Catholic life. . . . The Church will be with you and with your children. . . . Do not believe that the Church could ever have any question regarding Poland's future in the Recovered Territories. . . . Therefore with regard to the Pope and the Church, be quite reassured about your farms and workshops, about the Polish future of your homes and shops. . . . Stand without hesitation there where the wave of new national life has brought you. . . .'

By 1949–50 a yet further stage was to be noted in Polish treat-

(The rayon is produced from celulose, which up to now has been obtained from Sweden. 'But in two years or so we will have our own celulose factories. The other raw materials needed, caustic soda and carbon bisulphide, are produced here.')

On 1 May 1946 the factory was set going. Ever since it has been in a state of development. They now have 75 per cent of the machines going. They hope by the end of the Three-Year Plan (1949) to have 100 per cent operating. The difficulties are great because the machines were in such a state that most technicians would say they were hopeless, that it would be impossible to set a factory going with such equipment—'but we are used to endeavour'.

There are 1,600 workers, about 40 per cent of them women. Some came who had worked as slave labour. They arrived as mere skeletons. He emphasized that the industry is a very difficult one, a mixture of chemical, textile and mechanical processes: yet these people, he said, had to master it. They had to use country people as workers. Initially the workers from Tomaszow, an old textile centre, instructed the others; now they are department managers and so on here. Workers came, many of them, from the Eastern territories now ceded to Russia, and also from central Poland; also some repatriates from England, Germany, and France. 'It is a very great social experiment.'

'Up to now we have to produce on old machines and can only use little rationalizations. In order to live through this period we have to lengthen the life of these old machines: our workers work that way. Nobody will help us, we must help ourselves. It is not enough to work, we must work well.'

ment of the western territories question. The term 'Recovered Territories' had been dropped altogether. And presently even as 'Western Territories' these regions were no longer referred to as an entity. By 1951 it was impossible to find statistics dealing with the progress of the region as a whole. The work of physical and social reconstruction was considered to have progressed to a point where these lands no longer presented a separate 'problem'. They were to be treated as having been successfully integrated into the rest of the Polish economy.

CHAPTER III

EARLY RECONSTRUCTION

I. POLITICAL BEGINNINGS

Apparently the early days of reconstruction in Poland saw a strange mixture of elements of civil war, continuing on a considerable basis down to the beginning of 1948, and a strong upsurge of support for the actual work of reconstruction engaged in by the new Government. It was in an appeal to all Poles to unite to rebuild their country as a new and better one that Poland's Left parties had put forth their slogans.

The alignment of political forces showed a great preponderance in the Government and in mass organizations of almost equally balanced Socialists and Communists (P.P.S. and P.P.R.) working closely together. They operated on an ideological and programme-making level normally associated with a Socialist rather than a Communist position. They differed sharply from Right-wing Socialist parties in approving of the Soviet Union. But for themselves, their own conditions were to make things very different. They were building a social system which had 'no historical precedent'. The idea was even expressed that there were three brands of Socialism: Soviet Socialism, Western (Social Democratic) Socialism, and Polish Socialism. The Polish type might serve as an ideological bridge between the other two. In any case, ultimates were to be definitely de-emphasized.

The existing Government of Poland had been an outgrowth of the Committee of National Liberation, composed predominantly of a coalition of Communists and Left Socialists, and itself an outgrowth of the Union of Polish Patriots formed by pro-Soviet Poles within the Soviet Union during the war. Once the Germans had been driven across the Bug, the Polish Committee of National Liberation established itself at Lublin and proceeded to operate as a *de facto* government, taking over the administration of territory as rapidly as it was liberated.

The representatives of the pre-war Government of Poland meanwhile had established themselves at London after the German invasion of 1939, with various changes in personnel. Their chief military forces, under General Anders, had withdrawn from the eastern theatre of war in 1942, and their underground 'Home Army' under General Bór-Komorowski had vainly led the Warsaw Uprising against the Germans in late 1944. They therefore had no strong centre of authority to oppose to the Committee of National Liberation when the latter constituted itself the Provisional Government at the end of December and established itself in Warsaw so soon as the capital had finally been liberated by the Russians. By June 1945 Britain and the United States recognized the new Government in return for the inclusion within it of several representatives, not of the London Government as such, but of the chief of the London political parties.

The subsequent influence of the London representatives rapidly declined. At first their leader, Mr. Stanislaw Mikolajczyk, former premier of the London Government and representative now along with two lesser men, of that Government's mainstay, the Polish Peasant Party, was given the portfolio of Agriculture—a highly strategic position for a dissident in a period of land reform. During 1946 accusations and counter-accusations led to splits within his party, and a number of months after the unfavourable outcome of the elections of January 1947, which Mr. Mikolajczyk insisted had been unfair, Mr. Mikolajczyk fled the country, bitterly condemning the régime.

The effective Government of Poland therefore remained the Socialist–Communist coalition, although an ancillary third party, a left Peasant Party that had broken off from Mr. Mikolajczyk's party much earlier, during the war, was well represented in Parliament as it had also been in the Committee of National Liberation. It held many of the less important Cabinet posts and after the January 1947 elections it received the portfolio of Agriculture. Two lesser, non-socialist parties held several posts each.[1]

Soon after the end of the Mikolajczyk dissensions, numbers of the

[1] The Cabinet roster after the 1947 elections ran:

Polish Socialist Party—7 ministries, including the premiership.

Polish Workers' (Communist) Party—5, including the vice-premiership and various important ministries.

Peasant Party—6, including Agriculture.

Democratic Party (drawing especially upon middle-class intellectuals)—3.

Christian Labour Party (Catholic, artisans largely, chiefly active in the new Western Territories)—3.

more violent opponents of the régime were successfully conciliated. In late 1947 large groups of General Bór-Komorowski's 'Home Army' and others came in from the woods during a three weeks' period and handed in their arms in response to a Government promise of amnesty. It was claimed subsequently that those coming in had numbered 20,000 men, and the trade unions were said to have done a 'remarkable job' in integrating these men back into normal work life.

The dominant political pattern of the 1945–7 period was undoubtedly formed by the Communists quite as much as the Socialists. Its most authoritative formulation was given by Mr. Władysław Gomułka, at that time Vice-Premier of Poland and General Secretary of the Workers' (Communist) Party, late in 1946, upon the occasion of a meeting of the two parties.[1]

His party, Mr. Gomułka said, believed in a new, peaceful form of society for Poland, as different from the Russian path of development via a dictatorship of the proletariat as the peaceful Polish revolution had been from the Russian Revolution.

'. . . the Polish Workers' Party established the conception of the Polish way of development toward socialism. This conception . . . eliminates the necessity of a dictatorship of the proletariat . . . the bloc of democratic parties exercises the power of government. This conception calculates on a peaceful, evolutionary development . . .'[2]

In Poland there had no longer been any powerful machinery of an old State by the time of liberation. 'We took power without applying the force of revolution against reaction. The weakness of reaction permitted us to apply democratic methods of exercising power.

'. . . The primary cause which permitted the peaceful overthrow of reaction in Poland was the complete shattering of the State apparatus in Poland as a result of the September catastrophe (i.e. the German invasion in 1939) and the utter illusoriness of the London delegates in Poland. . . .

'. . . . The main and basic armed strength of the Polish capital-

[1] See *Glos Ludu* (*People's Voice*), Warsaw, No. 330. Excerpts from an address delivered at a meeting of P.P.R. and P.P.S., activists, Warsaw, 29 November 1946, reprinted in *Political Affairs*, New York, April 1947.

[2] Mr. Gomułka added: 'Because this problem has so far not been discussed extensively in public by our party and because of its importance for strengthening the unity of action of both our parties, I consider it advisable to clarify it from the point of view of the party which I represent.'

ists, landlords, and reaction in general—Anders's army—was outside the country and unable to do much in defence of their interests. . . .

'At the time of the liberation of Poland, State power was simply lying on the street. It was picked up by democracy, which proved itself stronger than reaction.'

Foreign capital, moreover, had been weak in Poland.

'Another factor which facilitated our taking over power was the inertness of foreign capital in Poland. German capital could not act as a force at all; for, as a result of its defeat, it was eliminated; and the whole nation was inflamed with hatred toward the Germans. Foreign capital of other origin was actually taken over by the Germans, and that also paralyzed its power and prevented it from playing any independent role.'

Similarly, Mr. Gomułka held, once it had been peacefully established, the Polish revolution was in no danger of armed overthrow: there was no sizable domestic counter-revolution and there were no foreign capitalist states ready to come to its aid by armed invasion.

'. . . In Russia the necessity arose for the dictatorship of the proletariat . . . because the domestic counter-revolution . . . of the landlords, the capitalists, and the Right generally in city and village . . . allied itself with foreign interventionists. . . . If the October Revolution . . . had permitted . . . a parliamentary way of deciding the problems of social reconstruction, it would have been crushed by the landlords and capitalists, who would then have established their own dictatorship and would have exacted a terrible revenge. . . .

'We proceed on the basis that, under Polish conditions, . . . the dictatorship of the working class, the class which was and is at the head of the democratic camp, was unnecessary; for the resistance of reaction did not overflow into a wide wave of counter-revolution.

'. . . The working class in Russia, on attaining power in 1917, found itself faced with the catastrophe of war and with the threat of the rape of its country by world imperialism with which domestic reaction was allied.'

The common war of liberation against fascist Germany, Mr. Gomułka suggested, had changed the world balance of forces, so that the Polish revolution had not had to meet armed intervention. In all the important countries of Europe the democratic forces were now on the upgrade.

'When taking over power, we were confronted only with a boycott by world reaction, which at first did not recognize our democratic government. This [lack of interference] was due to the growth of strength of world democracy as a result of the defeat of fascism during the war. . . .

'We are witnessing the growth of democratic strength in the French nation after the Second World War. (This was written in 1946.) We also see the development in England . . . giving the majority of votes to the Labour Party. . . . Similarly in other countries, in Czechoslovakia, Yugoslavia, Rumania, and Italy, the strength of the democratic forces is everywhere growing.

'This power of world democracy is strengthening our democracy, for it is not permitting world reaction to extend such help to Polish reaction as the landlords and capitalists in . . . Russia received. . . .

'We should remember that the working class in Russia, when it took power, was confronted with armed intervention by fourteen capitalist states which wanted to strangle the October Revolution. . . .'

Internally also the new Poland was more advanced than the Soviet Union had been originally. Hence no such huge efforts would be necessary to achieve industrialization and an effective agriculture:

'There is furthermore the fact that the Soviet Union was able to erect a powerful industry only at the cost of tremendous hardships imposed on society and that, in close connection with the industrialization of the country, she was faced with the problem of the collectivization of agriculture.

'We, however . . . independently of the possibilities of receiving foreign credits . . . [have an] actual productive potential of our industry . . . far greater per capita than . . . Russia [had] before . . . its Five-Year Plans.

'Similarly there is not the slightest need for us to follow the Soviet pattern of agricultural economy. We have rejected collectivization, since under Polish conditions it would be harmful in the economic and political sense. . . .'

Mr. Gomułka closed with a recapitulation of the uniqueness of the new Polish system.

'. . . Our democracy and the social system which we are building and establishing have no historical precedent.

'Ours is not a country with a typical capitalist system. . . .

'Ours is not a country with a socialist system. . . . We have recognized the necessity and usefulness of individual initiative and non-socialized forms of production in a definite segment of industrial production; we have rejected completely the collectivization of agriculture. . . .

'Polish democracy is exercising power through a multi-party parliamentary system. . . .

'Our democracy has many elements of socialist democracy and also many elements of liberal-bourgeois democracy, just as our economic system has many features of socialist and capitalist economy.[1] Our type of democracy and our social system we have designated "People's Democracy".'

In a later chapter we shall see how the ideology thus presented by Mr. Gomułka was condemned in Poland as elsewhere during the summer and autumn of 1948, so that by the time the Socialist and Communist parties merged in a Unity Congress at the end of that year, the resulting United Workers' Party emerged with a stand far to the Left of the former 'Polish road'. Here it is sufficient to note that a policy well within the limits described by Mr. Gomułka was dominant in Polish Government circles throughout the early reconstruction period.

2. LAND REFORM AND NATIONALIZATION. THE EARLY 'THREE SECTORS' VIEW

The economic structure of post-war Poland was based on what was at first regarded as three different sets of property relationships—public, private, and co-operative.[2]

[1] Possibly one further ingredient in the view dominant in the two countries at this time and expressed clearly by various prominent Socialists should be mentioned here. This was the 'yardstick' view regarding private enterprise: that a modicum of private business was good for the economy, not only because of immediate need but to keep State enterprise alert and 'prevent bureaucracy'. This view was expressed warmly to the writer, for example, by a Czechoslovak Left Socialist Minister who had stuck to her Communist colleagues after the crisis of February 1948. She gave instances of what she considered the inexcusable conduct of private business in the field with which she was concerned, hence argued the necessity of nationalization here and everywhere else where it had been undertaken thus far; but in general favoured the yardstick idea.

[2] Later on, co-operative property came to be regarded as part of the 'socialized sector', as over against capitalist property. As will be seen in Chapter XV, this distinction had more than passing significance.

D

The co-operative sector, to be sure, was as yet infinitesimally small: not more than 2 per cent of the gainfully occupied worked in it by 1948. But it was destined to grow, and the Government from the outset set great hopes upon it. The stronghold of the public sector was industry, and the stronghold of the private sector was agriculture, and also, for the most part, trade.

Public property by 1948 included not only public utilities, transportation, and mining, but broadly speaking, all key industries and all big and medium sized industrial undertakings generally. Private property included virtually all agriculture, most of trade, and virtually all artisan production and very small industry.

In terms of the number of persons employed, about three-quarters of all the gainfully occupied were engaged in private undertakings and only one-quarter in public and co-operative. So small, however, was the scale of most private enterprises that in terms of output about half the national income was produced from the public and co-operative undertakings. 'Pure' capitalist production, indeed, i.e. production in private enterprises employing wage labour for hire, accounted for only about 15 per cent of the national output and about 10 per cent of the labour force. All the rest of 'private' enterprise consisted, not of entrepreneurs and their employees, but of the self-employed. They produced about 40 per cent of the national output and included two-thirds of the gainfully occupied.

This, of course, is only another way of restating the predominance of private ownership on the farms, in what was as yet a predominantly agrarian country. It also underscores the final disappearance in post-war Poland of landed estates and of most large farms worked by hired labour.

Land

The revolutionary land reform that brought about almost universal small proprietorship in the country-side dated back to 1944 when the war was still raging. It was promulgated on 6 September of that year by the Committee of National Liberation, in conformity with the Committee's July Manifesto, issued so soon as Polish troops had crossed the Bug River line. Unlike the attempted reforms of 1919 it was to be carried into effect at once.

The July Manifesto had read:

'. . . Fellow countrymen!

'In order to accelerate agricultural rehabilitation of the country and to satisfy the Polish peasants' age-old hunger for land, the Polish Committee of National Liberation will immediately proceed to carry into effect, in the liberated territories, agrarian reforms on a large scale.

'A Land Fund, subject to the Agriculture and Agrarian Reforms Department will be created for that purpose. It shall consist of landed property, buildings, and livestock included, heretofore held by the Germans and by traitors, as well as . . . estates of Polish landowners which exceed the area of 50 ha. (ca. 125 acres), and in the territories incorporated by the Germans into the Reich, 100 hectares (250 acres). Landed property belonging to the Germans and to traitors . . . shall be confiscated. Estates of Polish landowners shall be taken over by the Land Fund without . . . [payment in] proportion to the area of the estates, but the former proprietors will be compensated. Landowners who have patriotic merits in the fight against German oppression shall receive a higher compensation. The land taken over by the Land Fund, except for the areas specified for model farms, shall be distributed among small farmers . . . tenants, and farm labourers. The land to be distributed by the Land Fund against a very small payment shall constitute, equally with formerly owned landed property, the private property of its owners. The Land Fund shall set up new farms or complete the existing ones on the basis of 5 hectares (12½ acres) of agriculturally utilizable land of middle quality per average family. Those farmers who are unable to receive land on the spot shall be entitled to State assistance in moving to the territories with free land, especially those regained in the west.'

The 6 September decree provided for machinery to carry the reform into immediate effect throughout the territories already liberated, with a time-table for successive stages. On the one hand, the new Department of Agriculture and Land Reform was to set up District Land Offices which, aided by District Land Committees, were to inventory available land. On the other hand, small farmers, tenants, and land workers in each community were to elect Communal Agrarian Reform Committees to draw up lists of farms under the 12½ acre minimum, and of the families having no land or less than this amount. Working from the data assembled in this rough-and-ready fashion, and with a brief period for appeals and further claims addressed to the Department of Agriculture, the District Land Offices were to have the whole process completed within about three and a half months of the publication of the Decree, i.e. by late December 1944. No greater contrast in the manner of carrying out a land reform can well be imagined than the contrast between this reform and the one of 1919–25.

In content, it can readily be seen, the new reform was radically different from the old also. This time the upper limits of ownership were to be modest and absolute: no arable land over 125 acres in most of the old portions of the country, 250 in the Western Territories. This time, moreover, there was to be no problem of 'residual' estates and their owners left in the midst of the new farm plots. Estates above the permissible limit were to be divided *in toto* and the owners would have to move away.

In the matter of compensation also, this time there was to be no payment to the estate owners for the land as such, let alone letting them have a hand in settling its price. The former owner would receive a fixed pension *irrespective of the size of his lost property*; or, if he preferred, he could take up new land elsewhere, free of charge, but again fixed in amount. The new land had to be outside the district, which in practice meant in the Western Territories, and the limit for landholding would be the same for the expropriated owner as for other settlers, the only difference being that he would receive his land altogether free. As to the size of the pension, it was set at the equivalent of the salary of a civil servant of the sixth class, i.e. a lower administrative as distinguished from a clerical rating. The great majority of landholders apparently chose this latter alternative, as the pension could then be added to whatever salary or business earnings the individual might secure on his own account.

Treatment of the new peasant purchasers of land was also very different from that of the first land reform. The land was handed over unencumbered, the Government assuming the problem of previous indebtedness. Payment was extremely small in amount, supposedly the equivalent of a single harvest, and it was spread over a number of years. Attempts were made, in the midst of universal shortages, to supply the new occupants with cheap credit.

The new farms could not be divided, sold, rented, or mortgaged. Hence further splitting up of this land or its loss by the new owners, such as had occurred after the first reform, were forestalled.

However, the size of the new holdings, as will have been noted, was pitifully small: 12½ acres for cropland of average quality. The figure is an index of the extent of Poland's rural over-population and the low level of its agriculture. In the Western Territories, where rapid settlement was at a premium to get the deserted fields under cultivation again, the size of new holdings ranged up to 37 acres.

Industry

At a considerable remove in time after the decree on land reform came the legislation on nationalization of industry. The actual process of Government administration of major portions of industry, however, had come much earlier. Indeed the legislation, when it was finally promulgated early in 1946, meant the handing back into private possession of considerable properties hitherto in the hands of public authorities.

War, Occupation, and the Nazi methods of waging both, had left much property ownerless. Business leaders in large numbers had been physically destroyed by the Nazis. Jewish businessmen were gone and so were their relatives and heirs. Polish business leaders had been deposed and many of them were subsequently lost.

Not only owners but managers were gone. 'In the western areas, annexed to the Reich, Poles had been removed from large, medium and even small industrial and handicraft establishments. In the section of Poland which comprised the so-called "General Government" the Germany policy of extermination, though somewhat weaker, nevertheless provided for the annexation by the German State of private administration of all large and medium-sized establishments.'[1]

Moreover the Nazi method of conducting Polish business and banking had been such as to strip the country of its financial resources, leaving behind worthless German paper. In addition to material chaos, therefore, there was no private initiative available on a large scale for reconstruction.

In practice, as the front passed over a given neighbourhood and the Germans were driven out, Polish workers and engineers had struggled to get the surviving plants into operation again, and local and later national government organs subsequently had taken over guardianship of the ownerless property. The armies had to be supplied and the most pressing needs of the civilian population had to be met.

[1] 'Organization of Industry in Poland', National Economic Bank, *Quarterly Review*, Warsaw, December 1946, p. 1.

'The Polish workers—mostly spontaneously—secured the safety of industrial establishments. . . . Production in most cases started immediately, on whatever scale existing conditions and existing labours permitted. . . . It was not possible, under these conditions, to allow unsettled legal forms or the question of uncleared ownerships to obstruct the development of economic and social life.'[1]

The State met the crisis by passing on 6 May 1945 a Bill concerning the temporary care of abandoned and ownerless property.

Eight months later, on 3 January 1946, the Nationalization of Key Industries Act was passed, and together with it, a new law protecting future private undertakings.

The nationalization law provided for the taking over without compensation of all establishments, irrespective of size, previously belonging to the German State or the Free City of Danzig or to their citizens. Enterprises belonging to Polish citizens or to citizens of other foreign nations were to be compensated for if taken over (in the case of citizens, payment would normally be by government bonds), and their taking over was to depend upon their kind and size.

In principle the nationalization limit for industrial establishments was set at the very low figure of a capacity of 50 employees per shift, and there were certain key types of industry that were to be taken over altogether. On the other hand, in the building and installation industries, private establishments irrespective of size were to be left unmolested. Also in industries with little mechanization and in industries of a luxury or pioneering character the limit was to be set higher: at 150 or 200 workers.

In describing the Nationalization Bill Mr. Hilary Minc, the Minister of Industry, and himself a Communist, stated: 'The course of the war on Polish soil, the extent of destruction and the need for a speedy reconstruction . . . brought about *de facto*, with the logic of objective facts, the nationalization of industry on a still wider scale than envisaged by the Nationalization Bill. The question to be decided was not which undertakings should be taken over by the State, but rather which undertakings under State administration should be returned to private owners. That undoubtedly is the peculiarity of the Bill which has, up to a point, mitigated the spontaneous force of post-war events. . . .

'The limit laid down of fifty workers in one shift is justified by the [low] degree of mechanization and concentration of industry

[1] Ibid., pp. 1–2.

in Poland. Undertakings employing over fifty workers play an important part in the economic life of Poland where output and profitability are considered. If the State deprived itself of these undertakings it would deprive itself of the economic basis for the larger industry which at the moment calls for great investments for restoration and development.'[1]

The matter of compensation, although serious for a ruined country, was not regarded as impossible, provided it were undertaken gradually. Counting the Western Territories and the numerous German, traitor, and derelict properties in the old country, it was calculated that not more than a third of the enterprises in number and not more than a fourth in terms of value would be eligible for compensation.

Apparently a number of deputies objected to the payment of any compensation, but the Government insisted on its stand, both on the ground that foreign capitalists should be paid so as to establish as soon as possible normal economic relations with the West, and, more basically, on the ground that payment was in accord with 'the character of the social changes we are undergoing'. 'The confiscation of industrial property without compensation', said the Minister of Industry in his speech to the deputies, 'would mean embarking on the road to social revolution. This is not our road. ... We are not making a socialist revolution and are therefore paying compensation.' The Minister added: 'We have, however, carried out an agrarian revolution . . . in the shape of the Land Reform. This revolution was delayed here, as compared with other countries in the west. . . . And that is why we have, in common with France (at the close of the eighteenth century) carried out the expropriation of landowners without compensation.'[2]

At the same time as the Nationalization of Key Industries Act, the National Council passed the decree on 'The Setting Up of New Enterprises and the Encouragement of Private Initiative in Industry and Trade'. The two Bills were presented by the Government for joint discussion and acceptance. The New Enterprises Bill provided that private industrial undertakings started after its passage would not be held to the fifty-employee limit or indeed to any limit, nor would existing small plants be forfeit if they sub-

[1] Preface to 'The Nationalization of Industry in Poland: Speech by the Minister of Industry, Hilary Minc, at the Ninth Session of the National Council of the Homeland', Warsaw, 1946, pp. 8, 9.

[2] Ibid., p. 26.

sequently grew. The whole nationalization process must be completed before 1 January 1947, and all industrial enterprises not coming under the decree were guaranteed that they 'are an inviolable private property'.

On the strength of this decree a number of thousands of small new enterprises were started. How many of them exceeded the fifty per shift figure the authorities made no attempt to ascertain. A large number of small enterprises previously held by the State for lack of owners were also turned over to new private owners. This was especially true in the Western Territories, where about two-thirds of all small enterprises were sold at a low figure to new Polish owners, rather than being grouped under municipal or co-operative management.

Certain types of private industry were especially to be favoured. In the Economic Reconstruction Plan Law of 2 July 1947, it was stated that 'special protection and assistance of the State' was to be furnished to those branches of small industry where 'resourceful and direct participation of the private owner' gives the best economic results, 'particularly in industrial precision production'. Beyond that, private production was to be helped where it 'supplements and assists State industry'. Also to be helped were 'pioneering activities in new branches of production', 'residential house-building', 'export activities of private entrepreneurs', and, in general, 'the activities of private entrepreneurs in the Recovered Territories'.[1]

Trade

Trade, it should be noted, had remained altogether outside the nationalization law: no limit was placed upon either the size or the kind of commercial undertakings that could remain private property. Wholesale and foreign trade, as well as retail merchandizing, could be engaged in by private individuals. In general, in contrast to farming and industry, trade and handicrafts continued to be governed by the property laws in effect before 1939. Control and direction of trade were attempted, not by any change in property status, but by a changed system of trade licences and by the grouping of traders and small industrial producers in Chambers of Commerce and Industry.

The co-operative sector of the economy, as stated earlier, though exceedingly small as compared to the other two, was to be

[1] Art. 97, and see Part XI, chap. 2 of the law, *passim*.

encouraged. Decisive increase was looked for in its historic field, that of the village co-operative store and in marketing co-operatives. 'The co-operative sector', stated the Economic Reconstruction Plan Law, 'is to become the chief and decisive factor in the trade between the country-side and the towns.'[1] In the city also co-operative trade was to grow, albeit more slowly. However, in the words of Mr. Minc, 'co-operative societies should also take an important place in production in various branches of industry. . . . This applies in the first place to the food industry, i.e. the processing . . . of agricultural produce.'[2] The co-operative sector was also to become an important factor in building and house management.

In addition, general co-operatives of a new type were looked to, to furnish social amenities in the country-side and to protect their members against speculation and fraud. Mentioned in only the most general terms in the Reconstruction Plan, this type of organization subsequently had a rapid and important growth.

In handicraft and small industry production, the co-operative sector had the advantage of a post-war start: ownerless small enterprises were sometimes turned over to co-operative groups, among them often the remnants of the surviving Jewish population.

In agriculture, temporary farm co-operative groups were permitted in the earlier post-war years in the Western Territories, on land where scanty inventory and centralized buildings made division at first unduly difficult; but it was understood that after three to five years the groups must dissolve and the merged lands be divided up among the members, who must meanwhile have built themselves houses upon it.

This was the state of affairs at the beginning of the Three-Year Plan. How much existing property relations were beginning to change by the end of this period, must be reserved for discussion in a later chapter. Here suffice it to say that the legal framework changed but little, while administrative and economic policy began to push sharply in the direction of further socialization.

3. THE THREE-YEAR PLAN

The Three-Year Plan of National Reconstruction, the first general plan to be undertaken by the Polish Government, was drawn to cover the calendar years 1947–9. Preceding the launch-

[1] Arts. 92, 94, and see Part XI, chap. 2, *passim*.

[2] 'The Nationalization of Industry in Poland', p. 29.

ing of this Plan there had been a nine-months' investment plan covering the last three quarters of 1946. And preceding that there had been a series of fractional plans, for various branches of industry.

The first of these was contained in a resolution of the Council of Ministers in April 1945, setting basic production figures for coal mining. A second stage was reached during the last quarter of 1945 when plans were drawn for a series of industries under the control of the Ministry of Industry. At first this planning 'covered only matters of production and employment, afterwards it was extended to matters of technical supply and supply of raw materials'.[1]

The second half of 1946 saw a third stage, with the beginnings of cost accounting and the main rudiments of an economic and financial plan being incorporated into the industry plans. A fourth development, parallel in time with the third, was the setting up of numerous separate plans in yet further fields, outside industry proper. 'Parallel with sector plans in industry', stated Mr. Minc in September 1946, 'sector plans in other fields are developing, firstly the transport plan of the Ministry of Communications. The plan for the reconstruction of the ports was created; the plan for settlement and the reconstruction of industry in the Western Territories, the plan for sowing and harvesting, the plan for sale of industrial products to the country-side—the first such plans in our history—the plan for the purchase of agricultural products by the State through the supply fund [all these plans] have been created this summer and autumn; the nine months' investment plan has been accepted, the plan for the extension of the co-operative system has been created and realized. We are dealing with a mass of sector plans of varying degrees of precision and covering various periods, covering territory after territory.

'The period from the 1 April 1945, from the first plan of the coal industry, up until now, has been the time of a mass planning school, a lesson in planning.'[2]

Conditions of life, however, were still extraordinarily difficult. 'What have we achieved during 1946 in spite of the awful war damage? We have achieved about 40 per cent of agricultural production, about 70 per cent of industrial production, about 50 per

[1] The Speech of Minister Minc on the National Economic Plan . . . at the Session of the National Council on 21 September 1946, *Information on Poland*, Ministry of Foreign Affairs, Warsaw (1948), p. Hx2.

[2] Ibid., p. Hx3.

cent of national income taken as a whole in comparison with 1938. Taking into consideration the reduced number of the population, we have calculated that we have achieved *per capita* more than 55 per cent in agricultural production, about 100 per cent in industrial production and about 70 per cent of the national income. . . . [However] if we have shown the figure of industrial production per head as being nearly 100 per cent, it should not be forgotten that in those figures a big part is played [by the increase] in . . . electric power and coal. With a more detailed analysis the picture looks worse. For instance, the production of cotton fabrics per head in comparison with pre-war days is 64 per cent, the production of sole leather only 24 per cent and upper leather less than 50 per cent. . . . The average consumption of food per head is now 2,000 calories. . . . We must realize that our miners have been working without picks and shovels, without safety lamps and with breaking transporter bands. We must realize that our foundries have old and unrenewed rollers working at the end of their life, we must be conscious of our locomotives requiring more fuel to run than would be required in their construction, we must be conscious of the soil of our farmers being deprived of natural fertilizers, deprived of draught power and often covered with weeds. . . .'

'All this means that, owing to the enormous effort of the nation, we have obtained high production indices, but this should not close our eyes to the two basic questions, the destruction of productive apparatus and the wear and tear of the vital forces of the men who direct this apparatus.'[1]

The quantitative goals of the Three-Year Plan were to raise gross industrial production over the pre-war level—thanks to the new opportunities of the Western Territories—but to raise gross agricultural production, in view of lost lands and the slower pace of agricultural recovery, to only 70 or 80 per cent of pre-war.

In the case of industry, *per capita* production (taking into account the loss of nearly a third of the population) was to reach 125 per cent of pre-war for consumers' goods and no less than 250 per cent of pre-war for producers' goods.

The level of investment was to run very high, around 20 per cent of national income. (Before the war, in 1938, in spite of military preparations, it had been only 13 per cent.[2])

[1] Ibid.

[2] For 1946 the figure had been 24 per cent. For 1947 it was to be 22·4, for 1948 19·5, and for 1949 19·3.

The key branches of production whose output was to increase rapidly were still electric power, coal, and iron and steel. The generating capacity of power plants within Poland's present boundaries was before the war almost twice as great as that within old Poland, but power stations had been so thoroughly destroyed by the retreating Germans that by the end of 1945 power output was down to about 15 per cent. By the end of 1949 pre-war output within the new boundaries was to be substantially exceeded; this meant nearly two and a half times as much power as Poland had had formerly. Coal was the heart of the Three-Year Plan, both for servicing domestic industry and for export, to bring in desperately needed foreign equipment. Even by the first year of the Plan, 1947, coal output had exceeded that of old Poland by more than half. By the end of the Plan it was to be twice as great, and was to exceed substantially (by 12 per cent) even the pre-war production within the present boundaries.[1]

In the case of the steel industry, reduced at first to some 60 per cent of pre-war, both pig iron and rolled steel production were by 1949 to exceed old Poland's by almost half.

Metallurgy had been particularly hard hit with the destruction of its Warsaw plants: at the conclusion of hostilities it was down to 40 per cent of pre-war. However, though denuded of machinery, numerous factories in the Western Territories, such as the famous Pa-Fa-Wag railroad car concern, could be and were rapidly rebuilt. Rolling stock was given an especially high priority in recovery investments. Agricultural machinery and tools were also emphasized.

The principles governing investments were those of emergency endeavour. No new investments were to be undertaken during the life of the Plan, unless they were absolutely essential to make old investments operative or to bind together the old and new parts of the country. And priority in restoration was to be accorded to the less damaged plants and structures, to the kinds of undertakings that would give quick output results, and to industrial 'bottle-necks', i.e. to key items whose scarcity held back other production. The extent of the devastation and the modesty of the means at the Government's disposal may be seen by the Plan's explicit statements concerning 'decapitalization', i.e. further ruin

[1] The extent of destruction and the tremendous preliminary recovery efforts may be judged by the following figures: 1945—29 per cent of 1938 production, 1946—68 per cent, 1947—86 per cent.

through unavoidable deterioration from neglect. In 'certain branches' of the economy sufficient investment was to be made in the initial period of the Plan to insure that 'upon the termination . . . of the Plan decapitalization will be completely checked'.[1] The checking was to proceed by stages. 'The liquidation of the decapitalization process will take place first in industry and in agriculture. Later on it will embrace waterways and roads; finally, the building and construction industry.'[2] 'Outlays . . . are to be such as towards the final period of the Plan will check decapitalization in respect of buildings.'[3] In other words, ruined buildings would have to wait for salvaging, if necessary, until 1949, while the essential business of life went on.

In the country-side the first restoration investments with State assistance were to be to make habitable one structure per farm for the shelter of the farmer and his livestock, 'one combined building for all purposes per farm'. This would enable farming to be re-established in burned-out areas and would prevent further deterioration of large tracts.

In the cities investment was to concentrate on the least damaged buildings and equipment. 'Industrial investments are in principle to consist in the rehabilitation of establishments whose capital equipment has been damaged only in part. The reconstruction of establishments whose capital in buildings and installations has been damaged to more than 50 per cent of their former value may only be started in justified cases.'

In transport, heavy investment was to be made in rolling stock, but road-beds would have to wait, even though this slowed up train runs.

Within the capital goods industries, preference was to be given where possible to investment 'in respect of goods requiring a short period of manufacture and giving quick results in production'. In individual manufacturing establishments, investments were to be made 'according to the criterion of volume of production, swiftness of productive effects and diminution of manufacturing costs'.

In general, the programme in respect of building investment shows well the system of Plan priorities. First, the most essential

[1] Art. 44—1. See also Art. 6—1.

[2] 'The Economic Reconstruction Plan for Years 1947–8', National Economic Bank, Warsaw, *Quarterly Review*, September 1946, p. 4.

[3] Art. 51, section 2. For this and succeeding quotations, see Arts. 23, 51, 47, 53, 55, 56, 75, 76.

services, living centres and regions; were to be rebuilt sufficiently to function. These included essential industrial production, rehabilitation of idle land, the Warsaw region, the Western Territories. 'These investments are to be concentrated first and foremost in the most damaged centres and in those which are of the greatest importance to the economic structure.' Second, building investments were 'in principle to be confined to repairs and reconstruction, maximum use being made of the least damaged properties'. Maintenance expenditures meanwhile were to be such as 'will check decapitalization . . . towards the final period of the Plan'. Third, as in the case of other investments, 'building investments are to be made according to the criterion of swiftness of productive effect and their importance to output'. Fourth, the solution of the housing problem by new construction to adjust differences between different regions, etc., would have to wait for the period of the next Plan. At this time, there could only be provision of working-class flats and prefabricated houses sufficient to make possible 'uninterrupted production activity'. And in the countryside, as mentioned above, investments with State assistance would cover, in general, only 'one combined building for all purposes per farm'.

The tremendous emphasis on production is shown by the final investment plan figures. Half the total investment funds were to go into industry, and another third into other forms of production, while residential building was to receive only 7 per cent, and health, education, etc., about 6½ per cent.[1]

Consumption predictions were highly optimistic. 'Such conditions are to be established as will make it possible to reach in 1948 the pre-war level of consumption in respect to the majority of goods consumed.' The improvement during the period of the Plan itself was to be very great. There was to be a *per capita* rise of from 50 to 250 per cent between 1947–9 in the *per capita* consumption of such foodstuffs as green vegetables and fruits, sugar, milk, meat, fish and eggs, fats. There was also to be an increase of 50 to 150 per

[1] Art. 53: 'The following distribution of investment outlays in the final period of the Plan is hereby established as a guide for the various branches of the national economy:

Industry	49·8%
Other productive activities	34·2
Residential building	7·2
Health, welfare, education and culture	6·4
Miscellaneous	2·4

cent in *per capita* consumption of such clothing materials as cotton fabrics, woollen fabrics, knitted goods, hard and soft leather.

In the field of employment, the Plan envisaged a shift of 400,000 persons out of agriculture in the old territories, and an increase of 200,000 in agriculture in the Western Territories—making a total shift out of agricultural employment of 200,000. In non-agricultural employment there were to be big increases all along the line—900,000 additional workers in the old territories, 400,000 in the western, making a total of 1,300,000.

To conserve scarce skilled labour, there was to be wherever possible substitution of less for more skilled workers, upgrading of women, etc. 'Such conditions are to be established in manufacturing establishments as will make possible the replacement of skilled workers by semi-skilled and an increased participation by women in trades previously carried on by men.' White-collar occupations, particularly in service and trade, were to be combed for further recruits for industry. 'A frugal and proper use of manpower is to be made possible by . . . abolishing over-employment in branches of work not directly connected with production . . . restricting employment in services and . . . trade within . . . proper . . . limits.'

In the actual carrying out of the Plan, two sets of factors beyond the control of the planners created great difficulties, beginning in its very first year. One was the sudden withdrawal of U.N.R.R.A. help in the summer of 1947, and the difficulty experienced by Poland in securing American commercial credits and subsequently in receiving clearance for various types of goods already paid for. Machine tools, tractor parts, penicillin, began to be banned. The other and more devastating difficulty was the extraordinarily bad weather of 1947:[1] first a destructive winter freeze

[1] 'In agriculture intense frosts with a lack of snow cover . . . inflicted serious damage upon the winter wheat. In the Recovered Territories where imported wheat having but slight resistance against severe frosts was used during the autumn sowings, the losses were particularly painful.

'Railway traffic in the second half of the winter, owing to snow-drifts and severe frosts had to limit the volume of its services. The necessity arose to limit the passenger traffic for the sake of goods' transports. In spite of this, transport difficulties have rendered impossible the regular supply of raw materials . . . to industry. . . .

'In March, the period of snow-melting and drift-ice, despite preparations made beforehand and the use of military detachments as well as heavy airplane bombardments, the damage inflicted by both drift-ice and river-inundations assumed in the middle and lower stream of the Vistula and Warta rivers the

immobilizing traffic, especially of coal, then spring floods destroying great areas of cropland and tearing down bridges, finally extreme summer drought ruining harvests and fodder and giving a head start to weeds and pests. The Soviet Union sent in large grain supplies, and famine was averted; but losses had been very great and the effect upon the meat and milk supply especially could not soon be made good.

Reconstruction, nevertheless, went forward rapidly in 1947 and it was announced that the industrial portion of the year's Plan had been fulfilled 103·4 per cent. Moreover, incorporation of the Western Territories with the rest of the country, i.e. their rate of settlement, the rebuilding of their economy, and the tying in of their transport and communications network, were declared to have exceeded plan.

In physical reconstruction, the rate of restoration of damaged buildings and equipment in industry had proceeded so rapidly during 1947 that by the beginning of 1948 it was stated, 'The expiration of the period of repairs is clearly marked. While in former plans . . . repair works (i.e. on only partially damaged factories) were a characteristic feature of industrial investments, in 1948 this type of investment is vanishing.'[1] Plants damaged beyond 50 per cent now comprised the overwhelming bulk of restorations, while investments for overdue renovations began to be permissible on a wide scale. Above all, new investments now comprised nearly half of all industrial investments.[2]

In building construction, greater investments for 1948 were undertaken than originally planned for in three important regions. Large funds were concentrated on the rebuilding of Warsaw; reconstruction of the port, town, and province of Szczecin (Stettin), and the erection of workers' dwellings, with a large concentration in Silesia.

extent of an elemental calamity. Owing to damaged protective embankments, about 110,000 hectares of arable land, meadows and pasture-grounds were flooded. The farm buildings situated on these grounds were for the most part destroyed. The population from the endangered areas was in good time evacuated. The spring inundation has also demolished many bridges, causing temporary difficulties in both railway and road traffic.' (National Economic Bank, *Quarterly Review*, Warsaw, June 1947, p. 6.)

[1] *Information on Poland*, Hc 19.

[2] In the entire national investment plan, the proportion of new investments had doubled, but was still only about a third of total (1947, 16 per cent; 1948, 34·5 per cent).

Summing up the situation in regard to new and old construction, it was said: 'The scale of the processes allows the statement that the first stage in the reconstruction of Poland progresses more rapidly in several economic fields than was anticipated by the Three-Year Plan and therefore the stage of economic reconstruction in Poland will be finished earlier than the end of 1949.'[1]

During 1948 both industry and agriculture did better than planned. Industrial production exceeded Plan by some 10 per cent.[2] Agriculture exceeded Plan in all fields except pork production, doing particularly well in the rate of reclamation of idle lands, and in horse and cattle raising in spite of the previous bad years.

Railroad transport substantially exceeded Plan, with an excess of 13 per cent in freight and 20 per cent in passenger traffic.

Speaking in the middle of December 1948, upon the occasion of the unification meeting of the Socialist and Communist parties, Mr. Hilary Minc, Minister of Industry, summed up the production achievements and the structural changes wrought by the first two years of the Plan. Gross industrial production, taking 1937 as base, had increased from something over a third of pre-war in 1945 to over three-quarters of pre-war in 1946, over 100 per cent in 1947 and 140 per cent in 1948.[3] Comparing November 1948 with November 1937 the figure became 150 per cent. On a *per capita* basis the proportion had risen from slightly over half in 1945 to double the 1937 output in 1948.[4] In the composition of the total national product, there had been a marked change from less than half industry and more than half agriculture in 1937 to practically two-thirds industry and one-third agriculture in 1948.[5] Within industry there had been a more than proportional increase in producers' goods, and a base for mass production had been laid in a number of new fields such as the production of tractors, trucks, machine tools.

Private production in industry (excluding artisan production) had fallen from 8·8 per cent in 1946 to 6 per cent in 1948. All the

[1] Ibid., Hc 27.

[2] A part of this overfulfilment was ascribed to the special efforts put forth by the trade unions in furthering the so-called 'Congress Deed' movement, pledges by groups of workers to finish their part of the Plan in time for the Unification Congress of the Communist (Worker's) and Socialist parties held early in December 1948.

[3] The exact figures were: 38, 77, 107 and 140·5 per cent.

[4] 55 per cent to 199·5 per cent.

[5] 45·5 and 54·5 per cent to 64 and 36 per cent.

rest was now national or co-operative. In domestic trade, wholesaling was rapidly becoming co-operative or public, so that private enterprise now accounted for not more than 20 per cent of the whole. In foreign trade, it accounted for only 0·6 per cent of imports and 1·5 per cent of exports.

In agriculture, idle land had been reduced from over a third of the country's arable surface in 1946 to less than 10 per cent in 1948. Harvests on the country's present territories very nearly equalled those of pre-war on the same lands. Yields per hectare of the chief crops equalled or exceeded the pre-war. On a *per capita* basis the production of Poland's three chief grain crops was 20 per cent above pre-war. Hence the country was now not only self-sufficient in grain but had something of a surplus for export. The number of cattle *per capita* of the population, however, though it had trebled since 1945, was still only about 80 per cent of pre-war. Total *per capita* production of meat was some 90 per cent of pre-war, of milk less than 75 per cent. The grand total of *per capita* agricultural production had increased two and a half times since 1945 and now exceeded that of pre-war.[1]

In foreign trade the pre-war level had now been surpassed,[2] and on a *per capita* basis it was two-thirds above pre-war. A trade agreement concluded with the Soviet Union early in 1948 had ensured the importation of investment goods to the value of £112,000,000. In general, trade with the Soviet Union had risen from 0·4 per cent in 1938 to 21·5 per cent in 1948; and trade with her and the other countries of planned economy now accounted for over a third (37·8 per cent) of Poland's total foreign trade.

Railway freight traffic now exceeded the pre-war level and passenger transport had more than doubled. Even harbour traffic now equalled that of the same harbours before the war.

In the Western Territories there now lived almost 6,000,000 Poles, 5,000,000 of them new-comers. The share of the Western Territories in total national investment had increased from a quarter in 1946 to well over a third (38 per cent) in 1948. The territories now furnished over a fifth of the total output of nationalized industry.[3] In agriculture, almost 8,000,000 acres of idle

[1] 1945: 45 per cent; 1948: 110 per cent.

[2] 1946: less than 30 per cent of the 1938 level; 1947: less than 60 per cent; 1948: 115 per cent.

[3] Electric power, 37 per cent; coal, over 32 per cent; coke, over 50 per cent; cement, over 25 per cent; machine tools, over 20 per cent; coal cars, almost

land had been ploughed and sown. The ports of Danzig and Stettin had been rebuilt and the smaller ports on the western shore restored.

The 1949 Plan, embodied in a Bill passed by the national Diet at the end of March 1949, carried further the trends already described for 1948 by Mr. Minc. Investments were now to be nearly three times as great as during the first year of the Plan and total investments, including both those within and those outside the Plan, were to be 2·5 times pre-war. Major emphasis continued to be laid upon the capital goods industries: they were to receive three-quarters of all industrial investment. However, in production the highest rate of increase was to occur in the consumption goods industries, with the textile industry leading. Social services moreover were to increase to 8 per cent of all the country's investments, and housing to 8·4 per cent.

In the field of agriculture, the Plan called for a 25 per cent further rise in output over 1948, 1948 having been a year of good crops. The value of agricultural output *per capita* was already considerably higher than pre-war. The planned output of grain and potatoes was to be sufficient not only for domestic needs but for an export surplus.

Very significantly, as reflecting the policy changes of the previous autumn, increased emphasis was now to be placed upon the output of state-owned farms. They were now expected to 'pave the way for agricultural progress'. The 1949 Plan also for the first time provided for aid to various types of co-operatives and the development of co-operative villages.

Along with the new emphasis upon larger scale forms of agriculture went increased provision for mechanization. By 1 July 1949 there were to be 15,500 tractors in use. This represented an upward revision of over 50 per cent over the original Three-Year Plan figures for 1949. The figures for livestock production were also revised upward substantially, by 25 per cent.

In the field of domestic commerce, the 1949 Plan called for much further development of socialized trade. All told, State-owned, co-operative, and local government trading enterprises were to increase their turnover by almost 50 per cent.

In foreign trade, exports and imports were each to amount to some £150,000,000, with a slight favourable balance of trade. Of

70 per cent; cotton goods, 25 per cent; paper, almost 30 per cent; sugar, over 30 per cent.

the imports, slightly over a fifth were to be investment goods, two-thirds raw materials and subsidiaries, 10 per cent consumer goods. In exports coal would continue to lead, and there would be increases in the export of foodstuffs and other agricultural products.

Taking into account both the planned rise in industrial output and the planned savings in operating costs, the national income for 1949 was to reach a total exceeding the gross pre-war level by about 15 per cent. In *per capita* terms this would be about 50 per cent above pre-war.

By December 1949, it was announced that all these goals had not only been met but substantially exceeded. The Three-Year Plan as a whole had been finished ahead of time, a large part of the third year's portion of it one or two months ahead, so that the total of over-fulfilment by January 1950, turned out to be about 15 per cent. Plans for 1950 had meanwhile been launched, and preliminary figures given out for the new Six-Year Plan as a whole that was to occupy the years 1950–5. The task of initial reconstruction was now declared to have been finished, and the new longer-term Plan would be able to begin transformation of the economy along socialist lines.

II

BASES OF CHANGE: CZECHOSLOVAKIA

CHAPTER IV

INDUSTRIALIZED CZECHOSLOVAKIA

Like Poland, Czechoslovakia during the period between the two world wars went through the experience of being re-created as a nation, carved out of the pre-war imperial structure of central Europe. It differed from its northern neighbour, however, in almost all other important respects.

The country was small, with a population of about 15,000,000, landlocked, and for the most part highly industrialized. Its two western provinces, Bohemia and Moravia, had served as the workshop of the old Austro-Hungarian empire, sending out their wares to a domestic market of 67,000,000 population. Besides the majority Czech nationality here there was the sizeable German minority amounting to nearly 25 per cent of the whole. The small eastern section of the new country, Slovakia, had, as its name indicates, a different Slav majority nationality. The Slovaks had been kept far more retarded than the Czechs, both economically and culturally, under the harsh rule of the Hungarian Magyars, who constituted a very small part of the population. In contrast to the Czech lands, Slovakia had furnished part of the agricultural hinterland of the Austro-Hungarian Empire.

When the first World War was over and the empire was finally broken up, the new nation was thus faced with a double difficulty. One was that of reconstituting its economic life in the face of heavy trade barriers and the beginnings of rival industrialization in the other parts of the former empire. The other was that of assimilating Slovakia into really effective economic and political partnership: a retarded section of the country that for excellent reasons had strong separatist tendencies. There was also Carpatho-Ruthenia, a province still more retarded than Slovakia but lost to Czechoslovakia after World War II.

The methods of amalgamation pursued by the new republic after the first World War were those of an advanced liberal régime,

Politically all the national minorities were given extensive rights, including education in their mother-tongues and access to public office, and Slovakia especially made very rapid strides. Elementary education at public expense was for the first time made available there on a wide scale, and the illiteracy rate fell decisively. (The Czech provinces had already been the most advanced in literacy of all central Europe.) Economically, private industry made some brilliant advances in the Czech lands, the Bat'a shoe concern at Zlin being especially notable, and production costs were cut sufficiently to build up the necessary export trade. New concerns, however, when any were built, tended to cluster where industry was already well developed, leaving the backward regions, and more particularly Slovakia, still backward. It did not pay to invest there.

Indeed, in many ways it was convenient to have Slovakia remain as something of an economic hinterland. Slovak labourers came to the Czech lands when wanted, and Slovak agricultural products remained cheap enough to help Czech industry compete on international markets.

Agriculture in Czechoslovakia may be described as varying between the eastern and western European pattern, with Slovakia nearer to Poland in the degree of its rural over-population and the backwardness of its tillage, while Bohemia and Moravia were nearly as advanced as Germany. In the immediate post-war period, in fact twelve days after the establishment of the republic, the country had enacted the beginnings of a land reform. In the Czech lands much division among smallholders actually took place, but in Slovakia many of the great Magyar estates at the end of twenty years still lay untouched. Altogether by 1937 some 4,400,000 acres of land had changed hands, amounting to about 10 per cent of all arable and over 18 per cent of all forest lands. Some 639,000 applicants received land, about half the total number of those applying.

As in Poland, the original land reform scheme, enacted to meet a wave of irresistible popular feeling, was subsequently watered down, although in Czechoslovakia the watering down process never went so far as in Poland.

The operation of the reform was in the hands of a central Land Office, headed by a permanent presidential appointee and manned by twelve members elected by the Chamber of Deputies. Throughout its history the Land Office was in the hands of the Agrarian

Party, which soon became the leading conservative party in the young republic, numbering among its membership leading businessmen as well as landed proprietors. Great discretionary authority rested with the Land Office. 'It had to determine what estates fell within the law, in what order they were to be taken over, what estate industries . . . were exempt from the law, what part of the land might be retained by the owners, and what price was to be paid for the remainder.'[1]

The law specified that estates of over 150 hectares (370 acres) of arable land, or 250 hectares (618 acres) altogether, were subject to division. However, where it was 'in the public interest' for maximum production, land up to 500 hectares (1,235 acres) might be retained. Moreover, vagueness in the wording of the law left it unclear what claims, if any, could be made by the State against agricultural industries located on the estates. In actual operation, the great majority of these were left intact in the hands of their original owners. Even in the case of ordinary land, 'Land Office statistics show that a majority [of landowners] were left more than a strict interpretation of the law would have allotted them. In fact, nearly half the land taken into custody was returned to its original owners.' Also, 'large areas of forest were returned to their original owners'.[2]

As in Poland, the former landowner was free to sell land in excess of the maximum at his own price to prospective purchasers, subject to Land Office oversight. It was only if he failed to make a sale that the Government would take it over, in which case it was to pay him the full pre-war price.

Of the land distributed, very considerable amounts were apportioned, not to smallholders, but in large lots averaging 100 hectares (247 acres) each to large settlers. These were the so-called 'residual estates', consisting of land grouped around farm buildings of the original estates. Professor Jászi speaks of them as 'middle-class farms for influential Czech people'.[3]

Taking the country as a whole, industry, agriculture, and other

[1] Lucy E. Textor, 'Agriculture and Agrarian Reform', in Robert J. Kerner (Ed.), *Czechoslovakia: Twenty Years of Independence*, Berkeley, 1940, p. 223.

[2] Lewis Bracket, *Democratic Czechoslovakia*, revised edition issued by Czechoslovak Information Service, New York, *Democracy in Czechoslovakia*, June 1943, pp. 30, 34. The author considers these modifications praiseworthy.

[3] 'The Problem of Sub-Carpathian Ruthenia', R. J. Kerner (Ed.), op. cit., p. 209.

occupations were evenly balanced.[1] But within industry itself there was a great differentiation between the very large number of individually unimportant small establishments in the finishing industries and the large concentrations of capital in heavy industry such as mining, steel, and chemicals. Out of a total of 720,000 business 'establishments' only 2·2 per cent employed more than twenty workers. On the other hand, over 90 per cent of Czech coal production was controlled by seven firms—99 per cent of all iron ore was produced by a single concern, four companies produced almost 85 per cent of coke, and so on. A large part of mining stock, moreover, was foreign owned.

It was significant also that, while less than a quarter of the total population of the country was German, the Germans were concentrated in the older industrial regions, particularly along the western frontier. A disproportionate number of industrialists, technical personnel, and industrial workers were Germans.

Much State intervention and State capital existed in the republic, although here too the process had not gone nearly so far as in Poland. The State owned almost all the railway system, while all the tram-cars and the electric, gas, and water works were owned either by the communities or by co-operatives. There were also increasing numbers of mixed concerns. The Government had large funds invested in key firms such as the Skoda works and certain of the leading banks. The depression brought much more of this, including a mixed Grain Purchase monopoly and subsidies in the field of foreign trade.

The status of the industrial worker in Czechoslovakia was much higher than that of the small farmer, and strikingly higher than that of workers in Poland.

Membership in trade unions was large, amounting to nearly half of industrial wage earners. (It had increased fourfold during the twenty years of the republic.) Altogether some one and a quarter million industrial workers and, even more striking, nearly a million white collar workers and government employees were organized. However, these large numbers were split up into a number of different local and central organizations, along political party and religious lines, thus greatly weakening their influence.

[1] The 1930 census showed 35 per cent of the working population engaged in industry and crafts as over against 30 per cent in agriculture, 13 per cent in trade and transportation and no less than 17 per cent in the professions and public service.

At the time the Germans entered the country there were no less than eighteen competing trade union centrals with their countless branches, as well as numbers of unattached regional and local groups.

In the field of labour legislation and social services a number of reforms were achieved and held during the inter-war years. A sweeping eight-hour day law was passed in the early revolutionary period (December 1918) breaking sharply with the old Austrian legislation based on an eleven-hour day. It applied to all categories of labour, set limits to overtime, and also prohibited night work for women and juveniles.

A sickness insurance law was passed soon thereafter, in 1919. It covered all wage workers, even agricultural labourers, and the members of their families, and provided a twelve-week maternity benefit. Health facilities for the insured were built up continually thereafter, winning high international reputation.

Public unemployment insurance was never achieved, although in the early days it was promised for the future. Instead, the so-called Ghent system of unemployment benefits was established, providing for compulsory insurance of trade union members, financed by the trade unions with substantial subventions by the State.

Works councils laws were achieved in 1921, first for mines and then for factories as well. The councils were alloted 10 per cent of the profits of each establishment for welfare work.

Vocational training was built up successfully during the period of the republic. The status of women was ensured by the Constitution, and was in practice high in industry as well as in public life.

Czechoslovakia had many political parties split along national and religious lines as well as class lines. Among them were three that adhered to a more or less Socialist position and that secured a considerable part of the trade union vote. There was the original Socialist Party, the Communist Party that split from the Socialists in 1921, and the moderate and far smaller National Socialist Party that had been formed so early as 1897 and appealed particularly to the white collar worker. It was to this party that Beneš belonged.

The largest proportion of votes ever won by a single party was the 25 per cent reached by the Socialist Party in the first elections, before the split with the Communists. No party thereafter ever succeeded in winning more than 15 per cent, although the Communist and Socialist parties between them at all times polled nearly 25 per cent of the total. The second largest party at this time was the Agrarian Party, representing the landed and later on the leading business interests of the country as well. Together with the Socialists it formed the centre of the first, 'Red-Green' coalition. In the subsequent election the Agrarians became the first party and the Communists, who remained outside the coalition, the second. It is to be noted that the Agrarians were at all times the fulcrum of the Government bloc, and that there was at no time any serious rival bloc. The bloc was very large and variegated, and in addition to the Agrarians and the two Socialist groups it contained the powerful Catholic Party. Had the two Socialist parties and the Communists ever chosen to combine they would have mustered twice as many votes as the Agrarians, but this never happened.

During the opening years, the reforms enacted under the urging of the Socialists included constitutional matters such as marriage and divorce legislation and non-sectarian instruction in the public schools. Next came, not public ownership, but establishment of the principle of State control of railroads and hydro-electric power, and the guaranteeing by law of workers' councils in industry. Beyond this the 1919–20 ministries did not go, and thereafter they did not have the opportunity. The country at this time badly needed foreign loans. 'Czechoslovak socialism rapidly moderated its economic programme. . . . Any far-reaching experiments would undoubtedly have weakened the new Republic's financial position. . . . Czechoslovakia did not abuse the confidence which her Western protectors and benefactors reposed in her.'[1]

During the subsequent Agrarian Party periods, while at times the coalition could be called 'Green-Black' (Agrarian-clerical), the basic complexion of Parliament and the conduct of successive Governments shifted but little. The Agrarian Party remained permanently in control of the Department of Agriculture and the Land Commission, hence of the Agrarian Reform, and headed various other important ministries as well. However, the other eligible parties received their share, and in fact so stable was the line-up that many of the portfolios were said to be regarded as the private preserve of particular political parties, irrespective of the momentary complexion of the Government.

[1] Melbone W. Graham, 'Constitutional and Political Structure', in R. J. Kerner (Ed.), op. cit.

Party control over Cabinet and Parliament hinged upon the voting system and the authority of extra-parliamentary leaders. Voting was by the list system and party discipline was exceedingly strict: the voter could not split his ticket or scratch a name, candidates were declared elected in the order of the list preordained by the party managers, and once elected, any M.P. voting contrary to party orders could be withdrawn and another substituted. At the top of the party manager system was the joint group of the leaders of the largest parties, known as the 'Petka' or Five. Extra-parliamentary and indeed extra-constitutional, these leaders quite openly directed the policies of the country: Cabinets and Parliaments carried out their bidding.

The intricate combination of numerous parties, strict discipline, and successive Government blocs so variegated in composition as to be meaningless, gave the country its exceedingly stable—toward the end of the régime deceptively stable—appearance. It was not until the sudden growth of the Henlein Party under Nazi inspiration, sweeping rapidly into its orbit the majority of all the German votes in the country in 1935, that the coalition balance began to break up.

It was at this same critical period, following the prolonged effects of the great depression and the successes of the Nazis, that the weakness of Czech administrative policy in Slovakia revealed itself: the clerical and separatist Slovak People's Party (Hlinka Party) gained strength, with its slogan 'For God and Nation!' Most of its organizers were Catholic priests and they were able to combine with their Church grievances—the spread of public rather than parochial schools and the predominance of Protestants among Slovakia's political leadership—a series of nationalist complaints. The republic's government was said to be too centralized, one had to run to Prague for every adjustment, under Hungarian rule the counties had had more home rule; as to the republic's governing class, what were all these Czech bureaucrats doing in Slovakia? They were as arrogant as the old Hungarian officials, they even received higher incomes than the Slovaks, special living allowances because they lived away from home. . . .

Actually there was some fire beneath the smoke. 'After ten years [of the republic and the new education] Slovaks left school only to find that many positions were being held by Czechs.' Then came the economic crisis and retrenchment. The Government had to limit the number of new appointments and it hesitated to relinquish the services of any of the faithful Czech officials—who unfortunately often held unpopular posts. 'They were often gendarmes, policemen, or tax collectors.'[1]

Once the Germans began their Munich policy of piecemeal absorption, both the Agrarian Party and the Slovak Catholic Party compromised themselves hopelessly for any future leadership in a revived nation. But collaborationism was made easy at first.

German occupation policy throughout Czechoslovakia was very different from what it was soon to be in Poland. Here there was no attempt to drive out and kill off the native population, nor even to despoil them totally. Treatment was highly selective, with terror reserved for Jews and any who could be associated with signs of the resistance movement. There was also a sharp difference between the status accorded the Czech provinces and Slovakia. Whereas Bohemia and Moravia were a 'Protectorate', Slovakia was 'Autonomous' and had its own fully established quisling government under Father Tiso. Slovak separatism was assiduously fed with hopes of complete independence at a later date.

Very important economic consequences flowed from these distinctions. Relatively few industrial establishments or cultural monuments were razed, manpower was not seriously decimated, businessmen and intellectuals for the most part were not physically destroyed, the country-side was not devastated on a large scale. The losses in the Czech provinces were chiefly those of reckless wear and tear and neglect, selective looting, and the usual Nazi financial manipulations, siphoning off the country's currency and credit resources to Germany.

In the case of Slovakia there was actually an expansion of industry. A number of new factories were built and there was more demand for labour than ever before. On the surface there was apparently prosperity. Agricultural products were in demand, food was not rationed. Some Jewish-owned land was even taken over and distributed in the name of land reform to Slovak farmers. Once the fighting began heavily on Slovak soil, however, in the concluding stages of the war, heavy war damage occurred, especially in the eastern sections of the country-side. Partisans had been active in eastern Slovakia for some time before this and in early 1944 an uprising against the Tiso Government occurred that held wide stretches of the country for some time. In the later stages of the war, moreover, taxation and requisitioning had been much

[1] A. Kussosi, *The Basis of Czechoslovak Unity*, 1944.

heavier. Both politically and economically, therefore, the effects of the war upon Slovakia were exceedingly mixed.

For all Czechoslovakia the process of liberation and the setting up of an initial liberation government was much simpler than for Poland. As in the case of Poland, the bulk of the liberating was accomplished by the Red Army. But unlike Poland, there was no question here of a sharply divided political allegiance. There was no opposition 'government in exile' here in competition with a local one formed in the course of the fighting, there had been no rival military undergrounds, the whole situation was less sharp. Beneš, with his followers, was the 'London Government' and all groups acknowledged him. This was indeed a unique situation in Europe: to have a government-in-exile that had consistently received the allegiance of the people at home and was avowedly on friendly terms with the Soviet Union. So soon as the fighting had crossed the eastern border, therefore, a set of principles for the new Government, initiated by the Communists and known as the Košice Programme, was agreed to, with the approval of Beneš, by all the organized liberation groups.

CHAPTER V

REFORMS AND REVOLUTIONS

I. LAND REFORM AND NATIONALIZATION, FIRST AND SECOND STAGES

The National Front

Nationalization in reconstituted Czechoslovakia at first did not go so far as in Poland. Although the Czechs referred to their 1945 situation as a 'revolution', the degree of continuity between their pre-war and post-war régimes was far greater than in Poland. Their pre-war régime had, of course, been far more democratic, middle-class, advanced, and prosperous than that of the Poles: there was less of a striking nature for them to flee from. Besides, the Czechs had never gone through the revolutionizing experience as a nation of fighting the Germans with arms in hand, nor had they met the full force of the German's eastern policy. Destruction for them had been purposely selective and on a moderate scale.

To meet the economic crisis of the post-war therefore required no such extraordinary means as it did of the Poles. Government intervention, yes. Some government ownership, undoubtedly. But there was not the same appalling wreckage everywhere, not the same absolute dearth of capital, means of production, business ownership even. More particularly, the vacuum created by the war in the ranks of the business class was much less. Therefore, on the one hand there was no such crying need to take over medium-sized business, and on the other by the same token there remained a much larger group of highly vocal business and upper professional men to be reckoned with in framing national policies.

Political factors in the Government itself were also different. As suggested earlier, the government-in-exile group headed by Beneš never constituted an intransigeant opposition, ultimately defeated and individually absorbed, as happened finally in Poland. It itself accepted a radical programme and Beneš was unopposed for the presidency.

The political party mixture also was unique. Instead of a fairly even balance between Socialists and Communists as in Poland, in Czechoslovakia the Communists, taking the country as a whole, were by far the largest political group, with the Socialists much smaller. In the Czech lands the Communist plurality was very large. However, in Slovakia the leading group was a powerful Church party—which subsequently became involved in separatism once more. In the Czech lands there was also a far smaller Church party, the People's Party, much more moderate in tone, but opposed to more than a minimum of nationalization. And there was President Beneš's National Socialist Party which, even more than the People's Party, now had become the haven of the business interests of the country, the Agrarian Party having disappeared because of its collaboration with the Germans.

The whole spectrum of parties, it will be seen, had shifted to the left, and most of the smaller parties, as well as the collaborationists, had disappeared. The remaining groups, all of them with a claim to some Resistance activity, had joined together in a 'National Front of Czechs and Slovaks', and it was this grouping which accepted from the Communists the Košice Programme and undertook to remain together to carry on the government and give shape to the promised reforms. Irrespective of actual size, the four Czech parties agreed to an equal representation in the initial Parliament, and on all committees. By a gentleman's agreement, moreover, a unanimity rule on the reporting out of legislation was agreed upon: every reform Bill must have the approval of all four of the party representatives on its appropriate committee before it was to be presented to Parliament as a whole. By these means the more conservative parties were to be ensured against dominance by the numerically stronger Communists.

In addition to the political parties, two politically important institutions with a strong leftward orientation existed from the outset in the new society: the National Committees and the trade union organization. As revolutionary organs of the Resistance, representing the organized underground groups rather than merely the population at large, local 'National Committees' had been explicitly recognized by the Government-in-exile through President Beneš so early as the summer of 1944. He had called upon them to oust the Germans and to set up local administrations. Subsequently, in April 1945, the Košice Programme confirmed this role for them throughout the republic and called upon them to elect a Provisional National Assembly. Declaring that the gulf between government and people in pre-war Czechoslovakia had been too great, it stated that henceforth the National Committees were to be the new organs of State and public administration. Such a substratum of potentially revolutionary organizations was to prove important in the subsequent history of the Government. Even at the time, it was recognized that the powers of the Government were to be in a sense derivative, with the National Front, somewhat equivocally, representing not only the six political parties but to some extent, on a local level, the Resistance movements.

The other self-declared revolutionary organization, with its leadership shared by Communists and some Socialists, was the United Revolutionary Trade Union Organization. Formed during the days of the Underground out of the fragments of the old disunited trade union organizations, this one was more highly developed and centralized than anything that developed in Poland in the early days. It rapidly secured a unique place for itself, upon various crucial occasions formulating political policies which were subsequently adopted by the Left political parties, rather than vice versa.

The initial programme agreed upon at Košice was purposely left vague in its economic sections. Expulsion of Germans and Hungarians and confiscation and distribution of their landed property and that of collaborators to small peasants was stated in so many words. Even here, however, there was subsequently much debate as to how rapidly this programme should be carried out. There were some three million Germans, and their loss as manpower, in both industry and agriculture, it was felt by many of the more conservative elements, was too serious to be undertaken lightly. In Slovakia, where many large estates remained, actually the whole Hungarian expulsion and land programme lagged until after a political overturn in November 1947.

As to nationalization of industry, the Košice programme merely spoke of seizing and placing under national 'administration' the business properties of Germans, Hungarians, and their collaborators, and the placing under general 'government control' of 'the key industries, the insurance system and all sources of power' as well as 'the entire financial and loan system'. It also made promises to help the non-speculative, private initiative of 'employers, traders, and other producers' by loans, the furnishing of raw materials, etc. That was all.

The interpretation given to this programme as soon as the new Government was established was broader than the original words seemed to indicate. It was, however, unquestionably along the lines desired by the most vocal groups in the country, more particularly the trade unions. Even so, the resulting nationalization was much less sweeping than that of Poland.

Industry

The Nationalization Decrees of October 1945 applied, in general, to all industrial enterprises employing more than 300 to 500 persons. In a number of cases the limit was 400. In certain others the criterion was size of technical capacity rather than number of employees. In various 'key' industries, however, such as mining, iron and steel and electric power, all establishments were nationalized irrespective of size. The building industry was not covered, and neither was printing, although special regulation was provided for the latter.

The resulting extent of nationalization was such that in the Czech lands in the course of a year roughly 60 per cent of industrial employment was in the nationalized sector. But the 60 per cent was very unevenly distributed. It ranged from 100 per cent in mining and approximately 75 per cent in iron and steel, metallurgy, and chemicals, to 60 per cent in leather, 46 per cent in textiles and clothing, 39 per cent in food, and only 10 per cent in building. These variations were subsequently to prove significant.

Compensation was to be paid on the basis of the current price of the property at the time of its taking over. A Fund for Nationalized Economy was to issue bonds to cover the payments out of the proceeds of national industry. In cases of personal hardship, owners might receive a small living allowance subsidy.

Enemy and collaborationist property was of course to be confiscated outright without compensation, irrespective of size. As in the case of Poland, the medium-sized enemy concerns were to be either attached to nationalized enterprises or handed over to local authorities, while small ones might be sold to private owners. Some with obsolete machinery were closed down.

Land

In its first post-war stage, the Czechoslovak land reform also did not go so far as that of Poland. As in the case of industry, the immediate need here was not so critical. The country-side in the interior was less overcrowded and the peasants less desperate. By far the largest number of remaining great estates were situated in the border regions where German and Hungarian landlords had managed to perpetuate themselves in spite of the 1919 reform. Their lands, often lying in continuous stretches, would now be forfeit in any case and would furnish much land for settlers. And on the side of government, the same factors making for a cautious approach toward property rights were operative in land as they were in industry.

The Košice Programme had said nothing whatever about the land of nationals. As indicated above, it had concentrated on the confiscation and division of enemy and traitors' land—accepting the action already taken by the Slovak National Council and the local Land Committees in this respect, and promising to apply similar measures to the rest of the republic. A series of decrees in accordance with the Košice Programme were promptly passed during 1945. As in the case of similar Polish legislation, they provided for confiscation without payment of all enemy and traitor holdings irrespective of size. The only exceptions were for enemy nationals who had personally proved themselves anti-fascist. Distribution was to be exclusively for the benefit of small farmers and landless labourers, and purchase prices were to be very low. Also as in Poland, the whole machinery of assessment and distribution was changed from the pre-war official pattern to one based on local Land Committees in co-operation with the National Land Office.

It was clear, however, that with more settled conditions a revision and fulfilment of the original 1919 reform as it applied to Czech and Slovak nationals, would also inevitably have to be undertaken. It was their holdings that constituted the great majority of the often over-sized 'residual estates', as well as perhaps 10 per cent of the original, inadequately divided big estates.

A Land Reform Revision Bill was finally passed late in 1947, providing for a thorough re-examination of the implementation of the old Reform, with power to annul and reverse all illegal and ambiguous decisions taken under it. The provisions of the Act were to be carried out before the end of 1948. In practice this would have meant that the upper limit for the original Czech and Slovak landlords would have been fixed strictly at the 600-odd acres overall originally intended, while the 2,000 'residual estate' owners would have been pared down from 250 acres or more to 125 each. If carried to completion, this process in itself would have provided nearly 2,000,000 acres for distribution, more than the total that all the smallholders had received during the twenty years of the original Reform.

For practical purposes, however, the really profound changes undertaken by the 1945–7 reforms remained those of the handling of enemy land. It was the German and Magyar aristocracy that had held 90 per cent of the original 2,000 great estates covering 10,000,000 acres before the 1919 Reform. Of their average of 5,000 acres each at that time, no less than 2,800 acres each still remained to them in 1938, or some four and a half times as much as the supposed upper limit. The big German estates in the Czech border districts with their rich forest lands and the big Hungarian estates in southern Slovakia had been especially untouched and formed large, often contiguous areas. In terms of available land, the total German holdings in the Czech districts alone amounted to over 6,000,000 acres, about 2,500,000 in forest and 3,500,000 in arable surface. Of the latter, almost all lay in the strategic border regions. Breaking up these great foreign concentrations, nationalizing the forest holdings, and opening the arable portions for settlement, meant a weighty social change.

The February Events

Within three years of the first stage of Czechoslovakia's revolution in industry and landholding, namely in February 1948, came a second stage. It occurred in the midst of the country's Two-Year Plan and just before the framing of the country's new Constitution. The revolution was a bloodless one, but far reaching for all that. The 'February events', as they were called, consisted initially of a series of mass demonstrations and a token general strike, ushered in by a Cabinet crisis: these thereupon resulted in a series of revolutionary governmental changes.

The political tensions between Left and relatively Right groups in the country had progressively worsened as East-West relations worsened in the outside world. In February 1946, in elections generally conceded to have been free, the Left parties in the Czech provinces had had a majority of two to one over the two more conservative parties. The Communists were the largest single party, with 40 per cent of the vote, and the Socialists had 16. In the much smaller and less urban population of Slovakia, where the Socialists had no strength, the proportions were reversed: the Communists had 30 per cent of the vote and the very conservative Slovak Democrats had over 60. Combining the two parts of the country, the Communists still had 38 per cent of the total, the Socialists about 13, and all conservative groups together nearly 50. This made an extremely delicate balance if once relations became unfriendly.

During 1947 an impasse had gradually been reached in passing legislation through Parliament, including both promised reform Bills and the draft of the new Constitution itself. It will be recalled that under the unanimity rule agreed to originally, representatives of all parties in each parliamentary committee had to agree to every Bill before it was reported out.[1]

The Communists maintained that the impasse was being purposely created by the minority parties, more particularly the National Socialists, to poison the popular mind against the Government in preparation for the coming elections. The conservatives asserted that the Communists were losing ground anyway and were preparing to take over power.

A crisis was precipitated when the representatives of the conservative parties in the Cabinet sought to stop the Minister of the Interior from promoting certain Communist police officers. They resigned in a body in protest, without, it was said, consulting their parties. For a period of days President Beneš, who himself belonged to the National Socialist Party but was regarded as independent, apparently remained undecided whether to accept their resignations. Meanwhile a series of tremendous demonstrations took place in Prague, and it was these, together with a token one-hour general strike, closing down, it was said, everything in the city, that really gave the 'February events' their character of a second stage of revolution. President Beneš finally accepted the resignations of the Ministers concerned, and the Government continued in office, with new representatives of the more conservative parties replacing those who had resigned. Technically the process was constitutional.

The demonstrations had been peaceful and no counter-demonstrations were held by the more conservative parties with the exception of a demonstration of university students. There was a

[1] A moment's reflection upon such a rule would suggest that only a majority unusually trustful of continued co-operation from former opponents could have agreed to it.

national Congress of Works Councils representatives and a Peasant Congress. At these were voiced not only support of the Government and condemnation of the policy of blocking legislation, but a series of concrete demands for further and more radical legislation. More important still, the demonstrators demanded that the political parties and national life generally be 'cleansed' of elements determined to 'sabotage' the National Front programme. And they demanded the addition to the National Front of representatives of the trade unions and other mass organizations.

All over the country now were set up so-called Action Committees to carry out the programme of the National Front within their respective organizations and to cleanse them of hostile elements. They were formed within all organizations in the country, even in educational and welfare institutions and within the Catholic hierarchy itself. In a short while the Action Committees of the various organizations dissolved again, their work supposedly done; but those of the National Front itself remained and greatly activized its local branches, which now consisted explicitly not only of the political parties but of the trade unions and other local mass organizations. It was, in a sense, a reconstitution of the state of affairs existing when the original revolutionary National Committees had taken hold and been given authority to call a Provisional Assembly into being.

Further evolution came in the spring and summer. In the period immediately after the February events the various political parties remained officially as before, as constituent elements of the National Front, each with its independent organization. The two more conservative parties, more particularly the National Socialists, had gone through an extensive purge of leadership at the hands of their respective Action Committees. The Socialists, who had in 1946 commanded 12 per cent of the vote, had not gone through as much of an overhaul, since they already had a stong Left wing; this was now in control, with the Right wing lopped off.[1] All the parties joined together once more, as in 1945, in a common slate of candi-

[1] The policies of the right Socialists had been successfully discredited when they had nearly engineered a tie-up with the two conservative parties during the course of the Cabinet crisis; had they succeeded, the dissidents in the Cabinet would have formed a majority. Much was also made of irregularities said to have been discovered in departments headed by certain of the dissidents, after their departure.

dates at the general elections of June.[1] Cabinet seats as well as those in Parliament itself were divided once more according to a political key; only this time harmony had been assured beforehand.

Meanwhile the Socialist Party had been having a series of discussion meetings, and soon after the elections the party voted to dissolve and join the Communist Party *en bloc*. Thereafter only the two conservative parties retained their identity. Apparently they confined their activity to protecting the interests of their remaining members, in the administration of laws affecting private business and so on. Certainly they no longer attempted to swing legislation. For all serious policy formation the Communist Party was now responsible, not only in the mass organizations but in all branches of the Government.

It would have been extremely interesting to see what would have been the next steps in Czechoslovak economic policy under these circumstances, if the outside world had meanwhile stood still. But instead, that summer saw the Tito-Cominform split, and with it a turn to the Left of all the Communist parties of eastern Europe. In external policy all these parties now advocated a closer drawing together of their several countries with the Soviet Union and against the influences of the West. And in internal policy, all advocated a consolidation of the Socialist elements of their economy *vis-à-vis* the capitalist and a more rapid and decisive march toward the final goal of socialism. Indeed they accused their former party leaders of having fallen into a more or less static view of the composition of a 'Popular Democracy': a neglect of its essence as a purposefully transitional form and a glossing over of the class struggle going on within it. The centre of their new approach was a changed peasant policy. Instead of the more radical of the peasants being held back, all the smaller peasantry were now to be urged forward toward ultimate co-operative farming, and they were to be warned and helped against their 'class enemy', the larger farmer. Less central, but a part of the same policy, was the competing out of existence of the private trader by public and

[1] Running in opposition to the common slate was permitted, but the only two opposition candidates of whom the author heard at the time withdrew their names before the day of the election. Balloting moreover was only optionally secret, so that at the polling place the author observed, some voters demonstratively refused to enter the booths. Wherever this occurred *en masse* a voter wishing to cast a negative ballot in secret would certainly have hesitated to do so.

co-operative trade, and the drawing together of handicraftsmen into production co-operatives.

In the case of Czechoslovakia this meant that, no sooner had February been well digested, when a yet further series of social-economic changes began to be undertaken. These, however, will be left to a later chapter for discussion.

New Legislation

Once the 'February events' were over, the log-jam on legislation that had been developing in Parliament during 1947 was of course broken. The National Insurance Law, the Education Law, the project for the new Constitution itself, were finally reported out by their respective Parliamentary Committees and passed by Parliament. Most important of all in the economic field, a further Nationalization Law and a further Land Reform Law were quickly adopted. The new Nationalization features had been demanded of the Government by the trades union and works committee demonstrators during the 'February events'. Similarly the increased Land Reform had been demanded at that time by the peasant demonstrators. It had already been projected previously at the end of 1947 by the Ministry of Agriculture, a key organ headed ever since Liberation by a Communist, but nothing approaching it had had a chance of passage in Parliament.

The new Nationalization Law went as far as the Polish law and even somewhat further. Considering the more highly developed state of Czechoslovak industry, it represented a definitely more revolutionary change. (As a Pole said to the writer soon after, 'Revolutions which come later are always more radical.') The new absolute limit for industrial establishments was to be fifty persons overall, not fifty per shift as in the original Polish decrees, and without free invitation to future capital to exceed the limit.

Certain further key branches of industry, moreover, were to be added to the original list of branches to be nationalized in their entirety. They included key branches of the building and building materials industries, various key branches of the food processing industry, all distilleries, breweries, and wine-making establishments, all sugar mills, the entire pharmaceutical industry. All told, it was estimated that over 90 per cent of industrial production would now be in the hands of national or local authorities or co-operatives, only about 8½ per cent in the hands of private enterprise.[1]

In addition to all this, important steps in nationalization, having no counterpart in Poland, were to be taken in the sphere of trade. All foreign trade was now to be nationalized, and all wholesale trade.

Furthermore, all health resorts and watering places were to be nationalized without regard to size, and all hotels and restaurants employing more than fifty persons. Similarly with all department stores and other retail establishments employing more than fifty persons. In general, in contrast to Poland, one may say that the fifty-employee ceiling in Czechoslovakia was to apply not only to industry but to virtually all forms of private business enterprise.[2]

In the field of farming, the new legislation was likewise sweeping and very simple. In the first place, 125 acres was henceforth to be the upper limit to private landholding. Any surplus land above this amount would be trimmed off and paid for. In contrast to Poland, however, the owner could continue to work the rest. Secondly, as also in Poland, no land whatever above 2½ acres could be held if the owner did not work on it himself. 'The land to him who tills it', had been the slogan of the peasant demonstrators. Hence many of the 'residuary estates', those that had formerly been held by townsfolk and rented out to tenant farmers, would be forfeit in their entirety. By the combination of these two principles it was easy to see that tenancy would be eliminated altogether and wage labour in agriculture considerably reduced. The implementation of the new reform, moreover, was obviously likely to be strengthened by the revamping of the National Committee machinery.

2. NATIONALITY QUESTION: SLOVAKIA

Unlike Poland, for Czechoslovakia the question of a permanent national minority was not automatically settled by the war, the Nazis, and national boundary changes. Slovakia was to remain an

[1] It is interesting to note that this percentage is just what Poland had had in 1946. By the end of 1948 Poland reported only 6 per cent of industrial production in private hands.

[2] However, one might also point out that Poland had little need of such an explicit ceiling. In Poland there were few private concerns in these lines capable of employing 50 persons.

integral part of the republic—but with a difference. How the difference was to be implemented became a social-political question of the highest importance.

The handling of a backward area—still more a backward partner—is a difficult test for any government. This was what had faced the new Czechoslovak régime after Liberation.

Politically the Košice Programme, in this as in other respects presented by the Communists and accepted by the London Government, had promised a sharp break with pre-war national structure. The Czechs and Slovaks were henceforth to be treated as two 'nations', with parallel government structures in all respects save at the top level of administration where the powers of the Slovak National Council were of necessity limited. At the outset the parallelism was carried over into political party, trade union, and other structures as well.

Personnel policies proceeded to follow a new pattern: Slovak nationals wherever available now occupied Slovak posts, whether in industry or administration—to the detriment, it was frequently observed, of immediate efficiency, but to the undoubted satisfaction of the Slovaks themselves.

Some such radical break with the past was considered as inevitable by most groups in the liberation process, if only to cut the ground from under the remnants of the Tiso 'autonomous' clerical-fascist régime. However, it had its dangers too. On the one hand, it was precisely in Slovakia that the bitterest final struggles against the Nazis had taken place: the partisans here knew what they wanted and had earned. On the other hand, it was in Slovakia that the forces of the old order were strongest. The Church hierarchy here was more consistently wedded to the past and had a far stronger hold upon the population than in the Czech lands. During the Tiso régime it had had charge of the entire school system. It was deeply opposed to any change in the old agrarian order, the beneficiaries of which were still very much in evidence even though their pre-war political parties were now to be banned. Hence the parallel political structure set up for Slovakia was bound to result in very sharp tensions there, with maximum opportunity, as the event showed, for the opponents of the new régime as a whole to entrench themselves.

The results of the 1946 elections had confirmed the cleavage. Here as in the Czech provinces, of course, all legitimized political parties had become members of the National Front and had subscribed to the common programme. For Slovakia there were two parties (with last-minute minor additions), the Democratic Party, harbouring the more conservative elements, and the Communist Party. The Democratic Party received 62 per cent of the vote and the Communists 30 per cent. Counting in the additions, it would make two-thirds of the vote for the conservative grouping and one-third for the Communist-Socialists. (The Socialists had received but 3 per cent of the total.)

It soon became evident, moreover, that the animus of the Slovak Democratic Party was much more bitter in its anti-Socialism than the corresponding Czech parties. Difficulties between the Slovak National Council, dominated by it, and the central Government culminated in November 1947 in accusations by the Government of an actual armed plot in Slovakia and a reorganization of the Democratic Party and the Council. Warnings of brewing trouble had been given by observers for some time. 'The fact is', wrote a British economist in a study of the country early in 1947, 'that officials of the fascist Slovak Republic still hold positions of authority, that a reactionary clergy is still powerful in Slovakia, that the Democratic Party . . . draws heavily upon the remnants of the now outlawed clerical-fascist parties. . . . The Democrats . . . will hold a key position in the National Assembly [for their vote was required on any question affecting the status of Slovakia]. . . . While these conditions remain, the Slovak problem will continue to be a threat to Czechoslovakia.'[1]

The November 1947 changes in Slovakia anticipated by only a few months the nation-wide changes of the following February. Slovak land reform and the removal of Hungarians and pro-Nazis from estates and businesses at last began to be speeded up. So did the beginnings of serious attack upon the black market that kept Slovak prices higher than Czech. Nominally, of course, the same basic legislation on nationalization, land reform, and related matters had been applicable in both parts of the country all the time. But even after February the retarding effects of the Slovak social situation were very evident.

The basic attack upon Slovakia's difficulties, advanced originally by the Communists in 1937 and accepted in principle by all parties of the National Front after the war, was industrialization. It was a difficult proposition for any Slovak politician openly to

[1] William Diamond, *Czechoslovakia Between East and West*, London, 1947, p. 53.

oppose, since it was to be effected through aid from the richer Czech lands. However, nothing could be more calculated to undermine the strongholds of the old order—more particularly as the bulk of industrialization now was bound to come from nationalized rather than private industry.

For twenty years under the First Republic Slovak industrialization had been held up for the simplest of reasons: it did not pay. In common with other East European nations that had been bypassed by the first wave of the industrial revolution, Slovakia lagged behind at a permanent disadvantage: more advanced neighbours—in Slovakia's case, the Czech lands—offered a more attractive field for investment for the very reason that they already had a good industrial and communications network and because they already had a prosperous internal market. The retarded agrarian lands, on the other hand, had little purchasing power and poor facilities. In the case of Slovakia, lack of coal aggravated her unattractiveness to the investor, cancelling out any advantages she might have derived from her considerable deposits of iron ore. And the mountainous nature of much of the country increased the poverty of her agricultural population and hence of her internal market. Finally, during the First Republic the over-expanded state of parts of Czech industry in relation to foreign markets made it highly unlikely that Czech capital would find it profitable to cross the border and start yet further competition.

The degree of Slovak backwardness was very great. The 1930 census figures showed less than 20 per cent of the Slovak population engaged in industry, as against 57 per cent in agriculture—a ratio comparable to what Bohemia had had eighty years earlier. Transportation was only about half as developed. Industrial wages were low because of the pressure of workers for jobs. And the living standards of the rural population, by all available criteria, were hardly more than half those of the Czech farmer. Farms were small, overcrowded, poor, and poorly cultivated.[1] The birth-rate continued extremely high. Such industry as there was was very badly distributed, clustering thickly in a few centres and contributing little to the prosperity of the poorer regions.

[1] The typical Slovak farm averaged around 12 to 13 acres as compared to the Czech 25. In part this could be accounted for by inheritance laws. In the Czech lands, following Austrian law, one heir inherited the whole land. In Slovakia, following Hungarian law, the father divided his inheritance among his sons.

The war gave a sharp temporary stimulus to industrialization. Metallurgy increased greatly and so, to a certain extent, did textiles. Not many new plants were built, but many existing plants were greatly enlarged and modernized. This, of course, further increased the cluster-pattern of industry, but it put money into workers' pockets.

With the end of the war and the widespread destruction in rural eastern Slovakia, affecting about a quarter of the Slovak population, the prospect of restoration by other than governmental means was of course negligible. So was the prospect of attracting private capital for industry into such a situation. In the words of a trade union leader, 'For us nationalization is not even a question, nationalization is a necessity, there is no other possibility'.[1]

In the first period after Liberation, aid to Slovakia took the form of direct relief and rehabilitation supplies and the transfer of some factories from the Czech border districts whence the Germans were being removed. Under the Two-Year Plan direct commitments were made to transfer enough additional plant and machinery to provide employment for 26,000 further Slovak workers. This would represent a considerable net addition to the labour force, since its total at the time was probably about 140,000. Total investments in Slovakia under the Plan were to amount to about a third of the country's total. As Slovakia contained under 30 per cent of the country's population and furnished only about 15 per cent of the national income, this was a generous allocation. (Later on, under the Five-Year Plan, the programme was stepped up yet faster: new industrial jobs were to be provided for another 90,000 workers, a quarter of whom were to be skilled.)

In spite of political troubles the industrialization programme proceeded above expectations. Almost 25,000 new workers had been absorbed into industry in the first year of the Two-Year Plan, most of them into large nationalized industry. Attempts were made to utilize all the war-time gains in productive capacity possible, even if some of the plants had to run temporarily at a loss.[2]

[1] Interview material, May 1948.

[2] Thus, in 1948, half a dozen factories with over 5,000 employees each were said to be operating which before World War II had had less than a thousand workers or none. (e.g., Svit, a large artificial silk plant located in what had been bare country near the Tatra mountains, was one of these. It now gave employment to 8,000 workers and had developed into a flourishing factory town.) A considerable number of 1,000- to 2,000-employee plants were also operating which before the war had not existed at all. In 1948 6 metal

Some of the absorption of new workers into industry had, however, apparently been accomplished by somewhat questionable means. The factories complained of were small and medium sized private ones, and curiously enough the blame was placed by more conservative elements in the Czech lands upon the Slovak Communists for having created an atmosphere of 'industrialization at any cost' so that anyone was welcome. Be that as it may, during the first stage of nationalization, fly-by-night concerns had managed to break off from larger units about to be nationalized in the Czech lands—or else they bought up their equipment—and set up shop with their machinery across the border. 'Parcellizing factories', the process was called, and the claim of the Slovak trade unionists was that these runaway concerns thereupon competed with nationalized Slovak industry for raw materials from abroad, and also broke the labour laws. (The difference in attitude toward planned and unplanned migration was interesting to observe.)

In the textile industry the migration process was facilitated by the existence of a war-caused surplus of spindles in Slovakia, which the Slovak industry apparently was loath to sell to the Czechs. Spindlage in the Czech lands meanwhile was short, also for war reasons, with an ensuing shortage of thread for the Czech weaving mills, some of which were said to be running short time. Small entrepreneurs seeking quick profits would therefore pick up looms and join the migration—with results not healthy in the long run for stable industry.

During 1948 the events of February had brought many of these small and medium-sized plants under nationalization, and the resulting technical problems were immense. The second stage of nationalization presented difficulties quite different from the first. The proportion of nationalized industry throughout Slovakia was now to be 80 per cent as compared to some 50 per cent before February, but the additional 30 per cent were precisely the less well organized and less stable concerns. 'We now have a big and difficult task', said a textile executive, 'to make these mills produc-

plants with over 1,000 workers each were matters of pride to the trade unions. One was a Siemens plant in Bratislava with much skilled personnel. Of two other large metal plants nearby, one with 4,000 and one with 6,000 workers, the 6,000-man one was said to have operated with as many as 10,000 workers the previous year, though at the moment it was short of materials; before the war its capacity had been 3,000.

tive. It is a question of the rationalization of the medium-sized mills, those of from 50 to 300 hands.'[1]

Various methods of rationalization were in process of being worked out. For example, in the textile industry 180 small factories had recently (spring of 1948) been taken over. The effort now was to group and concentrate them into units of economic size, each specializing in what it was best equipped to do. A full horizontal organization of the industry was aimed at. There were at this time two horizontal trusts: the Slovakian Cotton Works and the Slovakian Woollen Works. Two more, Flax and Clothing, were about to be set up.

The actual problem of location was a difficult one. Under existing social conditions it was undesirable to take any enterprise away from a district, however badly it might have been placed in the first instance. 'We won't move away factories from a region, only from a place,' said a trade union officer, citing the case of a plant 28 kilometres from a railroad. This particular plant would have to be moved a short distance. Or again, a textile factory might be situated among woods: in that case, he said, it should be converted into a lumber mill.

Labour problems in Slovakia also bore a special character. Here there was a superabundance of unskilled labour, coming from the great reservoir of the country-side, but an acute dearth of skilled workers and technicians. In 1948 half the industrial workers were said to work in agriculture also—hence there was much seasonal absenteeism. Many of the young workers from the country greatly needed dormitory accommodation, both because of the distances they travelled and to improve working discipline. Many of them had been for six years under fascist youth organizations. The nationality problem was still there. The trade unions had a task in teaching Slovaks to get along with Czechs—to realize that there was still some need for Czechs in factory and trade union posts.

Wage scales in nationalized industry were officially similar to those in the Czech lands: the nominal difference in 1948 was said to be only 1·5 per cent. But living standards remained much lower, because of the necessity of buying on the still uncontrolled black market. Moreover the smaller proportion of skilled workers lowered the income of the industrial population as a whole. Finally the considerably larger families of the Slovak workers and their

[1] Interview material, May 1948.

close ties with a far more poverty-stricken rural population meant that the effective industrial incomes per family member were small indeed.

The wages policy of the Slovak authorities was to hold the line of nominal wages, increase the real wage by lowering prices—i.e. overcome the black market—and build up a system of incentive wages. (At the time referred to, a long-overdue system of ration cards had just been introduced. In the words of a Bratislava hotel keeper complaining to the writer: 'We never had rationing once during the war.')

To secure skilled workers an energetic programme of technical education was under way. It comprised large numbers of factory evening courses, several small full-time schools with a six months' training course, and the sending of Slovaks to Bohemia for specialized training.[1]

Land reform since Liberation was complained of as having been less thorough in Slovakia than in the Czech lands, still its results were far more important. The proportion of lands at the end of the First Republic still lying in great estates, almost all of them Hungarian-owned, had been much larger. With the end of the war, 65 per cent of these large estates were eliminated at once. After February 1948 the remainder were scheduled to go. The shortage of land, however, still remained acute. Before the war, average peasant holdings in Slovakia had run around 12½ acres as compared to 25 in Bohemia. And there had been an army of 60,000 landless agricultural labourers. Obviously, only a successful industrialization programme to drain off the 'hidden unemployed', accompanied by great qualitative improvement in agriculture, could raise the social level of the country-side.

Evil social factors meanwhile had operated during the war. The Nazis had set up their own brand of 'land reform'. Between 125,000 and 150,000 acres of land formerly belonging to Jews had been seized and some 75,000 acres of it had actually been distributed

[1] The cultural department of the trade union organization was in charge of this work. Its director described his program of the night before to the writer. 'You now have three hundred workers,' he had told a factory meeting, 'soon you will have five hundred. You (the old-timers) therefore have the chance to raise your qualifications to be sent to higher technical schools.' Two hundred had signed up, and he predicted that at the end of six months there would be fifty to sixty graduates, out of whom they would find thirty to forty foremen, ten or more with qualifications higher than foremen, and two or three technicians.

among Slovak peasants. Even after the war, a pogrom against surviving Jews had broken out in one of the rural districts.

One of the major elements in the new land reform was the careful settling of peasant 'colonists' on the great stretches of land left vacant by the Hungarian gentry and the Germans. Chiefly the settlers were poor mountain peasants from eastern Slovakia, accustomed to primitive conditions and knowing nothing of the farming methods suited to the western part of their country. They had to be, and apparently were, taught everything, from what crops to grow and how to plant them, to how one lived in a western village. The minimum holding for settlers here was 25 acres, enough to use a tractor on. Remarkable results in learning intensive methods were reported concerning the mountain folk, and striking individual instances were to be seen. Housing, however, still constituted an acute problem, and Government funds were going into housing credit.

Evidences of the help of land reform to local peasants were everywhere to be seen. Poverty-stricken villages with their holdings eked out by estate land now looked decidedly prosperous.

A third feature of land reform had been the setting up as State farms of certain of the large estates that were too poor for successful cultivation by the small farmer. Portions unsuitable even for extensive cultivation were being turned into grazing land and the once private forests were being conserved for public use. One such estate, near Bratislava (named after the absentee owner's favourite racehorse), at the time of the writer's visit was having its manor turned into a convalescent home, its stud farm into a State horse-breeding station, the infertile portions of its land into pasture, and its better fields into a plant experiment station. The forest portions were being preserved and restored.

By the end of 1949 the Slovak industrialization programme had progressed according to plan and apparently somewhat better. In the case of the textile industry, for the time being seven large factories were growing up in Slovakia. As they were getting the advantages of the newest equipment available, it was felt that they might prove better than those in the rest of the republic. The productivity of textile labour in Slovakia at this time was said to exceed that of the rest of the country by 10 per cent.

A 'contradiction' here was pointed out to the writer. 'In Slovakia we have much manpower, yet automatic machines. It is comparable to the American South.'[1] In the Czech lands, average machinery was said to be fifty years old. However, a new native textile machine production industry was beginning there now. Since major investment funds were still going to heavy industry, the Slovak textile industry was for the most part running in two shifts. When the whole expansion programme for the industry had been rounded out, it was planned to have about 25 per cent of the total national textile production located in Slovakia.

A good deal of specialization, however, was planned for. As Slovakia had very good climatic conditions for cultivating flax, a whole new linen industry was to be built up. Similarly with hemp. The country moreover was unusually rich in forests, hence rayon production was being increased. On the other hand, the Slovak cotton industry was also being increased, with materials to be imported from the eastern countries.

A textile engineer stressed the increasing output in his industry and its effect upon living standards. 'In Slovakia the work-people value their jobs—they want to learn.' The new post-war factories had been built in the poorest regions and drew predominantly upon the rural population. As the labour force was not concentrated in the regions where the largest factories were wanted, it had been necessary to provide housing and cultural facilities for the new workers. Moreover, earlier war-time renovations in machinery and equipment, when Slovakia had had the opportunity to be in business communication with Switzerland and Germany, were now being taken advantage of fully. During the war many workers had been transferred from the textile industry to metals. 'The people who stayed have a very positive attitude toward innovations. Out of 250,000 textile workers, 50,000 are in "socialist competition"—overwhelmingly so in the automatic works.'[2]

[1] Besides, Czech industry had started small. The average mill there had had from 80 to 120 looms—'an industry of small masters'. In Slovakia, on the other hand (as also in Poland), big plants had been founded in the nineteenth century by French capital.

[2] Interview materials, November 1949. Before the war, one worker was said to have tended 20 automatic looms; now, up to 80.

CHAPTER VI

TWO- AND FIVE-YEAR PLANS: CHANGING OBJECTIVES

The Two-Year Plan, 1947–8

Czechoslovakia's Two-Year Plan Act was passed in the summer of 1946, before international and domestic tensions had become acute. It was adopted easily and quickly, with the unanimous approval of all political parties. Two years, 1947 and 1948, were considered sufficient to repair war-time dislocations, restore the pre-war standard of living and prepare the country for further long-time development.

Losses and damages had been considerable, but the most serious of them were concentrated in the agricultural regions of eastern Slovakia where losses in cattle and especially in horses would take some time to make good. All told, about 125,000 dwelling units would have to be restored, most of them in Slovakia. In the Czech lands some big industrial plants had been bombed. Compared to Poland, however, the task of physical reconstruction would be light indeed. This difference is reflected in the considerable allocations the Two-Year Plan was able to give at once to such long-term needs as housing[1] and the reconstruction of railroad road-beds.

Industrialization as such was also not considered a major need for Czechoslovakia. She already had an excellent base of heavy as well as light industry. Indeed in the period of the First Republic excess capacity was recurrently complained of along with heavy unemployment, especially in the older industrial regions, the light industry sections along the west. The only place, it was now considered, where further industrialization in the sense of new capital construction was needed on a large scale was in Slovakia, and here the need was chiefly for social reasons, to raise the level of living of the Slovak population, rather than to add to the coun-

[1] The ambitious housing plan was, however, never fulfilled. By the end of the Two-Year Plan it was still about 50 per cent short.

try's overall capacity. Some of the minor procedures for increasing Slovak output therefore consisted of the physical transfer of textile plant equipment across the border. For the rest, the considerable investments to be made in building new industry in Slovakia bespoke the relatively large resources of Czechoslovakia's Plan.

The country also did not have the problem of settling alien territory. The border districts where the majority of the German population had lived had always been part of the republic, and a large minority of the population was Czech. There had also been no wholesale destruction in these regions. Hence the problems here were of an altogether different order from those of Poland's Western Territoeies.

However, the loss of the Germans as manpower was a serious matter, not alone for the border regions but for the country as a whole. Before the war the Germans had constituted nearly a quarter of the country's total population, and for Bohemia approximately a third. To expel the remaining 2,000,000 of them at this time meant reducing the overall population of the country considerably below what it had been for the same territory as long ago as 1930. The Census at that time had registered 14,000,000; the figure now was to be only twelve. The loss of this many Germans would mean spreading the remaining working population a good deal thinner for the whole country. The more conservative parties had made much of this point, endeavouring to slow down the rate of expulsions. The process, however, was consummated before the Two-Year Plan was ready to be put into operation. By October 1946, over 2,000,000 Germans had been expelled and 1,300,000 Czechs and Slovaks had taken their places. Five hundred thousand Germans were allowed to remain.

Another problem to be faced by the Plan was the general repopulation of the Czech country-side. Unlike Poland, the Czech lands had never had a large surplus agricultural population. The country's economy was too well balanced for that. Now under the conditions of the Occupation and the war there had been a considerable flight from the land. When added to the shortage of draught power and agricultural machinery, necessitating greater recourse to hand labour, the manpower shortage for agriculture was serious.

In industry manpower had gone up sharply during the war, under pressure of the Germans. By the end of 1944 it was nearly double pre-war. Then it broke, and by October 1945 it was still only 80 per cent of pre-war. However, even this 80 per cent was unevenly distributed. Coal mining was operating with 30 per cent more workers than in 1947, textiles and clothing with about 40 per cent less.

The shortage was aggravated by a lack of straight production workers. A characteristic occupation phenomenon throughout Europe had been the increase in administrative overheads. The German war machine had been exceedingly complicated, with endless record-keeping, and, as a reaction to occupation bondage, the flight from production to white-collar jobs continued after the Germans left. In October 1945 the ratio of non-manual to manual jobs in industry was said to be more than double what it had been ten years previously.

As was to have been expected, labour productivity had fallen greatly. Men as well as machines were in poor condition, the new labour brought in was unskilled. Key branches such as coal-mining had to be kept going at a maximum by a policy of over-manning, robbing Peter to pay Paul. 'The coal was mined by dint of the fact that the labour supply in the mines was greatly increased. Extra rations were given to miners . . . incentives . . . special bonuses. . . . Voluntary labour brigades were recruited for temporary work. Deteriorated machinery. . . . It was impossible to open new and more productive seams of coal, for all labour had to be concentrated on the job of coal-getting. . . . Coal was produced, but the coal problem was not overcome.'[1]

A final and exceedingly serious problem for Czechoslovakia was her export trade. She had always been dependent upon the export of a large proportion of her finished products, especially those of light industry, to pay for raw materials. Her dependence in this respect was probably greater than of any other well developed country in Europe, except England. To regain her one-time markets, or others like them, she would have to catch up with the technical progress made abroad while her own light industries had been neglected and deteriorating under the Occupation. Yet it was these very industries that had already begun to fall behind in the days of the First Republic. It was they that had suffered most from the cutting off of the old Austrian internal market, that had shown the most unemployment, that had had the greatest difficulty in meeting adequate living standards for their workers; and it was they that had been the most largely manned by the now

[1] William Diamond, *Czechoslovakia Between East and West*, London, 1947, p. 76.

departed Germans. To renovate these industries from within sufficiently to meet foreign competition would be difficult indeed; to shift gradually to a greater dependence upon heavy industry exports would, it was felt at this time, be a long-time process. (In the event, the shift took place more quickly than anticipated.)

The Two-Year Plan as adopted outlined six basic tasks. Four of them applied to the country as a whole. In industry the overall level of production was to increase to 10 per cent above that of 1937. In agriculture the pre-war level of production was to be reached. In building, 125,000 dwelling-house units were to be erected or restored. In transport the pre-war carrying capacity was to be restored.

In addition there were special provisions for the under-developed parts of the country. Slovakia as a whole was to be given aid, 'to speed up the process of raising Slovakia's economic level to that of the Czech lands'. Included in this it was stated specifically, 'The scheme for the transfer of plant and machinery for factory and workshop production from the Czech lands to Slovakia will be completed on a scale sufficient to provide employment for 26,000 persons'.[1] An enumerated list of under-developed districts in the Czech lands, in the south of Bohemia and elsewhere, were also to receive some additional industrial enterprises. These were to be 'transferred to, and, in certain cases established' there. Something less than a quarter as large an investment allocation was to be made to these districts as to Slovakia.

In the process of setting up its tasks the Czech Plan, like the Polish, had concentrated upon production, and, within that, in the first instance upon key or 'bottle-neck' sectors of industry. These were considered to fall into four groups: first, power production, comprising coal, electricity, and fuel; second, the basic industries of iron and steel and artificial fertilizers; third, production of the most important capital goods such as railway rolling stock, trucks and tractors, and agricultural machinery; fourth, the principal consumer goods, especially footwear and clothing.

Next after the key branches came planning for the so-called ancillary branches of production, those essential to the products and processes of basic production—for example, tyres; or again, those supplying indispensable capital equipment, such as machine tools or plate glass. In general, it was only these main branches and related processes that were directly planned, in the sense that

[1] *The Two Year Economic Plan Act*, Prague, 1948, Sections I and IV.

definite production figures were originally fixed for them. Outline figures finally given to various less important branches of industry, it was stated, represented only indirect planning, they were derivative. That is to say, these branches were to have apportioned to them what remained over of labour, raw materials and industrial credits after the more pressing requirements of the basic industries had been satisfied.

Finally there were portions of local industry altogether outside the Plan. These would have to make shift for themselves as best they could. 'Investment programmes not included in the Two-Year Plan can be carried out in the years 1947 and 1948 only in so far as the necessary raw materials and labour can be provided from local resources without drawing on raw materials and labour required for the tasks laid down by the Two-Year Plan.'[1]

In general, within the Plan, key industries were to reach something approaching 150 per cent of pre-war output and the remainder only about 90 per cent. (However, even the latter, in view of their neglect by the Germans, would have to rise sharply.)

For agriculture, detailed figures were given for the output targets of livestock and of various crops, as well as figures of the estimated manpower requirements. But it was stated strongly that a major necessity for reaching any such targets would be the required supply of agricultural machinery—in other words, a requirement from key industry once more.

To reach pre-war output in agriculture and 110 per cent of pre-war in industry would mean a great increase in the labour force as well as a heightening of its efficiency. This point was emphasized and re-emphasized in official analyses of the Plan. Two hundred and seventy thousand additional persons would need to be directed into industry, 90,000 into building construction, 230,000 into agriculture and forestry—practically 600,000 additional persons out of a total population of some 12,000,000. Or, to put it in another way, in spite of a 2,000,000 (or 15 per cent) population shrinkage since pre-war—including a very special shrinkage in industrial personnel with the departure of the Germans—total industrial output was not only to equal the pre-war but to exceed it by 10 per cent. Ergo, the best that could be expected would have to be a working force equal to that of pre-war and working, in spite of all handicaps, at 10 per cent *per capita* greater productivity. This, according to Prime Minister Gottwald,

[1] Ibid., Section VI.

would represent an increase over the present low labour productivity of something like 40 per cent.

Obviously, much vocational guidance work would have to be done with young people, offices, and shops and administrations must be combed of superfluous personnel, women and pensioners, and the handicapped encouraged to part-time work, and so on.

As to renovation of equipment, the vast majority of it would have to come from the output of native industry itself. Any machinery imports would in general have to be balanced by comparable exports. Imports on credit would naturally be welcome, but 'the Plan is not based on the assumption of foreign credits'.[1]

Finally, the export problem was emphasized, particularly in the case of the textile and clothing and leather goods industries. In these fields large exports would be essential. They must be sufficient, it was stated, to cover the costs in these fields of raw material imports, not only for the exported portion of their output but for their entire domestic consumption in these fields as well.

Course of the Two-Year Plan

The first year of Czechoslovakia's first Plan was marked by the same catastrophic drought that struck Poland. Agricultural production for 1947 was down to only about two-thirds of Plan, in the case of sugar-beets to half, and, most serious of all, the lack of fodder brought a great slaughter of livestock in the ensuing autumn and winter. (Milk was down to 40 per cent in the latter half of the year, while meat was momentarily abundant.) Famine conditions had to be averted by importation. The Soviet Union granted a five-year trade agreement, under the terms of which large amounts of grain and fodder were furnished at once, and Yugoslavia and Rumania also sent large immediate supplies. Subsequently the Soviet Union sent additional amounts.[2] Altogether Czechoslovakia's crop and animal losses were estimated at about £125,000,000

The industrial part of the Plan for 1947 nevertheless was fulfilled approximately 100 per cent. The heavy industries as a whole exceeded their quota. But among consumer's goods industries, not only food processing but clothing fell short. And in construction the ambitious housing programme was less than half fulfilled.

[1] *The First Czechoslovak Economic Plan*, Prague, April 1947, Explanatory Memorandum, p. 93.

[2] Soviet Union: 200,000 tons each of grain and fodder, and subsequently another 200,000; Yugoslavia: 300,000 altogether; Roumania: 150,000.

Such facts lent ammunition to those who saw in private industry a readiness to sabotage the Government's programme, for the industries with the serious shortages were all of them industries with much private capital. Other pulls, both Right and Left, combined with the deepening East-West tension abroad at this time, helped bring on the February 1948 crisis, with all its economic as well as political consequences. Nationalization entered its second stage, quite unforeseen by the original Plan.

During 1948 the 1947 trends were only partly reversed. Agriculture recovered from the worst effects of the previous year, but crops delivered still fell below expectation. The building industry still lagged badly. Textile production, however, had improved greatly. And the whole heavy industry sector equalled or exceeded Plan. Early in the year, soon after February, a slogan to complete the Plan by 28 October, the anniversary of the founding of the republic, had been put forward by the trade union organization and had helped to cancel out the disturbing effects upon production of the February events themselves, although actual completion by 28 October was by no means generally reached. By the end of the year production was above Plan and the Two-Year Plan as a whole was declared to have been achieved.

The Five-Year Plan, 1949–53

To begin with 1949, a planning period of no less than five years had been agreed upon. At the time the initial decision was taken the five-year block of time was regarded as only in moderate degree representing a qualitative change from its predecessor: the end of the new period, 1953, was to see the country yet further developed industrially, with a better regional balance, and in a much sounder position in international trade; its social structure, however, would be evolving only very gradually.

The actual course of the Two-Year Plan period had changed these perspectives very materially. Between the time the Five-Year Plan had been projected in its initial outlines, at the close of 1947, and the time it was put into action, at the opening of 1949, the 'second stage' of Czechoslovakia's revolution, of February 1948, had had full time to take effect. Moreover, no sooner were these effects absorbed than there supervened the yet further policy changes of the summer and autumn of 1948 common to all the planned economies after the Tito-Cominform split. The result for the structure of the Five-Year Plan meant, first, a skewing upward of many individual indices, particularly all those having to do with the larger scale operation of agriculture—machinery, chemical fertilizers, trained agricultural personnel. But there came also a more rapid pace all along the line in further intensive industrialization, embracing all the main branches of heavy industry. In terms of trade, increasing difficulty in securing needed equipment from the West—for Czechoslovakia and for the other smaller planned economies as well—had only raised yet further the country's emphasis on heavy industry development at home. And, as the other side of the shield in trade, the Soviet Union's willingness to furnish scarce raw materials in exchange for finished consumers' goods, more especially textiles and footwear, had proceeded to solve a part of those industries' export problems. Hence these industries too had expanded more than expected.

A picture of the situation at the time the original outline for the Five-Year Plan was adopted and the arguments then in use for the future reorientation of industry are given in Prime Minister Gottwald's preliminary speech at the session of the State Planning Commission in October 1947.

'It is necessary', said the Prime Minister, 'to change the structure of Czechoslovak economy, which in its essence originated in the days of Austria-Hungary. . . .' The country's industry was to be reoriented, away from such former low-wage export branches as gloves, toys, etc., and partly also glass and textiles; and to those where Czechoslovakia could compete on favourable terms, such as the metal industry, especially heavy machinery production, and the chemical industry.

Under such changes the textile industry would lose its primary position. 'That place corresponded more to the needs of the Austro-Hungarian monarchy, where our textile industry had a large stable market, than to the needs of to-day. It is known that already before the Second World War we had to face some difficulties when our textile industry, which had originally been built up as an industry producing principally for the home market, was to become our main export industry.'[1]

Another reason cited for the proposed structural changes was the need to secure the Czechoslovak economy as much as possible

[1] 'Long-Term Planning in Czechoslovakia. A Speech by Prime Minister Gottwald at the Extraordinary Meeting of the Central Planning Commission on 10 October 1947', Czechoslovak Ministry of Information, Prague, October 1947, pp. 7–8.

against the disastrous effects of foreign business cycles. A sub-head in the printed speech is entitled 'Czechoslovak Economy Must Be Safe from Fluctuations'. Under this head the need is emphasized to increase trade with the countries of planned economy, which obviously would have a great demand for Czech machinery.

Further reasons cited were the need for the metal industry at home 'for the development of our own forces of production, for the modernization of our industry, and for the increased security of our State'.[1]

Finally, an international reason cited was the opportunity to replace to some extent on European markets, and especially for eastern Europe, the supply position once held so dangerously by Germany. 'Germany has temporarily vanished as a competitor in the international market, especially in the chemical and machine industries. Our Five-Year Plan should help us to take her place more than hitherto.'[2]

In its final form the Plan more than came up to the specifications proposed. It called for an extremely rapid rise of industrial output, 57 per cent overall for the country as a whole, and for Slovakia 75 per cent. Within industries, particular priority was to go to machine-building. This branch was almost to double its output and was now to be the largest single branch of Czech industry, considerably outdistancing the production of the textile and clothing industry with which it had been about equal in 1948. In absolute size among heavy industries, iron and steel still came next after machine building; then chemicals, then coal. In speed of development, however, the chemical industry was to exceed steel: it was to increase by something over 60 per cent. Iron and steel and electric power meanwhile were to rise about 50 per cent, mining 35 per cent.

Among the light industries, by far the largest, textiles, was to increase its output rapidly, well over 60 per cent. Next in importance came leather and rubber with an increase of well over 40 per cent. Footwear for the domestic market was promised at a somewhat less than proportional increase, at the rate of something over one additional pair of shoes per person per year.

As the one industry which had notably failed to come up to plan, the building industry was to have a serious overhauling. It had achieved less than three-quarters of its public construction

[1] Op. cit., p. 9.
[2] Ibid., p. 14.

programme under the Two-Year Plan and only about half of its housing. Now its output was to be stepped up by 130 per cent. Chief among the means to achieve this output were to be increase of mechanization, with use of prefabricated standardized construction parts, and a 50 per cent increase in labour force. (This figure was subsequently increased yet further.)

Aside from the production of industry proper, handicraft output was to continue to fill an important place in total Czech production, particularly in food processing, clothing and metal work. Altogether its output was to increase 20 per cent.

Foreign trade was planned to increase 40 per cent, with emphasis upon the conclusion of long-term trade agreements, particularly with other countries of planned economy.

Agricultural output was expected to rise at something over half the rate of industrial, 37 per cent in all, taking as base the reduced agricultural plan of 1948, following the drought. Within agriculture great emphasis was to be laid upon the more valuable form of production, animal husbandry. (Crops were to increase only 11 per cent, livestock production nearly 90.) Nevertheless the total value of agricultural output would now form less than a fifth of the whole national income.

Further emphasis was to be given in the Five-Year Plan to regional development, particularly to the continued industrialization of Slovakia. Ninety thousand 'new work opportunities' were to be given Slovak citizens in industry. The mechanization of Slovak agriculture was to be pushed further. Intensive surveys for possible mineral resources in Slovakia and other under-developed areas were to be undertaken. Altogether, the proportion of funds to be assigned to Slovakia under the Five-Year Plan was rather more than equal on a *per capita* basis to that allowed the Czech lands; and since the country was incomparably less developed to start with (to say nothing of furnishing a several times smaller *per capita* contribution to the total national income), the effect of the funds upon its existing industry and agriculture would be very much greater. It should be noted that the Czech lands were hereby making a net contribution to the raising of Slovakia to their level.

By the time a year of the Plan had run its course, yet further increases in production were called for. In February 1950 the Plan's production targets in heavy industry, building, and agriculture were all revised upwards. Especially to be increased were the heavy engineering trades, for the making of major capital equipment goods. Trade restrictions from the West were now spoken of in much more definite terms. By late 1950 Mr. Gottwald, now President of the Republic, was saying flatly:[1] 'Further development of mining . . . coal and ores . . . and of the chemical industry mean still more raw materials from our own resources.

'As to export . . . we know that we have found better and more lasting markets for . . . our heavy industry in the people's democracies which need them for their own work of construction.

'In this way we shall also best be able to get rid of our dependence on the capitalist countries which in their economic policy do everything possible to hamper our economic development and choke our socialist construction. That is why we are concentrating chiefly on the building up of heavy industry.'

The tone, both of the Five-Year Plan itself and of subsequent statements by political leaders, was still sober and thrifty, with constant emphasis upon conservation of labour and materials and the most efficient deployment of all resources. Again and again it was stressed that the results looked for in better living standards —an increase of 35 per cent in individual consumption and a like increase in social services—would require the utmost economy. There would have to be an increase in labour productivity of the following order: in industry by 32 per cent, in agriculture and forestry by 20, in transport by 30, in building by over 50.[2]

Along with sobriety of tone, however, the Plan itself and subsequent comments upon it contained many statements that would not have been heard during any of the Two-Year Plan discussions. Socialist goals were now for the first time spoken of as something immediate and indeed pressing. February had quite plainly done its work before the final version of the Plan was launched. 'Capitalist elements', the Five-Year Plan stated flatly in its opening section, '. . . will be progressively restricted and eliminated from *all* sectors of the national economy.' The Plan as a whole was to mark 'an important step in the progress of the Czechoslovak People's Democracy towards Socialism'.[3]

[1] Address on Miners' Day, 10 September 1950, quoted in *Recruitment for Mining in Czechoslovakia*, Orbis, Prague, January 1951, p. 12.

[2] It was pointed out that no further great increase in total man-power was to be looked for. The overall increase was to be less than 6 per cent, with a pronounced shift away from agriculture, now to be more mechanized, and into industry. Industrial man-power as a whole was to increase by over 18 per cent.

[3] *The First Czechoslovak Economic Five Year Plan*, Orbis, Prague, 1949, Section 1 (italics mine).

Early in 1951 it was announced that all the main goals of Czechoslovakia's Five-Year Plan were being surpassed and that 'it appeared that the whole of the original plan could be carried out in three and a half years instead of five'. The Minister of Planning accordingly gave out various 'revised targets for the Five-Year Plan'. Industrial production by 1951 was to increase by 98 per cent over 1948 instead of by 57 per cent. Consumption was to go up 49 per cent instead of 41. The non-agricultural labour force was to increase by 780,000 persons instead of 486,000.

As for Slovakia, industrial production as a whole had gone up 19 per cent in 1951 over 1950, and 50 per cent in 1950 over 1948. Hence for 1952 'In Slovakia, the output in heavy industry in 1952 will be twice that originally planned', while light industry was to be 15 per cent above original plan. 'A new foundry combine with a yearly capacity of 1,000,000 tons of pig iron will be built by the end of 1952. In 1955 Slovakia will produce as much power as the whole of pre-war Czechoslovakia.'[1]

[1] International Labour Office, *Industry and Labour*, Geneva, vol. VI, 1951, pp. 450–2, and vol. VII, 1952, pp. 254–6.

III

THE COMMON PATTERN

CHAPTER VII

PLANNING METHODS AND THE GROWTH OF CONTROL

I. POLISH EXPERIENCE: THE AREA OF CONTROL

Like everything else in post-war Poland, the process of national economic planning had started under difficult circumstances. Records had largely been destroyed, the simplest necessities for new record-keeping were at first lacking. The Office of the Plan for the Rebuilding of Warsaw, for example, began without typists and typewriters, without sufficient desks, chairs, paper, and even pencils. Trains were not running, and before coming to his office the director would have spent some time standing in line for water to bring his wife for her household. Production itself was at first chaotic and prices wildly unstable. Moreover, among the survivors of the Occupation and war there was a great lack of planning personnel. Statisticians and clerks alike had in no small part to learn their tasks on the job.

As for foreign examples and foreign aid, the precise methods employed by the Soviet Union apparently remained undisclosed to the Polish planners. Soviet planning literature, in Russian, was available to some extent in libraries.

As indicated earlier, planning began at first on a sectional basis, led by the production plan for the coal industry, with other industries following; and by the latter part of 1946 there was a nine-months' financial plan. Finally planning widened to embrace the whole economic structure, with full-fledged plans for both production and investment, the whole 'creation and distribution of the national income'. It is to be noted, however, that within the scope of the Three-Year Plan cultural and health services were not yet actually planned. Overall figures for their development were indicated, but no detailed plan was drawn up. Also in the whole sphere of consumption, while numerous figures were given indicating *per capita* estimates, these were as yet only derivative from the corresponding production figures. Consumption as such was not yet planned.

As it broadened, planning also lengthened and deepened. It lengthened to embrace both a multi-annual plan, at first for three years, then for six; and it deepened, with each successive annual plan becoming more precise.

The multi-annual or 'perspective' plans were regarded from the outset as furnishing the general framework within which the one-year plans operated. 'There is, of course, no reasonable reply to the question, which of the two is "better"; practice shows that both types are indispensable, . . . the long-range plans making possible a solution of basic economic problems once for a number of years, and [the short-range] permitting real planning, based not only on bold strokes and ideas but also adapted to actual conditions.'[1] The first segment of a multi-annual plan becomes automatically the One-Year Plan for its initial year. However, the succeeding One-Year Plans will be modified in their details, upward or downward, by the success of the preceding ones. Hence by the end of the series there may be considerable divergence from the original 'perspective' plan. This is indeed what happened with the concluding section of Poland's Three-Year Plan. As seen above, over-fulfilment of many of its second-year goals made its third year skew considerably upward beyond the levels originally set, with the consequent prospect of finishing the original Three-Year total substantially ahead of time. Specific policy changes, moreover, in the course of a long-term plan, as in the case of the increased emphasis upon mechanization of agriculture in 1948, can cause marked ultimate divergencies in the case of a particular item, to which then not only a greater amount but a greater total proportion of investment funds may be allocated. This is what appears to have happened specifically in the case of tractors in the 1949 Plan, after a more rapid approach to large-scale agriculture had been decided upon. As noted above, in its final form the new 1949 Plan provided for an output of tractors over 50 per cent above its original allocation under the Three-Year Plan.

When all this has been said, however, the basic characteristic of the Polish, as also the Czech type of planning, should not be lost sight of—its focusing of all agencies upon plan fulfilment. The goals set are by no means targets, but rather government commands, to be carried out in the allotted time. And for this purpose they must be understood, not only by the specialist but by the layman. 'The national plan . . . corresponds, so to say, to the order

[1] *Polish Planned Economy*, Warsaw, 1948, p. 12.

of a commander-in-chief to his forces engaged in a battle. . . . It must comply with the requirements of mobilizing the population. . . . On the other hand, it must comply with the demand of precision, it must resemble an operative order prepared by the general staff.'[1]

The source of the Plans was, from the outset, as authoritative as possible. In Poland they were drawn up by the Economic Council[2] of the Council of Ministers with the aid of an operative body of experts, the National Planning Board (subsequently renamed the State Council for Economic Planning). They were then accepted by Parliament and passed as special Acts. Thereafter it was a prime duty both of the Planning Board and of the respective ministries to check up continuously on Plan fulfilment and to marshal resources to break bottle-necks and obstacles. 'The planning apparatus must at the same time be the reporting apparatus, for the very reason of not losing touch with reality. In a planned economy the plan is not an object of art, and planning is not "art for art's sake": the aim of preparing a plan is its realization.'[3]

[1] Ibid.

[2] The Economic Council was made up of the various ministries of industry, agriculture, commerce, marine, labour, finance, reconstruction, i.e. of all those dealing with economic affairs. The Chairman of the Planning Board was appointed directly by the Prime Minister.

In formulating a new Plan, (1) the Planning Board drew it in outline in accordance with the objectives set forth by the Government. (2) The Economic Council thereupon worked it over and actually decided upon it, although formally it was the whole Council of Ministers that passed it. (3) Parliament accepted the Plan. (4) In the case of local industry, the State Council, as the administrative agency concerned, gave it approval.

Provinces and smaller local government divisions, and originally also the executives of the co-operative movement, themselves drew up comprehensive summaries of plans for their organizations and presented them to the Planning Board.

However, 'The territorial and other self-governing units are bound to execute the regulations of the respective Ministries'.

In general, it was the Ministries upon whom the primary executive responsibility fell.

'Organizing and executing the segmental plans and supervising their execution is the duty of the respective Ministers. . . . Ministers issue regulations to the institutions under them and these in turn to their subordinate units.'

Some local modification was, however, allowed for. 'In questions of the execution of segmental plans, the institutions and enterprises concerned may submit proposals for their modification.'

[3] Ibid., p. 13.

Of course, at the time of the Three-Year Plan it was only the nationalized sector of the economy that was subject to direct methods of control for Plan fulfilment, and it was here that non-fulfilling agencies could be held most strictly to account. The small co-operative sector at this time still functioned semi-autonomously, and here controls had to be chiefly indirect, through persuading the co-operatives to 'produce their own economic plans on the basis of the line and the instructions of the National Plan',[1] and through the mechanisms of credit, purchase and sale, and so on. In the case of the private sector, including all of peasant farming, controls remained wholly indirect. But the degree of involvement of private and co-operative sectors, their dependence upon and their meshing in to the planned production of nationalized industry, had been increasing greatly.

The emphasis upon fulfilment of Plan ran throughout the planning machinery organization. Each year the Council of Ministers made a report to Parliament concerning the previous year's plan fulfilment. And each year Parliament voted the next annual Plan (in spite of having already voted the longer-term Plan). The individual ministries then handled the Plan and its fulfilment on a three-months' basis, and the individual industry director did the same on a monthly basis.[2]

In checking, both the individual ministries and the Central Planning Board had the duty to check. Finally, the whole matter of successes and failures in each Plan was aired each year before Parliament and the public in the most conspicuous manner, at the

[1] Ibid.

[2] In addition, 'The Chairman of the Central Planning Board is empowered to verify the execution of particular sector plans, as well as the conformity of orders issued . . . and to present to the Council of Ministers motions to this end'.

There was thus a series of plan-making mechanisms and a double-check on execution. In plan-making:

(*a*) The original total plan was drawn up by the Central Planning Board in conformity with the general objectives (and means) laid down by the Council of Ministers, which had of course consulted them during the process.

(*b*) Segmental plans were drawn by the respective Ministries, again working with the Planning Board.

(*c*) But local government divisions and the co-operatives drew up their own plans, submitted directly to the Planning Board.

(*d*) And institutions might raise questions themselves; that is, after the plan travelled down from above, it could be modified from below.

same time that maximum publicity was being given the discussion of the succeeding Plan.

Beginning with December 1948 when the two Left parties merged, basic problems of planning were thrashed out in advance at the United Workers' Party conferences. Party and Government were now at one on all important questions and public policy could be sharply focused. Before that the Socialist Party and the Communist Party had each had planning proposals of various sorts that were ultimately adjusted to a common denominator. The Planning Board itself at the time was under Socialist direction. So early as the beginning of 1948 we find Mr. Hilary Minc, a Communist and at that time Minister of Industry, criticizing at length the methods of the Planning Board at an inter-party conference: its assessment of national income and its under-emphasis upon production were said to be un-Marxian. Subsequently these methods were changed. More particularly, after 1948, production was no longer classified as public, private, and co-operative, with the co-operative sector treated as independent and the private sector lumping together large and small producers indistinguishably, divided only into agricultural and non-agricultural branches. So-called small commodity producers, the class of self-employed peasants and craftsmen, were now sharply to be distinguished from the capitalist employer proper and the large farmer. Statistical distinction here had a highly practical bearing, for the whole social emphasis of the country's planning from 1948–9 on was to cease relying upon even the small employing capitalist and the large farmer as positive forces, however much they might be hedged about by public controls. They would have to be dislodged by discriminatory competition. The small producers meanwhile could be persuaded into co-operatives. And the co-operatives in turn would no longer be making autonomous plans as a separate, 'third' sector of the economy: they would form an integral part of the socialist sector, alongside State and local enterprise. As such they would fall under direct planning. As a Polish co-operator said to the author in 1949, 'There is no longer any co-operation outside of Plan'.

2. CZECHOSLOVAKIA: COALITION PLANNING?

So far as technical factors went, Czechoslovakia had from the outset a great advantage over Poland for successful planning. Her economy was incomparably more advanced, tidy, skilled, and less destroyed. It was not such an excruciating question to decide where to begin. The population was less in flux, the border districts were not in the deplorable condition of the 'Recovered Territories.' The prerequisites, moreover, for assessment and estimation were there. Records had not all been lost. Statistical services and statisticians were available.

The whole structure of Czech industry was more rational. Czechoslovakia had long had concerns outstanding for their efficiency methods. The wage structure itself had been more rational. Business accountancy had reached a high level.

Moreover, Czechoslovakia had from the outset the great advantage of a much smaller agricultural population: hence the proportion of people for whom planning could at best be only indirect was greatly reduced.

The one negative feature technically, and this was a serious one, was Czechoslovakia's greater dependence upon exports. Having no major raw materials resource comparable to Poland's coal, the country had become a 'country of finishing industries' and was now highly vulnerable not only to world price vagaries but to trade discrimination from the West.

The actual structure of the planning mechanism in Czechoslovakia was not very different from that of Poland, but greater technical means and centralization were indicated from the outset by the frequency of reports to Parliament. The progress of the whole Plan was reported on to the Economic Committee quarterly.

We find the same distinction as in Poland between 'global' and 'operative' or detailed plans. As in the case of Poland, we find that the Central Planning Commission 'divided up the global tasks laid down in the [Two-Year Plan] Act, . . . in industry, among the enterprises and workshops; in agriculture, among the various units of public administration. . . . In working out the operative plans a distinction was maintained between tasks expressly laid down in the Act and auxiliary tasks.'[1]

In checking on fulfilment of the operative plans, however, the Czech planners were from the outset able to be more precise. 'In addition to political control', we read in the 1947 statement by the President of the Planning Commission, Dr. Outrata, prefacing the Two-Year Plan, 'it is necessary to carry out systematic opera-

[1] *The First Czechoslovak Economic Plan*, Prague, April 1947, p. 9,

tional control', to see whether the Plan was being fulfilled not only in its stated amounts and on time, but 'whether the . . . production costs . . . and the prescribed quality are being maintained'.

Three devices were used for this purpose. Current, so-called 'running' reports were sent to the State Statistical Office, worked up by its staff, and submitted to the central organs. (Subsequently in the Five-Year Plan the Statistical Office was itself taken over by the Planning Commission.) Secondly, a system of 'regional observers' was set up. These were to serve as the chief agencies of operational control, not only reporting back to the Planning Commission but serving as a permanent link between the Commission and the lowest economic units. In case of urgency, it was stated, they could immediately discuss proposals for overcoming obstacles. Thirdly, a bold step was taken in business accounting. A law passed in May 1946 had provided for the setting up of 'a unified system of accountancy . . . in all departments of industry. This permits of a comparison of the results in the individual economic units.' In doing away with free competition, Dr. Outrata noted, it became necessary to find 'some other gauge of a rise or decrease in the efficiency and in the profit-making capacity of industry and one which would, at the same time, act as a lever for the regulation of prices'.[1]

Various further developments in planning, the Memorandum on the Two-Year Plan Bill pointed out, would have to wait until a later Plan. Regional planning was not yet begun, save in an embryonic form in the case of Slovakia and the especially needy Czech districts. 'The Plan . . . is in principle a sectional plan for it consists of separate plans worked out by the various branches of industry . . . and then co-ordinated in the General Economic Plan. . . . Regional planning, on the other hand, would take as its starting point the economic needs and productive potential of the various zones and would merge the various regional plans into one national plan. In fully developed planning both types are required. . . . Perfect planning thus demands the most perfect co-ordination and balancing of sectoral and regional planning.

'The Two-Year Plan is, however, only a beginning. It is necessary to concentrate our main effort on the basic industries. . . . The erection of electric power stations in Slovakia, for instance, or the expansion of the food industry in the poorer districts of the Czech lands, will only be possible if the industry supplying the necessary

[1] Op. cit., p. 10.

plant or the mining and energy-production industries which supply the required power realize the production figures fixed by the Plan. Nor will it be possible for either the one or the other regional scheme to be carried out unless the general plan for the national mobilization of labour is successful.'[1]

The Two-Year Plan also was a plan frankly one-way in direction, with tasks distributed from the top down. It would take further time and experience to be able to deal with lower level plans proceeding from below up. 'Finally, the Two-Year Plan is a *centralizing* plan, for it is top-level planning, defining first of all certain basic aims and distributing the tasks which their fulfilment entailed. . . . It was impossible to make inquiries of all the enterprises in the republic as to what plans they have and what they would like to do and then co-ordinate these plans.'[2]

In the Five-Year Plan, definite places were assigned both to regional planning and to planning from below. Regional planning now occupied a portion of the Plan to itself. All details, however, were left to the later, operative plans. The Act confined itself to statements of principle, such as that the less developed regions, where possible, have priority.[3]

[1] Ibid., pp. 23–5.

[2] Ibid., pp. 25–6.

'*Paragraph 29:*

[3](1) It is the aim of the . . . Plan gradually to attain a balance of the economic levels of the regions. . . .

'(2) Regional progress shall be attained chiefly by means of an effective distribution of production and investment targets under the . . . Plan. . . .

"(*a*) Priority in the allocation . . . shall be given to economically backward regions, provided that the realization of the Five-Year Plan [i.e. the necessary total of production] is not jeopardized thereby.

"(*b*) . . . new equipment shall be allocated to those regions where the greatest facility exists for the utilization of local resources (labor, raw material, power, transport, etc.).

"(*c*) Excessive concentration of production targets in . . . centres . . . [where it may interfere with the ultimate aims of the Plan] shall be guarded against."

(*d*), (*e*), and (*f*) then provide that in regions unfavourable for other economic activity all existing facilities be used to develop tourist traffic and recreation, that 'modern principles of town and country planning' be used for the development of cities and villages, and that 'a systematic investigation be carried out in all regions', assessing their natural resources and needs.Machinery for this last provision, it may be remarked parenthetically, had already begun to function very effectively during the concluding months of the Two-Year Plan. The writer had occasion to see such regional surveys at work.

Other sections of the Plan spoke of the development of new regional organs of the planning service, and of their close co-operation with local mass organizations. 'In the preparation of regional plans they shall rely on the direct participation and initiative of the working population and of the national committees.'

'Production accountancy' was to be developed further. Planning was to be extended fully into the spheres of incomes, prices, taxes, consumption, and trade; costs both of production and distribution were to be planned. 'The premisses for the preparation of global financial plans shall thus be laid.'[1]

In spite of her advanced technology, social factors in Czechoslovakia at the outset had presented serious difficulties for planning. Industry, to be sure, was much larger than in Poland, but a greater proportion of it at first remained in private hands. Czechoslovakia's 300 to 500 man limit during the first stage of her nationalization was some six times as high as Poland's, leaving fully a third of industry outside the sphere of direct planning.

By the same token, the representatives of this third in the National Assembly and the Government were much more vocal. In fact in Poland their *vis-à-vis*, owing to the Nazis' occupation policy, were for the most part no longer alive. In Czechoslovakia the middle business and professional classes had not only survived, but during 1946–7 were increasingly in strategic positions in the political parties, once the first efflatus of the May Revolution of 1945 had worn down.

Relations between the management of private industry and the powerful United Trade Unions organization were precarious, with the unions demanding further nationalization, additional business taxes, and the enactment of a broader national insurance law. Meanwhile, especially after the bad harvest of 1947 with its consequent need of exports of manufactured goods at all costs and its strict rationing, the complaints of black-marketeering against the textile and clothing industry, the food and liquor industries, and the building industry, took, as we saw, the form of charges of deliberate sabotage against their private owners. Similar unrest affected the sector of agriculture, where small farmers were demanding completion of the land reform, while the Church parties were in opposition. After the 1947 drought there was difficulty in collecting the necessary proportion of crop deliveries for the cities. All these forms of unrest were bound to hinder smooth Plan fulfilment.

[1] Paragraph 28.

The February events of 1948 sharply altered the balance of the planned to the merely controlled sections of the economy. As previously recounted, over 90 per cent of industry was now to be in public hands, together with all of foreign trade and wholesaling.

Controls over the private sector had also increased. A greater proportion of what remained of private industry was now working either for orders given out by nationalized industries or with materials furnished by them. The tax structure had been tightened, and banking, credit, and price controls were firmer. Adherence to plan by private businessmen could therefore be rewarded and non-adherence penalized much more effectively than before.

The old dispute with the unions concerning the long-time limits of private enterprise had also come to an end. Complete socialism ultimately was now accepted explicitly in the Plan itself with a corresponding shift in policy. The Two-Year Plan had said nothing about Socialism as such, and in its concluding section had stated: 'Full equality is guaranteed to all forms of enterprise—whether . . . national, co-operative, or private enterprise—in the carrying out of the Two-Year Plan, by according to all the same opportunities and conditions for the development of their economic activities.'

The Five-Year Plan, on the other hand, in its opening section declared: 'The Five-Year Plan constitutes an important step in the progress of the Czechoslovak People's Democracy towards Socialism, principally in that it aims to strengthen and consolidate nationalized industry. . . . Such capitalist elements as remain will . . . be progressively restricted and eliminated from all sectors of the national economy.' It was obvious therefore that no claims on the part of private business that this or that measure was discriminatory would be allowed to interfere with Plan fulfilment. On the contrary, measures making for the still further increase of the public sector would be considered *ipso facto* desirable, provided they did not interfere with Plan fulfilment in some other respect.

The Action Committees set up in consequence of the February events had increased the opportunity to bring various forms of popular pressure to bear for getting plans carried out. On the negative side, the temporary Action Committees in all the various organizations of the country had served to eliminate so-called obstructionist elements. And on the positive side, the continuing local Action Committees of the National Front (enlarged 'National Committees') were now much more active than the original

National Committees had been in recent years. The trade unions, moreover, had now been given a direct voice both in the Government and on the local National Committee level. These changes were reflected in the Plan machinery.

For the Two-Year Plan, political conciliation of the more conservative parties had been a delicate business. To make sure of representing adequately all political views, the Central Planning Commission had been itself composed of experts nominated by the various political parties. Working, as pointed out earlier, in the relatively peaceful atmosphere of 1946, they had reached decisions concerning the working out of the Government programme by compromise, not by voting each other down.

Beyond the Central Planning Commission at this time lay a series of lay commissions, also political, going over detailed portions of the Plan before it reached its final form. The process was described by Dr. Outrata in his preface to the Two-Year Plan Act.

'Democratic control was ensured by referring the working out of the various sections of the Plan to special commissions made up of representatives of all political parties, and, it may be said, of all sections of society whose interests were affected. The work of planning was carried out by eighteen such Commissions. . . . The 250 members of these Commissions along with the Central Planning Commissions, comprising five members . . . [received suggestions from the public], especially the clubs of the political parties and the members of Parliament.

'The work of planning was not carried out by a staff of State officials within the framework of departments, but by the Working Commissions organized as above. The bureaucratic staff was thus under the direction of the Working Commissions and had to accept their decisions. It is of interest to note that the Central Planning Commission . . . reached its decisions always through the medium of discussion; not in a single instance did discussions among the fifteen experts, *representing different political parties and nominated by them*, lead to decisions being forced to the vote. Thus in all questions of principles complete unanimity was achieved.'[1]

Dr. Outrata added that the method employed in the task of planning 'should also dispel most effectively any doubts . . . as to

[1] *The First Czechoslovak Economic Plan*, Prague, April 1947, pp. 5-11 (*our italics*).

the possibility of introducing planned economy into a state which wishes to preserve a multi-party system of democracy.'

Twelve months later, after the Plan had been in operation for nearly a year, we find Prime Minister Gottwald making acknowledgment of the services of Dr. Outrata as follows: '. . . . The Central Planning Commission has been able to balance and bring to a common denominator not only a number of questions arising out of departmental disagreements, but also a number of party-political issues. In my opinion, therefore, the Central Planning Commission has rightly played the part of a factor furthering the consolidation of the National Front. This is a highly honourable role, and I hope the Central Planning Commission will not relinquish it in future.'[1]

The Plan itself also provided for a politically constituted committee of oversight for Plan fulfillment. In paragraph 14 we read: 'The Constituent National Assembly shall elect, on the basis of proportional representation [i.e. of parties], a commission of thirty-six members for the control of the operation of the Two-Year Plan.'

In contrast, under the Five-Year Plan we find no mention of any similarly constituted top-level machinery. It is merely stated that the National Assembly is to appoint a committee for Plan review. On the other hand we find various statements concerning Action Committees and mass organizations.

Thus we read: 'The national committees shall participate in the drawing-up of the operative plans, . . . participate in the implementation of the Five-Year Plan and, within the framework thereof, plan, carry into effect and supervise economic, social, and cultural development within their territories. . . . Organs of the regional planning service . . . shall in the preparation of regional plans rely on the direct participation and initiative of the working population and of the national committees.'

Again, concerning the unions: 'The united trade union organization shall participate in the preparation, implementation, and supervision of the Five-Year Plan.'[2]

Obviously the temper of the planners had changed very much between 1946 and 1948–9.

[1] Ibid.

[2] Paragraphs 37 and 38.

3. LATER DEVELOPMENTS IN PLANNING

'The fundamental task of the Six-Year Plan', said Vice-Premier Minc of Poland in mid-1950, '. . . . is to bring about a significant development of productive forces, and in the first place, of the production of means of production. . . . That is why the highest rate of development . . . has been projected for all the branches of the machine-building industry.'[1]

This and other main items of the Plan had been considerably increased over its original version of a year earlier. The Three-Year Plan had been 'systematically and considerably over-fulfilled', and it was on this basis that the six-year aims were being raised upward. The final draft 'sets much wider tasks' in output, in investments for new construction, and in social change. 'As a result of experiences resulting from the development of the country since that time (i.e. the time of the Unification Congress of the United Workers' Party, December 1948) these guiding principles have undergone considerable changes. . . . The present draft provides for much quicker development. . . .'[2]

The original draft had called for an increase in the output of industry by 1955 of around 90 per cent. The present draft called for almost twice that, namely around 160 per cent. The original draft had called for an increase in agricultural production during the six years of less than half of this, or around 40 per cent. The present draft raised the sights for this goal somewhat, calling for over 60 per cent above original 1949 estimates.[3]

As for social evolution, the socialized sector of the economy had already grown faster than projected, and by the end of the Six-Year Plan, employment in it, excluding agriculture, was to increase by almost 60 per cent. This was chiefly a matter of the growth of industry. But expulsion of remaining capitalist elements was also a factor. Already some 90 per cent of combined industrial and handicraft output was in state and co-operative establishments. By 1955 the combined figure was to be almost 100 per cent. In trade also, sweeping changes had already taken place,

[1] Speech of Vice-Premier Hilary Minc, 15 July 1950, in 'The Six-Year Plan', Warsaw, 1950, pp. 25–6.

[2] Vice-Premier Minc, quoted in *Polish Facts and Figures*, Polish Embassy, London, 21 July 1950.

[3] Actually 50 per cent over the unexpectedly good harvest results obtained in 1949.

and by the end of the Plan period, to all practical purposes all of trade would be socialized.

In agriculture, however, the situation was very different. As yet fully half the population were still making their living in agriculture, a proportion comparable to that of Slovakia; but the living was coming from 3,500,000 peasant farms. These produced well over 90 per cent of all marketed produce, and of this amount perhaps a third came from the 300,000 larger, over 50-acre holdings. No wonder that 'the social, economic, and organizational reconstruction of peasant farming' was held to be 'the basic problem of the workers' party policy at the present stage'.[1]

Meantime, planning in the field of agriculture had to be on a limited and altogether different basis from that of industry. 'Our agriculture is based at present and for a certain time will still continue to be based predominantly upon small commodity economy. . . .[2] We do not as yet have direct planning in the preponderant part of our agriculture, and the influence of the State on its development takes place solely by means of planned regulation. The stronger the position of the State in the field of socialist industry, in the finance system, and in trade, the more effective does this planned regulation become.'[3]

Regional Planning

Regional planning in the planned economies is conceived of very broadly, as a part of the long-run, all-around economic development of each region and of the country as a whole. 'A long-term process aiming to obtain a more even distribution of productive forces,' Vice-Premier Minc called it. The persistence of large purely agrarian areas is deplored: however useful it might be thought to the outsider to have some specialized, purely 'bread-basket' regions, this is not the view of any of the countries moving toward socialism. Every sizeable area must have built into it its own core of industry and industrial employment. None must be allowed to remain hinterland. This is for two reasons: one, the

[1] President Boleslaw Bierut, *Tribuna Ludu*, Warsaw, 2 December 1950.

[2] A Marxist term, denoting production for the market by petty independent producers, self-employed.

[3] Hilary Minc, 'The Six-Year Plan', pp. 62–3. During the Plan period, Mr. Minc continued, planned relations between town and country were to be greatly extended 'in the form of planned purchasing of agricultural commodities'.

urgent need declared by all these countries for a great increase in industrial production generally; the other, the deep effect of industrial employment upon the local population. Socially, it is held that only by furnishing every region without exception with its own centres of industry can the standards of living of the more backward populations be raised rapidly. And politically, the rise of a working class dissolves old rural habits and prejudices, brings in carriers of socialist thought and new technology.

At the same time the planned economies, like town planners the world over, urge the avoidance of continued accretions of further industry to centres already amply stocked, unless there is some overriding reason for a given addition. The gravitational tendency for industries to settle where initial facilities are cheaper, regardless of overcrowding and ultimate economic ill effects, is strongly combatted. Here, as also in the case of the agricultural regions, it is the long-run results that are aimed at, even at higher unit costs to begin with.[1]

In their willingness to sacrifice immediate income advantages even in the face of pressing need, as indeed in their policies of regional balance generally, the planned economies have been seeking to follow Soviet practice and experience. However, they have not needed to go so far. The effort to industrialize broadly in a short time is of course difficult in any case. But the special regional problems of the Soviet Union had originally been complex to a degree quite unparalleled in the smaller countries.[2]

In Poland in the early 1950's the task of 'reconstructing the economic geography of the country' was beginning to get under way at three different levels.

(1) Country towns in 'neglected' areas were to receive 'econ-

[1] At the same time, what are known in Britain as conurbations are also here aimed at in cases where previous satellite or related cities had grown up without plan. This is especially to be seen in Czechoslovakia which was more heavily industrialized to begin with. A striking case there is the great shoe centre of Gottwaldov, formerly Zlin, the earlier history of which is described in Chapter X.

[2] The U.S.S.R. is so vast and varied that its regional policies obviously operated on an altogether different scale. But also, its social-political structure as a multi-national State was extraordinarily complex. Republics and administrative districts were delimited in so far as possible on the basis of nationalities; socially speaking there were regions within regions, and, to begin with, the variations in initial living standards of the various groups and sub-regions were altogether out of scale with anything to be found between the more and the less developed portions of Poland and Czechoslovakia.

omic animation' by being seeded with socialized small industry, drawing upon their own unused resources of materials and labour.

(2) Throughout the country there was to begin a more even spread of the larger, national industry establishments, chiefly of course in the non-industrial cities.[1]

(3) In no less than five different parts of the country there was to begin a deliberate building up—on the whole very quickly—of massive new areas of heavy industry concentration, large enough to contain the major complementary processes. Hitherto in Poland there had been only one such major area, the Silesian basin. 'In all other places heavy industry establishments are scattered and do not form compact industrial regions. . . . The industrialization of Poland is inconceivable on the basis of solely one large heavy industry district.' Moreover, 'The building of the foundations of socialism calls for . . . a considerable raising of the level of economically backward districts . . . and for the creation in the entire country of concentrations of the working class—the principal driving force in the building of socialism.'[2]

Much the largest piece of industrial construction listed for the Six-Year Plan was the great steel combine of Nowa Huta ('New Foundry'), near Cracow. Deliberately planted in the most poverty-stricken and probably the most traditional-minded province in Poland, a region of dwarf farms, the new 'socialist city' when completed was to house 100,000 persons.[3] Another characteristic note was that the entire equipment of the foundry and its related works had been furnished out of the proceeds of the 1948 long-time investment loan granted Poland by the Soviet Union, and that all the major parts were actual imports from the Soviet Union, complete with all their technical documentation.

[1] In 1949, Vice-Premier Minc pointed out, two-thirds of the persons employed in industry had lived in the four most highly industrialized provinces of Poland, with all the rest of the country having only one-third. 'This state of affairs is unacceptable.'

[2] Minc, op. cit., pp. 33–4.

Even for Warsaw a good deal of further industrial construction was called for, in accordance with its new position as 'the socialist capital of a people's State'. 'Warsaw', it was stated in the press, 'is to be given a strong proletarian backbone through the expansion of industry in the city itself and in its suburbs.' (*Polish Facts and Figures Supplement*, London, 5 August 1950.)

[3] Twenty thousand of the future workers, most of them local people, and untrained, were said to be engaged in the first year in building their future city.

A popular brochure[1] describing the founding of the new combine and city illustrates some of the regional planning points involved.

In answering the question, Why at Cracow?, the authors first go into the technical factors of raw materials, power, and transport, explaining that for lack of Polish iron ore, the combine will get its ore floated down by a great canal (to be built during the Six-Year Plan) direct from Krivoi Rog in the U.S.S.R.; that it will get its coal and coke from nearby Silesia, and that in turn Silesia will be a great consumer of Nowa Huta products. In answer to the further question, Why not in Silesia itself, then? they state that 'Silesia is already too well stocked with productive establishments to put another giant industrial investment there'. Silesia has 'a negative balance of manpower'. And 'it would be impossible to find there a large enough area not lying over valuable beds of coal'. Cracow, on the other hand, though 'lying close to the centre of our heavy industry, is itself a non-industrialized area'. It 'holds promise of a great future'. Also Nowa Huta has plenty of water, whereas 'much of Silesia has barely enough water for its existing needs'.

As for social-political reasons, Cracow is 'a region of overcrowded farms, which can well afford to have some of its population drawn off into industry without injury to agriculture'. Nowa Huta can 'give these people work and opportunity for a better life'. And 'Nowa Huta changes the face of the Cracow region and even . . . the face of Cracow itself; bringing into its core of rich cultural tradition . . . many thousands of people belonging to the working class, young people, full of enthusiasm and faith in the future.'[2]

Another illustration of regional principles is found in a non-popular article on Katowice,[3] one of the long-established great coal and heavy industry centres of Silesia. Here the author is dealing with the meshing in of provincial planning to the national Six-Year Plan and its objectives. He describes the rise of the provincial planning authorities in Katowice, their local projects, and

[1] Z. Morawski and I. Weyrocz, 'Nowa Huta', Warsaw, September 1951 (in Polish).

[2] Op. cit., pp. 11–13. For technical estimates of Nowa Huta, cf. Jan Aniola, 'The Role of Nowa Huta in the Technical Progress of the Steel Industry', *Gospodarka Planowa* (*Planned Economy*), July 1951 (in Polish).

[3] M. Ziomek, 'The Province of Katowice in the Six-Year Plan', *Gospodarka Planowa*, October 1950.

their share in the national Plan. Then he explains the chief difficulties currently met. These were both technical and social. Important portions of the province had previously been German. Hence there were all the technical problems of abolishing the former demarcations between 'old' and 'new' territories, in communication lines and so forth. And there were sharp social differences in housing and other amenities to be levelled up. Katowice inherited in large part 'very old working and housing conditions—a former chaos and agglomeration of population—no running water, no lighting'. Housing improvement therefore had come first in the local plans, and next, more rational exploitation of natural resources, more particularly coal.

This last point was being worked out in a large-scale way under the national investment policy of the Six-Year Plan. 'The Six-Year Plan calls for no more new industrial enterprises in the area, only for the development of coal and kindred processes': i.e. there were to be a number of new mines, certain electric power stations, iron ore mining, lime kilns, foundries, and a number of coke mills, but that was all. As a result, Katowice's share in the total industrial output of the nation would fall: by the end of the Six-Year Plan it would be about one-fourth instead of one-third.

Large ancillary projects were to be invested in nationally, to conserve coal, operate the related industries, and help the local population. More particularly, there was to be very heavy investment in water reservoirs, to be constructed by the Regional Water Commission. And a large sand reservoir was to be built for the coal mines. (The Poles used a process, described in Chapter IX, to fill in the floor and all successive levels of coal chambers with sand as cutting proceeded.) A new ample supply of sand would make possible, it was stated, a greater extraction of coal, would diminish losses and protect against accidents.

The tone and pace of the Six-Year Plan, and more particularly its great regional construction works of heavy industry, could also be directly related to worsened East-West relations. There was specific reference in many public speeches of the period to the need for increased industrial strength for defence. The fulfilment and over-fulfilment of each man's task in the Six-Year Plan was urgently spoken of as 'a blow to the warmongers'. And it was, of course, obvious that such changes as the beginnings of co-operative farming on the one hand and the building up of the steel, chemical, and basic machine industries on the other would be of especial service if the country were again at war.

The relations, contradictory or otherwise, between what must have been two sets of motivations for Czech and Polish planners, and the relative weight of each in the final version of the Plans, is of course a matter for speculation only. It is to be noted, in any case, that contemporaneously with the defence-of-the-country note, there was much publicity at this time on the need for long-time peaceful construction and on the losses entailed by war and its preparations. An exceedingly widespread campaign was carried through during these years, on war as the greatest of social evils. There was also at this time much publicity concerning 'the transformation of nature' as an important peace-time project. Very great space was given in Czechoslovak and Polish scientific literature, as also in popular descriptions, to recent vast undertakings of the Soviet Union in this respect. The idea was that the face of a country could be changed permanently and increasingly for the better if only sufficiently large investments of manpower and material were made[1] in long-term, linked projects of afforestation, shelter-belt planting, creation of new water-levels, acclimitization of plants and animals, and so on. Limited beginnings of such work were to be made here and there now in the smaller economies plans. But for the real 'transformation', it was emphasized, a long perspective of time and meticulous care was needed: the linked

[1] 'Execution of these giant undertakings (i.e. the centralized construction portion of them) places extremely heavy demands on manpower resources and on the steel, cement, and heavy electrical engineering industries. . . .' (U.N., E.C.E., *Economic Survey . . . for 1951*, Geneva 1952, p. 132.)

Much larger manpower investments were called for in the agricultural parts of the Soviet programme. As was pointed out in the United States at the time of its opening stages, early in 1949, the tree planting part alone would have cost in America some 30 billion dollars, for it involved the handling of 15,000,000 acres of trees with nearly 34,000,000 pieces of planting stock, in shelter belts totalling over 3,000 miles. Even more absorptive of manpower and organizational effort was held to be the establishment of cropland and meadow-land rotations on all of the 77,500 collective farms of the region. Affecting some 230,000,000 acres of land, this part of the programme was to be completed in 1955, i.e. in 6 years, and was stated in America to 'far overshadow the vast tree planting programme in complexity, magnitude, and economic implications.' (Soil Conservation Conference, Russian Research Center, Harvard University, 14 January 1949.) Further 'minor phases' of the programme included local irrigation projects with the construction of over 44,000 ponds and reservoirs.

projects required not only great material resources but uninterrupted peace for many years to carry through.[1]

Techniques of Planning

The tasks of the planning organs in this period of critical pace, with its disproportions between rates of development of industry and agriculture, had become very difficult. However, the areas of direct control of the economy in both countries had grown very much with the increase of socialization; hence a rapid development of planning techniques was called for as feasible and necessary.

In descriptions of earlier planning in all the planned economies, faults are commonly stressed, so that it is easy to see where progress is held to be imperative at the given time. In the case of Czechoslovakia, a good analysis of what were considered the worst of the technical sins of the old Two-Year Plan period is found in the published lectures of a well-known Czech economist, dating from early 1949.[2]

In the field of materials requirements planning, he declared, no proper norms had been set up. 'In the Soviet Union the raw materials requirements come from each factory, along with and derived from the factory's production plan. In the Soviet Union they have worked out definite norms of materials requirements for each article of each type of product. . . . We did not even begin to work out such norms. . . . We did not provide proper planning organs. It is not possible that five to ten or twenty clerks from the Planning Board should work out, check and prove, and afterward lay down the norms for twenty industrial branches which account for thousands of enterprises and factories.'[3]

In investment planning the situation had been even worse. 'In raw materials planning we at least gained some valuable experi-

[1] A third publicity note on the anti-war theme was the particularly hard effect war was supposed to have on a socialist economy. For such an economy, it was said, war preparations could have no compensating employment effect: full employment existed anyway. This indeed was one of the arguments put up for the 'peaceful coexistence' of the socialist with the non-socialist world. If only competition could be reduced to economic means, the 'economies without crises' could show their superiority before long.

[2] Dr. J. Goldman, 'Some Problems of Planning Method and Technique' (lectures delivered 5–10 January 1949), *Planned Economy, the Economic Law of Socialism, A Collection*, Prague, 1949.

[3] Op. cit., pp. 77, 78.

ence from key branches—so that in key branches we are already not bad. But in investment planning we are still in the dark. . . . Everyone who has worked in the Planning Service knows the feverish mood surrounding the discussions of investment planning. It actually came to open war of each against all *re* the investment quotas.'[1] It was on this account that the plan for industrial construction had fallen so badly short of fulfilment. 'The investment budgetings were simply inadequate.' This side of the situation did improve in the course of the Two-Year Plan.

But proper investment planning, just as raw materials planning, had to be based upon detailed production planning. 'If you have to produce a certain metal product, you have to work out how many hours of work of each type of machine are required. . . . Only thus can you tell where the bottle-necks in machinery are. We don't everywhere have these machine norms.'[2]

As to manpower planning, 'With all due self-criticism, we must say that here the situation is even more unpleasant. If in investments we reached only 40–50 per cent of plan, we must point out that between manpower planning on the one hand and the progress undoubtedly achieved on the other, the connections were very small. Influx of manpower occurred right enough, but obviously it was not due to planning. . . .'[3]

Quality planning in terms of labour productivity had also not been a full success. Total output had increased to the degree foreseen, but with a slightly larger working force than planned for. 'For the Five-Year Plan we have not yet adequately developed the planned productivity of labour.' In 1948 the productivity estimates had been too low: the plan was overfilled, but the goals set proved to have been inadequate.

'The most serious infantile disorder of our planning is the insufficient mobilization of workers for the Plan. In many factories the Plan was left to lie on the leading organs, the planning organs, and life in the factories remained just as it did before the Plan.' Following February 1948 the initiative of workers improved. And 'political fights with the anti-planners ended'. 'The workers began to try to find out what unused production resources there were in the factories.' It was only during 1948 that the workers could know how much was specifically expected of them: with a precise plan it became possible to counter-plan.[4]

[1] Ibid., p. 78.
[2] Loc. cit.
[3] Loc. cit.
[4] Ibid., p. 80.

Similar criticisms were voiced from Poland. During the Three-Year Plan, it was declared, check-ups had been very loose and original standards had often been set too low, due to faulty enterprise planning. 'Planning was incomplete. For example, in some of the enterprises there had been no planning of costs of production, and sometimes not of technical standards. Therefore in some whole branches of industry plans were surpassed by as much as 100 per cent. . . .'[1]

Even in mid-1950 Polish planners were still complaining of the lack of enterprise planning. 'Our planning organizations . . . have not as yet tackled seriously many fundamental fields of planning, such as inner-establishment planning or local planning.'[2] In these respects, as in their accounting practices generally, the Czechoslovaks were held to be considerably more advanced. Later it was stated that in Czechoslovakia's 1951 Plan a sharp distinction had been made between real enterprise planning and branch

[1] Andrej Karpinski, 'For the Highest Level of Plan Control Fulfilment', *Gospodarka Planowa*, Warsaw, December 1950. On the other hand, the author states, where plans were very far underfulfilled, the reason was often bad organization of supply and/or lost time due to breakdowns, which in turn were due to lack of adequate repairs planning.

Charges were also levelled against the earlier Plans on the ground that various of their underlying theoretical assumptions had been mistaken and could only lead to bad task-setting and task-fulfilment.

Thus in the same volume as the Czechoslovak criticisms just referred to, published in 1949, the then Vice-Minister of Industry of Poland listed three main mistaken theories to be discarded henceforth by planners. The first was 'wrong, anti-Marxist accounting of the national income', the second, 'so-called "independent" planning for co-operatives, artisans, small traders', the third, 'the theory of the primacy of consumption planning as over against production and investment planning'.

These theories have already been referred to in the earlier part of the chapter. The proper national income classification according to the view later prevailing was:

- (1) Socialist economy
  - State and local government
  - Co-operative
- (2) Petty commodity economy (the self-employed)
  - farmers
  - artisans
- (3) Capitalist economy
  - the employer
    - in industry
    - in agriculture
  - the merchant

(Cf. State Statistical Office of Poland, *The National Income of Poland in 1947*, Warsaw, 1949.)

[2] Vice-Premier Minc, 'The Six-Year Plan', p. 64.

planning, and that the former had been developed with success.[1]

Plans of the 1950–2 period showed rapidly increasing subdivision. At the same time there were calls for more realistic co-ordination between the parts, both major and minor.

'The Financial Plan as a whole', it was claimed, 'was not tied in closely enough with the Production Plan. And the whole National Plan was not sufficiently tied in with the Budget.'[2] 'With us there exists to be sure a formal unity of the technical-industrial-financial plan,[3] but the individual parts of this . . . the technical plan, the plan of production, the plan of material supplies, the plan of employment and wages, the plan of real costs, the investment plan, and the financial plan—proceed in effect independently, each in its separate compartment.'[4]

By the time the 1952 Polish Plan was being framed, serious attempts were made to make for better co-ordination, and Soviet example in this and other matters was cited. 'It is on the basis of the experience of the Soviet Union that we are making some changes in our plan.'[5]

However, the author goes on to say, in utilizing Soviet planning experience, 'We cannot take over the planning methods of 1930–1, but those of 1950–1'. And even these could not be taken over mechanically, but had to be adapted to Polish conditions. It was to be remembered that Soviet planning had developed by stages; it would be nonsense if one tried to follow all the stages.[6] 'We have the advantage of being able to take the experiences of the Soviet Union for the latest period, that of the building of Communism, with its "tempestuous" development of technique on the basis of a wide development of heavy industry.'

[1] For the connection between this and the results ascribed to organizational changes within industry itself, see Chapter IX.

[2] Bronislaw Minc, 'Changes in the Methodology of Planning for the year 1952', *Gospodarka Planowa*, Warsaw, July 1951, p. 10. (This Minc is not the Vice-Premier, but his brother, a well-known economist.)

[3] This expression is taken directly from the Russian 'techpromfinplan', a triple combination occupying a central point in Soviet plan formulation.

[4] Stefan Jedrychowski, 'Some Conditions for Fulfilment of the Six-Year Plan', *Ekonomista*, Third Quarter, Warsaw, 1950, p. 31 (in Polish).

[5] Bronislaw Minc, op. cit., p. 9.

[6] This does not mean of course that one should not [also] take advantage of Soviet experience in the period of the building of the basis of Socialism. . . .'

[7] In Marxist-Communist theory a sharp distinction is drawn between the first, or lower, or 'Socialist' stage of development after capitalism has been replaced, and the later, or higher 'Communist' stage. In the first, rewards are

Such 'tempestuous' technical development could be approached, even from afar, only with something approaching the Soviet Union's closely fused plan structure.[1] In Poland's 1952 Plan, following Soviet example, several entirely new sections had been added, dealing with various material, technical and financial 'balances', i.e. meshings-in of one part with another.[2]

The outline of the 1952 Plan consisted, first, of a series of sections centering around production, along with the programme of technical development and that of investment-and-construction. (The latter two were put under a single heading.) Next came a pair dealing with various components for increased living standards on the one hand and the plan for employment and wages on the other. Then came the plan of real costs and the financial programme. Then came a general 'balance of the national economy' and a schedule of provincial plans. Finally, before the concluding plan of foreign trade, there were a series of balances and norms newly introduced for 1952—the 'balance of income and expenditures of the socialist economy', the 'norms of consumption for the most important raw materials and fuels', and the 'material balance and plan for material technical supplies'.[3]

on the basis of services rendered ('to each according to his work'); in the second, on the basis of need. In neither is there equalitarianism. But the second is said to depend for its establishment upon an abundance of material goods and the development of new motivations. (Lenin claimed to find this theory clearly formulated in Marx's *Critique of the Gotha Program.*)

[1] 'On what pattern will our detailed . . . economic plan be drawn up? That arrangement is based upon the experience of the Soviet Union, with due consideration for our conditions.' (Ibid., p. 10.)

[2] As, for example, the 'balance' of the delivery of industrial supplies to agriculture and of agricultural raw materials to industry. The two were patently not expected to be in balance in the sense of equilibrium, but to be related to one another.

[3] As set up, the outline looked as follows:

1. Summary of Plan.
2. Programme of Production: (*a*) Industry; (*b*) Agriculture and Forestry; (*c*) Communications.
3. Programme of Technical Development.
4. Programme of Investment and Construction.
5. Programme for raising the material and cultural level of the working masses. (*a*) Internal trade; (*b*) Social and cultural services; (*c*) Communal economy and housing.
6. Plan of Employment and Wages.
7. Plan of Real Costs.

The system of balances was very elaborate. Thus the single heading 'Balances of the National Economy' as a whole included 'the balance of global production; the balance of industry and agriculture; the balance of the formation of the national income and its distribution among classes of consumers; the balance of the objects of consumption; the balance of the pecuniary incomes and expenditures of the population; the balance of permanent landed property; the balance of labour.'[1]

Provision for investment naturally occupied a strikingly increased place in the new planning. And much emphasis was placed upon having its purely formal, financial side tied strongly in to its concrete end results. Investments were made after all to be put to use. 'Only on the real programme of the institution to be constructed should final figures be based.'[2]

For every object of investment a separate plan should be made for the final stage of the work, when the object was to be ready to start operations. 'Thus you can see whether all parts were finished harmoniously and are really ready to operate. You can thus check back on the investment plan.'[3]

8. Financial Programme.
9. Balance of the National Economy.
10. Diagram of Provincial Plans.
11. Balance of Income and Expenditures of the Socialist Economy.
12. Norms of Consumption for the most important raw materials and fuels.
13. Material Balance and Plan for material technical supplies.
14. Plan of Foreign trade.

[1] Ibid. In Czechoslovakia by the beginning of 1952, fixed annual 'wage funds' for industry had been introduced, embodying 'both the increase in productivity and the raising of wages for which the plan has made provision' . . . The National Planning Office was to be responsible for setting the total 'and for allocating it among the Ministries and Departments responsible for the various branches of industry, which in turn must fix the share of each establishment'. (I.L.O., *Industry and Labour*, vol. VI, Geneva, 1951, pp. 194–6.)

[2] K. Sekominski, 'Changes in the Methodology of Investment Planning', *Gospodarka Planowa*, July 1950, p. 540. The author calls this kind of investment planning 'factual', i.e. substantive. Others also use the term 'contents planning'.

[3] Ibid., p. 542. It was also possible now, it was said, to have much closer planning of supplies for objects of investment. It was no longer going to be necessary to keep on hand a 'pool' of essential imported parts. 'Now the supplies coming from the Soviet Union and the People's Democracies are planned on the same basis as those produced at home.' (Ibid., p. 541.)

In connection with investments, various writers at this period cited the effect of recent local government reorganization upon a better division of

This principle was embodied in the 1952 Plan. 'In the overall Investment Plan strong emphasis is placed upon the plan for putting investments to use. For this reason the National Economic Plan embraces a wide list of construction projects, with concrete obligatory terminal dates. . . .' It was also to include a schedule of 'given unit-times', apparently for typical stages in the final process of readying for operation the object constructed.[1]

As might be expected, further development of technical planning was provided in the new Plan. Subheads of the Technical Plan ranged from the introduction of new processes, new or substitute materials, new methods of mechanization and so forth, to 'the plan of working out prototypes', including entire new model plants appropriate to different kinds of industry, and to the huge topic of 'the plan of working out standards and norms'. There was also the general 'plan of the work of scientific research', 'constructional', and 'experimental'.

Co-ordination of the technical plan with all the other plans was also provided for. 'In the State Economic Plan for 1951 the technical plan was not sufficiently connected with the total plan. . . . For 1952 . . . its programme is so worked out as to be closely connected with the total plan and with each of its indices.'[2]

In the schedule for getting the annual plans prepared there had also been a change. Formerly there had been a certain amount of doubling back of the planning process between State Planning Commission on the one hand and enterprises and their ministries on the other. Apparently the latter had been called upon to make very full plans which were subsequently altered. The procedure had been that, on the basis of very general preliminary directives,

planning. The classic dichotomy between 'state' and 'local' organs was said to have been done away with, without the evils of centralization. In Poland the dominant authority in the regions and townships had been made the People's Councils, bodies popularly elected, but responsible to carry out national policy in economy as well as government. The title of the law defining their status indicated this drawing together of functions quite plainly: 'On Local Organs of the Uniform Authority of the State.' The Councils were each to have its own planning organ. These were responsible for elaborating in detail provincial economic plans for a year or more, and for planning and setting up local industry and handicraft, distribution, and local communications. A certain number of undertakings totally projected by the central authorities also required prior approval of their plans by the provincial or local authorities.

[1] Bronislaw Minc, op. cit., p. 13.

[2] Ibid., p. 13.

'locally there were prepared . . . very detailed plans, the Technical-Industrial-Financial Plan in Industry; the Trade-Financial Plan in Trade; the Transport-Financial Plan in transport, and so on.' As a result of this, the enterprises 'had the heavy task of working out entire plans'. 'On the basis of the complete plans prepared by the enterprises, the corresponding ministries worked out combined plans, which went thereupon to the Planning Commission, and then usually were revised upward—increasing the task of the Plan. As a result of this it was necessary to make changes in the plans prepared by the separate industrial enterprises, commercial enterprises, and so on, and in consequence the National Economic Plan was only approved in February and came to the enterprises in March or even later. . . .

'The rate of the working out of the National Plan for 1952 provides therefore acceleration of dates [i.e. 1 January for final publication of Plan] and at the same time it provides the working out of financial concrete task planning in five stages.' These were: (1) The working out of the general directives by the Planning Commission. (2) The working out of their outline projects of the Plan by the enterprises, central managements, and departments. (3) The working out of the full project of the National Plan by the State Planning Commission. (4) The approval of the Plan by the Government. (5) The working out of their own details of the Plan by the enterprises.

'In this way, before starting Plan fulfilment, all will know the tasks set out by the Planning Commission.' The new methods, it was added, required a very precise observance of dates and a very thorough analysis of the contents of the Plan. Great importance was attached to the original directives, as being the 'organizational factor' of the Plan. They 'must be set neither too high nor too low: they must be realistic, mobilizing. They must comprise, of course, not all the details of the Plan but only the most important elements.'[1]

A final matter, that of better check-up on Plan fulfilment, was approached by a provision concerning the country's banks. Under planned economy banks have the duty not only of checking on such matters as the formal solvency of the concerns under their care, but of acquainting themselves directly with the extent to which these concerns are fulfilling their share of the Plan. The banks were always supposed to pass on this information where

[1] Ibid., p. 10.

necessary to the higher administrations in industry, etc. But the Planning Commission also made its own check-ups. Now, under the Polish 1952 Plan, the two sets of checks were to be co-ordinated and the banks were to make available to the Planning Commission whatever material they had that was pertinent.[1] How thorough this material might be will become evident in the next chapter.

[1] Formally speaking, the latter procedure had already been provided for in a Council of Ministers' Decree of early 1950. (Cf. Karpinski, op. cit.) But the Plan provision amounted to implementation.

In Czechoslovakia, in conjunction with the fixed 'wage funds' for 1952, referred to earlier, the banks were given a yet further duty. '. . . If an undertaking were to pay out in wages more than it produced', it was explained in the press, 'the State Bank responsible for providing the undertaking with the necessary funds would have to inform the competent ministry; the latter would then study the reasons for that situation and take the action necessary to rectify it.' (I.L.O., *Industry and Labour*, Geneva, vol. VI, 1951, p. 196.)

CHAPTER VIII

SOCIALIST BANKING, SERVANT OF THE PLAN

Intermediate between Plan and national economy in the countries moving towards Socialism lies the banking apparatus. As servants of the Plan, the banks naturally do not themselves initiate basic financial policy: the Government does that. But under the Plan, they directly control the operations of the economy by their handling of credits and investments. Numerous devices are invented to keep the closest possible check by the banks upon the concrete details of production and construction.

Originally the requirements of their new planned-economy banking had been worked out more or less independently by the Czechs and Poles, for lack of intimate knowledge of Soviet experience in the field—there was said to have been lack of familiarity with source materials, language, and also a lack of adequate personal banking contacts. By 1948, however, Poland and Czechoslovakia had learned a good deal from each other through systematic conferences and exchange of experience.[1] And by the end of another year rich technical materials from the Soviet Union and the experience of Soviet bankers were said to be fully available and taken advantage of.

As technical experts, the banks were given a free hand to devise what machinery they wished to make their controls effective. Their work began with the detailed formulation of the Financial Plans themselves, aside from the budget, which was outside their competence. The other two main portions of the Financial Plan,

[1] Common problems, it was said, had led in the main to a common pattern of controls. Apparently the initiative of the Polish system had been greatest in the general sphere of domestic credit operations, and Czech banking delegations profited subsequently from this. On the other hand, the Czech system had taken a lead in foreign exchange operations, from which, again, the Poles were learning. Also, *ex post facto*, Czechs and Poles found that many of their devices duplicated what had been worked out long since in the Soviet Union. (Interview material, 1948 and late 1949.)

the Investment Plan, and the Credit Plan, were worked out in all their detail by the appropriate central banks.[1]

How strong the control of national enterprises early became through this initial financial planning can be seen in a 1947 article by a Polish economist describing the new banking system:[2]

'As the authoritative economic organ, the Bank holds financial control of the nationalized industries. Such control is exercised irrespective of credits granted and also extends to firms to which no credit has been given. The basic purpose of this control is to make sure that the principles of the planned financial economy are strictly adhered to and that the functions it assigns to the various economic units are properly carried out.

'The Bank's control takes effect even before the financial economic plan of a given enterprise has been approved. The Bank studies this plan from the viewpoint of its conformity with the overall national programme and with an eye to the financial possibilities and technical facilities of the enterprise. On the basis of this study, the Bank renders an opinion on the plan itself and suggests what capital will be required for its implementation. It further determines what part of this capital will be derived from the firm's own working funds and what part will have to be supplemented by credits. From then on, the Bank assumes permanent control of the enterprise, thus keeping it in line with the general principles of the country's financial policy.'

To maintain planned control both countries found it necessary to make a sharp separation between investment and working credit operations. And in course of time both sets of bankers came to reorganize their banking systems to make this distinction central.

The reason was highly practical. As explained by the Czechs and Poles, the tendency of the individual manager of a nationalized enterprise, of course, is to over-invest, to want to extend his particular business beyond the limits of the Plan. Similarly with current credit: he tends to continue to be 'a good business man', to want to keep plenty of stocks on hand against any emergency, to hoard, i.e. to overbuy supplies. The Bank therefore must always

[1] Thus, in the matter of credits, the National Bank of Poland had to make three major financial plans: A Credit Plan, a Foreign Payments Plan, and a Cash Operations Plan.

[2] Ludwik Kostowski, 'The Role of the Polish National Bank in the National Financial System', *Polish National Bank Bulletin*, August 1947 (in Polish).

pay great attention to the rational and correct use of the enterprise's means. If enterprises are left free to switch funds back and forth between their credit and investment accounts, the standing of neither can be kept clear. The two sets of balances must, therefore, in any case, be kept separate. An increasing functional division of the banks themselves along these lines is hence only logical. Then the enterprise goes to one bank for its investment credit, to another for its operating credit.

Originally, of course, both the Poles and Czechs had a multiplicity of banks, and for a time during the early period of mixed economy it looked as though division of banking by 'sectors' might persist indefinitely. The State (nationalized industry) sector was only one among many. The local government sector, the co-operative sector, the private enterprise sector, and agriculture, each had its own banking institutions. Thereafter, during the general transition to socialist forms, these sectoral divisions were first minimized and then in so far as possible given up altogether. In their place the emphasis upon division according to function—investment *or* current credit operations financing—became paramount, and the banks were specialized accordingly.[1]

The Czechoslovaks, as a small nation already well industrialized, had advanced the most rapidly to the clear-cut structure called for. During 1949 the country had liquidated its separate Agricultural Bank, which had handled both investment and current credit for farmers. Thereafter the farmers went for investment credit to affiliates of the Investment Bank, and for current credit to either a branch of the State Bank or, if they were very small farmers, to a savings bank. The Poles at this time continued to have a mixed Agricultural Bank but did not intend to keep it permanently. Their separate Co-operative Bank had already been liquidated and its functions divided.[2] And the greater part of

[1] In the Soviet Union banking was both highly centralized and specialized by function. In addition to the great State Bank for note issue and credit operations, with its many thousands of employees and many branches, there were four different all-Union Investment Banks, for industrial, commercial, agricultural, and communal investments. Savings Banks on the other hand were decentralized.

[2] Under Socialism, it was pointed out to the writer, the practical difference between aiding co-operative and State enterprises is unimportant. A jam factory of a given size that is co-operative has quite similar operating and financial problems to one like it that is under nationalized industry: the criteria for servicing it are no different.

Polish investments had been concentrated in a single Investment Bank.

By 1951, in Czechoslovakia all credit operations without exception were concentrated in branches of the one central National Bank, which was also the country's note-issuing bank: the various other big credit banks of the country had been amalgamated with it. And all investment functions without exception were carried on by the single Investment Bank.[1]

[1] The early history of Czechoslovak and Polish reforms had been as follows. When nationalization first began, the Czech system had inherited twelve industrial banks, several hundred savings banks and several hundred or more credit banks. A village might have several banks 'with nothing to do', and of course with industry nationalized there was still less for them to do. Simplification was effected in two stages. As described by a Czech official in 1948, in the first stage the number of major banks was reduced to about three in the Czech lands and three in Slovakia; after February 1948 the number was further reduced to only one bank for industrial credit in the Czech lands and one in Slovakia. Savings and mutual credit institutions were all amalgamated into the credit type, and multitudes of small local savings institutions were dissolved. A postal savings bank remained at this time. A single investment bank was in process of being created. The National Bank financed the credit institutions. There were thus four main sets of banks.

When the writer revisited Czechoslovakia at the end of 1949 the single Investment Bank was fully operative and a single State Commercial Bank had superseded the various credit institutions. The Agricultural Bank had disappeared and the Postal Savings Bank and other saving institutions were merged.

In Poland, pre-war banking had already been largely in State hands. There had never been a real stock market here, and the whole banking system was considered very feeble. 'There were no capitalists in Poland big enough to finance industry in a big way.' (Interview material, October 1949.)

After wartime destruction and the depredations of the Germans it would have been out of the question to start up private banking effectively. Reconstruction taxed all possible State resources as it was. Instead, the old forms were carried over and successively modified. In some cases, however, purely Polish historical forms were found good and used. Thus there had already been in old Poland the rare tradition of combining successfully in one and the same bank the functions of note issuing and direct financing of the economy. The old Bank Polski, formed in the Kingdom of Poland during the Partition Period, i.e. under the Russian Empire, combined these two functions with great apparent success. The ensuing period had been one of rapid economic development, especially of the building industry in Warsaw. The Poles pointed out that in Soviet Russian history there was no such tradition. This characteristic was carried over in the National Bank of to-day.

A Polish writer points out that during the period of adaptation of the banking system to the needs of a planned economy, the necessary reorganizations were not carried through by laws but on a more *ad hoc* basis by Government decrees

In Poland changes had been less complete, chiefly because of the problems of a large peasant population with low economic standards. Here the 'functionalizing' of the banking mechanism had stopped short for the time being at agriculture. A single Agricultural Bank provided both for investment and credit needs, and there were also some less important exceptions.[1]

However, major banking reforms had been prepared in Poland in the second half of 1948 and went into effect at the beginning of 1949. 'We had to adapt our system to the growth of the socialized sector and to the growth of planning.'[2] In the new system the National Bank granted credit directly to almost the whole nationalized portion of the economy and indirectly to the rest. 'It is our aim to concentrate all short term and working credit in the National Bank.' The Bank constituted the 'control point', the

and by instructions of the Ministry of Finance. Thus a Council of Ministers' decree in August 1947 had provided that the National Bank was to draw up a Credit Plan and check up on its fulfilment. It also introduced the principle of the concentration of the cash of each enterprise in one credit institution only, and forbade mutual credit between enterprises. A recent decree, of March 1951, had 'decreased the number of agent banks, and, over those that remained, strengthened the position of the National Bank of Poland as the central bank of the State'. (T. L. Michalowski, 'Outline of the Development of the Banking System of People's Poland', *Gospodarka Planowa*, September 1951, p. 14.)

The same writer points out that 'Different economic and social conditions made the manner of our nationalization of banking differ somewhat from that of the Soviet Union, although it aimed at the same ends.' 'The wide range of activity of our Agricultural Bank derives from the small-scale structure of our agriculture' (pp. 13, 15). He also points out that although the Bank is included in the list of economic 'enterprises', it differs from all other enterprises in being 'not merely an economic unit operating according to principles of economic accounting, but also an organ of State power'. (Ibid., p. 16.)

[1] The Agricultural Bank received its credit funds from the National Bank and its investment funds from the Investment Bank in lump sums. The Agricultural Bank had over four hundred branches and agencies, in order to service adequately the small farmer—one or even two branches in every county. Local credit operations were bound up with it. It gave both long and short term credit, investment loans and non-investment loans. The Agricultural Bank also financed the rural trading co-operatives.

For the time being also the construction industry, because of its swollen proportions, received both sets of services from one agency, in this case the national Investment Bank. In all the rest of its work the Investment Bank remained a strictly one-function agency. Another special case was local government activities and enterprises: all of these were financed, both for investments and current credit, by a special national Communal Bank.

[2] Interview material, October 1949.

'commanding height' of the economy.[1] The Investment Bank did the same for the nation's investments.

In both countries a national Investment Bank had functioned since 1949 with the sole function of collecting national investment funds and dispensing them. The role of the State in the investment field in both countries was to plan and to make decisions concerning the hierarchy of different investments, deciding which industries and enterprises required priority. The whole technical task was carried out by the Investment Bank.[2]

Socialist Credit

Two phrases sum up the principles of Socialist credit: 'The Bank holds all the keys to the factory', and, 'No plan, no credit'. The concept of a good credit risk changes fundamentally. The size of a client's assets is no longer the chief criterion. It is not amount of collateral but degree of adherence to Plan that is decisive.[3]

Methods of control were various. 'Control over the actual operations of the concern', a Polish economist pointed out, 'is exercised by the Bank in two ways. Firstly, it sees that operations are carried out in accordance with the original plan, and, secondly, that the stipulated capital is used up within a stipulated period of time. Thus production is controlled by a financial factor which is

[1] Under the National Bank were a set of member banks directly state-owned or corporate in form. The National Bank itself by 1951 had some 400 branches.

[2] In both countries, prior to 1949, a large part of investment funds had come from long-term State credits, the rest from grants. Czechoslovakia still continued this twofold system. Poland, however, in its 1949 reorganization went over to a single system, that of direct budgetary grants for virtually all investment purposes. 'The Government budget and industrial investments are now one.' (Interview material, October 1949.)

[3] As it was put by a Czechoslovak banker, 'It is the justification of credit itself within the framework of the state economic Plan which is decisive, and the realization of the Plan is the most appropriate guarantee for the credit granted.' Or, as it was put by another Czech banker, 'It is here that we find ourselves confronted with the dynamic conception of valuation of credit, contrary to the formerly urged static conception, according to which the immediate solvency of the debtor was decisive. The new standpoint is applied not only in production but also in respect of agricultural credit.' (Written materials from Czechoslovak National Bank, winter 1948.) The Agricultural Credit Law of March 1948, provided for State-guaranteed loans to working farmers, based not on farm area and inventory, but on the farm's recent production record and on the personal qualities and schooling of the applicant.

especially concerned with operating costs and with the proper use and rotation of working capital; this financial factor acts as a stimulus to careful and thrifty management in running the enterprise.'[1]

Inspection of a concern's credit sheet could tell much. The credit requirements of national corporations were shown in their budgets. After its budget had been approved, the enterprise might draw operational credit. The normal amount of credit under the Plan for each period of time for each business was known in advance—in fact, it was entered at the head of each customer's sheet. 'A clerk reports if the business asks for more. Thus you can prevent the accumulation of excessive stocks of one kind or another.'[2]

In general, by following the balance curve of an enterprise, the Bank could see whether something abnormal was going on. Thus a decline of a balance was held to mean either that higher costs were at work or that dispositions were being made outside the Plan; unless indeed some payment had been made ahead of schedule legitimately, as, for instance, in the case of a chance to make advantageous immediate purchases. An increase in the balance might mean that stocks were being sold out, which might prove unsound, or that production was restricted; unless indeed more economic realization of the Plan was sufficient to account for it.[3]

If the reasons for the deviation appeared unsatisfactory, the Bank reported to the central management of the nationalized industry and, if necessary, to the Ministry concerned and to the Ministry of Finance.[4]

By 1950 a Polish regulation provided that in addition the banks

[1] Kostowski, op. cit.

[2] Interview material, April 1948.

[3] Written material from Czechoslovak National Bank, winter 1948.

[4] 'If the Bank ascertains that there is a marked disharmony between the budget of the national enterprise and the development of the current account, or if it arrives at the conclusion that the granting of a new credit may involve the risk of loss, it is its duty to report . . .' as above. (Ibid.)

Supervision in Poland was equally close. 'Control by the National Bank of Poland in enterprises falling within its competence begins with the purchase of raw materials and continues up to the sale of goods. It is carried out in the form of preliminary, current, and additional control. The Bank is presented quarterly with budgets of the enterprises, the need for working funds is ascertained through a comparison of estimated expenses with the initial working means and anticipated receipts for the respective period. The debtor is allowed to

were directly to pass on the results of their financial check of the enterprises under their care to the planning authorities, national and regional. 'All the shortcomings discovered by the banks are to be reported to the Planning Commission.'[1]

Credit control had at times been drastic, as in the case of Polish anti-inflation measures following the drought of 1947. That autumn the Bank made very stringent restrictions on credit to State industries, forcing them to throw masses of merchandise on the market, so that there was, as one banker put it, 'almost a direct flow from the machine to the market'. He added that, 'It was a shock to the economy, but a successful one.'[2] For a normal situation, the writer was told, the Bank merely kept the national enterprises from accumulating stocks of fuel, supplies, and so on. Since all accounts were open to the Bank and all receipts and expenditures were effected through its intermediacy, it could tell what was happening. In the case of the autumn 1947 operation, the throwing of the masses of merchandise on the market was accomplished through the co-operative and State stores. Private merchants, it was felt, would have hidden the goods for a rise in price.[3]

In Czechoslovakia the device of blocked accounts had been used by the National Bank to prevent development of excessive credit. Unlike Poland, Czechoslovakia started out with indirect rather than direct financing of most of nationalized industry, by the National Bank via operational banks. With the consent of the Government, the National Bank could require a financial institution to maintain a certain percentage of its entrusted assets in a

draw credit but gradually according to economic demands. He regularly submits to the bank documents (invoices, payrolls, etc.) which are examined as to whether they are in compliance with the plan and anticipated by the plan; unplanned payments may be rejected. Through its officials the National Bank may undertake a check on the spot in the enterprises. . . .' (Ibid.)

[1] Andrej Karpinski, 'For the Highest Level of Plan Control Fulfilment', *Gospodarka Planowa* (*Planned Economy*), Warsaw, December 1950 (in Polish).

[2] Interview material, July 1948.

[3] Wages, meanwhile, were not allowed to rise. This was hard on the workers at the time, but, it was pointed out, inflation was avoided. In Czechoslovakia wages had not been kept down as strictly, with a resulting price rise. Direct price control, outside the operations of the bank, was also attempted during the 1947 difficulties. But this method—the fighting of speculators directly in the market—proved far less effective than the 'stock-pile dispersal' operation. (Interview material, July 1948.)

blocked deposit, so that it would be unable to use it as a basis for further credit.

As indicated earlier, the most important single principle in credit control, as in that of investments, had been to make sure that funds were actually used for the purposes intended and were not hoarded or clandestinely reinvested. Hence national enterprises were under no circumstances allowed to use for investment any funds assigned to them for operating credit, and vice versa. Checking on this was facilitated by allowing each enterprise to keep only a single credit account covering all payments.

A second preventative of confusion and concealment was the prohibition against national enterprises paying one another in credit balances. Every payment between them had to be cleared through the Bank (the so-called 'control by the crown', as the Czechs put it). Invoices were payable at sight. Enterprises might not grant each other suppliers' credit. Moreover the amount of cash balances was kept moderate and was checked on.

Thirdly, national enterprises, in Czechoslovakia at least, had since 1948 had a uniform system of accounting: book-keeping, statistics, and budgeting. The Poles were following in this as rapidly as they could.

In the case of residual private enterprise, both countries had sought to mesh in the small producer and trader to the nationalized part of the economy by strict credit controls, and subsequently to cause him to combine with his fellows in co-operatives. No credit from State sources was available without certification from industry or trade associations, and every attempt was made to keep a running check on its use.[1] Together with market controls—priorities in scarce materials and bulk purchases—this made a strong triangle of control.

Latterly, pressure to join co-operatives was exercised in various ways that will be dealt with in a later chapter. The share of credit

[1] Special conditions and requirements apply to banking credits granted . . . to small traders. . . . The applicant is . . . obliged to attach to his application for credit the decision of the Traders' Association. Credit may be drawn only by dealers keeping books legally prescribed and owing no sums to the State Treasury.

'Even in these cases the use of the credit is supervised. The customer must make all his transfers and remittances to the account of his supplier exclusively, through the respective bank, the bank deciding on the ceiling of invoices admissible, and in this manner the bank controls also credit granted to retail dealers.' (Written material from Czechoslovak National Bank, winter 1948.)

control in this was quite direct. Better credit terms were made available to co-operatives than to private individuals, and to smaller artisans than to larger ones. Moreover, the larger artisan had to keep precise accounts according to prescribed forms and to secure his credit from the Credit Bank affiliate, while the smaller man dealt with the Savings Bank and could receive credit on the basis of his personal standing. (Similar distinctions applied to the large and small farmer, irrespective of whether the two dealt with the same bank or not.) By clubbing together in a co-operative, the larger artisans could cut down their overhead and get a bookkeeper between them. It was the business of the banks to point this out and thus to accelerate the progress toward more socialized forms.

Increased socialization and increased planning in turn were said to speed up the changes in the banking structure. 'The necessities of planning push us toward centralization and integration.'[1] Elimination of countless small credit and savings banks had not only meant a considerable saving, but had increased the opportunity of the central credit bank to know precisely what was going on in the country. Similarly with foreign and domestic trade: increase of socialization brought opportunity and need for more accurate banking analysis.

Very considerable activity in what might be called operational rationalization was therefore to be seen in both countries. New methods appeared to be exceedingly popular. For example, pleasure was expressed in Warsaw in 1949 over a recent rationalization in the National Bank's current accounts sections, whereby daily results could be given three hours earlier. Similarly with statistics of international payments: they were now being kept current to a degree not possible before. A 'very complete account of balance of payments' could now be made every month. As socialism was approached, the question of establishing a balance of payments, the writer was told, became 'no longer a question of estimates, but of good statistics'. 'In capitalist countries, you can only make estimates of the balance of payments, in socialist economy we are able to gather complete and very detailed data concerning the actual record of payments.' That is, all international payments being openly recorded at a central bank, the data for statistical analysis and classification were already there. 'The balance of payments is the execution of the Plan.'[2]

[1] Interview material, October 1949.

[2] Ibid.

Operations of the Bank and Plan possibilities were said to be subjected to running analysis, with quarterly Plan discussions between division head, section chiefs, and trade union representative. In making up a plan for the quarter and presenting it to his subordinates the division head would have to 'be specific and take into consideration fixed conditions. For example, "Can you do this without overtime or not?" Consultation goes on with the knowledge that the subsequent responsibility will be shared.' In turn there would be 'counter-plans' from discussions within the sections. 'Upon this we base our final Plan.' Present progress would then be discussed similarly in monthly meetings, again at both levels. This banker insisted that initiative from below had increased greatly in his institution and that it was comparable to what was going on among the personnel in industry. 'Hidden energy' was being tapped. 'It was as if they slept before.'[1]

Meanwhile a very firm grip indeed was being kept upon the national machine. Banks, Plan, and industry were part of one whole.[2]

[1] Ibid.

[2] In the matter of currency reform also the functioning of the banks as instruments of national policy was very clearly laid down. Thus in Poland, in October 1950, a currency reform destined greatly to strengthen the zloty (it was put on a gold basis at the same value as the rouble), was at the same time operated in a manner to cut down drastically the holdings of the remaining private traders and wealthier farmers, and conversely to lift debt burdens from the smaller farmers. Old zlotys in cash to any amount could be turned in for something over a week and no questions asked; but they could be exchanged at a ratio of only 100:1; while for prices, wages, savings deposits, pensions and ordinary private debts the ratio was 100:3. But debts owed by a small or medium farmer to a large one were to be accounted at the 100:1 ratio. The wealthier farmer therefore stood to take a 3:1 loss on any hoardings plus any debts owing to him.

The most serious effect of the currency reform, however, must have been upon the remaining mercantile classes. Not only the illicit dealer in currency as such, but all private traders who had substantial sums in bank deposits other than savings accounts fell under the 100:1 ratio. Small bank deposits were treated like savings accounts, i.e. 100:3, but larger ones at a scale of rates culminating in 100:1.

CHAPTER IX

THE STRUCTURE OF NATIONALIZED INDUSTRY

Pre-war experience in both Poland and Czechoslovakia had made the liberation movements extremely wary of 'statism'. The new nationalized industries were under no circumstances to be run like the old State Monopolies, nor like the mixed or all-State industrial concerns of the depression period. Here there could be no 'cold socialization' of the losses of friendly concerns by a friendly government, with yet more powerful interests freely operating outside, and the whole bound together by cartel agreements. Still less were the new industries to form part of the government public service apparatus, like the post office. The laws on the status of nationalized enterprises explicitly stated that they were to be organized into national corporations operating on a commercial basis. 'The Board of Management and the Director shall run the national enterprise with the care of good businessmen,' says the Czech law. The enterprises were to pay regular taxes and possess their own legal personality, including the right to own property. The State assumed no legal responsibility for their debts. In all these technical respects the conception of the nationalized enterprise in the planned economies closely resembled the 'public corporation' conception familiar to Britons after the war.

Early Structure

In structure also, so long as one remained within the framework of the original industry grouping, the Polish and Czech patterns at the outset had little to distinguish them from the British. Each industry group had a Central Directorate or Board which was a controlling and planning body, not an operating body. In each country there were about twenty such Central Boards to begin with, so that the groups were very large. These Central Boards in the case of all the larger industries were subdivided into two or more separate Branches, on a functional or regional basis or both. The functional basis itself varied between industries: it might be similarity of raw materials or of product or of process of production. Each Branch bore immediate responsibility for the enterprises under it, so that the whole arrangement was hierarchical. The active operating unit however was in every case the single National Enterprise, itself as a rule a multiple-plant corporation. The enterprise had its own balance sheet and profit and loss account. The enterprise received the use of land and buildings and enjoyed full proprietary rights over movable property.

In cases where originally large firms had had holdings in what were now different industry divisions—for example, coal and foundry combines—the constituent sections went under separate National Boards. In Poland the process had been facilitated by the form of the nationalization law itself: it applied to the physical property, not the ownership unit, so that from the outset different parts of a concern might have been handled differently. In the great majority of cases, however, a national enterprise comprised not one but several former firms, in the case of small plants often a considerable group. In Poland the common range was said to have been from two to ten plants.[1] In Czechoslovakia the average was apparently much higher. Thus in the first wave of nationalization about 2,000 firms had been nationalized: these were thereupon amalgamated into less than 250 national enterprises, or an almost 10 to 1 ratio. The new enterprises employed on an average almost 2,500 people each. During the period when a political contest was going on concerning the limits of nationalization, an active question had been the fate of numerous small enterprises, the former property of Germans and collaborationists, that had been sequestered under 'national administrators'. Should these be sold to private businessmen or should they be added to the growing national enterprises? The question was settled in the main by adding them to national enterprises. By the time the second wave of nationalization took place, this question of course no longer existed: now the problem was precisely the rendering efficient under government auspices of the smaller firms. The answer by and large at the time was to amalgamate them into large enterprises even though the physical plants remained separate. Establishments of a local nature, to be sure, were left in the hands of local

[1] Cf. M. Doroszewicz, 'The Organization of the Enterprises of Key Industry', *Gospodarka Planowa* (*Planned Economy*), Warsaw, July 1950.

authorities or occasionally co-operatives. But where it was possible to do so, operation in sizeable groups as part of the national industry network was considered to have the initial advantage of making rational management easier. How this opinion was shortly modified we shall see a little later.

It should be noted in any case how different in content in spite of various structural similarities, were the problems of the individual national enterprise in Poland and Czechoslovakia from those of the public corporation as usually conceived of, operating in the midst of an otherwise stable economy. Here the process of nationalization had engulfed an incomparably greater part of industry and an incomparably smaller size of business unit than was attempted in the West—in fact in the case of enemy property, which was the majority of all business property, units without any lower limit. These properties had, to put it mildly, for the most part been in unusually poor condition—in the case of Poland very largely physically emptied if not destroyed. In any case, except in Slovakia, they had all been under German occupation, with all the confusion of finances, book-keeping and personnel that this involved. Moreover the process of nationalization had been incomparably more hasty, with no time for fine adjustments. In the early stages it had commonly followed upon an initial period of control by local workers' organizations and then national administrator rule which had perforce been upon a catch-as-catch-can basis. Even the post-February 1948 nationalizations in Czechoslovakia had been very hasty by Western standards. Finally, the whole process had taken place in the midst of economies far more shaken by the war than, say, the British. Improvisation consequently was necessary at every step.

Within Industry Boards at the outset the power of the Branch was very great, certainly greater than its counterpart in the British coal industry. In principle it was the Branch that allocated supplies of basic raw materials to the individual factories under its jurisdiction and distributed orders among them. It was the Branch that prepared in final form the financial and economic plans for the individual establishments. The managements of the individual establishments under this system were supposed to be free to concentrate on production problems only. The system also was supposed to make for a rational use of scarce managerial personnel.

Under this initial system the top management of the individual industry agglomerate, the National Board, dealt only with overall policies. Its Chairman carried a good deal of authority, but he might be overruled by the members of his Board.

The Early Polish Ministry of Industry and Trade

In the case of Poland, above the individual national industry boards there was at the outset an interesting development of the general Ministry of Industry, far above anything to be seen in its counterpart in Czechoslovakia. The Ministry wielded very strong powers through a set of nine functional Departments, cutting across industry lines but working closely with the industries themselves.

The reasons for this special development were not far to seek. Separate business undertakings and even industry branches as a whole had been with few exceptions in too fluid a state for the industries by themselves to set up their own machinery for standard setting. The Ministry of Reconstruction was busy with the concrete tasks of building. Each of the production industries had its own troubles. Some undertakings were operating at a profit, others at a loss, others were moving rapidly from one category to the other as the work of restoration progressed. Conditions of work differed correspondingly.

It was in these conditions of flux that the functional Departments of a single Ministry of Industry and Trade proceeded to play a major role in rationalizing management. Among the departments the Control Department at this time had the difficult task of maintaining financial checks that should be adequate but quick and as simple and direct as possible, to keep pace with the rapid changes of Polish undertakings. The Department, it was said, tried to delegate as much as it could of its inspection work to agencies directly connected with the individual industries. For example, the Sales Department in each industry checked on orders. Thus in the Steel Industry, an inspector from the Sales Department kept track of the amount that was going to each firm—if a given firm appeared to have twice as much as necessary, he could draw the appropriate conclusion. The General Department of the Ministry, among other things, drafted laws dealing with industry. The Planning Department, besides drawing plans for future industrial development, prepared the current raw materials and marketing plans. The Technological Department conducted research on inventions and supervised the construction of new industrial establishments. The Distribution Department directed the commercial prices policy and also the imports and exports policy.

The Departments between them conducted a type of research and standardization that it would have been impossible at the time for individual industries to undertake. The Planning and Technological Departments, for instance, were in 1948 concentrating on the development of a 'progressive technological coefficient'.[1] The Ministry held that, whereas originally the main thing was to get industry going again at any cost, and after that had come the question of gross production, and then that of financing, now a chief question was that of the technological plan. Such a plan had to be based on 'the movement of coefficients', and it was held to be no longer merely empirical, but scientific. 'A technological plan makes it possible to compare one plant with another. Is a given plant technologically dead? If so, liquidate it.' In this second stage of planning, the issue was said to be not merely a financial question but one of the general advantage to the country of having a given plant operate or not. It might even pay to get rid of an old factory and use some substitute for its products.

Again, the Investment Department had exceedingly specialized work, closely linked with technology. How long would it take to build a given establishment before production would be ready to begin? There was a Central Bureau of Industrial Products, specialized for different industries. It studied 'typical' construction, the best types to be standardized for different kinds of establishments within each industry. For example, there were special enterprises for all sorts of steel construction—for hydraulic, electrical, metal construction, high tension installations and so on. How economize most effectively on steel for each of these?

The Financing Department was considered 'rather ingenious'. It had sought to develop a method on the one hand to enlist all establishments in the competition for profits and on the other to make it possible for each to do its best, given its conditions. The question had been how to compare the efficiency of management and men in factories some of which were old or half-destroyed, others new. The method used was to fix beforehand individual sales prices for the product of these factories on the basis of what they were reasonably capable of producing. In practice, this meant setting up a series of group classifications according to the degree

[1] Interview material, July 1948.

of handicap. An average factory sales' price was then fixed for the use of the Ministry itself, by a combination of these individual prices. But the high-cost firm did not have to meet this average price.

Such a device was said to enable each firm to compete against a standard reasonable for itself in reducing costs or exceeding output, thus becoming eligible for the corresponding bonuses to management and workers for extra effort. At the same time the Financing Department made good the planned deficits below average price of the high-cost firms, out of the planned surpluses accruing from the low-cost. This was done by means of a revolving fund in the National Bank.

The revolving fund was also fed by planned surpluses accruing from some entire industries that were purposely given a higher sales price than necessary; the surplus from them revolved to the others.[1] Again, some industries, for example, shipbuilding, have a very long cycle of financing, whilst others, such as textiles, have a very short one. Here, too, the money from the more advantaged went into the Revolving Fund to help out others.

The Social-Economic Department was said at this time to be elaborating a basis for more scientific treatment of comparative wage levels in different industries, a matter which hitherto had been treated empirically only. The process of introduction of rational criteria would have to be gradual, it was stated, as it was considered impossible to take away privileges to which people had become accustomed. The three criteria usually cited—skill, conditions of work, social importance of the work—often operated in contradiction to one another, and the Department was trying to work out rational criteria with these as ingredients. As an illustration of existing difficulties, in the mining industry which was socially important and where the work was hard, even the workers above ground had been getting a differential wage, which they personally did not deserve.

The Personnel Department had an important sub-department on trade schools. An interesting feature of this was the wide developments of *internats*, apprentice boarding schools for village youth, some 35,000 of whom were receiving instruction in 1948. The *internats* served young people who presumably would be

[1] In all the planned economies the practice was, broadly speaking, to keep the prices of heavy industry products low, to encourage reconstruction and further industrialization.

coming into industry anyway, but who would enter unprepared and unskilled. In the *internats* they received at this time a minimum of a year's training. Subsequently the amount was to be increased.

It can readily be seen that some of these functions of the various divisions of the Ministry of Industry could apparently just as well have been undertaken by other agencies instead. Indeed in Czechoslovakia this was notably so in the case, for example, of labour standards and trade schools. And it will also be noted that the Ministry itself, in the case of the Control Division, already felt the need of trying to 'de-bureaucratize' its work by delegating all it could to intra-industry agencies. However, an interesting residue remained, of standardization and research, for which at that time an inter-industry agency, operating under the pressure of immediate need and with wide responsibility and authority, was apparently considered the only answer.

Original Relations of Nationalized Industry to National Planning

In both Poland and Czechoslovakia at the outset the relations of the national planning apparatus to industry were general. Nevertheless, the scope of nationalization had been so broad as to create qualitatively different inter-industry relations from those of, say, the portions of nationalized industry in England during the régime of the Labour Government.

In the first place, the relations between public and private industry from the very outset were reversed. The scale of nationalization, reaching down to the fifty-man level, had removed all large private competition, and by the same token the representatives of that competition in Parliament and governing bodies. What remained of private industry even by the opening of 1948 was frankly ancillary to the operations of public industry, it existed on sufferance, however good its rate of profit for the moment, and its buying and selling were increasingly from and to public or co-operative agencies, hence subject to a degree of planning. Two years later private enterprise had all but disappeared from industry altogether and was on the way out even in trade.

More important, by virtue of initial full acceptance of a planning system as a part of socialization, the operations of the various industries could be, and were, planned for together. Making them harmonize was not an exceptional or extraneous procedure, involving the ironing out of conflicting claims that were already full grown. The whole machinery of planning and controls was posited on a co-ordination of the various industries and their plans from the outset, with overruling priorities accepted. The individual nationalized industries were in no sense sovereign states in the economy of the nation; at best they were provinces with some self-government. The difference between an economy with some elements of planning here and there and a 'planned economy' is nowhere more evident than in this set of relationships.

Finally, again by virtue of the degree of their nationalization, the nationalized industries of Poland and Czechoslovakia were said by those working in them to be no longer subject to general business fluctuations, at least so far as their internal market was concerned. Bad harvests, as we saw, could have their damaging effect, and so could trade policies and business fluctuations abroad, in so far as these directly hindered or helped vital imports and exports. But internally the trade cycle as such was held to have disappeared along with the predominance of private industry that was said to have given birth to it.

Problems of Rationalization

Within the nationalized industries problems of securing more rational operation were much emphasized in spite of the degree of disorganization out of which much of the attempted rationalization had to proceed.

Thus in the case of the Polish coal industry, a managing engineer expressed great satisfaction that it was at last possible to cut coal with a maximum of conservation, irrespective of ownership lines and unhampered by the demand for quick profits. In large chambers, for example, instead of cutting from ladders as the ceiling grew higher, which was dangerous and wasteful, standard practice was now to fill in the lower layers by forced pumping with sand as they got cleaned out of coal—a method the former owners had considered too expensive. 'The interests of our mines found themselves completedly protected by the law on nationalization,' concluded the technician.[1]

On the other hand, both business structure and technical problems had been acute in the mining industry at the outset. In Czechoslovakia, for example, the large coal companies had been organized horizontally with coal, iron, coke, steel, chemical products, and some landed estates. (The German *Berg und Hütten-*

[1] Interview material, June 1948.

werke had held one of these companies.) With nationalization this structure had had to be split up, only some closely related departments being left in the coal industry. Moreover, even before the War, ownership in the Czech mines had been chiefly foreign. The profit had gone abroad, largely to Germany and Vienna, and Czechs were of the opinion that this had further engendered a quick-profits attitude on the part of the owners. Of the personnel, however, only the higher administrative posts had been occupied by Germans. The workers had been Czechs.

During the Occupation the Germans had of course worked the mines recklessly, without repairs; and technology had remained at the 1939 level or worse. Hence in the post-war, in spite of some initial aid from U.N.R.R.A., the import of mining machinery was a serious problem. The prevalent German-Czech type of mining, with very low ceilings at times, required small, German-type equipment which was not at the time available.

As for personnel problems, in the course of liberation the managing personnel had come together and manned the mines. Then with the nationalization decree of October 1945 these same men had stayed on. The personnel for the higher positions were appointed at once by the Minister of Industry. Trained mining engineers were sent in for the Central Board at Prague as well as for the Districts Boards in the country. The haste of all these changes is obvious.

Once set up, the Central Board for the coal industry had been organized along lines now more or less familiar in the West. It consisted of a Managing Director with seven groups under him, social, technical, research, commerce, etc. A manager and a group of senior engineers directed each group of mines. And each mine had its pit manager. The miners themselves at the pit elected a Works Committee and a Production Committee. The Managing Director originally had been appointed by the Minister of Industry, by 1948 it was by the Cabinet. Methods of work had at first to be improvised. Subsequently they were more carefully checked. For very important matters, such as a decision to build a new works or close an old one, a monthly gathering of Division Managers met with representatives of the Government. Or again, if the National Mines General Manager wanted to appoint a Division Manager for a given region, he could only do it with the approval of the leading personnel in that division.

In the Metal and Machinery Industry rationalization had taken various forms. It was more difficult in this industry to measure degree of Plan fulfilment for the individual worker or even group of workers than in, say, the shoe industry, because of the great size and complexity of some of the products. For example, a Czech administrator pointed out that producing a sugar mill would involve the work of several different national enterprises, all under the Metals and Machinery Administration. On the other hand, very important rationalizations could be effected here because of the size of the investments and the length of time involved in production. The prolonged planning periods now possible for orders made a great difference here. 'To-day you can buy equipment that will only be needed three years hence.' Moreover, it was now possible to see that only the most necessary machines were produced, 'because the whole investment agenda is concentrated right here, at the Central Office'.[1]

Technicians in the Polish Heavy Metals Industry management reported similar experiences. 'Take a rolling mill under free enterprise—for every profile which it rolls it has to change patterns. It can't know in advance, when it has a one-hundred ton order of this pattern to-day, whether three months hence it may not have an order for another fifty tons of the same pattern. With us a rolling mill knows ahead for the year. I am speaking as a technician, not as a man interested in politics. The results are certainly striking. Three years after World War I we could show no such accomplishment, although destruction now has been incomparably greater.'[2]

In Poland the Machine and Metal Industry Administration inherited the remains of what had been a highly competitive industry before the war, exceedingly sensitive to business fluctuations. 'Before the war every manufacturer wanted to protect himself against crises, hence he made as many different kinds of products as possible.' The multiplication of products had run to great extremes. For example, the Warsaw factory 'Parawoz' had had seven different divisions with nothing whatever in common between them; yet the whole factory had less than two thousand workers. Since nationalization, stages of rationalization in the industry had been as follows:

'(1) In the first two years we left in each factory only one or two articles, or perhaps three in big factories, choosing whatever products the particular enterprise's costs were lowest in.

[1] Interview material, April 1948. [2] Interview material, July 1948.

'(2) Next came standardization of different articles, "typization". For example in the case of agricultural machinery, Polish factories before the war had been producing seventeen different kinds of threshing machines. To-day the number had been reduced to four, with real type differences between each. "And the peasants are getting used to it."

'(3) The third stage, the working out of new techniques in the production process, the modernization of machines and the widespread installation of techniques already known but requiring scarce equipment, was only beginning.' (For example, the conveyor system had only lately been installed in two factories.)

The difficulties involved in reaching even this degree of rationalization had been great. Plants and equipment had had to be rebuilt with whatever was at hand or else 'demobilized' from German war production, new workers had had to be trained, scarce steel had had to be—and still had to be—conserved, for the prewar steel industry had been small compared to the metal industry's present needs. Indeed one important aspect of the present rationalization effort was the saving on valuable raw material.[1]

The pressure for more and better machinery production was to be heard in Poland from all sides. Thus a mining engineer at the great coal centre of Katowice: 'Our mines were not actually destroyed, but they were devastated. Before the war almost all our mining machinery was imported. We bought it from the Germans, had practically none made at home. The Germans disappeared and so did the German machinery. Now we have thirteen plants making our mining machinery. But the number isn't enough to extract our 70,000,000 tons of production that we are making today—while in five years we shall have 500,000,000 tons production.'[2]

Rationalization in the textile industry in the form of a more economical grouping and selection of plants has already been referred to in the chapter on Slovakia. In the Czech provinces the departure of the Germans had left manpower in the industry nearly a third short, many of the older plants had been in bad condition even before the war, and during the war the whole industry had been allowed to run down, since it catered chiefly for consumers' needs. 'What the Germans "lost" here was 200,000,000 crowns' worth of debt.'

Rationalization had involved immediate regrouping of the

[1] Interview material, August 1948. [2] Interview material, August 1498.

nationalized concerns, the closing down of the oldest and least efficient, and the concentration of production in those best equipped for the various specialities. Size as such had not been a criterion. Thus in the textile town of Nachot, the leading concern, Mautners, had originally had 2,500 workers; yet beside it had existed a prosperous firm specializing in poplins with only 150 workers; similarly in another town where a 200 worker concern specializing in handkerchiefs had operated successfully within a few kilometres of a 2,000 worker general establishment. In its post-war reorganization, the industry had put together in Nachot 72 firms into one concern with Mautners at the centre. This Nachot National Enterprise now included about 10,000 employees.[1]

In Czechoslovakia an important item of rationalization, cutting across industry lines, had been the introduction of the standard accounting system referred to earlier. This was now uniformly prescribed for all nationalized industry. The changes it involved were emphasized by an accountant from the old Pilsen Brewery. The previous year, 1947, he pointed out, special evening accounting and book-keeping courses had been opened in many centres, so that on the appointed date, 1 January 1948, the change-over could be made. The regular commercial schools also now taught this new system, including wage accounts. Before the war at the Pilsen Brewery incredibly antiquated book-keeping had been used. All accounts had been written out in longhand. A single person, the head of the book-keeping office, carried the system in his head. In 1945 this old gentleman, who by this time must have been very aged, had been pensioned off and the office had 'sat up nights trying to figure out the accounts'. The man from the Accounting Department now was delighted to have a new national system.

Personnel Problems

Some of the managers of nationalized industry in Poland and Czechoslovakia were men who had held high administrative posts in the industry while it was still in private hands, some of them came from the lower ranks of technical and managerial personnel. Thus in Czechoslovakia the then head of the textile industry had been formerly manager of the country's largest spinning concern,

[1] Interview material, May 1948. Subsequently such large composite concerns were not favoured.

where his father had been a director before him, while in Poland the head of the industry had been formerly head only of a weaving section in a large mill. Higher technical personnel at that time seemed to be largely men who had occupied closely similar posts before. Thus a former vice-president in charge of industrial relations from a large Polish coal concern, a highly trained engineer, was now in charge of industrial relations at the country's chief mining centre. And so on. However, it was stated that great numbers of young men presently graduating from the technical and professional schools and, more striking, very great numbers straight from industry with only a minor technical training, were rising into important industry positions. It was noteworthy that in Czechoslovakia where the pressure for trained personnel had not been so overwhelming as in Poland, entrance requirements for the technical schools were at that time actually being raised: a passing mark in graduating from secondary school had formerly been sufficient; now special entrance examinations were to be required.

Political questions had from the outset played a considerable role in administrative posts in industry. During the first period there had been an effort in both Poland and Czechoslovakia to divide up posts, as the Poles put it, according to a political 'key': i.e. if Party X's man is given this job, his deputy must come from Party Y, and so on. In Poland it was predicted that with the merging of the two Left parties at the end of 1948 this whole system would disappear in economic administration. In Czechoslovakia the system was said to have made it particularly difficult to get rid of superfluous white-collar jobs: parties with many white-collar adherents had been ready to abolish other parties' jobs but not their own.

Salaries in Nationalized Industry

Upper managerial personnel in Czech and Polish industry were receiving incomparably less than before the war. Young engineers on the other hand were doing rather better, in view of the depressed state of the employment market before the war. A Czech mining engineer of high rank claimed that during the 1930's as a young graduate engineer he had been employed at a company for 12,000 crowns yearly (between £150 and £175), while the general manager of the company received 1,200,000 crowns, a ratio of 100 to 1. He still resented the fact that during the five or six years of this depression period he and his like were paid 'like day labourers', i.e. could be laid off, told any day, 'You need not report to-morrow'. At the present time, he pointed out, even manual labourers could not be treated thus.

In the Pilsen Brewery the pre-war managing director was said to have been paid about 300,000 pre-war crowns. Now (1948) the man occupying this post was still paid 300,000 crowns, but they were post-war, equalling about one-third the former pay. In addition, moreover, the former manager used to receive a handsome percentage on the sale of waste products from a small brewery near by, so all told he had received about a 1,000,000 crowns a year (close to £15,000). The old administrator, whose record in his old post had apparently not satisfied everyone, had been pensioned off—in addition to which he was now in the administration of another industry. The present general manager had formerly been production manager: to-day he was filling both posts at once, for the aforementioned 300,000 crowns (£1,500).

Again, in the international Bat'a concern, the former active manager after Thomas Bat'a's death and John's departure for America,[1] was said to have earned and received in real estate and other outside holdings a net income of many millions of crowns a year. The present General Director of the Zlin plant, Dr. Holiš, received 25,000 crowns a month, or £1,500 a year.

The Works Manager

In both Poland and Czechoslovakia the question of board versus one-man control in the actual operation of industry had been much mooted in the early days, but even by early 1948 it had been solved on the whole quite definitely in favour of one-man control. Subsequently the principle was extended much further. Each national enterprise was supposed to be directly in the hands of its manager. However, he had a supervisory board to deal with, unpaid and meeting monthly, which was responsible for his management in a general way. Towards the higher administration of the industry the Board's function was chiefly financial: it approved the manager's annual report, authorized financial expenditures for purposes other than the ordinary conduct of the business, such as extraordinary expenditures for prize money for workers, and so on. In addition the Board had one important non-financial duty: it reported to the Divisional or Branch Administration any sugges-

[1] See Chapter X.

tions for structural changes in the enterprise or in its relation to other enterprises (e.g. that it absorb another).

Any advice given him by the Board, the manager, according to the law, was entitled to contravene if he felt it necessary to do so: however, he had to report the fact promptly to the Divisional Board.

As indicated previously, the one overriding function of the works manager, under this conception, was production pure and simple. It was the aim of the nationalized industry authorities to relieve him entirely of concern with the problems of the market. These were supposed to be handled by separate buying and selling organizations, operating for the branch at large, not for the individual national corporation. There was even, in the case of Poland, a separate economic administrator in the establishment to concern himself with financial and plan questions. Subsequently this sort of specialization was held excessive. Even so, very hard work as well as responsibility already fell upon the individual works manager. The amount of improvisation, in Poland especially, that had to be undertaken in the initial years of reconstruction would frighten away a routine mind.

Relations with Labour

Managers seen by the writer claimed that day to day dealings between management and workers, as well as major dealings, were now free of hostility. They held that, with considerable overall voice in political and economic affairs and with nationalization of leading industries accomplished, labour demands, even local ones, had become reasonable, and interest in production had increased radically.

Complaint concerning the new interest, however, came to the writer, not from active management but from an efficiency expert, formerly the head of a firm installing efficiency systems and now a technical adviser in a Czech government institute. This older man complained of the waste of time occasioned by workers wishing to know about everything. 'You have to explain everything to workers' committees. What can they understand? Now they want me to give two-weeks' courses to them on "The Problems of Management". Two weeks! They were much happier before. The Germans, in spite of their faults, had wonderful labour relations in Germany itself under Hitler. I saw them. Every man knew his place and they took pride in their work. The discipline was perfect.'[1]

The industrial union structure now prevailing was stressed by many managers as a welcome change. Each management had now only a single organization to deal with. Thus in the Polish coal industry, a man who had been a pre-war industrial relations manager recalled that formerly getting contracts signed by four different unions had been a harassing experience. Each would have promised its members something impossible as over against the others. After long fencing and face-saving, 'the affair would always end in the hands of Mr. X'—Mr. X being the Inspector-General of Mines who heard arbitration cases. Now the miners were reasonable (this particular manager was continuing to do the same work as before) 'and we ourselves have nothing to gain by beating them down'. There had been no strike in the coal industry since Liberation for more than half a day, and then on a purely local basis.[2]

The point at which the new attitudes undoubtedly met their severest test was that of production effort pure and simple. Pre-war experiences during a prolonged period of depression had made speed-up greatly hated. Then had come the years of exhausting labour under the Nazis. Old workers, and for that matter newcomers from the country, too, it was said, would say, 'This is our industry now. Why do we have to work so hard?' Management had had to see that work loads were reasonable and that, where necessary, as in the case of the Bat'a efficiency system, more hands were put on a unit.

In general it was stated on all sides at this time, that there could be no question now of workers being driven. Even the old efficiency engineer insisted upon this; in fact it was one of his complaints, that consent now had to be obtained for everything. Both the law and the activity of union representatives in the shops, the writer was told by both management and men, now made it exceedingly difficult for any individual to be discharged. Moreover full employment itself was said to be dispelling the fear motive. 'Before the war there was a line at the factory gate. But where is it now?' In later chapters we shall see how these problems had to be faced and how the installation of incentive wage systems and other devices for increasing output were being handled in the planned economies.

[1] Interview material, May 1948.

[2] Interview material, June 1948.

Later Developments

The structure of nationalized industry underwent a series of changes in 1948–50 as the two countries moved from the stage of their short-time reconstruction plans to their Five- and Six-Year Plans of longer development. As we have seen, originally the responsibility for co-ordinating the work of separate establishments had been aimed at through business amalgamation of the physical units into larger concerns and multiples of concerns. National plan projections had been as yet experimental and the supreme task of the moment had been one of co-ordinating supplies, filling in equipment deficiencies, allocating scarce personnel and so on. A drawing together of the administrative apparatus at a succession of levels, and the avoidance of any diffusions of responsibility to the lowest units was hence natural.

Sharp changes in this set of relations were undertaken in 1948–50. Chronologically they began at the top and worked down, but presumably both aspects were in the minds of the planners simultaneously. In substance, intermediate links in industry were to be cut out and the functions of the top and bottom units were to be strengthened and made more specific.

First the joint Ministry of Industry and Trade was split. Separate Ministries of Foreign Trade and Domestic Trade were set up, and separate trade corporations now functioned all along the line, so that the industrial units were freed from trade responsibility. The industrial Ministry was now split up into several separate Ministries for various main industrial divisions, and each Ministry was charged with much more direct management of the Central Administrations under it. In Poland indeed the Central Administrations were spoken of as 'prolongations' or 'arms' or even 'branch departments' of these highly functional Ministries.

The series of Ministries initially formed in Poland were Mining and Power, Heavy Industry, Light Industry, Food and Agricultural Processing, Internal Trade, Foreign Trade, and Construction, the last being not a new Ministry but a reorganization of the former Ministry of Reconstruction, whose old functions were now accomplished, Somewhat later, with the rapid spread of socialization in the small production field, a new Ministry of Small Industry and Handicrafts was set up. It was evident that in both countries further creation of ministries might take place as circumstances dictated. It was pointed out that in the Soviet Union there were about fifty industrial ministries.

The various Central Administrations under each Ministry were in turn split up, on the principle of forming only one Central Management for each industrial branch. There were no longer to be composite Central Administrations; these were now regarded as left-overs from the old capitalist form of 'trust'.

Below the Central Administrations there had also often been sub-trusts, called in Poland 'unions' or federations of enterprises, themselves mixed in character and/or scattered about the country. This whole structure was now to be swept away: there was to be no intermediate link between Central Administration and enterprises.

The whole principle of industrial organization was now said to be that of the 'territorial-production' (or area-production) basis, a term used in the Soviet Union to denote that it was productive physical enterprises located in definite neighbourhoods and regions that were being organized, and not abstract business 'concerns'. The 'territorial-production' basis was declared to be 'the only right form for a socialist industry'.[1]

At the bottom end of the industrial scale the enterprises themselves were now reorganized. It was held that this process was part and parcel with what had happened at the top. 'The influence of this change (i.e. the splitting-up of the original Ministry of Industry) upon the structure of industrial enterprises was decisive.'[2] In both countries the enterprises were trimmed down to smaller and more specialized proportions. Inappropriate or physically distant branches were lopped off. But, under a 1950 decree, the process of whittling down went farthest in Poland. 'The main principle of the decree is the statement that the basic unit should be the single-establishment enterprise. This signifies a fundamental change from previous practice which was based on multiple-establishment units.[3]

Absolutely no enterprises, of whatever size, were to continue if their plants were widely scattered. Only in the case of very small establishments or in the case of a small establishment making

[1] Stefan Jedrychowski, 'Some Conditions for Fulfilment of the Six-Year Plan', *Ekonomista*, 3rd Quarter, Warsaw, 1950, p. 31 (in Polish).

Cf. M. Doroszewicz, 'The Organization of the Enterprises of Key Industry', *Gospodarka Planowa* (*Planned Economy*), Warsaw, July 1950, p. 330. 'The new decree provides a uniform system of management and internal structure for all the organizational links of industry. This system in the Soviet Union is called "territorial production".'

[2] Doroszewicz, op. cit., p. 327.

[3] Ibid., p. 329.

parts for a larger one, could two or more remain grouped together, and then only if all were in the same locality.

Within the enterprise in both countries responsibility of the single manager was to be made more far-reaching. In Poland, with plant and enterprise now normally one, this meant in itself a closer connection than previously of the enterprise head with production processes. At the same time, he was given broader economic duties than before. Previously there had been two other 'directors' beside the manager: an 'economic director' and a 'technical director'. These posts were now abolished and the Manager was merely to be assisted by a chief engineer and a chief accountant, both technical specialists only. However much the Manager might consult his assistants, full reponsibility for Plan fulfilment and the correctness of the framing of establishment plans in the first place, rested upon him.

The same principle of one-man responsibility was emphasized in the operation of the Central Administrations of industry in both countries, and as the chain of relation, Ministry-to-Central Administration-to-single establishment had now become very direct, it was intended that Plan fulfilment could be exactly located and insisted upon. At the same time, operational initiative of the individual works and its manager as over against the Central Administration was intended to be fuller than before. Various cautions were reported against Central Administration interference in local affairs.

Inter-industry relations were spoken of in Czech and Polish publications in three contexts. The first two were in connection with the splitting-up process of the Ministry of Industry. On the one hand, problems of the respective allocations of materials, manpower, etc., as well as all price relations, now became, concretely as well as in original projection, the province of the State Planning Commission. On the other hand, many of the general technological and other problems that had formerly been handled centrally by the functional departments of the single Ministry of Industry, were now split up among resulting separate Ministries. One technical problem of intense interest for all the Ministries and their industries together, however, was for the most part kept centralized. This was the problem of model types of construction and building materials for all the different industries. This now became the predominant concern of the Ministry of Construction, whose main orientation had become a technical one.

The third problem was that of on-the-spot relations between individual enterprises belonging to the same or to different industries. This problem obviously became more important with the split-up of industrial units from multi-establishment to single-establishment management. It also inevitably became important because of the underlying transition from a period of restoration to a period of intensive new investment: with new plants being started, there were new chances for lack of co-ordination. The chief method of meeting this was a provision for inter-establishment contracts of a special type.

It has already been mentioned in the previous chapter that the banks had found it necessary at an early stage to have the Government forbid concerns' borrowing back and forth from one another's accounts or investing in one another's properties. It was, however, not only permissible but useful to have concerns of a similar type upon occasion given access to one another's supplies—e.g. in the event of breakdowns. Contracts setting forth this type of operation were therefore to be found. More important naturally was the use of special contracts between finished products enterprises and those manufacturing parts. This was especially significant in heavy industry where, for instance, in machine tools some 30 to 40 per cent of the cost of production went to the semi-fabricates. With the multiplication of Ministries it was commonly the case that the parts suppliers belonged not only to a separate Central Administration but to a separate Ministry.[1]

The special character of these contracts was that they were binding not only between the enterprises themselves as business entities, but between the contracting parties and the State, for the fulfilling of whose plans the contracts were undertaken. The form was intended to ensure that even if an individual business unit could not prove material damage to itself from its partner's breach of contract, the State could. Contracts of this general type, it was pointed out, had long been in use in the Soviet Union.

Relation of Industry to Governmental Units

With the growth of socialization, all governmental administrative divisions became directly involved in the fate of the industries

[1] Cf. J. Sawiczewski, 'Improvement of Co-operation in Industry', *Gospodarka Planowa*, September 1951, p. 3. 'In Heavy Industry every factory depends on half-products, some of which come under the Ministry of Small Industry and Handicraft.'

on their territory. Much small industry, too small to be operated well as a part of nationalized industry, had been placed under local government administration. Moreover there was now a secondary growth of socialization by way of co-operatives in the field of small industry and handicraft.[1] Hence a further mass of enterprises now fell into the general orbit of local or regional governments. And outside industry proper, there began to be a major movement of co-operative trade chains and also municipal retail shops and department stores. Finally, there were the State national enterprises located in the territory of the city or province.

For the first group the locality had direct administrative responsibility, for the second general aid functions, in helping them to secure local supplies, etc. And even for the last the locality was supposed to further Plan fulfilment through its local National Council.

The National Councils, of which mention has been made earlier, had had their powers greatly augmented and had finally been made the sole organs of local and provincial government. The change came in 1949 in both countries in connection with the expanded economic functions of the local administrations and their necessarily close relation with Plan fulfilment. Instead of a double set of agencies and powers, local and central, there was now to be in the localities a single organization, popularly elected but responsible also to the national government. From one point of view it might be regarded as a devolution of central government powers, from another as an extension. It was certainly decentralization in method and certainly not devolution in ultimate authority. The new organs were called, in the laws setting them up in the case of Poland, 'local organs of the uniform authority of the State', and this very well described their function. There was no longer in the localities any remnant of the old central prefect system of State appointees on the one hand, such as had been criticized earlier especially in Czechoslovakia, nor of the purely autonomous type of locally elected and directed organs of classic local government, which were now criticized also. The Poles and Czechs boasted of the ending of this previous 'dichotomy'. The Councils, then, were universally and locally elected, and, among other things, they were in duty bound to frame and carry out for their localities economic plans that should be in consonance with the larger

[1] More will be said of this in Chapter XV.

economic plans of the nation. Whatever administering or aiding of local industry went on, was in the hands of the Councils.

In city structure itself, very definite changes were taking place at the same time. Urban geography was to be adapted to city planning and the latter to the needs of industry. Boundaries between old city areas could be changed, usually in the direction of including lesser adjacent industrial towns into one major city. This multiple-city would then have a central administrative apparatus and a unified industrial and residential planning system. The original constituent units, if sufficiently large, might keep their own identity and local administrations for local affairs, as branches of the larger unit.

In the country-side, the corresponding administrative changes were as yet on a smaller scale but perhaps of more immediate economic significance. The smallest village units were in process of being grouped together, to form so-called communes, two to four villages perhaps per commune. The new entities might average in the neighbourhood of 3,000 inhabitants each. There was also the beginning of an attempt to form effective area groupings midway between commune and province. These would normally be centred upon a sizable market town.

In all the planned economies a comparable pattern of consolidation of regional-local administrations had been taking place at about this same period, 1949–51. The general idea was already familiar from Soviet practice. The economic bearing of these changes will be made clear as we come to deal with the process of agricultural transformation in Chapter XIII.

The ultimate picture of the relations between industry and government, therefore, as also between economic and political life in general in the planned economies, was one of increasing fusion in Plan fulfilment as a whole, and of increasing devolution of administration in execution. Throughout the pattern of administrative economic devices ran the emphasis on the theme of maximizing economic output, trying to clear away whatever structures interfered with this, and speeding the adoption of whatever technical methods in industry had come to be known.

CHAPTER X

A CASE STUDY IN NATIONALIZED INDUSTRY: THE BAT'A-SVIT CONCERN

Thomas Bat'a[1]

To a Czech twenty years ago Thomas Bat'a would have represented much the same achievements that Henry Ford did to Americans. And the Bat'a shoe concern would have meant far more than the Ford empire ever did to its country, because of Czechoslovakia's small size and because Bat'a had so utterly outdistanced his competitors. To see what happened to this highly efficient industry under nationalization is therefore interesting, the more so since it presents in most acute form Czechoslovakia's dominant problem of exports.

Like Ford, Thomas Bat'a began single-handed and without capital. The son of a shoemaker, at the age of eighteen in the year 1894 he formed a 'company' in the remote country town of Zlin in the border region of Moravia near Slovakia, with his sister and brother to help him. He was said to have travelled with ten to fifteen pairs of shoes a week to provincial city markets. He knew nothing of business and became involved in debt in two years. By 1901 he had recovered and realized about 2,000 guilders (£330). He had read of machinery and determined to master the new methods and apply them in his native region where he could take advantage of a cheap labour force. In 1904, accordingly, at the age of twenty-eight, he went to the United States and worked as an ordinary labourer at a shoe factory in Lynn. When he came back he at once started a steam-driven factory with fifty employees and produced 1,000 pairs of shoes a week. By 1910 he employed 1,500 hands. (Zlin at this time had only 3,600 inhabitants altogether.) After this his business expanded rapidly and spread into many related fields. By the time of his death in 1932 his home

[1] The writer does not claim accuracy for the biographical accounts of Thomas Bat'a and his family. They were drawn primarily from interviews with and memoranda submitted by various of Bat'a's former employees.

factory alone was employing 18,000 hands and producing 100,000 pairs of shoes a week.

The Bat'a System

Thomas Bat'a's system contained six ingredients. First and foremost came his basic policy of low price and small unit profit with the widest possible markets. His shoes were mass-produced and cheap enough to undersell competitors even in the hardest times. They did not last long, and his ambition is said to have been to enable all his cutomers to have three or four pairs a year.

His second speciality was an original cost-accounting system. Along with all possible mechanical devices for efficiency output, Bat'a introduced a method of his own for checking on productivity in every department. Each section of his works competed with every other on a costing basis, each 'bought' and 'sold' its output to the links above and below it in the production chain, with weekly balance sheets; so that at any moment management could adjudge the profitability of each of its divisions and hence presumably the efficiency of each of its sub-managers, from superintendent down to foreman.

A third ingredient of Bat'a policy was anti-unionism. This policy was pursued with determination and marked success, in spite of the highly organized state of Czech labour generally and the great numbers of employees who ultimately came to work for Bat'a. Having once broken the leading union in the industry, the leather workers, in 1925, Bat'a for the rest of his life worked open shop. For his working force Bat'a relied upon a maximum number of young workers coming chiefly from the rural regions. Large numbers of them were housed in dormitories, and after hours attended apprentice schools set up by him. This system of so-called *internats* was operated paternalistically and strictly, but gave the rural young people a higher standard of living—especially a chance to purchase better clothes—than they had been accustomed to at home.

A fourth Bat'a feature was the widespread establishment of both branch factories and retail sales outlets. These presently spread not only all over Czechoslovakia but widely in Europe and even into other continents.

A fifth feature was Bat'a's expansion into related fields. This included many different fields of manufacture, both within Zlin and elsewhere. And, more important, it included a very wide expansion into the raw materials field. In some cases Bat'a owned his own sources of raw material production—in Africa, for example, in the case of some of his rubber—but more frequently he relied upon a widespread network of his own purchasing agents. These persons were permanently stationed at their posts and were kept closely tied in with the home office by means of frequent reports on purchase quota fulfilment, comparable in accuracy to the production reports covering quantity, quality and costs.

A final feature of Bat'a's system was the building up of a great export organization, *Kotva*, which dealt not only in his own products but in the leather and rubber field generally and also in a great many unrelated lines. It, too, had branches all over the world.

Expansion under Bat'a

Bat'a's great opportunity came during World War I. He had already by this time begun to export his shoes abroad and started a tannery. In 1914 he went to Vienna to get military orders and ultimately secured them—it is said with the help of his marriage to a lady whose father was the Emperor Francis Joseph's physician. His initial order for 50,000 army boots came in 1916. By 1918 he had 2,000 employees and was producing 10,000 pairs of shoes a week.

During the post-war depression in 1922, according to one story, he called his Zlin employees together and said that he was going to cut prices virtually in half and wages almost as much, but that if they would agree to this he would get them food and lodging equally cheap. The story at least indicates the power ascribed to the great man. It was during this period that Bat'a established his retail shops all over Czechoslovakia and abroad. He succeeded in pushing his sales greatly, at the expense of handicraft shoemakers as well as manufacturers.

In Zlin presently Thomas Bat'a founded his trade and technical school. He built a hospital and opened a park, part of a feudal estate which he had purchased, to the public. He bought the local railway, opened an airfield, built a gas works, laid the foundations for a new industrial town, started to manufacture tyres and began building a department store.

Community Relations

Bat'a's relations to Zlin were highly paternalistic and also profitable. Bat'a's employees lived in well-built company houses, a provision considerably stabilizing the labour force. On the other hand, evictions could be had 'on ten minutes' notice', as old-timers put it to the writer. 'The truck came from the factory and the house would be locked up.' In the early 1920's there had been a good deal of friction between Bat'a and the town over who should pay for street paving, lighting, and so on—with the result that improvements were said to have been often delayed. Then Bat'a captured the city government and thereafter trouble ceased. The change came in 1924 when Thomas Bat'a ran on his own ticket (calling it literally 'the Bat'a Ticket') and had himself elected Mayor. Thereafter the schools were built by Bat'a, the roads by Bat'a, the electricity and gas supply—again Bat'a. Bat'a was said to have paid virtually no taxes, on the strength of his generosity to the town, and on the other hand he received rents and rates for the services provided. Luckily, said the citizens, the town hall had been built in 1923, before Bat'a became mayor, 'so it belonged to the town'. Town officials, police, and school teachers, over and above their regular salaries were said to have received substantial retainers from Bat'a. Those of whom he disapproved could apparently be dismissed without trouble.

In the factory, as noted earlier, Bat'a did away with the Leather Workers Union in 1925. When the collective agreement expired in that year, Bat'a discharged the union president and the local collapsed. Not being organized, the workers now could not get benefits under the Ghent system of unemployment insurance, the system prevailing in Czechoslovakia at that time. They were therefore doubly dependent upon the goodwill of their employer. There was, to be sure, a Works Committee as established by law in 1923. However, according to older workers, Thomas Bat'a nominated the head of this committee, a Mr. Bruna; thereafter Bruna, who had been a plain production worker, stopped working in the plant and built himself 'several fine houses'.

In 1930 Bat'a introduced the five-day work week with an eight-hour day. Operations were further speeded up. It is said that a red light would wink if the conveyor stopped and the man responsible would be fined. There was profit-sharing for personnel in responsible positions, with the higher executives receiving a major part of their pay in this way. In the shop each self-contained group of eighty people had a task of 12,000 shoes a day. This output task, amounting to fifteen pairs per man, was to be completed in eight hours. But in order to finish, the shops frequently stayed open after hours. The clerical force also habitually worked late; on Thursdays, pay day, it was claimed, they sometimes sat up all night. There was no overtime pay.

By 1931 the world crisis again threatened Bat'a and he declared his business must counteract it. He gathered together a committee to go with him to the Far East. As a consequence, before the outbreak of the Second World War several hundred retail shops had been opened in India alone. Raw material stations also were opened here, as they had been earlier in Argentina.

Bat'a undertakings had become very complex and played into one another's hands. There were factories in Switzerland, France, Belgium, England, and Yugoslovia. Shoe-making and auxiliary process machinery was exported by Bat'a often at grossly undervalued prices, to beat tariff regulations. In Zurich he founded a special company, Lieder, Inc., to establish subsidiary factories in foreign countries. It dealt in shares only, operating as a holding company, in order to circumvent the objections of the Czech National Bank to the export of capital. Thomas Bat'a himself was the owner of 40 per cent of all the shares of all these companies, and the Lieder Company owned 60 per cent. But Thomas Bat'a in turn was the 100 per cent owner of the Lieder Company. He was thus able to export all sorts of properties and values.

Later Events

In 1932 Thomas Bat'a was killed in an aeroplane crash, and by a little-understood will the entire business went into the hands of his stepbrother John. John had held a minor post in the business and had been treated with little respect by his brother. The terms of Thomas's will, drawn in 1931, provided that the business be 'sold' to John at a token valuation, said to be about one-five hundredth of its real value. Thomas's wife and sixteen-year-old son were effectively by-passed: each was to receive half the proceeds of the token sale. Among the workers there was also disillusionment, as rumour had had it that the business, or a large portion of it, was to be willed to them. This last point illustrates an attitude not at first appreciated by the modern visitor: Thomas Bat'a as employer, in spite of his intense discipline and his turning everything to profit, commanded much admiration from those who worked for him. He had been 'a good man and a master'. Brother John was not nearly so impressive.

Between 1932 and 1938 the momentum of the business carried

it forward in spite of the absence of the founder. The local head of the concern was a Mr. Cípera, Thomas Bat'a's manager since 1919, remembered now as a strong man with no sentimentality, 'a man of figures'. Around Cípera was a group of experts.

When the Germans occupied Czechoslovakia John Bat'a escaped by plane a day ahead of them, then after some further delay left again for the United States. Arriving in that country with a rather large technical staff, he built a factory in Belcamp, near Baltimore, where the concern's methods of handling its labour force were to be transplanted to new territory.

Early in 1940 John Bat'a left the United States for a stay in Brazil where there was a small self-contained Bat'a unit. He finally stayed on there. The United States had meanwhile become involved in the war and enacted very strict wartime commercial measures. John Bat'a settled down in Brazil and after the war was said to have become permanently established there. He never returned to Czechoslovakia, and the Czech post-war regime condemned him roundly, even before the February events. The changes in the subsequently nationalized industry took place without any traces of the Bat'a heir.

Bat'a-Zlin under Occupation and Liberation

Dominik Cípera did not long remain the effective head of the Bat'a concern. In 1940 a German director was installed by the Nazis, in accordance with their common policy in the occupied countries. Outwardly the business prospered exceedingly: footgear could not be turned out fast enough. Eighty per cent of production was now for war orders. Good leather shoes were exported to Germany, Italy, Spain, Sweden, while cheap wooden-soled shoes with textile uppers were produced for the Czechs. In 1948 special types of extraordinarily heavy wooden-soled sandals could still be seen that had been made at Zlin for concentration-camp inmates. They must have been intolerable for the feet but would never wear out. Certain of the Bat'a personnel had also been sent to set up a branch factory to make these concentration-camp shoes. The machine department directly made military machines.

Bat'a's was also said to have sent some 6,000 young men and girls to Germany to the German Labour Office. In Zlin was erected a special gymnasium, capable of accommodating 600, for the particular benefit of the Germans, for the use of eighty German children.

The partisans came to Zlin several times. When the Germans

had not yet collapsed, Cípera, it is said, gave the partisans some 3,000,000 crowns and thousands of pairs of shoes and stockings. In turn, when the Russians came, he welcomed them in his capacity as Lord Mayor. In return for the aid he had given the partisans he had been continued in his mayoralty post.

For a month after Liberation, Cípera and his aides remained in office. But presently a certain Dr. Ivan Holiš was put in as National Administrator of Bat'a and Cípera was displaced.

This marked the end of the colourful private period of the Bat'a concern. As a national enterprise in later years it was to try to continue many of the business innovations established by its founder, and to add others to them. But the great financial network was gone. Branches were no longer to be planted in other lands, expansion and contraction were no longer to succeed each other dizzyingly. And the labour force was to become something dealt with under new terms and requiring new handling. But for the initial post-war months the first question was survival.

Liberation

When the Nazis were driven out of Zlin, the Bat'a plant was in serious condition. A few months previously, late in November 1944, the Zlin works had been heavily bombed by American aircraft. Twenty buildings, containing about half the total productive capacity of the plant, were destroyed thereby and about 60 per cent of the shoe manufacturing capacity. Fires burned for six weeks.

In their retreat the Germans had destroyed communications, all bridges in the region were blown up, there were no means of transportation for workers, no raw materials. However, the equipment of the plant itself had been left nearly intact by the Nazis, thanks to the haste of their retreat and the vigilance of the workers. Toward the close of the war, before the front reached Zlin, illegal groups had set up small committees in the plant. They removed spare parts of importance from crucial machines. In this way, stated old workers, when the Germans left and thought they had rendered machines useless by taking key parts away, the workers were able to bring their duplicate parts from hiding and set the machines going again immediately. The Germans finally left in the opening days of May, and on 14 May the plant started production once more. Participants emphasized that these original Workers' Committees that started up production were not political organizations nor were they as yet trade union organizations, but groups for production first of all. It is evident therefore that the post-war emphasis of the unions upon production runs all the way back to this period of their genesis.

It is to be noted also that from the same underground organizations as the Workers' Committees that became unions sprang the new civic organizations, the 'National Committees', that became the new organizations of local government and the agencies for preliminary nationalization. In Zlin the Bat'a works were taken over formally on 13 May when the National Committee of Greater Zlin appointed Dr Ivan Holiš National Administrator for Bat'a-Zlin and its affiliated companies. At the same time a Workers' Council for the entire plant, later also including subsidiaries, was formed with a functioning Chairman and Executive Committee. After some months of manœuvring, during which the former owners and their supporters in the town tried to obstruct final nationalization, the presidential Nationalization Decree of October confirmed the new régime. Bat'a became a National Enterprise.

In 1948 Bat'a and its affiliates accounted for perhaps four-fifths of the country's entire shoe production. (This was in addition to Bat'a enterprises in other lines, subsequently cut off.) The rest of the shoe industry at this time was said to consist of only four or five large plants and four to five very small ones, aside from handicraft production. Bat'a also had large production in other types of rubber and leather work.

Shoe output at Bat'a in 1948 was said to be nearly back at pre-war and was on the increase. *Per capita* production, however, was lower. Not only was the Zlin plant at that time still suffering from great overcrowding of workers and machines, because the bombed-out buildings had only begun to be replaced, but there was said to be less driving of workers. In various forms of assembly-line work the speed, formerly very taxing, had been reduced somewhat and/or additional workers put on the line. Bat'a's famous work units which just before the war had operated with 100 workers each, now were manned by 115 to 120. The stint of shoes for each group, at first lowered, had been restored to the pre-war level.

Labour costs had markedly increased. The wages especially of lower-paid categories of workers had been raised. This applied especially to women workers who comprised virtually half the labour force. There were also various forms of so-called 'fringe benefits' that had been increased. With the hoped-for increase in productivity following plant rebuilding and the installation of better equipment, it was said, unit labour costs should go down. But apparently they would never go down to the original Bat'a level, because of the new emphasis against speed-up and for a larger proportion of benefit to the employees.

The earnings of administrative personnel, particularly in the higher brackets, had been cut sharply. Bat'a had paid his top executives well.

Taking 1939 prices at 100, changes in wage and salary rates at Zlin were estimated in May 1948 to run approximately as follows, leaving out of account the gains in 'fringe' benefits:

Index of prices	274–290
Index of wages of the unskilled and untrained	350–400
Index of wages of the skilled, experienced workers	250–300
Index of wages of the women workers (approx.)	400
Index of wages of the clerical and administrative staff and officers (approx.)	230

As to current wage rates, the average for the whole works was reported to run about 18 to 20 crowns per hour (1s. 10d. to 2s.).[1] Average clerical pay would be about 2s. 2d. A skilled workman in the machine shop would average 3s. 6d., in the rubber department 3s. 9d., in the shoe factory 2s. 9d. In the lowest category of work, such as cementing soles, the girls would average about £2 10s. per week. Unduly low average wages were still being complained of in the textile (hosiery) department—a heritage of low pre-war textile wages generally. Before the war the lowest-paid girls here had been earning the equivalent at present prices of 15s. to 20s. per week. Now the average was £3 10s., but this was still lower than the average for comparable skills in other departments. The girls were waiting for better rate equalization some weeks hence when the chiefs of all the production departments were to meet on the subject. A revision of the whole national textile wage schedule was also being awaited. And above that, the men in the local rate-setting department were expecting a general change in the national wages classification to go into effect the following year.

Marked changes had occurred since the war in the status of apprentices and of women workers. Thomas Bat'a had had an

[1] This was at the official rate of exchange. Actual prices of most goods were much higher than this would suggest. On the other hand, social amenities and housing were cheap.

advanced apprentice system in his day, but like everything else in the plant, it had to pay for itself on the spot. Schooling for the apprentices took place after the full eight-hour day, and school hours ran until 10 p.m. Young workers not preparing for any skilled trade, who formed the great bulk of his juvenile labour force, received the minimum legally required hours of continuation-schooling (12 per week) and for the rest worked like everyone else in the factory.

Since nationalization, no one under 18 could work full time. All apprentices, which now meant all young people aged 15 to 17, worked from 7 to 12 in the morning and attended a specialized school of their trade in the afternoon. Hours of work were 5 a day, 5 days a week, a maximum of 25 hours in all. Apprentices received free board, lodging, and schooling, and received a small cash allowance, increasing with the length of their service. The boys and girls lived in separate groups of dormitories, with a head of house who was also a trade teacher in charge of each. They also had their own house representatives. Meals were taken in a central cafeteria.

The old dormitories in 1948 were still very crowded because of the great post-war influx of young workers, but those being newly erected were excellent, with unusually good facilities, including a sun-lamp room for the girls and spare kitchens where the girls from the country could cook food sent them from home. Regular food and service in the cafeteria were ample, in spite of the strict rationing prevalent at the time.

Newly introduced for the young workers were better library and recreational facilities. The girls at this time were finishing the building of an outdoor volley-ball court. The spade-work on it had been done in one of their Sunday brigade projects. Altogether the evidences of self-activity were considerable and the air of the place was unmistakably like that of a school—a co-educational school at that, catering for country youth. The illusion was at its strongest in the spring evenings, with the hillside 'campus' alive with couples and groups, and the trees hiding the factory buildings below.

After finishing the three years' apprenticeship course young workers could, if they had the ability, go on to foremanship training courses or technical high school courses. From these, in turn, they might go on to university or higher managerial work. The process of selection was said to be stiff. Since the war special schooling facilities had been instituted for older students desiring commercial school or home economics or even general high or normal school education. Before the war a factory worker might have attended evening primary school, but it would have been 'his own affair', it was said, after finishing the full day's work. Now students were given special short hours in the factory, seven to twelve or seven to two, depending upon the nature of their schooling, paid at regular rates, and had afternoon courses arranged for them at school in town.

Women Workers

The status of the 11,000 women at Bat'a had risen markedly. The question of equal pay as such was presenting no difficulty; the problem was how to fit women as rapidly as possible for the better paying jobs. For this, and to protect the interests of women generally, a special Women's Committee was functioning here, as elsewhere throughout Czechoslovak trade unions.

The Women's Committee had a representative in each department of the factory and a general chairman who sat on the Bat'a Factory Council. She stated that she received excellent co-operation from her male colleagues on the Council. 'It is really a question of skill. Before the war it was the men who did the skilled jobs, and women on the whole were unskilled. Now the task of the Women's Committee is to raise the standard of skill of the women.'

This work was carried on at various levels. At the most elementary, a woman seeking advancement would apply to her Women's Committee representative in her workshop. If there was not a place open for her there at the kind of work she wanted, she could be transferred to another part of the factory. A special school was provided for such people. There they received pay at an apprentice rate, partly earned and partly paid for by the Factory Council. This learning period lasted at the most for two weeks. After that the woman worked immediately on piece rates.

There were also so-called qualification courses to enable unskilled women to learn truly skilled work. Here it was not a question of mastering a single technique and acquiring dexterity. To be considered skilled a worker had to learn not only her job, say at the stocking machine, but to repair the machine as well. It was this higher kind of all-round skill that was being sought.

Women were also seeking entrance to the skilled trades not formerly open to women, for example, in the building crafts. The

Bat'a plant at this time was about to be the first in the republic to open its regular craft apprentice schools to women. This was to happen the following week. The girls would work half time and study half time precisely like the male craftsmen and could choose any craft they wished.

Two other types of training were being opened for women. Within the next few weeks Bat'a was to open a school for executives. The Factory Council's Women's Department had decided to reserve half the places in this school for women. And a week previously, a trade union school had been opened specifically for the training of women trade union functionaries. The trade union candidates were elected by the personnel in the workshops. The courses for executives were to be reserved for 'anybody who has the will for advancement'.

Care for married women and their children had increased tremendously since the war. About half the plant's 11,000 women were now married, and as they were almost all young, most of them had children. Crèche care for many children and even transportation to the crèche was now arranged for. Special shopping passes were issued for mothers so that they would not have to queue up after work for the family supplies. After-school care and holiday camp outings were provided for children. The general extension of vacation accommodation and emergency social care had also improved the living of women workers. And a marked improvement was to be seen in the quality of new family housing now going up.

Labour Organization

Most fundamental among the changes in Bat'a life was the active role now played by the workers themselves. The change from open shop to post-war organized labour was very great. And so was the change from the Nazi-imposed management labour combination that had served to collect its 10 crowns a month from most workers during the Occupation. Now the single industrial union for the leather industry had won its way to virtually 100 per cent membership at Bat'a. (The textile division or the chemical plant, as long as they were part of Bat'a, would fall under the Leather Workers' jurisdiction.) An applicant for work was given a union application form by the personnel department. If he did not apply for union membership, one of the union representatives stated, he would be urged by the employees in his department. 'But if he insists "No"

—nothing will happen to him.' The Factory Council was charged with the duty of protecting his rights in this respect. If his fellows in the department insisted that they would not work with him, the Factory Council had to find him another job in the plant at equally good rates, up to his abilities. 'We have good experiences here,' i.e. with individuals thus transferred, maintained the representative, illustrating with the story of a man who had signed up voluntarily after a successful transfer, saying, 'This is decent treatment,'—i.e. because he found the Factory Council had actually protected him, and his new assignment was equally good.

The Factory Council in Zlin consisted of 27 members for 32,000 workers; 22 of these members worked in the shops, 5 were executives. During their incumbency, the excutives received their previous wages. They could not be promoted to a higher pay rating while in office. Young people had their special representatives on the Council, as had production workers, clerical workers, and women.

The Factory Council was said to be in a delicate position: it had to protect the workers, and at the same time before the management it was co-responsible for production. Discharges could not take place without its consent. Promotions on the other hand were the affair of management. However, it was said, the Council would have a say if it felt the man being promoted was not really qualified as a specialist. ('The Council is reponsible before the law for the prosperity of the works—with this goes the necessity for the promotion of able people.')

Grievance machinery normally operated through departments. For instance, if a worker had a complaint against a foreman, he would normally bring it first before the trade union section of his department. If they could not iron it out, the trade union section and the foreman jointly would bring it before the Factory Council. ('The authority of the foreman must not be broken down.')

Wage scales, general piece rates with production standards, were set 'by the State'. The Rate Department of the plant operated within the given limits. Employees could disapprove the Rate Department's rates, via the trade union of their department. Rates were finally set with the concurrence of Management, Works Council, and the trade union in the department concerned.

The right to a job was almost absolute. Discharges appeared to be exceedingly difficult to secure. Where work was slack, e.g. due to shortage of materials, transfers were offered to other sections of the plant, or the work might be temporarily divided up. Thus, in 1947, 500 Bat'a workers accepted transfers to the building department.

The emphasis of the early post-war labour groups upon production was still very much in evidence. Workers' representatives spoke with surprise at the high spirit maintained during the past year when drought had brought down food levels, and clothing and consumers goods generally had had to be exported in such large quantities to make up for the deficit. Old Bat'a, they said, might have raised output levels under such circumstances, but only through fear of unemployment. To-day jobs were begging for workers, yet those at work kept increasing their output.

'Volunteer brigade' work was also much in evidence. A series of Sunday jobs in making improvements about the town and helping in the country-side brought out large crowds, especially of young people. And the talk among all ages of workers concerning production and records was striking.

Action Committees

An interesting feature at Bat'a was the small effect apparent there of the February events. These had occurred only a few weeks previously, but evidently there had been very little upset. Interest was expressed in the new legislation promised and in the general purport nationally of the events, but locally there appeared to be little to report.

Out of the 54,000 Bat'a employees in the country, 350 all told were said to have been removed from their posts by the Action Committee. These were people who had been in key or at least important positions where it was felt they might do harm. Of these 350, five were actually discharged. Conspicuous among these was an executive of the purchasing department who, it was said, had collusively raised prices to Bat'a in the purchase of hides: instead of buying direct from the tanneries, he had had the tanneries sell the hides to certain shops from whom he then purchased them. The rest of the 350 were offered transfers to less important posts in the company. One hundred and twenty-seven of them refused to be transferred to lower positions and instead gave notice themselves. A number of them subsequently asked to be reinstated, but were now refused, and had to go to the Labour Office to seek jobs elsewhere. The 218 who accepted transfer were now working in Bat'a in their new posts.

Export Difficulties

The most serious problem that Bat'a was facing at this time was the export trade. The combination of dollar shortage and the 1947 drought had forced increased exports upon the shoe industry at the same time that fewer hides could be imported. A higher grade of shoes than hitherto was accordingly being planned, to maximize values in relation to raw materials. Already during the Occupation Bat'a designers had been working secretly upon quality improvements for the post-war, with emphasis upon greater durability than the Bat'a products had shown before. It was felt that the old Bat'a system had relied too much upon the colonial trade that would accept shoddy wares, to say nothing of the great present need of the domestic market for well-made shoes that would last. Kotva, the Bat'a export organization, was meanwhile working within all its branches on sales. During 1948 production was proceeding at the rate of well over 40,000,000 pairs a year. For the exportable portion of these Kotva would also be responsible.

New Zlin

The town of Zlin in 1948 was a lively affair, with a new city government and a changed relation to Bat'a. 'No more a republic within the Republic,' said the new mayor. The mayor was now a purely civic official, the presiding officer of an active town council. He himself, a former electrical worker by trade, was a Communist, his deputy was a Social Democrat. In 1945 the four Czech parties had formed this town council. It consisted of twelve people, all of whom, he stated, he had to consult before he could take action on anything. The council met on Fridays with a regular calendar of matters coming up for action. Everything had to be voted on. This was a great change from the old Bat'a system. A number of town employees worked under the council. Some of these had changed in the course of two years, some additional ones had been let go in February.

Financially as well as legally the town was now independent of Bat'a, and Bat'a taxes had been multiplied several-fold over the 1932–8 rate in spite of the destruction of half the factory buildings.

The new Zlin had an ambitious new Town Plan, and the administration was inclined to disparage the achievements of the previous régime. These had included a huge hotel, excellently appointed, at which Bat'a visitors in great numbers could be entertained, a large department store of Bat'a products and general household ware, open at regular retail prices to both Bat'a employees and outsiders, an interestingly equipped trade school with machinery models and a miniature natural history museum attached, the fine estate grounds turned into a park, that were mentioned earlier, and a first-rate small town hospital with a fine industrial diseases section. Possibly the feeling was that these institutions, except for the hospital, had been too much for show. Certainly this was true to some extent of the workers' housing arrangements: the buildings, though attractively placed and built for their day, were box-like inside, and the families had been forbidden to have kitchen gardens as this might spoil the effect of brick on green.

'The town which we inherited was advanced industrially but it was poverty-stricken in social institutions,' declared the mayor, 'no bathing establishments, libraries, kindergartens, gymnasium.' So now it was a problem to put in all the amenities at once. However, housing had had to come first.

On the outskirts of the town a number of blocks of new apartment houses were to be seen, in groups of three-story buildings, each housing six families. Each apartment had good outside exposure and a balcony. The rooms consisted of kitchen, bath, and three or four other rooms. Kitchen equipment was furnished complete, with electric range and refrigerator. Also included in the rental was central heating from the Bat'a works. The rent was 500 to 600 crowns per month (£2 10s. to £3). This, the writer estimated, would have run to nearly 15 per cent of wages.

Rentals in the old housing were much lower, £1 to £1 10s., or around 5 to 6 per cent of wages. They had been frozen after Liberation, as had rents throughout Czechoslovakia. But at such a return—especially with building materials up 300 per cent—no new private building could have been undertaken. To encourage new building, rents on new construction were allowed to be higher. The old Bat'a apartments, though pleasant to look at from the outside, were said to have walls that were too thin, to be hot in summer because of flat roofs, and to have inadequate bathrooms.

Included in the new Plan, though not yet built, was an additional eating place for workers at the noon hour. It was to accommodate 10,000. At present the workers were eating in shifts in a very large central cafeteria.

One new crèche had been built since the war and fourteen more were now to be completed. The old Bat'a, it was said, had had one poor day-nursery where children of all ages up to six were left, with the woman in charge 'sitting and knitting stockings'.

Kindergartens at present numbered 8, 5 pre-war and 3 new. The Plan called for 54 classes of 3- to 6-year-olds. Several new schools were also be built.

A long-distance heating system was to be installed, operated from waste steam from the factory, to reach all the boarding-houses and also many one-family dwellings. There were still no public baths in the town, that would have to come later.

The town had never had a public reading-room. All there had been before the war was a very small lending library, for both adults and children. In the past three years the town had bought well over £18,000 worth of books. Bat'a was said to have been 'afraid of new books'. A new library was yet to be built.

The town had never had a theatre. In 1946 they had fitted up a makeshift theatre in what had been a small moving picture-house. In 1948 a town music school, the theatre, and a warehouse, still shared the same building. But the theatre had made a name for itself.

The policy of the Plan was to scatter town cultural institutions out into the outlying districts, beginning with a better distribution of moving picture-houses. Hitherto there had only been one very large, Bat'a cinema, in the centre of town, and two tiny neighbourhood houses.

A good deal of civic improvement work had been completed recently by the volunteer brigades before alluded to. Parks and streets had been excellently restored from war-time abuse and were pleasing to the eye. In two weeks young people had torn down a whole row of houses that had been waiting for clearance. But it had taken time to get people interested to this extent, 'two and a half to three years, you may say'. They had to see for themselves that the city government officials were not getting money out of it for themselves. Formerly Zlin had been careless of community property.

Regional Relationships

All around Zlin lies rather poor agricultural country. The farms had been small and overcrowded. Bat'a, in its rapid growth between 1920–40, had been able to continue drawing largely upon the local population, but land subdivision continued. During 1948 a thorough investigation was under way to determine optimum crops and land utilization policy. The study was in charge of the regional Department of Agriculture office, whose head was a member of the National Section on Methodology and Economic Planning. The regional office was full of admirable charts and tables illustrating the needs of the region. One set of charts showed the points of origin of Zlin workers, indicating the transportation routes followed by those commuting daily or at week-ends, and the time and money consumed. For the region the findings indicated that more workers could profitably be drawn from east of Zlin, from Slovakia, where a new highway was now being constructed, and that much of the commuting now being done was exceedingly wasteful.

Other sets of charts showed the land held by Bat'a workers, and here one reason for the long commuting was evident. Thousands of Bat'a workers possessed smallholdings of land, of from 2 to 12 acres. Particularly uneconomical, it was said, were those sized 5 to 12 acres. Such a piece was too large for a family garden, too small for a farm. Altogether 2,800 scrapholders in the 5- to 12-acre category were occupying a third of the Zlin district's arable land.

The situation of the Bat'a workers had come about originally, it was said, by a twofold process: poor peasants in the region had had 'nothing to export' to the town except their children who entered the factory; and workers once established in Bat'a had held on to their bits of land or even bought new ones as 'depression insurance'. Bat'a had wanted his workers to keep such scraps. But economically they were absurd. For heavy work such as ploughing, such a holder had to call in his real peasant neighbour anyway; he himself would have no horse, no cow perhaps, inadequate fertilizer, 'and worst of all socially, the woman in such a family does most of the work'.

The desirable solution, it was said (this was in 1948, of course), and one that must be worked out gradually, was to get these scraps consolidated and given into the hands of real peasants. About 25 acres in this region was necessary for an adequate peasant farm. The agronomist told of a regional meeting the day before on farm legislation at which both smallholders and peasants had been present. During the discussion one man had said, 'I inherited 5 acres and bought two more—I'll not sell'. A peasant answered him, 'O.K., then we'll give you eight more acres and make a farmer of you—but then you can't work in the factory any more.'

The agronomist felt that the process would begin to take place amicably after there had been a few good harvests. 'When once the black market prices equal the established prices, the operation will become painless.'

The Old and the New

Looking at Bat'a Zlin as a whole, one could say that the technical foundations of the great Bat'a system had withstood social change. Thomas Bat'a's extraordinarily successful rationalization processes in production had been preserved, as also his unique unit-purchase-and-sale accounting system. In fact the latter during 1948 was in process of being applied experimentally to yet other industries, especially textiles. The only change of importance here was a softening of the tension under which the workers had formerly laboured, with the use of additional workers per unit.

Per capita productivity was now lower than pre-war, and labour costs were up. Bat'a, however, had formerly been so extraordinarily profitable that a considerable margin apparently remained.

A very great change had occurred in labour relations. Labour organization had taken hold on a tremendous scale and with much initiative: group output effort was now very strong.

Community relations were in process of change in the same direction. The former 'totalitarian' hold of Bat'a over the town, as the new administration put it, had been broken. However here, too, Bata's original technical achievements—housing, hospital, parks, hotel, department store—were still a matter of pride to the company. The new community features could add to this development.

In the country-side the beginnings of change were much more pronounced. Here, for the first time, rational development of the region on a wide scale was taking hold, with orderly planning of rural areas and town-country relations.

The most serious problem for Zlin's future in 1948, as for that of the country at large in large measure, remained the question of exports. Inevitable in a country of Czechoslovakia's resources and history, and worsened greatly by the desperate foreign exchange situation of the post-war, the export problem was in 1948 beginning to be added to by purely political factors. The history and extent of the East-West trade restrictions in which Czechoslovakia found herself involved are, however, matter for a later discussion.

After 1948 some interesting structural changes took place in both company and town. Beginning with January 1949, it will be recalled, new policies had gone into effect nationally concerning specialization and decentralization of oversized industrial units. Bat'a, of course, had been a prime target for change. The writer well recalls a conversation with an enthusiastic young Bat'a engineer in 1948, a great admirer of the technical system developed in his factory, who nevertheless pointed out a series of reasons why he thought Bat'a had originally over-expanded. A smaller unit, with less diversification, he felt, would have been more economical in the long run. As it was, hosiery, chemicals, and many other lines had been superimposed upon the original leather business, and the welter of branches all over the country was very great.

Under the 1949 reorganization a beginning of subdivision was made. The Bat'a enterprise, now renamed Svit ('light'), was henceforth to control only the production in the town and its surroundings, centering in leather. All the former production branches of Bat'a were now separate new National Enterprises. The aim was to have them of medium size. It was felt that perhaps 3,000 to 5,000 employees in leather would be the optimum per establishment, but of course no such degree of redistribution was possible. By late 1949 there were perhaps twenty to thirty national corporations in the former Bat'a domain, each with over 1,000 workers, with Svit itself remaining very large. In so far as possible each plant had a specialized line of production.

Bat'a's original export-import organization, Kotva, had also undergone a transformation. In 1948 it had still been doing a general export-import business for all Bat'a products, whatever their nature, and also for all leather and rubber products of other Czechoslovak manufacturers. But in November of that year it was reorganized to become the nation's monopoly commercial enterprise for leather and rubber. It was now separated completely from the producing units of the leather and rubber industries, of which Bat'a, though the largest, was only one. And it had had lopped off from it the numerous Kotva excrescences in unrelated fields. Its name was changed to 'Exico'. In accordance with the principle of specialization, it had lost glass and textiles, but had been given the fur trade as a part of hides.

The town of Zlin had also undergone changes. The name Zlin now applied only to Zlin proper, the immediate centre where the factory stood. The whole rapidly growing urban region of which Zlin had been the centre and point of origin was now drawn together administratively into a single city. Zlin now became only one of eleven component towns of this complex, although of course overwhelmingly the most important. The development of the whole was being planned for as a unit. The new city in its entirety was named Gottwaldov after Czechoslovakia's President.

CHAPTER XI

LABOUR AND PRODUCTION

I. THE TRADE UNION MOVEMENTS

That a society cannot distribute more than it produces is a truism that hardly needs proving. But that a labour movement should fix its attention upon this point, even in a society-moving-toward-socialism, is another question. Is not the very function of a labour movement to wrest what it can away from the managers of industry? Has not labour's historic attitude been, Let the managers concern themselves with getting their money's worth in return?

In spite of all the recent discussions about what constitutes responsible union leadership, this is undoubtedly the fundamental position expected of a labour movement by its members in a competitive society. The question is, To what extent, if at all, are these positions modified once the competitive, capitalist basis disappears? Some would maintain that along with the basis goes the need for a dichotomized superstructure; others, that a loss of dichotomy means a going over to the enemy—since the State, under this view, is only the old enemy multiplied a hundredfold.

Whatever the merit of these views, there is no doubt that in Poland and Czechoslovakia, as in all the new planned economies, the very same labour movements that struggled most strongly against the private employer and the Occupationists, turned rapidly to problems of production and broad social policy once their new states were established. And there is no doubt that in the course of this turn, taken on a mass basis, many new forms of wage administration, labour recruitment, distribution of social services and the like, were worked out. Examination of these changing institutions appears more fruitful to the writer than assigning praise and blame for their establishment.

Early History

The perspective in which the post-war Polish and Czechoslovak labour movements viewed their earlier history was in terms of its fragmentation and abortive attempts at unity. At all costs, such a history was not to be repeated.

Czechoslovakia had of course had a much larger and less harassed series of unions than the Poles. Relations with the Government were for the most part friendly. Union membership amounted to nearly half of both industrial and white-collar workers; but this was largely because of the form of Czechoslovakia's unemployment provisions, the so-called Ghent system whereby the Government added a subsidy to trade union out-of-work benefits. During the depression years, under pressure of labour unrest, the Government's subsidies became large. Such a system, of course, put a premium upon union membership, but in Czechoslovakia at any rate it also made for a large proportion of 'sleeping' members who looked upon their unions as benefit-distributing agencies. Fragmentation was not only by craft and locality, but by nationality, religion and, most destructive from the point of view of the post-war unions, by political party.

The initial split of importance occurred in connection with the break between Socialists and Communists in 1922. Thereafter each of the leading Czech parties tended to claim its own adherents in a separate trade union centre, and the Agrarian Party in particular became head of a large membership of so-called Yellow or employer-sponsored organizations with large funds at their command, considered company unions by the rest. By the beginning of 1938, excluding the purely German unions, there were said to be 709 different unions, 485 of them combined into no less than 18 different centrals. The remaining 224 unions were totally unattached. The strongest central was the Social Democratic, with almost three-quarters of a million workers; the next the National Socialist, with over a third of a million; the third the Agrarian Party 'Yellow' centre, with a quarter of a million; the fourth and fifth (in 1937) the Communist and Catholic with 136,000 and 124,000 respectively. The Communist unions by this time were under very bitter attack.

Social legislation of an advanced character, as was noted earlier, had been achieved in the opening years of the régime. Moreover collective agreements were protected by law. During the later years of the protracted depression, however, attacks upon existing agreements became more frequent, and the disunited trade unions waged a series of bitter and often unsuccessful strikes to hold what they had won and to maintain adequate government enforcement of what still existed on paper. Native fascist movements were unmistakably gathering strength and Germany was becoming more threatening.

It was in the face of this difficult situation that a number of fruitless conferences were held in the closing years of the régime, between the leadership of the leading labour centrals, seeking unification. Finally, the Communist central in 1937 decided to dissolve its unions and have members join the Social Democratic central; but Munich supervened before this was completed.

Under the Occupation all the old unions and their centrals were forcibly abolished and two Nazi organizations were set up, one for private employees and one for public. The officials of the former 'Yellow' unions were given leading posts in them. Underground, however, illegal trade union groups came together almost at once and formed at last a single trade union centre. Members of different political parties adhered to it and it never had a rival. It had the record of functioning uninterruptedly throughout the Occupation, the Germans never being able to uncover it as a whole: individual members who were seized refused to betray it. This central organization (U.R.O., or Central Council of Trade Unions), besides taking a lead in resistance activities, projected a nation-wide industrial labour organization (R.O.H., or United Revolutionary Trade Union Movement) to function in the post-war. It itself meanwhile performed unique political-economic functions. It drew up projects for various reform laws that were subsequently passed, such as the Social Security Act, it kept in touch with the London Government, and it had an important hand in the Košice Programme published in Slovakia a month before the liberation of the Czech lands. It also worked out in great detail the necessary procedures for the carrying on of economic life during the liberation process itself. Hence, according to its historians, when the 'May rising' came, aside from skirmishes with the retreating Nazis, the process was almost peaceful. '. . . revolutionary works committees took over, works militias protected the factories and helped to turn the Nazis out and to disarm them, national committees took over the local administration and looked after the population. . . . The relatively orderly manner in which all this took place was in no small measure due to the careful preparation by the underground revolutionary trade union movement.'[1]

[1] 'A Short History of the Trade Union Movement in Czechoslovakia' (Prace, Prague, 1946), p. 9.

In Poland meanwhile, pre-war labour organization had travelled a much more difficult road. After an initial period of rapid organizing following the establishment of Polish independence, trade unions had been increasingly attacked as the Pilsudski and post-Pilsudski régimes consolidated themselves. Hence the disastrous effects of fragmentation were felt earlier and more strongly here. As in Czechoslovakia, workers were split according to nationality, religion, political party, and craft; also, under Government pressure, into separate unions for manual and office workers. There were 9 different trade union centrals and 332 different unions, some affiliated to one or another central, some unaffiliated.[1] However, something approaching 25 per cent of the working population, or nearly a million, were registered in unions of one sort or another, and 600,000, or some 15 per cent, were dues-paying members. While this was only about half the proportion shown in Czechoslovakia, it was large considering the difficult political situation.[2]

By the mid-thirties, when the effects of the world depression had run their full course, a series of unusually serious strikes against wage cuts and social insurance decreases broke out in mining and transport. Suppression included police and troop action. Unrest amounting, it was said, to a serious political threat was only headed off by the final military steps preceding the German attack.

German Occupation policy was so much more severe in Poland than in Czechoslovakia and political strife was so much more marked, that a single trade union underground with elaborate programmes for the future was never achieved there. Resistance activity was carried out by individual unions. Hence when Liberation came, it was a congeries of individual union groups, springing up under the heels of the retreating Germans, that became a mass movement once more and attended the initial Congress of Trade Union Delegates in Lublin in November 1944. Subsequently the Christian trade unions, which had at first maintained their separate identity, declared their adherence to the new organization.

[1] Cf. International Labour Office, *Industry and Labour*, Geneva, vol. III, 1950, 'Trade Union Organization in Poland'. 'Before the war . . . a large number of trade unions . . . but they were split up into various occupational, ethnical, religious, and political categories. . . . According to 1935 statistics there were 332 different trade union groups.' (pp. 134, 133.)

[2] Moreover, because of the severe pressure under which they laboured, some of the craft unions, notably the building trades, had gone over to the industrial form. This lent them added strength.

From then on the story begins to become similar to that of the post-war Czechoslovak movement, except that the Polish movement never went through a stage of as high centralization as the Czech and never became as extraordinarily powerful politically.

Structure and Function

In both countries to-day the general pattern of union organization is a relatively small number of large unions, nation-wide in scope, all on a completely industrial basis. All workers in a given workplace, and in the industry comprising it, manual and auxiliary personnel, white-collar, technical and professional workers, deal as a unit with management. 'One enterprise, one union', is the formula. In Czechoslovakia in 1949 there were twenty-one such unions, in Poland there were thirty-one.[1] In the case of Czechoslovakia the three largest unions, those for the Metal Industry, Textiles and Leather, and Transport, comprised nearly half the total membership.

The National Unions have regional as well as local branches. And there are also regional federations and what we should call city centrals of all the unions in a locality. But the important distinction is the degree of power and influence as between the individual National Unions and the United National Central. In both countries the policy of the labour movement as a whole is declared to be paramount: any description such as that given the American Federation of Labour many years ago, 'a Congress of sovereign ambassadors', would be absurd here. But there appeared for a period of years to be a considerable difference in the degree of direction exercised by the national centrals in the two countries. In the opinion of the writer, the Czechoslovak movement started out with a wholly paramount Central and was only latterly moving out toward a good deal of initiative on a national level by the separate national unions,[2] and toward greater decentralization

[1] The International Labour Office, in the article cited above, presents in tabular form the Polish amalgamations up to 1 January 1949 (at which time there had been 36 unions), comparing the organizations of that date with those of 1935. It also notes the continuing increases in membership after the war, from something over half of all wage earners in 1945, to 87 per cent by the end of 1948.

[2] In Czechoslovakia it was only in 1949 that the separate national unions formed regional departments of their own. Prior to that, the Central alone had regional (i.e. mixed) Federations; and it was quite evident in 1948 that these Regional Federations were considerably more one-way streets for the perco-

generally. In Poland the evolution was, if anything, in the opposite direction; at any rate, there the Central had never been so powerful.[1]

In Czechoslovakia the relation between labour movement and Government was also for years a unique one. To a degree not encountered elsewhere in the writer's observation, it apparently was the United Trade Union Movement that, more than any political party, during the years preceding the February events, formulated the policies subsequently carried through in Parliament by Communists and Left-Wing Socialists. 'U.R.O. threshes things out first,' was the way an acute observer put it to the writer in early 1948, emphasizing that, while in U.R.O. all parties had some representation, it was the common workers' 'line' that eventuated, a line further to the left than that of the national Communist Party leadership at the time.

Once February had passed, and parties other than the Communist had sunk into insignificance, it appears to the writer that the functions of U.R.O. as, so to say, watchdog of the revolution, decreased *pari passu*. It ceased to operate so nearly like a political party, although it remained important and exceedingly active.

The history of U.R.O.'s unique position is, of course, bound up with the character of the original Czechoslovak National Front itself, a Front composed of an equal number of unequal partners, and with national sentiment at the onset far to the left. Once the National Front and Government had been established in power, all the parties composing it had at once recognized the United Trade Union Movement as the sole representative of labour in the Czech lands. (The only possible jockeying now would be to see to what extent the Socialist and other parties might succeed in rivalling the Communist within the ranks of the United union.) In Slovakia a similar organization that had kept in close touch with the United union before Liberation joined it in 1946 on a federative basis. Special legal recognition was extended to the new or-

lating downward of the Central's policies than for common formulation of regional needs and policies by the constituent unions. In 1949, along with the establishment of greater power and authority for the national unions and their branch divisions, the Regional Federations were de-emphasized.

[1] In Czechoslovakia the Central Council numbered no less than 130 members in 1949 as compared with the Polish 61. It was elected triennially. In Poland in 1948 efforts were being made to have annual elections with their expensive Convention machinery changed to biennial.

ganization, it was given the remaining assets of all previously existing unions, and broad powers were assigned to it—which it assiduously kept fresh with use. It had the right to a consultative voice in all discussions affecting labour carried on by either legislative or executive branches of government, it had the right to representation on all non-elective public bodies, and all public and private organizations were required to grant it full facilities for its work, including the opening to it of their books.

The political-economic detail work of the organization was carried on by the Central Council's seven permanent commissions, the Social-Political Commission and the Commission on National Economy being especially important. Major pieces of legislation of concern to labour, such as the Social Security Act, commonly had their origin in the Social Political Commission of U.R.O. and in every field of economy U.R.O. was in the habit of developing its own policy and presenting it to the Government with supporting data. For this purpose 'a whole series of sub-commissions work under this (the Economic) Commission on particular problems of industry, finance, insurance, foreign trade, internal trade, co-operatives, building, agriculture, forestry, food supply, voluntary activity, production committees . . . settlement areas, and so on'.[1]

Membership in Polish and Czech unions was voluntary, dues check-off was frowned upon,[2] and no closed-shop provisions were permitted. Some union branches, notably in the textile industry in Czechoslovakia, were however still being permitted the union shop (i.e. compulsory membership within a stipulated time after hiring). Dues were low and uniformly rated, at 1 per cent of wages.

All trade union bodies in both countries were elective, with the lower bodies sending delegates to conventions to elect the higher, as in unions elsewhere. The position of the basic membership unit, however, was unique. In both countries to-day so-called Factory or Works' Councils formed the lowest rung in the industrial hierarchy, and their relation to production was different from anything known to us.

Works' Councils

Factory councils had sprung up as militant bodies in many of the countries of the Continent and in various trades during or at

[1] 'The Trade Union Movement in Czechoslovakia', Prague 1947, (multigraphed).

[2] However, in Poland in 1949 the practice was still being combatted.

the conclusion of World War I and have had an interesting history, outside the scope of this book. Suffice it to say that they served as a means of uniting all workers in a work-place at a time when craft unions were split by politics and unable to cope with large-scale industry, that they won recognition from governments in many cases as an emergency measure to head off revolutionary unrest, and that in both Czechoslovakia and Poland they laid claim to a compulsory contribution from employers for welfare purposes. In Czechoslovakia such Councils were first won by the miners, and subsequently recognition of them was extended to other trades. In Poland, during the later years of the inter-war régime, the councils were almost completely wiped out, but, as a contemporary Polish source puts it, 'their memory remained',[1] and during the years of Occupation they were illegally revived, particularly, once more, in the mines. According to the Poles, it was these *ad hoc* committees that in their country proceeded to take over enterprises in the wake of the retreating Germans, protect them and start them running again. (The practical difference between this process and that taking place in Czechoslovakia a few months later was apparently that in Poland, with no single newly established and revolutionary Central to father the impromptu organizations, fewer of them would account themselves 'unions'.)

In both countries, within a few months after the establishment of their new National Governments, the Works' Councils were institutionalized: they were recognized for every productive establish-

[1] 'In 1918–19 there grew up in Poland in the larger industrial centres, in the mines, foundries, and factories, committees . . . working alongside the trade unions. . . . Due to craft unionism the workers within a single factory usually belonged to various unions. . . . Therefore, during campaigns concerning the workers' more important demands, the workers of the factory avoided unnecessary conflict by choosing their delegates or factory committee as the representative of all employees to put forward demands on their behalf and negotiate with the employers. It was often the case that even at the conclusion of a strike the committees did not dissolve. . . .

'As the forces of fascism in Poland increased, the number of factory committees shrank until they almost entirely disappeared.

'The memory of their fruitful activity remained, however, with the working class until the following world war. Even during the Occupation illegal works' committees appeared, in particular in the coal basins, and as soon as the Germans retreated, they sprang up in all enterprises, often taking over the role of management.' (Central Board of Polish Trade Unions, 'Trade Unions in New Poland', June 1949, multigraphed.)

ment and their powers, like those of the trade unions, were recorded—and delimited—in legislation.

Direct productive functions were obviously no longer held necessary or desirable. Establishments from which the Germans had fled were now in process of being formally nationalized or put into local government or co-operative hands. Here management would have to be definitely left free to manage. Thus in the Czech Works' Councils Law of October 1945, we read: 'The works' management shall be the concern of its managers who are exclusively responsible for the enterprise and its success. The works' representatives are not entitled to interfere with the management and operation of the works *by issuing independent orders*.'[1]

Even in the case of enterprises left in private ownership, the principle of single management would have to be respected.

Upon all managements, however, the workers, through their organizations, were to continue to have a check. There were to be periodic consultations on the whole economy of the concern, and books were to be opened to them. In the case of private enterprises, the works councils could make sure that national programmes were being adhered to—more specifically, that production was not being neglected for profits. But in all, a novel degree of what might be called 'supervision upward' was invited. Thus, in Poland, where managements were required to meet with and consult the councils at least monthly on broader technical and organizational problems as well as on those of immediate labour output and welfare, the writer had occasion to note the seriousness with which certain managements were treating this obligation. Managements were also required to present the councils with written quarterly reports on the state of the enterprise.

Not mentioned, obviously, in the legislation, but extremely important in practice in the early days of the régime, the writer was assured, had been the activities of the works' council organizations in the day-to-day furthering of nationalization. In border-line industries, such as pharmaceuticals, for example, in Czechoslovakia, the central managements of industry would be besieged by worker delegations demanding that their particular little plant, for such and such reasons, was so vital that it must be taken over. Trying to disentangle the absurd from the necessary became a difficult problem. The pressure from below was very great.

[1] Presidential Decree No. 104 Sb., 24 October 1945, Concerning Works' and Undertakings' Councils, Section 2. (Italics mine.)

On the other hand, private managements also frequently sought to attract and hold workers by paying 'black' wages out of 'black' or 'grey' market operations. Where this succeeded it naturally undermined union and works' council organization.

Under the Works' Council laws, everything having to do with personnel, both general and individual, had to be dealt with in advance with the works' council. Hirings, firings, promotions and demotions required their consent, as also the adoption of general policies concerning them (e.g. seniority). Individual grievances and also grievance procedure were dealt with through the council. The council supervised the enforcement of local collective agreements and gave approval to working rules, including hours and overtime distribution. It supervised enforcement of safety and sanitary measures. It set up social and cultural arrangements for the workers, receiving a subvention for this purpose in addition to its own funds.

Larger works' councils had, as a rule, a multitude of standing committees working under them and enlisting the efforts of a great many people. Typical committees were: Wages, Working Conditions, Placement, Social Security, Production Techniques, Education and Culture, Sports, Women's Committee, Youth Committee. Besides this, the councils themselves spent a considerable amount of time going over what we should consider problems of production purely and hence outside the functions of a labour body. The nearest analogy would be the activities of the most active of our war-time Production Committees; but even here the analogy soon breaks down, the range of production questions dealt with by the Czech and Polish councils being so much broader.

Within larger establishments there were various forms of departmental and shop delegates, in effect shop stewards. There was also provision for delegates dealing with social security and yet other delegates dealing with labour inspection. Collectively, following Soviet terminology, such persons were called trade union activists. In Poland the first country-wide elections for these three types of delegates were held in the shops in early 1951. According to the Polish T.U.C. Bulletin for April-June 1951, incomplete data showed over 157,000 workshop group delegates, representing from 10 to 30 workers each, besides well over 100,000 each in the other two categories.

2. WAGE AND OUTPUT PROBLEMS

General Wages Policy

Certain overall considerations are accepted in Czechoslovakia and Poland by all three parties at interest in the wages question: trade unions, management, and Government. It is agreed that total wages should not be inflationary—that they have to be limited by total production, and that much of total production as yet has to be devoted to producers' rather than consumers' goods. This is a silent premise underlying all wage considerations.

It is also agreed that the national wages structure, in all industries and localities, should be made increasingly rational and comparable, job by job; in other words that 'inequities' can and must be gradually removed. Individual managements, under this view, are not free to seek favourable balance sheets for themselves by 'nibbling' at rates. Unions, on the other hand, are not free to create disproportions in the total national wages picture for the benefit of their members only. The duty of the labour movement as a whole is to secure as much as possible for labour as a whole, consonant with the limits of production; the duty of individual unions is to make sure that any anomalies unfavourable to their particular membership are removed, and to protect the individual worker in securing everything he is entitled to.

The extreme emphasis of the Polish and Czechoslovak unions upon increasing production is closely bound up with these general considerations. Output wages are universally accepted in principle, just because they should enhance production. To introduce wherever possible piece rates instead of time rates, and systems of premium pay on top of the piece rates, is taken as an important and necessary part of wage reform.

Along with this goes the principle of equal pay for equal work for previously depressed groups. Women and young people are not to receive less than adult males for comparable service—'wages according to desert', 'pay for the job, not for the person who does it', are phrases constantly cited with approval.

In both countries the right of women to equal pay is embodied in law, in the case of Czechoslovakia, in the 1948 Constitution. In addition, women are accorded special privileges, 'special regulation of conditions of work, in view of the circumstances of pregnancy, maternity, and child care'.[1] In the case of young people, piece rates for juveniles have to be the same as for older workers; in Czechoslovakia, by regulation of the Ministry of Labour, even time rates may be only slightly less than those for adults.[2]

Yet another pay principle is accepted, directly related to the labour market: the principle that wage scales for hard yet 'socially important' work such as mining must run higher than for more attractive and less important trades. This principle is extended to social security provisions as well as to wages themselves. However, as we shall see later, there is also an attempt to influence the labour market directly through vocational guidance, the character of apprenticeship offers, improvement of the conditions of work themselves, and so on.

The Process of Wage Setting

The acceptance of general principles is one thing, their carrying out in so controversial a field as going wage rates is quite another. In both Poland and Czechoslovakia wage reforms had to be superimposed upon a crazy-quilt pattern of previous rates. The reform has been a spotty process, with more rational patterns resisted at times and with crudities in their application. Nevertheless the total volume and direction of change is unmistakable.

Historically rationalization of the wages structure in both countries had to start from the oppressive and abnormally complicated systems left by the Germans, with whom the creation of jealousies among the native working populations had been a deliberate instrument of Occupation policy. A Czech metal worker referred to the '460 laws plus 160 variations' existing under the Occupation in his industry. 'A jungle of rates,' he called it. 'Wage rates danced, mostly down.'[3] By 1948 there were three general wage regulations in force in his industry and everyone could understand them. In the early post-war, elementary simplifications were introduced, along with abolition of the 'hunger wages' of the depressed trades. But attempts at full-scale rationalization began only with the Two-Year Plan in Czechoslovakia and somewhat later in Poland.

A chief agency of rationalization in both countries was perforce

[1] Constitution of the Czechoslovak Republic, Section 26.

[2] The range is from 80 per cent of the adult day wage for juveniles of 15, to 95 per cent for those aged 19. Work under 15 is not permitted.

[3] Interview material, May 1948. '*Das war ein Jungel! Die Löhne haben getanzt —meistens herunter.*'

the Collective Agreement, local and partial at first, then made applicable to a whole industry by order of the Ministry of Labour. Considerable difference during the early period appeared to exist between the two countries in the amount of initiative exercised by the ministry in getting the final result. In both countries of course the sum total of wages and their chief subdivisions for a given industry for a given period were supposed to be limited in any case by that industry's Plan figures; but these themselves were subject to revision as conditions between industries changed. It was the business of the Ministry of Labour to see that an increasing degree of balance within and between industries should be achieved.

In Poland by 1948 there were about sixty nation-wide Collective Agreements, thirty-five of them in State industry, the rest in co-operatives, the building industry, agriculture, various forms of transport, private restaurants and hotels, and so on. (Private industry agreements, because of the small size of the concerns, were chiefly local agreements, most of them in food supply.) All told, of the total of about 4,000,000 wage and salary workers in Poland at this time, about 1,000,000, chiefly those in the public services, had their wages fixed by law and about 2,000,000 supposedly by collective agreements.

In some sixteen or eighteen cases the agreements had been made industry-wide, by order of the Ministry of Labour, and had been given the force of law, i.e. were directly enforceable by public agency, not merely on charges of breach of contract.[1] In such industries, accordingly, in so far as there were private employers in them, these as well as the public and co-operative employers would be subject to the agreement's terms. The three most important of the 'three-sectoral' agreements were in building, textiles, and printing. Since building at that time was carried on almost entirely by private contractors, so major an attempt at setting uniform rates there, publicly enforceable, was held especially important.

Collective agreements in Poland and Czechoslovakia, as in all

[1] Such contracts-having-the-force-of-law have had an interesting history in the labour law of various countries, notably in Mexico where 'contrato ley' is a familiar category. In Poland the category was first established under a 1937 law. Cf. International Labour Office, *Industry and Labour Information*, Geneva, vol. LXIV, 1937, pp. 13–14. "Agreements which are of predominant economic importance for the branch of production or the territory they cover may be declared generally binding.'

the planned economies, contained both standardized and unstandardized parts. The standardized portions consisted in a setting forth of the established wage scales and allowances[1] for the industry. The unstandardized portions contained a number of negotiated clauses regulating hiring and dismissals, hours schedules and overtime, special vacation and training payments, special health and cultural provisions.[2]

In Polish agriculture in 1947–8 a narrower form of collective agreement had been entered into. It did not specify basic wage rates at all,[3] but set general conditions of work, social security requirements, and overtime pay. A definite time-table of work and breaks in work was appended. Overtime pay in summer began after ten hours and was at double rates. There were also annual vacations.

In the absence of any general legislation on agricultural labour, the benefits of this Agreement were made universal by a special device. The Agreement had been entered into in the first instance by the State Farms and their employees, a relatively small number of workers at that time, represented by the Agricultural Workers' Union. But it was so drawn as to cover all members of the union, wherever working. And the union was granted the right of establishing union-shop membership. Hence the private farmer employing hired help was going to have to meet the requirements of the existing contract, including its highly expensive social security provisions for union members.[4]

In Czechoslovakia the collective agreement process as seen in

[1] I.e. allowances in kind. These were abolished after 1 January 1949.

[2] In form the Polish contracts began with an introductory statement of the general conditions of the industry, the social provisions to be observed in it, provisions for hygiene and so forth, and the general duties respectively of management and workers. The second portion gave the wage scales, job classification, and bonuses. As changes were made, new clauses were added.

[3] A large part of agricultural pay at this time continued to be in kind in any case. And rural living conditions in different parts of the country varied even more than in the towns.

[4] By 1951, with the fall in workers hired privately, the social security provisions were once more made applicable only to State Farm employees. But for the period in which it was operative, the enforcement machinery for private farm labour standards had been ingenious. Local Agricultural Workers' Committees were provided for, consisting of farmhands only, comparable to works' councils in factories. There was also provision for general local Agricultural Boards, on which farmhands were represented, to administer the social security and other benefits.

the spring of 1948 appeared to operate on a more elaborate scale than in Poland and under closer direction of the Ministry of Labour. New wage scales were in process of being established for a whole series of industries, and the position of trade unions and managers of nationalized industry before the Ministry of Labour appeared to be somewhat comparable to that of unions and management before the National War Labour Board in the United States during the war. However, the rates set were not maxima and minima, but specific rates for each occupation and locality —e.g. 'steam fitter with three years' experience in Prague'. In cases where the organized workers and organized employers at a local level were dissatisfied with a given wage and the matter could not be settled locally, the question would come up to the Ministry. There, the writer was told, what amounted to a bargaining process went on between employers and unions under the auspices of the Ministry. 'But it is the Ministry that in the last analysis accepts or rejects the Agreement arrived at: if the wages are not acceptable, given the economy as a whole, the Ministry may right them. The bargaining may go on a week, a month, sometimes several months. When finally the Ministry does accept the wages, the Ministry embodies them in a general decree on wage scales applicable to the entire industry.'[1]

The presence subsequently of considerable numbers of persons under compulsory labour sentences apparently caused no anomaly in the Czechoslovak wage structure. In October 1948, Czechoslovakia passed a law on compulsory labour camps, stating that it was being adopted in the interests of 'collective security', against 'persons who . . . are a menace to the economic and social régime because of their refusal to work or of their anti-social behaviour'. Persons liable to detention in a camp had to be between the ages of eighteen and sixty and the period of their detention could vary between the limits of three months and two years. Sub-committees of three of the regional people's committees were empowered to commit persons to such detention and to lengthen or shorten its

[1] Interview with the Ministry of Labour and Social Welfare, March 1948. Cf. also a 1950 statement: 'In matters of wage policy, the Ministry of Labour and Social Welfare is becoming a directing, co-ordinating and checking body, guided by the fundamental directives issued by the State Planning Office in respect to wage policy as a whole. The central management authorities will handle concrete individual questions. . . .' (Ministry of Labour and Social Welfare, *Report*, March 1950, p. 31.)

duration. Persons detained were to be paid normal wages minus maintenance costs.[1]

By 1951, in both countries the wage-fixing functions of the Ministry of Labour had begun to be split up and moved over into the separate ministries concerned with the various branches of production, trade and so forth. This was in consonance with the preparations going on for the absorption of all Ministry of Labour functions elsewhere. Thus, in Poland, minor wage changes were now negotiated directly between the administration of an industry and the executive committee of the union concerned; in that case the rates arrived at would be issued as a regulation by that industry. Important changes or changes involving long drawn out negotiations were referred up to the Central Council of Trade Unions and the Central Planning Board. In such cases the rates finally negotiated would be issued as an official regulation by the Ministry concerned.

By 1951 Polish industries had caught up with the Czech in having industry-wide agreements for all occupations without exception, and were preparing to draw up separate enterprise contracts for 1952 within the framework of the general agreements.

Beginning with 1951–2, Czechoslovakia took a further step in the central planning of wages. A National Wages Board was set up, chaired by the Prime Minister, with the duty of establishing 'compulsory wage totals' for each industry; and by 1 January 1952 these were to be formalized as separate 'wage funds', each closely tied to the industry's production plan. 'The wage fund', it was stated, 'embodies both the increase in productivity and the raising of wages for which the plan has made provision over a given period. . . .

'The National Planning Office is responsible for fixing the amount of the national wage fund . . . and for allocating it among the Ministries and Departments responsible for the various branches of industry, which in turn must fix the share of each establishment.

'The wages funds are fixed for one year.'[2]

[1] Parliamentary Report, No. 109, 1948; quoted in I.L.O., *Industry and Labour*, Geneva, vol. I, 1949, pp. 264–5.

[2] I.L.O., *Industry and Labour*, Geneva, vol. VI, 1951, pp. 194–6.

Wage Levels

In Poland the absolute level[1] of wages in 1948 was probably not over half that of Czechoslovakia, a disparity even greater than it had been before the war. This was in spite of Poland's more spectacular rate of recovery from the disastrous depths of 1945. Polish economists[2] considered Czech wages at this time to be already up to pre-war, whereas their own would do well to reach pre-war in another year and a half.[3] They estimated mid-1948 levels for Poland as follows: skilled wages, almost up to 100 per cent of pre-war, except in the metals industry which still needed special attention; unskilled wages, considerably lower, perhaps 75 to 80 per cent of pre-war; and white-collar wages, perhaps only 50 per cent. Higher managerial salaries, of course, were manyfold lower than formerly. In agriculture, real wages on the whole were probably higher than pre-war.

They stoutly defended the deflation of white-collar earnings. 'Before the war there was no equity between wage and salary rates.' The difference had amounted to a ratio of about 1 to 3·5. 'Now we are coming down to a ratio of about 1 to 2 or 1 to 1·7.' This was being accomplished by 'decreasing the *rate* of increase of salaries while greatly increasing the *rate* of increase of wages'.[4] However, it was granted that the absolute level of white-collar earnings was still far too low.[5]

[1] November 1947 data for insured wage and salary earners together gave an overall average of about 9,000 zl. a month, i.e. about £5 12s. at that time. For male wage earners in establishments of over twenty employees, the average was about 6,800 zl. (£4 7s.), and for female, 5,300 zl. (about £3 6s.). Full employment plus secondary jobs was said to have made low wages more tolerable, although of course it spelled overwork.

[2] Interview material, August 1948.

[3] In point of fact this level appears to have been exceeded by the time set, the end of 1949.

[4] Ibid.

[5] The largest rises in real wages at this time had been in the coal mines, next on the railroads and in the building trades. The railroads had been militarized before the war, with wages frozen at a low level. In the building trades, there was the matter of enormous need for construction, plus the tendency of building trades workers to leave the industry in the fall to go into other work, especially mining, where they could get free coal.

During 1949 and 1950 the general level of Polish real wages apparently continued to rise *pari passu* with increased production. But in the latter part of 1951 there was a serious recession. Following meat shortages and a bad autumn drought the cost of foodstuffs had risen markedly enough to make inroads on

In Czechoslovakia comparable considerations concerning relative wage levels had been at work, although here of course absolute need had been less desperate. During the crucial winter of 1947 a particularly serious struggle had been waged over white-collar earnings.

On the one hand, ever since Liberation, Government spokesmen had been inveighing against excessive employment of white-collar personnel in proportion to manual. Ratios in Czechoslovakia had gone up, it was stated, from a pre-war of 1:7, 1:8 and even 1:9 to about 1:5. Post-war bureaucracy was blamed for this, along with the unhealthy attitudes among workers engendered by the Occupation. Nothing specific was said about the use of political 'keys' as a factor, but undoubtedly these must have contributed. Each party was entitled to a proportion of the lower supervisory posts, hence the creation of new posts meant new opportunities, while job deflation and reassignment of employees became a political insult. In the nature of the case, moreover, white-collar personnel would be a natural stronghold for more conservative sentiment, as manual workers would for the Left.

On the other hand, it was undoubtedly true that the material situation of white-collar employees, particularly those in government service, had become deplorable. Before prices became stabilized, pay-scales generally had been multiplied roughly threefold to make up for currency inflation, but white-collar earnings had been allowed to lag, those of Government employees most of all. Now in 1947, following the drought, the issue occasioned a clean split along party lines. The question was, whether to raise at that time the pay of all civil servants, or to concentrate on the more poorly paid. The Communists contended that a further general rise now would be inflationary, the more conservative parties that it would only be just. In the end the Communist position won out and the pay of the higher ranking civil servants continued to lag. Even with the increases granted them, moreover, the lower ranking white-collar workers had by no means regained their pre-war earnings ratio. The end result therefore, in ratios, was not so very different from that in Poland. It is to be noted, moreover, that

consumer purchasing power in all other lines. How long the scarcities would continue it was impossible in the winter of 1951–2 to say, but it appeared at the time that a part of them at any rate stemmed from marketing rather than agricultural factors and might therefore be overcome more quickly than the physical effects of the drought and the decline in livestock.

complaints concerning the continued influx of workers into white-collar jobs continued to be made during the opening years of the Five-Year Plan.

Assertions concerning the absolute level of Czechoslovak living standards after the war and the rate of their subsequent increase would be difficult to make. The disastrous drought of 1947 had cut food consumption sharply for a time, even though a strict rationing system kept prices at bay. Similarly, to a lesser extent, with housing: rent control, subsidized housing, and, to some extent, distribution of new space and payment for that space according to need, caused a smaller proportion of the working-class budget than formerly to go for housing; but the amount of space available was much less than pre-war. Again, clothing throughout the earlier period was for the most part in short supply, partly a matter of production arrears, partly of the need to concentrate on export trades. Even by the end of 1949 very great changes in these respects were to be seen. Supplies were much greater and prices lower. Government figures, however, showed a continued intention to pursue a cautious policy, with basic industry, particularly the machine trades, developing far more rapidly than consumer output. Even for the end of the Five-Year Plan the goal set was to attain only a 35 per cent increase over pre-war living standards as compared to a 75 per cent increase of industrial output. A Polish industrial economist said to the writer, a little enviously: 'The saving of the Czechs is like that of a very rich man: he saves in order to have still more of what he has already amassed, for the future. Give them twenty years and the Czechs will be one of the richest nations in Europe.'[1]

[1] The 1949 figures quoted by the International Labour Office showed average Czechoslovak wages of slightly over 4,000 crowns a month (nominally £20 before devaluation of the pound). The I.L.O. further quoted the basic salary (aside from bonuses) of the best paid category of ordinary supervisory staff in industry as being only 5,000 crowns (£25) a month, i.e. only 25 per cent above the industrial average. (Actual monthly salaries received in the various leading industries on the other hand were given in tabular form as running from about 5,000 to well over 7,000 crowns (£25 to £30). How this was to be reconciled with the previous figure is not clear.) 'Contracts for salaries above this figure must be approved by the Ministry of Labour. The range of normal salaries is therefore fairly restricted. The current salaries of technicians who have great responsibilities vary, however, between 10,000 and 15,000 crowns (£50 and £60, i.e. 2 to 2½ times as much), less a heavy graduated tax.' (I.L.O., *Industry and Labour*, Geneva, vol. IV, 1950, pp. 495–8.)

Polish Wage Reform

An important step in the rationalization of wages was taken by the Poles at the beginning of 1949. What remained of wages in kind were abolished and all wages went over to a completely cash basis.

Originally the payment of wages in kind had been an emergency form of rationing and had served to keep all workers' families going. At the end of 1945 less than half of the average wage had been in cash. Nearly a quarter was represented by food ration cards,[1] and nearly a third by other allocations in kind, chiefly industrial products. These latter varied with the nature of the industry and the particular job, in an irrational manner (i.e. cloth for the textile workers, coal for the miners).[2]

As conditions eased somewhat, additional increments had been added, in kind as well as in cash; and collective agreements became very unwieldy affairs, as the early agreements drawn at first for only three to six months had been replaced by successive new ones, each with its added points and paragraphs.

There was also the question of disparities as between the workers in private and those in nationalized industry, for obviously the private employer could not be subsidized to the extent of his employees' food ration. He consequently had to be able to offer them more cash. There was also considerable trading-in of surplus rationed goods. (E.g. the miners were said to count on being able to sell a part of their generous coal allowance.)

Gradually during the period 1946–8 a part of the allocations in kind had been replaced by corresponding increases in wages. But what was left as each such payment in kind was liquidated by conversion into cash was an equally irrational cash wage.

By mid-1948, accordingly, one heard much of the need of a general overhauling of the wages structure, to run parallel with the change-over from kind to cash. Premium rates of pay were to be a main lever of change. During the latter part of the year negotiations along these lines were undertaken between the trade unions and the managements of nationalized industry. New collec-

[1] For rationed articles even in 1948, it was said, 'Price is symbolic'. Originally the prices charged covered only the cost of distribution, not that of the article itself.

[2] In 1948 the writer was told that a general wage agreement for the textile industry would be impossible as yet because of the existence of payments in kind.

tive agreements were to be drawn up, to go into effect at the same time as the abolition of rationed goods.[1] The Government had promised a total increase of 10 per cent in the wages fund, over and above the conversion of kind into cash, and it was the business of unions and management to distribute the surplus in such a way as to stimulate production, at the same time that the complexities of previous agreements were to be lessened.

The model of a general agreement was finally worked out, together with additional clauses for given industries, and in January 1949 the new collective agreements were signed. The wage reform was said to embrace approximately 3,000,000 employees, not only in industry, trade, transport, and finance, but in State and local government and in the co-operatives.

By late 1951 it was stated by the Economic Department of the Polish T.U.C. that 'accord' wages, i.e. piece rates and the other forms of output wage, had increased by 25 per cent in the previous two years, and that in all branches of Polish industry without exception well over half the workers were thus paid. In most industries the proportion was said to be about 70 per cent. The range of basic rates within a given industry was said to run about 1 to 2·5; however, in foundries it was a high as 1 to 3. Most industries had only eight wage classes, none apparently had more than twelve.[2]

Czechoslovak Job Analysis

During 1950 Czechoslovakia was completing a stage in her wage rationalization comparable, for her level of development, to what Poland had accomplished in 1949 with the change-over to cash wages and the standardization of collective agreements. For some years now the Czechs had been attempting to draw up job-ratings for various industries and to get them accepted as the basis

[1] On 1 January 1949, the provision of rationed goods, both foodstuffs and industrial products, did cease, with the exception of a priority on fats. Late in 1951, temporary rationing, as an emergency measure, was reintroduced. In Czechoslovakia a quite different system of rationing continued to be preserved right through both periods of the country's development. Rationed goods formed the mainstay of consumption; unrationed goods, also provided through State channels, were made available in considerable quantities after the beginning of 1950, at much higher prices: they served to siphon off spare purchasing power. So late as the end of 1951 some 80 per cent of consumer goods continued to be purchased through the ration.

[2] Thus chemicals had only 8 classes, metals 9, textiles 12.

for a general reclassification of wage rates. By 1950 the first new scales based on such ratings went into effect, and before the end of the year all occupations without exception were to have their job-ratings completed. However, the setting of specific output norms for all these occupations was a far more difficult matter and one that was proceeding more slowly. Yet it was the output norms that were at the centre of the Czechoslovaks' ultimate planning.

When the writer first visited Prague in 1948 the 'norming' process had begun. 'Job catalogues' were being worked out by a research institute connected with the Ministry of Labour and the trade unions.[1] It was the business of the institute to define the job content and set the time for the job, while the Ministry section defined the wage classification. The first industry to be worked on in this way was the metal industry, and at the time of the visit the textile industry and several others were to follow.[2]

Coal at that time was still on the old scale of pay plus 25 per cent, apparently a rather favourable situation. By the end of 1949 a rationalized scale for coal, with production standards, had been worked out, and at the beginning of 1950 it was applied—unsuccessfully, it was stated, for the first month, after that with good output results. In metals apparently better preparatory work had been done, for no initial drop in production was reported.

Czech administrators were under no illusions about the possibility of fixing rates based even upon time study once and for all. 'Hard' rates would sooner or later become 'soft'—i.e. the production standards set would become ultra easy to attain. However, constant warnings were issued to local managements not to jump

[1] The Trade Union Central by this time had a school for job estimators, i.e. time-study technicians.

[2] Engineers were being sent into the factories, to work with management and local unions on tests. The job classifications thus arrived at were then intended to be worked into an eight-fold wage classification to be defined by the Ministry of Labour. These eight classes of pay were supposed to be applicable to all industries and had a 12 per cent step-up between classes, so that the total range in base rates from lowest to highest was considerable. But not every industry in Czechoslovakia would have jobs in every category. As listed, the Metal Industry might have exclusively classes 5, 6, 7, and 8; the Textile Industry, classes 2, 3, 4, 5, 6, 7, and so on. Hence the range for a given industry might be considerably narrower than the total range would suggest. The average class for Metals in 1948 was said to be actually 6·5, indicating a heavy clustering in the upper categories. The Textile Industry, on the other hand, was at that time earnestly demanding a revision of its scale on the score that textile wages traditionally were low and bore no proper relation to skill.

into rate revision every time 'excessive' earnings were reported. Nothing would be more dangerous to voluntary effort than 'wage ceilings'. In work contracts, along with agreement on basic rates and conditions and on the workers' willingness to use norms fixed 'on the basis of up-to-date technique', must go iron-clad guarantees that during the Plan period, i.e. the year, these efficiency norms would not be revised—in effect, that rates would not be cut—no matter what the earnings.

Types of Premium Pay

In Poland the approach to working norms had perforce been much more elementary. When the writer visited plants in 1948 she found that in the heavy metal industry pre-war norms had had to be taken over and adjusted downward to allow for the poor condition of equipment and workers. The allowance had been 20 per cent at first. By 1948 output was said to be about up to pre-war, although damages still amounted to perhaps a 10 to 15 per cent handicap. But there was satisfaction that the previous welter of rates and rate systems was no more. 'Before the war', said a factory director, 'we had no common agreement with the workers. We had a different pay system in each factory! Now we have concluded an agreement with the trade unions for the entire metal industry.' In a large factory in Cracow the Works' Council reported that no stop-watch techniques were employed. Comparisons were made with previous production 'where possible'. An average was taken between the time required by 'a better, a poor, and a middling worker'. In yet other plants more precise methods were used to build up norms. But whatever the norm point, progression of piece rates above it was ordinarily very sharp.

In this connection it is interesting to note that the Poles quite as much as the Czechs were strongly averse to rate cutting. 'If a mistake has been made in favour of the worker', i.e. in setting the original norm point too low, said a Polish engineer to the writer, 'we leave it alone. If the opposite is true and we get a proof from the trade union, we alter it.'[1]

This man thereupon drew out tables to show the effect of an

[1] Subsequently under Polish law special mixed commissions of the works' councils and management were set up to keep continuous check on norms and their alteration. The law provided further that norm changes could not be introduced without the prior consent, not only of the trade unions and works' council, but of the workers directly concerned.

initial mistake upon wage costs throughout the range of possible earnings on the job. The effect would remain constant, merely a flat so and so many zlotys per hour extra. 'This is not a serious loss, particularly as we make every effort to set the rates correctly in the first place.'

As to the use of such steep rates of progression, even at a high cost per piece, the final increments of product, he maintained, were worth it. It was a case of considering the total output needed—the bulk of it at a lower cost, the last portions at a higher. 'Under planned economy, in our conditions, suppose you do have a little higher cost for the extra pieces: that is better than losing that much production and having to buy the balance abroad at a still higher cost!'

The actual rates of progression used differed, of course, with the nature of the job. The highest rates were paid where the work was particularly heavy and where it was difficult to exceed the norm point by much. 'We start from a certain norm, amounting to something above average output. Then we add, to begin with, a piece-rate increment amounting to 20–50 per cent. This is just in recognition of entering into the scheme. Secondly, if the specific productivity reaches a certain point, the worker will be paid at a double rate, a 2½-fold rate or even a 3-fold rate.'[1]

In the chemical industry, group premiums were often in use, since it was often impossible there to distinguish individual output. In a large Polish chemical plant visited by the writer the group premiums were steeply progressive and were awarded on two bases. The group received extra for exceeding the plan and for savings on raw materials. The union locals here also dealt with the assigning of 'A' and 'B' ratings for individual workers within their general job classifications.

Finally, in both Poland and Czechoslovakia, attempts were made to individualize responsibility and heighten output by special efficiency bonuses for foremen and higher personnel. With characteristic thoroughness the Czechs by 1950 had issued 'bonus scales for foundry foremen, for foremen in all sectors of the metal industry, and, on analogous principles, for technical personnel in mining. Our task now is to issue skeleton bonus scales for all pro-

[1] For example, in the rolling mill for plates where the process was not mechanized, the maximum was 200 per cent above normal piece rate; in the heat department it was 150 per cent above; in the mechanical department, 100 per cent above.

duction sectors. . . .'[1] Higher managerial personnel also were to be rewarded for unusual service by salaries above the customary for their grade, at the discretion of the general managers.[2]

For all grades of personnel, it was stated, it was essential to know directly and easily why extra pay was being given. In the case of workers, this meant premium scales that could be understood by everyone. There must be no mystification such as workers had complained of in so many of the pre-war systems. 'Our aim must be to eliminate the complex conditions affecting assessment of earnings . . . so that each wage-earner shall know at any time during his work how much he has been earning, without having to wait until pay-day to find out.'[3]

'*Socialist Output Competition*'

Various forms of production outside the regular line of duty have been practised in the Soviet Union and in all the other planned economies, their type varying with time. In Czechoslovakia and especially in Poland much early group activity took the form of 'work brigades' setting out after working hours to do emergency tasks. For example, in Warsaw in late 1947 the entire Old City, including the famous square, deeply buried in rubble, was cleared in this way by groups of citizens. Different unions also adopted specific streets of Warsaw for clearance. In general, the unions usually took a lead in brigade work.

In both countries more highly organized aid was also furnished to eke out manpower shortages in specific occupations. 'During 1949', the Czechoslovak Ministry of Labour reported, 'a total of 45,500 brigade-workers took turns in the mines, some 6,000 volunteers worked in the foundries; and over half a million were employed, for average periods of one to two weeks, in agriculture.' National youth organizations, moreover, at encampments comparable to American C.C.C. camps, though without the unemployment feature, laboured at various forms of agriculture, demolition and construction work during summer vacations. So late as 1949 when the Czechs were building their 'Gigant' pig-raising stations, most of the construction was done by volunteer youth

[1] Ministry of Labour and Social Welfare, *Report*, March 1950, p. 29.

[2] Ibid., p. 26. Here too, of course, the total of higher salaries permitted would have to fall within the allowance assigned the industry by the Ministry of Labour.

[3] Ibid., p. 30.

squads outside of Plan. In Poland the 'Service to Poland' youth organization also combined vocational training for country youth with its work programme.

The most important and highly organized form of extra labour, however, was within the workplace itself and hence quickly merged with other forms of work improvement and rationalization. This was the so-called Socialist Output Competition movement.

Again, as in the Soviet Union and in all the planned economies apparently, this movement started in Poland and Czechoslovakia as a production-and-quality race between individuals who challenged one another for a certain period of time. Then it was taken up on a team, plant, and in certain instances industry-wide basis; at which point the movement from below was met by one from above. Trade union centrals and Governments proceeded to reward and encourage the contestants most substantially, and the trade unions provided an organizational framework to carry the movement yet further.

In Poland the movement had apparently begun in one of the mines in Katowice so early as 1946 and spread from there. By early 1947 it had affected a substantial portion of the metal industry and was moving into textiles. At the time of the writer's first visit, in mid-1948, it had definitely become a mass movement in a series of industries but had not yet received any co-ordination or direction nationally. No one, even in the trade union movement at large, had been specifically charged with organizing and furthering it.

Now, however, at a plenary trade union central meeting the previous week the unions had agreed to set up a nation-wide competition organization. It was expected to get under way in another month. There was to be a central committee made up of the unions interested, of industry representatives, and of engineers. The separate national unions would have their organizations and the factories theirs. The coal industry had already set up an industry-wide organization. By 1949 it was claimed that the separate union committees had begun to analyse the practical results of the competitions and upon this basis to work on deficiencies both in pay and in production methods of their respective industries.

Up to the time of the central organization, declaring oneself a competitor had not brought any material reward, aside from the piece-rate earnings themselves. But now an Output Competition

Prize Fund was established, administered by the headquarters committee. To this the various nationalized industries, trade, and co-operatives, contributed an amount equal to 0·8 per cent of payroll. Outstanding workers might also, upon T.U.C. recommendation, be granted State decorations and tax reductions. And they would naturally be in line for promotion.

The scope of even an individual competition contract might be very broad. A number of qualifying conditions outside actual production were customarily included, in a sort of gentleman's agreement between the contestants. For example, the competitor must show no absenteeism, he must help his fellows improve their production, he must have followed safety regulations; and he would be automatically disqualified if he hurt his machine, left tools and equipment in bad condition or created an excess of spoiled work; also if he was personally disreputable or alcoholic.

Positive content of an individual contract would be quantity of production in a given time, sometimes quality of production, and —a point evidently stressed more in the more recent competitions —economizing in the use of raw materials, power, and fuel. For group competitions, yet further points would be included, such as fulfilment of the production plan ahead of time, improvement of safety and hygiene conditions, improvement of social services.

The writer discussed with an engineer, the former manager of a steel plant, who had had long experience with piece rates, the question of what happened under output competition to the production of those who refused to compete. He stated that he had observed 'an interesting psychological result'. 'We have found that in a given workplace, although only a certain group competes, it affects even the non-participants, like a magnet. Apparently even the worker who says outwardly, This does not concern me, is affected unwittingly to work better himself.'

When the writer revisited Poland in late 1949 a further stage in output competition was in evidence, combined with general rationalization of a series of related operations. This was in the large-scale building project of Muranow, referred to earlier, the quarter of workers' apartments being constructed on top of the ruins of the former ghetto of Warsaw. With extraordinarily little in the way of mechanical appliances and a great absence of hurry, small groups of workers were putting up houses of three and four stories in record time. No foremen were standing about. The workers concerned had gone into competition, and a great bulletin board on the site indicated the records of the various teams with their leaders on the different houses from day to day. The extreme rationalization of movement was obvious even to the outsider. The men, partly because of the shortage of skilled labour, had organized themselves for the most part into groups of three, one craftsman, one semi-skilled man, and a labourer. After finishing one operation on one room or house they would move on to the next, without loss of time. The different crafts, in so far as they knew one another's work, might be seen working interchangeably. What was not visible to the outsider, of course, was the technical side of the rationalization: the work of the engineers and chemists who had worked out new building materials and methods. But the labour side of the picture, and the place of a gigantic competition in it, was unmistakable.

Means of Spreading Rationalization

The years 1950–1 saw a rapid multiplication in both countries of means of making new techniques, once they were developed, available to other workers. Within the workplace itself, the giving of awards for outstanding performance or innovations took into account the willingness of the worker concerned to instruct others. If the innovation was important, after examination by works' council and management and approval at a general meeting of the workers on the job, it would move up the rungs of the trade union ladder. In Poland the process was that the district council of the union would call a conference of representatives of other establishments in the district, engaged in the same type of production, and would demonstrate the new method. (Larger establishments had a so-called instructor in rationalization and it was such men especially who would attend such a conference.) If successful on the district level, the method would travel up to the national executive of the union whose responsibility it would then be to make it known to other districts.

Exhibitions were also paying an increasingly specific part in spreading rationalizations. At a very large district exhibition organized in the autumn of 1951 in Wroclaw, workers upon leaving the exhibition were given a form asking what had interested them most. If a worker responded, he would be sent descriptions and drawings of the process concerned, so that he could show these to his fellows.

The Polish Patent Office was also furthering such publicity. It printed brief descriptions of new processes, in many thousands of copies. These were then sent to the various institutions, administrative boards and workplaces. An institution wishing to know more could thereupon write the Patent Office and receive a full description. The worker-innovator received a type of royalty upon adoptions of his device, in addition to the original premium for having made the invention.[1]

For fostering of the inventive turn of mind, there was wide diffusion of so-called rationalizers' clubs. In larger establishments the inventive workers could here meet with technicians and engineers. There were also larger city centres for such clubs, headed in Poland by the Warsaw Instructional Centre for Technique and Rationalization. And the trade unions, especially at the district level, were also said to be active in bringing together workers and scientists in their houses of culture.

3. THE LABOUR MARKET

Manpower Problems

Closely related to the problem of productivity was the problem of an optimum distribution of the national labour force. The two countries had moved into a period of tight labour markets. In Poland's case, as has already been noted, unemployment had at first been serious, especially in rural areas and small towns where

[1] This system was plainly an adaptation of one long in use in the Soviet. In the Soviet Union, besides inventions (which here as elsewhere have to meet the test of novelty) there are two recognized categories of improvements: (*a*) technical improvements, involving alteration in construction or technological process; (*b*) suggestions for rationalization of procedure, involving the use of new techniques, better use of equipment and so on. All are remunerated by a schedule according to the amount of annual saving obtained by their use. For inventions the top set in 1942 was 100,000 roubles, for technical improvements, 50,000, and for suggestions for rationalization of procedure, 25,000. The entire schedule was published in the text of the law. 'However, if no saving is realized and the invention or improvement results in better quality of production or in improvement of labour conditions or safety, the amount of remuneration is determined by the head of the establishment which accepts the suggestion.' (V. Gsovski, *Soviet Civil Law*, University of Michigan, Ann Arbor, 1949, vol. II, pp. 600–1.) 'The purpose of Soviet law governing inventions is the full and timely use of inventions . . . as well as the protection of the interests of the inventor.' (U.S.S.R., II *Civil Law* (1944), 253, quoted in Gsovski, p. 602.) By 1952 the Czechs had passed parallel legislation. Cf. I.L.O., *Industry and Labour*, vol. VIII, 1952. 'New Legislation on the Rights of Inventors in Czechoslovakia'.

industries had been destroyed and where many women after the war found themselves bereft of their menfolk. But this proved a temporary problem, met in part by the training centres and co-operative workshops set up by the Women's League, partly by the rapid growth of nationalized industry. The technical services on the other hand were at a disproportionate premium.

In Czechoslovakia, with full employment and the special man-power scarcity occasioned by the expulsion of the Germans, careful labour market planning had been essential from the outset. Both countries used more or less the same methods for labour recruitment and training, but as in many other fields the Czech system was for some time more highly organized.

Prior to 1951 the Czechoslovak Ministry of Labour and Social Welfare was in charge of the work.[1] In 1948 the writer found the Ministry speaking of its reserve powers for the actual direction of labour as important, but it appeared to have used them only negatively, i.e. to close the entrance to an overstocked trade. (This had happened, oddly enough, in the case of the furrier trade.) Permission to change from job to job was also supposedly a formal requirement, but did not seem to be administered with the strictness of American war-time regulations or those of Britain in the early post-war. In 1950 the Ministry was still writing, 'In the fulfilment of all these tasks we want to observe the voluntary principle.' Granting that 'this method of enlisting workers is perhaps a more difficult way and one requiring greater effort', it was yet 'politically and economically . . . correct'.[2]

Major emphasis was upon attracting labour into 'bottle-neck' occupations, such as coal-mining and, because of major construction needs at first, the building trades. Later, in addition to coal, more was heard of the need for younger men in iron and steel and the heavy engineering trades. In this connection it was said by 1950 that more girls were to be encouraged to go into precision engineering and light metal working than hitherto. There was also need for young men on the State Farms. And in Slovakia, where by 1950 industrial output for the first time was exceeding agricultural, the need for skilled personnel, especially in heavy industry was greater than ever: training of Slovaks in Czech institutions was therefore to be increased, while surplus untrained

[1] After that it was under a special manpower ministry, the Ministry of Working Forces. The Ministry of Labour as such had been dissolved.

[2] Ministry of Labour and Social Welfare, *Report*, March 1950.

Slovak labour was to be encouraged to come to work in Czech plants.

In Poland, by 1950, vigorous methods were being employed to secure and hold labour and technical forces. Three different laws bearing upon manpower were passed in the spring of that year. One aimed to hold in production or return to production trained engineers and certain other professional personnel who had gone over into administrative posts, one to direct new graduates of advanced schools to assigned posts, and one to check absenteeism among workers.

The law on professional personnel[1] was made operative for a period of a maximum of two years, and the types of profession to which it might be applied were subsequently defined by the Council of Ministers as including certain categories of engineers, technicians, accountants, and, on an individual basis, physicians, surgeons, and other health service specialists. The excuse given was frankly need.

'We never had enough engineers and other experts. But before the war the development of industry was very slow and it was thus unable to absorb even a modest number coming from schools. In consequence quite a number of engineers and technicians were employed in commerce, administration, etc., where they performed functions which had nothing in common with their training. During the six years of German occupation all the universities were closed. . . . The supply of experts from schools cannot fill these gaps at once. Hence the necessity to draw the existing force of experts employed in socialized economy, particularly engineers and technicians, from jobs where they cannot make use of their professional knowledge and to direct them to jobs adequate to their qualifications.

'Also the health service suffered serious shortcomings . . . impossible to secure physicians for many hospitals . . . large areas of the country where no physician was available. . . .

'This situation will improve gradually and reach a normal level . . . as new personnel from medical, nursing, and other schools become available.'[2]

The law on assigned employment for new graduates of advanced

[1] The so-called Law on Prevention of Fluctuation of Cadres, 7 March 1950 (J.L.P.R. 10, Item 107).

[2] 'Work Discipline and Planned Employment', *Review of Economic Legislation*, Warsaw, July 1950, p. 26.

schools[1] stipulated (Article 1) that such graduates 'may be obliged to work within their specialities in a defined State institution . . .' for a period of three years. The State Commission on Economic Planning was to draw up annually 'a plan of the number of graduates to be employed . . .' and the professional schools were to have a specially appointed Committee of Work Distribution for graduates.

Here the argument was need plus recompense, i.e. the return made by the citizen for his free higher education and in many cases maintenance scholarships. Unlike the law for older personnel, which was treated as a strictly emergency measure, it looked as if this law for young graduates might be a long-time institution. It followed closely a pattern long in use in the Soviet Union.

The law provided (Article 7) that, 'When issuing the order the wishes of the graduate as to the kind and place of work as well as other circumstances of personal . . . consequence' were to be taken into consideration. Also (Article 9) deferment of release from the duty could be granted 'in cases deserving special consideration and also if the graduate has been admitted to an academic school not figuring on the list'. Graduates of high schools for teachers, however (Article 10), were not to be granted deferment but 'are obliged to work in their profession for three years'. The deferment referred to in Article 9 was to be exercised especially for 'students who have proved to be particularly gifted and diligent and thus are expected to make prominent progress in further studies'. During the period of his obligation (Article 12) 'the graduate is entitled to salary and other services in accordance with . . . collective agreements'.

The law on absenteeism,[2] passed in April 1950, provided penalties both for the guilty worker and for the manager condoning him. An irregular worker could not be dismissed, but must on the contrary be penalized by wage losses combined with loss of his right to give notice.

Unjustified absence for a day was punishable by reprimand and/or loss of that day's wages; for two days, by deduction of the cor-

[1] J.L.P.R. 10, Item 106, 7 March 1950, 'Planned Employment of Graduates of Professional and Academic Higher Schools'.

[2] J.L.P.R. 20, Item 168, 'Law on Safeguarding Socialist Work Discipline'. Extensive extracts are given in *Review of Economic Legislation*, Warsaw, July 1950. An excellent summary in English is available in International Labour Office, *Industry and Labour*, Geneva, vol. IV, 1950, pp. 245–6.

responding wages; and for three days, by deduction of double the corresponding wages. This applied either to successive days or to days within the same calendar year. Since wages were ordinarily paid monthly, a worker showing absenteeism would have to finish out his month's work at the given place of employment before the deductions could be made and his record cleared. He would thus be losing for a month his right to give notice.

For four or more days of unjustified absence, i.e. 'in cases of persistent and malicious violation of work discipline . . . the offender shall be prosecuted before a Court of Common Pleas'. Thereupon 'the judicial punishment involves the obligation to remain in the same post for a period not exceeding three months, with a simultaneous reduction of from 10 per cent to 25 per cent of salary'. (Articles 7, 8.)

Responsibility for designating absence as justified or unjustified, for applying penalties for minor infringements and for submitting motions to the Court of Common Pleas rested with the manager of the workplace. 'The manager, after having heard the explanations of the worker and after having taken the opinion of the factory council or the representative of the board of the factory trade union organization, will render a decision.'[1] (Article 10, 1.) A manager deliberately reporting false circumstances for or against the justification of a worker's absence was to be liable to imprisonment for up to three months and/or a heavy fine.

In Czechoslovakia by the end of 1951 a much milder form of recruitment plan was announced. As quoted by the International Labour Office, the Czechoslovak National Planning Office had drawn up an 'Organized Recruitment Plan' to be used by the Ministry of Manpower (formerly the Ministry of Labour) for those firms and industries that would have especially heavy manpower needs under the 1952 Plan. Regional and district people's committees, 'having received prior consent of the management', were to 'establish contact with such workers as particular undertakings find it possible to release and to offer them contracts of employment in essential undertakings'. The undertakings concerned were also authorized to make 'independent efforts to secure the necessary staff . . .'.[2]

[1] The decision was to be issued in writing and was to be available to the workers on the job.

[2] Ordinance of 27 December 1951, quoted in I.L.O., *Industry and Labour*, Geneva, vol. VII, 1952, pp. 346–7.

Vocational Guidance

In Poland all vocational guidance institutions had been des-stroyed in the war and had had to be rebuilt from the ground up. Metallurgy and coal were the first to set up special vocational testing and research institutes for their industries. In Czechoslovakia no such wholesale destruction had occurred and much of the pre-war machinery of selection and personnel had been retained, sometimes with odd results, as individuals trained under old management ways were expected to adapt themselves to new. The research organization already referred to, the Institute of Human Work, in addition to its sections on rationalization and the setting of output norms, had two vocational divisions, one on selection and guidance and one on apprenticeship and vocational training. These worked in close conjunction with the Ministry of Labour and the vocational counselling service.

Mental tests were being reviewed and, as in all the planned economies, questions were being raised as to their structure and proper application. For example, it was being urged that the largest concerns, because of having a larger proportion of subdivided jobs, could well afford to take on a larger share of less qualified applicants, instead of combing the labour market for the best as had been their practice in the pre-war.[1]

The close connection possible between employment policies and the actual rationalization processes of industry is indicated in a Polish study of 1951 cited by the International Labour Office. The study aimed at better manpower utilization through a new attack upon the old problem of so-called dovetailing of seasonal trades. Comparing a pair of sharply contrasting food processing industries with respective winter and summer peaks, it recommended a double vocational training programme for their employees and also a mutual adjustment of the two industries' pay scales and working conditions, so that workers at the various levels, when seasonally redundant in one industry, would be able to pass to the other without loss of status.

The study dealt with the Industrial Meat Centre and the Industrial Vegetable and Fruit Centre at Warsaw. The common employment plan for the two, it was stated, 'should make provision for (1) the reorganization of programmes in the vocational training schools with a view to training workers capable of working in either industry, whether in the processing or the distributing of the products in question; (2) the adjustment of working conditions to make them similar in the two industries; (3) the standardization of norms of payment and payment systems so as to allow workers, according to the season, to pass from one undertaking to another without loss. (I.L.O., *Industry and Labour*, Geneva, vol. VII, 1952, p. 379.)

[1] 'When they had their own psychological laboratories they used to suck up

The system of vocational counsellors was highly developed and much more responsibility than before now rested on the counsellor's shoulders. The attempt was evidently to dovetail closely counselling with recruitment by labour market areas. The standard aimed at was to have every school-leaving child receive guidance in a series of stages described as follows.[1] Early in the final year (at age fifteen, unless the child was going on to complete secondary school) the child's teacher should have filled out a questionnaire concerning the child. By Christmas time the counsellor in the area should have assembled these questionnaires and know what the children in his area wanted. He was also to be well acquainted with local industry. Digests of the regional data were to be brought to Prague to the Planning Commission.

Meanwhile each region should have received from the Planning Commission its own detailed plan concerning work opportunities. The vocational counsellor, armed with this, was to go into the schools and lecture to the pupils. He 'cannot lie to the children', he 'therefore has to apply attraction'. 'He is able to tell them, for example, that the Coal Mines Administration now pays mining apprentices far more than other boys. Coal miners themselves may come into the schools and talk to the children.' Children in this way were 'worked upon collectively first'. They were also shown moving pictures of the various industries, paid factory visits, and so on.

It was after this background that the individual interviews came. However, the counsellor might still have some children he considered misfits insisting—or, more often, it was said, their parents insisting—on the scarce or unsuitable job. 'He cannot force them. But he can say, "There is no place for you here; better go home and think it over again." Still, in the end, he may have to yield.'

Besides the school report and the interview, the counsellor was to get his picture of the children from the teacher, doctor, and so forth. If the picture still was not clear, the child might be sent for psychological examination. In the early years of the programme some 6 to 8 per cent of the school-leaving children were receiving such an examination. As there were only about 100,000 children

the most promising young people, and then a disproportionate part of them would pick up and leave again because of boredom.' (Interview material, May 1948.)

[1] Interview material, May 1948.

a year leaving school annually in the whole Czechoslovak Republic, this would mean 6,000 to 8,000 children, not too great a number to examine carefully.

Apprenticeship

Czechoslovakia before the war had had a much more highly developed apprenticeship system than Poland, in consonance with its higher level of education generally. Subsequently Poland was trying to catch up, and both countries for some years were seeking to develop a type of interlocking general and special education that would keep doors open for all young people of secondary school age. The aims and their difficulties at that time were common to all the planned economies.

The idea was to get away from the old European—in the case of Czechoslovakia, German—patterns involving a maximum of specialization and a minimum of opportunity for later change of work or further education. Education had been bifurcated, or trifurcated, at an early age. The elementary schools did not open directly into the secondary, and those leaving them for work had at first no further educational requirement. If proficient, young workers might receive straight apprenticeship training on the job, but no more. Later this had been modified by the traditional and more or less perfunctory requirement of a stated number of hours a week at continuation school. (In Poland this requirement had been 6 hours, in Czechoslovakia 12 hours up to the age of sixteen.)

Under the post-war systems every child was to be required to continue regular education on at least a part-time basis up to the age of eighteen.[1] The regular school-leaving age had been raised to fifteen. And the intermediate three years, for those who had not gone on to general or technical secondary school but had entered industry, was in process of being filled in with apprenticeship work and schooling of an unusually many sided and long drawn out character. Industry meanwhile had to foot the bill: the 15–17-year-olds had to be paid for a full week's work—in Poland, 46 hours; in

[1] For example, the Polish decree of 9 April 1949 'stipulates that only juveniles who have a certificate attesting that they have passed through seven classes in the primary school . . . may be employed in Poland. Juveniles in employment are required to attend a middle public school, technical school, or an industrial school; the employer must require . . . a certificate of attendance. . . . The employer must release the juvenile worker for . . . 18 hours during the week, whether the teaching is given during working hours or not.' (I.L.O., *Industry and Labour*, Geneva, vol. II, 1949, p. 447.)

Czechoslovakia, 48—while 18 of the hours were spent away from the bench, at education.

For those young people who were later going to transfer to full secondary school or university the educational problem was one thing: the idea was that in three years of partial schooling they could be getting the equivalent of at least a year and a half of regular schooling. But for those who were continuing in industry, the curriculum problem was acute. The theory was not only that all children without exception should receive the benefits of a real further education; there was also apparently, at least in Czechoslovakia, a belief that all occupations without exception could have real educational content put into them.

The rub, of course, came in devising appropriate courses for the predominantly unskilled or narrowly specialized occupations, such as agriculture and the textile industry. The pattern in 1948 was to have approximately half the time of training spent on actual apprenticeship and the other half on school training. Of the school training in turn half was to be vocational in either the broad or the narrow sense and half was to be general education. The Institute of Human Work at that time was working out, in minute detail, standard courses for various industries and branches, attempting to fill in with background materials where the technical subject matter was thin.

The actual apprenticeship requirements at that time were a minimum three months' training for all school-leaving youth, and then a one, two, or three years' apprenticeship course, depending upon the nature of the industry. Except for mining, these courses were supposed to be open to girls as well as boys, and in various places one could see the young female carpenters and so on learning their trade.

Along with the enlarged apprenticeship programme had gone an enlarged system of boarding-schools or boarding-houses (*internats*) for working youth. These, too, had been a common feature in pre-war Czechoslovakia and were now extended in Poland. Especially famous in Czechoslovakia had been those at Thomas Bat'a's great plant in Zlin, now Svit, which was described in Chapter X. The *internats* catered predominantly to rural young people. Social features were much stressed here. In some cases young workers could continue living in the *internats* after they had completed their education. In both countries especial interest attached to the *internats* for mining apprentices. These boys received unusually high cash allowances and fine uniforms along with their board.

Trade education for older men was much stressed and highly organized. Financed by industry and Government, it was run by the trade unions. In Czechoslovakia a focal point of the movement was the unions' Skola Prace, or School of Work, a very large centre with various branches about the country. It operated numerous long- and short-term courses, evening and full time, for the different unions, and worked out, as the writer can aver, highly detailed educational programmes for them.

By 1951, the vocational picture had shifted once more. Dissatisfaction had been declared with the quality of the education offered in the revised continuation schools. And emphasis was laid upon the need for great numbers of seriously trained young technicians and skilled workers. In Poland, beginning with the academic year 1951–2, the 18-hour a week courses in vocational education with their corresponding reduction in work hours were to be given up altogether. Instead there were to be two types of shorter period full-time schools. One, to give a modicum of training to unskilled and semi-skilled young workers, was to provide full-time courses lasting from 5 months to 11 months for youths aged between 16 and 19. The other, to train more skilled workers, was to give introductory courses lasting from 1 year to 2 years to youths from 14 to 16. This programme followed in a general way the type of training instituted earlier in the Soviet Union. At the same time, the minimum age for general employment was raised from 15 to 16. There was also to be an expansion of the so-called technicums, the four-year technical high schools with students from 14 to 18. And within factories there was to be more systematic instruction on the job.[1] The individual worker, meanwhile, of whatever age, wishing to pursue courses of study after hours on his own account, would apparently continue to have the privilege of being freed from work for from 6 to 14 hours weekly whilst studying and of receiving 7 to 28 days' leave with pay when preparing for and taking examinations.

[1] 'Undertakings are obliged to organize and run training courses for young persons under 18 years of age employed by them. This training may be given individually, in groups, or in shifts, and should include technical work and refresher courses in the theoretical subjects connected with the young persons' jobs.' Such courses 'must terminate with an examination by a jury representing the undertaking. . . . The details of training . . . as also the method of appointment and rules of procedure for the jury shall be decided by the competent Ministers in conjunction with the head of the Central Office of Vocational Training. . . .' (I.L.O., *Industry and Labour*, Geneva, vol. VII, 1952, p. 82.)

CHAPTER XII

LABOUR AND SOCIAL SECURITY

In all the planned economies a counter-balance to extremes of wage differentiation has been the systems of social insurance and other labour amenities available on a wide basis to the working population. These systems have moreover served to take the edge off the burden for the wage earner of the high rate of national investment incident to industrialization. That all these economies regard social insurance as integral to their development can be seen from the fact that, beginning with the Soviet Union, they have established extremely broad systems, or greatly extended their old ones almost immediately, in spite of great material difficulties. And in all such systems the labour movement itself has played a decisive part.

At the outset the patterns of development followed have derived to some extent from the historical pre-war conditions of the particular country, and thus have reflected various of the classic problems of social insurance. Later on, with fuller development in a socialist direction, and with the increasing effect of Soviet example, a pattern emerges characteristic of the planned economies as such.

The Classic Problems of Social Insurance

The general development of social insurance as we have known it has been from scattered funds originally under the control of the employer,[1] to a more or less unified system under Government auspices, with more or less uniform benefits. Systems once established in a separate series of funds and benefit scales are hard to change over. But it can be done, as witness Britain to-day.

Historically, unemployment benefits were late-comers in the social insurance field, but they quickly rose to emergency proportions under it. The public had come to demand such protection more than any other kind, as can be seen from the history of the

[1] Germany under Bismarck furnished the classic example of such a system.

American Social Security Act,[1] but it was hard to include under an insurance framework. There was too much unemployment and it came too much in mass depressional forms.[2]

In the matter of financing, a whole series of problems presented themselves, a major one being the question of Government contributions and their size. Was the Government to become ultimately responsible for the solvency of the funds? This question, of course, applied particularly to unemployment benefits, but it was also important in the launching of old age programmes, before funds had accumulated, and in their alteration in times of inflation. In the case of sickness, the narrowness of medical care attached exclusively to a *quid pro quo* of previous insurance premiums led directly into the question of State responsibility for health.

An even earlier controversial question had been that of the respective shares of wage and payroll contributions in building up funds. To what extent, if any, should the worker be made by wage deductions to provide for his own security?[3] Historically the original attempt was to have the worker pay a major share; subsequently the employer's share was pushed up, and the State's added. In the case of serious unemployment, either the State's share had to become major, as in England in the 1930's, or the entire system broke down, as in Germany. The American system was not set up until after the last depression.

With periods of inflation following the last war a further edge was given the question of the State's share in financing. General taxation, being current, could of course take account of current price levels; whereas the proceeds of past payroll taxes could not. Old-age pensioners in France, for example, could hardly be expected to live on the pre-war franc. The same problem, in less acute form, has faced all provision on classic insurance principles.

[1] The original Act was to have stimulated bills in the several states for unemployment benefit only; it was only at the last moment that benefits for the aged were added and made Federal. Sickness benefits have never been provided in America.

[2] Sir William Beveridge turned the corner of the dilemma by going outside his insurance system and positing that a number of policy measures could and would be taken that would never allow unemployment in Britain to reach depression levels again. (*Full Employment in a Free Society*, 1944; *Social Insurance and Allied Services*, 1942.)

[3] In Britain all contributions for all forms of insurance have always included the worker, but they have also included the Government. In the United States unemployment contributions have been by the employer alone, old age contributions are joint: but in neither case does the Government contribute anything.

Some able students of the social security problem have accordingly viewed the line of progress as running away from the payroll method of provision altogether, and in the direction of final assumption of responsibility by the State through general taxation.[1] Whatever may be thought of this conclusion, it is not the method pursued by the existing planned economies.

The Soviet and Planned Economy Pattern of Social Insurance

The Soviet Union first set up the framework of its unified social insurance system at the beginning of the 1920's when the country's economy was still in ruins. All benefits were to be at the expense of the employer and the system was extremely comprehensive. Provision for unemployment compensation at that time was included in it. By 1931, when the economy had recuperated and the first Five-Year Plan was under way, involuntary unemployment was declared to have been ended and contributions and benefits for it ceased to be payable. Whatever may be thought of the move, certainly there has at no time since then been any recession in the country's economic activity. Industrial production, except in enemy-occupied territory during the war, has continued to go up rapidly and the drain on manpower from the country-side has been constant.

The example set by the Soviet Union has been followed at a greater or less remove by all the countries of planned economy. Each of them has endeavoured to set up a system of social insurance benefits on a very broad base, far beyond what would ordinarily be considered corresponding to its level of economic development generally. And each of them has excluded unemployment benefits from it.

In all cases the tendency has been fourfold: (1) As aforesaid, exclusion of unemployment from the list of calamities provided against. Purely transitional unemployment is characteristically provided for by other means. (2) A closely integrated and complete single system, to provide succour for all other disabilities. Except for its inner structure, this system can be compared roughly to the unification secured under the Beveridge Plan. (3) The opera-

[1] Cf. E. M. Burns. 'Social Insurance in Evolution,' *Amer. Econ. Review Supple.*, March 1944: 'In a country . . . where . . . this policy [publicly guaranteed minimum income] is regarded as a first charge upon annual appropriations, there is no risk to the objectives of the program in merging social insurance financing with the general budget.' (p. 207.)

tion of the system, both nationally and locally, by the trade unions, the provision of most benefits taking place directly at the place of work. This feature is unique with the planned economies. (4) The separation of medical services from cash benefits, and their administration by a National Ministry of Health (again comparable to the British system of 1948). In the Soviet Union health services had from the outset been free and universal, in spite of the extremely low level of economic development prevailing in the country at the time. In the 'people's democracies' these services are to-day in various stages of evolution from being tied in with social insurance provisions,[1] and hence available on a free basis to only the urban working population and their families,[2] to becoming truly universal. In any case, the level of distribution of the health services is high, in proportion to the rest of the economic development of these countries. (5) Retention of the nomenclature and part of the financial contributions of the conventional social insurance systems, but with a change of financial content. Individual benefits are no longer tied in to past individual contributions, whether by or on behalf of the given beneficiary. Instead they are, broadly speaking, charged as an additional cost to current payrolls generally. The significance of this will be discussed presently.

The Czechoslovak System[3]

In the individual 'people's democracies' the initial characteristics of their new social insurance systems have naturally varied with the stage of destruction of previous systems occasioned by the war, with the degree of social revolution in existence at the time the post-war systems were formulated, and with the level of living of the economies.

In Czechoslovakia the pre-war social insurance system had been advanced for its time.[4] It had provided a high level of medical care

[1] Public health provision for epidemic and major infectious diseases, as well as prevention work, has of course never been tied in with social insurance. It has been developed on a major scale since the war.

[2] State Farm employees are of course also included. But their number is not great. Poland and Czechoslovakia have also begun to have State Farms' medical and nursing personnel give free service to neighbouring farm producers' co-operatives.

[3] Cf. D. W. Douglas, 'Social Security in Czechoslovakia,' *Social Service Review*, Chicago, Sept., 1950.

[4] All but its unemployment features. The system in use had been the

institutions and had numerous provisions for sickness, accident, injury, old age and maternity benefits. There had also been some participation of representatives of the beneficiaries in the various governing bodies in the insurance centrals. However, administration was exceedingly complex. There were separate insurance systems for different categories of employees and a multiplicity of different insurance centrals and branches. There were also differences in the benefits granted non-manual workers as versus manual.[1] The system received no contributions from the State, costs being divided evenly between employer and employee. Under German occupation the funds had been partially despoiled. But after the war the previous system was restored for a time with temporary changes.

Czechoslovakia's new Act was introduced immediately after the February events of 1948. The proposed legislation had, however, been in the hands of Parliament, in committee, for a considerable period before that, and its nature bears evidence of the struggles and compromises of that period.

Projects for a new law had begun to be formulated so early as the Occupation period, and in accepting the Košice Programme in April 1945, the Beneš Government had pledged itself to the creation of a single national insurance system. However, although the Trade Union Council promptly proceeded to elaborate its project, it was two years before it was possible to get it considered politically by the six National Front parties of the time; and it was the better part of another year (January 1948) before it was possible for these to reach agreement and present the final Bill as a joint project to Parliament. By this time opposition in the party press had reached an acute point. The press of the National Socialist Party in particular was irreconcilable with the position taken by its party's experts on the commission. A stalemate was in sight.

It was at this juncture that the February events changed the political picture. Passage of the National Insurance Act had been

'Ghent' system, of trade union out of work benefits subsidized in equal shares by the government, without employer contributions.

[1] It was maintained subsequently that their splitting-up into special privilege categories was intended to split the common interest of these groups. The distinction had become particularly marked in the 1934 revision of the law, when white-collar benefits, in face of depression conditions, were increased, while manual workers' benefits were cut.

a prime demand of the Congress of Works' Councils. The Beneš Government agreed to back the Act and a government commission was at once appointed to go over it; a month later the commission's report was accepted by the Government, and after another month Parliament adopted the Bill in its final form.

The new Act provided that at an unspecified time in the future all benefits were to be paid for exclusively by the undertakings, at that time still in part private. But for the time being, it was stated, contributions from wages were to continue. All the previously separate social insurance centrals were amalgamated, with a decrease of overhead costs and personnel. However, at that time the administration of the new central agency remained autonomous, an insurance instution *per se*, with only partial participation by representatives of the trade unions. By 1951 the whole machinery was in process of being transferred into the hands of the unions.

Very great emphasis at the time of the passage of the new law was laid upon the 'national' character of the legislation. By this was meant, not only the centralization of funds and administration referred to above, but the extension of coverage of the system to include the self-employed as well as wage and salary earners. Indeed in the original version of the Act it was to include farmers as well. A subsequent amendment excluded individual farmers, temporarily, it was stated.[1] The cost of thus extending coverage would, of course, have been considerable, and it would have required a tax from the farmers themselves to which they were unaccustomed.

The new scales of benefit were much more generous than previously, total benefits being approximately doubled. The various forms of benefit were also closely integrated, so that a beneficiary would not fall between stools, and several new forms of benefit were introduced that were said to be original with the Czechoslovak system.[2]

[1] By early 1950 a Ministry of Labour report stated that under the amendment 'exemplary' United Agricultural Co-operatives were to be admitted to health insurance benefits, even though they had no employer to help defray the cost. 'We want National Insurance to play its part', said the Minister of Labour, 'as an effective instrument in increasing the productivity of labour. Therefore we must make the services of National Insurance available first of all to those who . . . introduce new working methods. . . .' (Ministry of Labour and Social Welfare, *Report*, March 1950, p. 51.)

[2] For example, 'housewives' pensions', for the house-working wife of the insured when incapacitated.

The health system at that time remained attached to the insurance central; there was no establishment of a universal free public health service. However, coverage was extremely extensive, health services free of charge accruing to all insured persons and their families, including dependent relatives.[1] It was thought at the time that with the inclusion under insurance of farmers as well as other self-employed, free services would be available to 95 per cent of the population.

The costs of the new system were to be high, nearly 18 per cent of payroll,[2] contribution rates being 10 per cent for old age and invalidity, 1 per cent for accidents, and 6·8 per cent for sickness. This was in addition to Government subventions. The total burden on the national income was expected to be about 13 per cent as compared to the old system's 8 per cent, with joint payroll and wage taxes meeting almost three-fourths of the extra costs and the Government something over one-fourth.

It was stated that this appeared to the State Planning Commission to be about as much of current income as the country could afford to apportion from the earning portion of the population to the non-earning. In this connection it was suggested that the retention, for the present, of worker contributions would serve to bring home to the working population the real costs of such a system.

Thus the problem was formulated in April 1948, at the time that the new social insurance law and its attached documentation, a substantial volume, went to press.[3] By 1949 a 'Minor Amendment' to the Act had been passed, postponing, as indicated above, its application for the present to the bulk of farmers. And by 1951, a previously promised 'Major Amendment' had been added, transferring the operation of the whole system into the hands of the trade unions. In addition, a beginning was made of transferring all the health functions of the previous Insurance Central to the Public Health Service. The Ministry of Labour and Social Welfare

[1] Brothers and sisters, as well as children, grandchildren, parents and grandparents.

[2] Properly speaking, of the 'basis of assessment', a somewhat more inclusive term, coined by the Czechoslovaks to denote the basic scales of earned income imputed not only to wage and salary earners, but to the self-employed and farmers as well.

[3] An excellent translation into English is available, prepared for the 1948 session of the International Labour Organization, *Czechoslovak National Insurance: A Contribution to the Pattern of Social Security*, Orbis, Prague, May 1948.

was abolished as such, its manpower functions going over to a Ministry of Working Forces, and its welfare features being transferred to the unions.

The Polish System

Poland's pre-war social insurance system had been less extensive than the Czechoslovak, but it, too, had been non-contributory as far as the Government was concerned, with joint financing by workers and employers all along the line, and its administration also had been divided among a series of separate centrals. Distinctions between manual and non-manual workers' benefits had been even more marked than in Czechoslovakia.

In Poland war-time destruction and despoiling of funds had been so much more severe that there was no chance to revive existing benefit systems. Moreover the new Government was more radical than that of Czechoslovakia. The original Committee of National Liberation had already in September 1944 decreed that henceforth all insurance payments were to be at the expense of the employer.

During the next few years, cash benefits were gradually increased, beginning with the present working forces and their families. Family allowances, available only to the children of workers and employees, were begun in 1948 and subsequently added to. Old age benefits perforce remained at a much lower level. The range of insured occupations was increased, benefit periods were lengthened, and naturally with the sharp growth of industry the proportion of the national population that came under insurance went up rapidly.

Meanwhile the range of health services had also increased greatly, starting from a low point immediately after the war when much medical personnel had been lost without replacements and much of material facilities had been destroyed. Public sanitary and preventive services worked together with industrial physicians and insurance doctors. The sources of funds and the various administrations differed, but many of the patients were the same. Polish writers reviewing this period make much of the fact that insurance medicine was already operating on different and broader principles than before.[1] However, the organization of the separate

[1] 'The organization of separate health services for the insured, in pre-war Poland amounting to about 16 per cent of the population, could of course be criticized from the point of view of comprehensiveness and rationality. But

insurance centrals remained as before, and so until 1950 did the multiplicity of medical authorities. In that year two preliminary laws were passed providing partial amalgamation of the insurance funds and extending the general authority of the Ministry of Health over insurance medicine.

The passage of a complete new social insurance law was thus delayed in Poland much longer than it had been in Czechoslovakia.[1] It was only by early 1952 that the new legislation was due to be presented. By the same token, the changes embodied piecemeal in Czechoslovakia had a chance to be presented as a whole and at the outset of the new legislation in Poland.

It was foreseen that the new law would, following Czechoslovakia in 1951, and Hungary and Bulgaria somewhat earlier, adopt the pattern first established by the Soviet Union in 1932: that is, abolish altogether the Ministry of Labour and Social Welfare and divide its welfare functions between the trade unions on the one hand and the Ministry of Health on the other. Only in the case of Poland, the transfer of social insurance administration to the trade unions could take place simultaneously with the final unification of the existing insurance centrals and funds, not at several years' remove.[2]

considering the set-up of the separate-fee institutions of social insurance at the time, there was as a matter of fact no other possibility.... It is worth remembering that (workers' attempts at health protection) . . . had to be argued as side issues to insurance interests. In order to justify the creation of their own hospitals, etc., they had to appeal to the savings that would be effected in the payments required for the sick and invalids, as if health protection itself were not a sufficient motive. . . . Under socialism . . . it is different.' (Roman Garlicki 'Foundations and Significance of the Present Reform in the Structure of Social Insurance', *Praca i Opieka Spoleczna* (Labour and Social Protection), Warsaw, July–August 1950, p. 83.)

Cf. E. M. Burns, op. cit., p. 199. 'It [the original, classic form of social insurance] was the ideal instrument for effecting a significant break in the deterrent treatment of insecure workers, because its apparent analogy with private insurance made the change acceptable to a society which was dominated by business ethics and which stressed individual economic responsibility.'

[1] 'Notwithstanding the profoundly significant transformation of social insurance in contents and extent in the course of the past six years of People's Poland . . . the basis structure dating from 1934–5 remained unchanged up to the first half of 1950.' (Garlicki, p. 80.) Even then the changes were slight, anticipating the general transformation of structure to come in 1952.

[2] In general terms the first Trade Union Congress in Poland in 1945 had already put forth the demand for the transfer of social insurance to the trade unions.

As to the scope of the social insurance, Poland had never made the attempt to make her legislation 'national' in the sense originally intended by Czechoslovakia, i.e. to include the self-employed and the individual peasants under it. Of course Czechoslovakia, even in 1948, had hardly more than half as large a proportion of peasant population as Poland had in 1952. It is noteworthy that the Soviet Union, also with a large peasant population, even though it was engaged in a collective farm system of agriculture, had never made such an attempt either. Cash benefits there were exclusively the affair of the collective farmers' mutual aid societies,[1] although, of course, collective farmers as well as all other citizens benefited from the free National Health Service.

The absolute level of benefit provisions, in cash as well as kind, would obviously have to remain for a long time lower in Poland than in Czechoslovakia, because of lower incomes and incomparably less initial equipment. But in terms of proportion of the total national wages bill, direct costs appeared very similar. In 1951 the sums laid down in the National Plan (i.e. for social insurance proper, exclusive of 'Social Action', etc.) ran to 15·5 per cent of payroll. This, it will be seen, in percentage terms approximated fairly closely to Czechoslovakia's 17 to 18 per cent.[2]

Analysis and Comparison of the Two Systems

As we have seen, by 1951–2 both countries were in process of turning over their cash benefit systems to the administration of the trade unions and their medical care systems to the Ministry of Health. Actual distribution of benefits by the trade unions at the place of work however had begun earlier.

As to coverage, as a more urbanized country Czechoslovakia of course had fewer persons outside her insurance system. By 1950, however, Poland had very close to 50 per cent of her population covered.

In both countries, the qualifying of an individual for benefit, once he was working in a covered occupation, was easy. In Czechoslovakia the mere fact of present employment served as sufficient

[1] Wage earners on State Farms, in the Soviet Union as in all the planned economies, are of course insured.

[2] However, in Poland family allowances are included as a special branch of social insurance, in Czechoslovakia they are outside. On the other hand, in terms of direct pressure on wages, it must be remembered that half of Czechoslovakia's 17 to 18 per cent premiums were as yet paid by the worker.

qualification for sick benefit. In Poland the worker qualified for sick benefit of all kinds after four weeks of employment; but in case of an acute or infectious disease he qualified from the first day of work here also. In the case of old-age benefits in both countries, a four-to-five-year period of employment was required. With the great extension of occupational coverage in recent years there was thus in both countries a problem of those aged who could not at present qualify. In the case of Czechoslovakia, a special form of eleemosynary pension known as 'social benefit' was established at a statutory but lower rate of pay than the regular pension. For the initial years of the system's operation many persons were expected to qualify only for this.

In both countries transitional unemployment was cared for by special measures. Czechoslovakia provided vocational training provisions under the Ministry of Labour, coupled with temporary cash benefits, outside the social insurance system. The Ministry's fund was supported by a ½ per cent payroll tax and a similar sum provided by Government.

In terms of percentage of the original wage, benefits in both countries ran high. In Poland, because of war-time destruction, first emphasis had had to be concentrated on the main field, that of the shorter-time benefits of the active worker and his family, while the smaller field of long-time pensioners' care, had been allowed to wait longer to have its standards built up. This latter form of benefit had naturally borne the main brunt of the wiping out of all pre-war reserves.[1] Thus sickness and accident benefit in Poland ran 70 per cent of wages, with somewhat more for the lowest wages and less for the higher. Old age pensions, on the other hand, in spite of having been trebled since 1946, ran in 1951 at only about 40 per cent of wages. They were, however, about to be increased further. In Czechoslovakia, with its lesser degree of destruction and possibly with its lesser emphasis upon industrialization in 1947–8, a much greater proportion of funds was assigned, at least potentially, to the care of the aged. Under the Czechoslovak law, sickness benefits, sharply scaled to favour the lowest wage earners, averaged about 50 per cent of wages. Pensions, at age sixty after twenty years of work in insured occupations, also ran about 50 per cent. Of course, for the present many pensioners

[1] Cf. Franciszek Krogulski, 'The Development of Social Insurance after the War in Figures', *Praca i Opieka Spoleczna* (*Labour and Social Welfare*), Warsaw, January–February 1951.

would have served less than that, and so might get anything above the minimum of about 25 per cent of the average wage. But potentially the rates ran very high, to a maximum of 85 per cent of actual wages.[1] Once the system was well established it looked as if a large proportion of pensioners might approximate the 85 per cent limit.

In both countries maternity benefit was at 100 per cent of wages and ran for a long period, in Czechoslovakia for eighteen weeks, in Poland, prior to the passage of the new law, for twelve weeks. There were also cash grants at the birth of a child.

Medical care was altogether free for insured persons and their families, including dependent relatives. But latterly Poland had introduced a charge of 10 per cent of the cost of medicines used in the home, to prevent waste, it was stated; medicines given out in clinics or institutions remained free.

Certain class differentials previously existing in the level of benefits granted were removed in both countries, and in both there was a beginning of attempts to create some new differentials of a different sort. Non-manual workers had formerly had longer vacations and more favourable pension terms than manual. These distinctions were now abolished. On the other hand, all round higher benefits, sharply distinguishing them from other workers, were granted to miners, as being engaged in both an essential and a hard occupation. Miners qualified for pensions earlier, received much higher sickness and accident compensation, and had longer annual holidays. It was intended to extend this system to other arduous trades.

As to methods of financing, it will be recalled that both systems intended to rely entirely upon enterprise contributions, although the Czech law provided for wage deductions as well, as a temporary measure. This was in accord with the principles originally applied in the Soviet Union and long demanded elsewhere by radical workers, 'insurance at the expense of the employer'. But why should this principle have been adhered to, once all, or virtually all, employing enterprises were State-owned?[2]

[1] The scale ran from age 60 after 5 years' insurance to age 65 after 30 years' insurance.

[2] It might, of course, be thought that in a socialist society the difference between wage and payroll deductions would itself become unimportant, that it would be merely a matter of book-keeping on which side of the ledger that particular section of the national wages fund should be placed. The worker's

The principle, it could be argued, can undoubtedly be of great importance during a transitional, mixed-economy stage. Such was certainly the case in the early period of social insurance provisions in the Soviet Union, when the requirement of paying heavy payroll taxes was an added means of siphoning funds from the private employer, such funds forming unquestionably a net addition to wages. The same thing holds true in China to-day,[1] where a 1951 law provides social insurance benefits financed by the employer for all large establishments in the country. But once an economy is socialized, why adhere to the payroll basis of collection at all? Would not straight State support be simpler? And how about the positive advantages claimed elsewhere for financing out of general current taxation? That is, its spreading of costs from the particular enterprise to those most able to pay in society generally?[2]

Apparently in these societies the functions of general taxation are no longer regarded in this way. Actually the chief sources of public revenue are the taxes paid by the nationalized industries in any case; income tax, on the other hand, plays a very minor role. Under such circumstances, the only way to shift the incidence of social security costs away from the industries of the country to any extent would be to shift it on to the farmer—and this is the very opposite of what these countries are trying to do when they are seeking to bring farmers on to mechanize and improve their agriculture by selling them machinery and chemical fertilizers cheaply.

Conversely, a heavy payroll tax upon a given industry does not operate here to set any necessary ceiling upon that industry's wages nor to make it restrict operations. The relative profitability of different industries is already planned for, and their expansion or contraction takes place upon quite other principles. A good illustration would be the high social security costs, combined with high wage costs, set for the mining industry—in spite of the fact

instinct, however, probably remains sound here: a pay cheque unencumbered represents one aspect of the job's status, its social security perquisites another; and in a socialist society as well as a capitalist, the two can operate separately as well as jointly.

[1] Chu Hsueh-fan, 'Labour Insurance in New China', *People's China,* Shanghai 1 May 1951.

[2] The argument about its freedom from past price fluctuations apparently does not apply here, since all these countries claim to be achieving stability and avoid building up large reserves.

that the price of coal is kept low. Coal prices and the degree of expansion of the mining industry are based upon the needs for fuel in other industries and upon foreign exchange.

The positive advantages felt for the payroll tax are probably its clarity and directness. It forms a convenient means for expressing the real relationship between current wage bills and security payments and thus focuses attention upon the means of lessening the hazards and disabilities of different employments and upon the real costs to the community of each set of payments.

In discussing points of view, administrators of the new systems made much of the distance they had travelled from the original private insurance conception which in their opinion dominated the older systems. Classic social insurance represented a claim to specific benefits corresponding to the kinds and amounts of previous contributions either by or on behalf of the beneficiary. Now the ideas of the 'actuarial balance', of 'saving' for 'one's own' security, of a *quid pro quo* accounting on an individual basis, of the building-up of national reserves from the 'past' to take care of the 'future'—all these were to go. Instead, society was to be regarded as a living body that did not, like its individual members, grow old. It was continually supported by the current labours of the present working population and continually had to take care of those not yet or no longer able to work. Social security fulfilled this latter function. What proportion of current production should be thus set aside for the current needs of the non-workers might be an open question; but note that both sides of the equation were considered current. The matter was clearly put by the Czechoslovak Minister of Labour in introducing the new Czechoslovak Act to the public in 1948:

'A society living within a certain territory is a permanent and self-renewing organism, consisting, first of all, of working members, further, of members about to become able to work, and finally of persons no longer able to work because of sickness, disability, or advanced age. All three groups of the population must be supported *from the current results of work*: it is the duty of the working members to devote part of the fruits of their labour to the care of those other two groups. . . . It is clear from these considerations that the current benefit of social insurance must be financed from funds provided from the current national income.'[1]

[1] *Czechoslovak National Insurance: A Contribution to the Pattern of Social Security*, Prague, 1948. Introduction by Evzen Erban, pp. 17–18 (italics mine).

Other Forms of Social Benefit

Although social insurance is the largest of the protections afforded the worker, it is treated as only part, and the oldest part, of a whole. Emphasis is put upon the connectedness of the various benefits, their mass character, and the closeness of their administration to the individual worker.

The total amount of effective supplement to cash earnings outside of insurance would be difficult to assess, but it has unquestionably been substantial. A Polish administrator estimated total social insurance benefits, in cash and kind, in Poland during 1949–50 as having amounted to an addition to wages of between 18 and 20 per cent.[1] And for total social benefits of all sorts during 1950, the trade unions estimated an addition of nearly 40 per cent. The difficulty of assessment can readily be made clear. The matter of housing itself should properly be included in part under the head of social benefits, since workers' new housing has been heavily subsidized by industry and Government, and rents are correspondingly cheap. Old housing also has had its rentals frozen at far below present costs. Thus in the new housing developments of the Skoda works near Plzen in 1948, approximately half the total costs, including upkeep, were being borne by the concern, and another fraction by the Government in return for adherence to certain building standards. In Poland average housing costs for wage earners were said to run from 4 to 10 per cent of earnings; in Czechoslovakia perhaps from 8 to 10 per cent. However, Czech rentals might be graded according to the income of the renter, so that the same apartment might cost less to one man than another. (In the Skoda housing project referred to above, the rent for an identical apartment appeared to vary about one-third from the lowest paid manual worker to the best paid white-collar worker. Of course there were also different rentals for apartments of different sizes; but the idea seemed to be, not to force a large family into an apartment built for a small one for money reasons alone.) On the other hand, housing was also being used to some extent as a labour market force: miners and other especially needed kinds of workers received housing priority, and so did 'leading workers' in any trade.

Family allowances and 'education allowances' also made a net

[1] Roman Garlicki, 'Social Insurance as a Factor Improving the Condition of the Working Masses', *Praca i Opieka Społeczna* (*Work and Social Welfare*), Warsaw, January–February 1951.

addition to budgets. The payments were so rated as to mean most to the lowest wage earners. In Poland when the allowances were first introduced in 1948 the allowances for wife and three children were said to make approximately a 50 per cent addition to an unskilled worker's wage, and were subsequently raised further. (Children after the first child had higher allowances: for the third and subsequent children 140 per cent of basic.) Education allowances in both Poland and Czechoslovakia could be continued during higher education up to twenty-four years.

Other cash perquisites above a straight wage were the provisions for overtime pay and paid vacations. These were embodied in basic law, increased to some extent by the provisions of collective agreements. Poland had a basic 46-hour week, Czechoslovakia a 48-hour one. (The Polish law represented a reversion to the standard won during the revolutionary period following World War I and subsequently lost again.) Both countries had an 8-hour day, with less for dangerous trades. (In Poland under a 1950 law, 6, $6\frac{1}{2}$, 7, and $7\frac{1}{2}$ hours for trades of varying severity.) For the shortened hours wages might not be cut. Overtime work, where permitted, was paid at time-and-a-half rates for the first two hours, double time after that. In 1950 the Czechoslovak Ministry of Labour was urging that more afternoon shifts be introduced instead of permitting so much recourse to overtime.

Paid vacations of considerable length were granted by law. In Poland a 1950 revision required 12 days'[1] paid vacation after 1 year's service in a given establishment, 15 days after 3 years, and 1 month after 10 years.[2] Here, too, there was additional allowance for hard or dangerous occupations, following a precedent set in the so-called Miners' Charter of 1948. In the building industry, seasonal workers, in lieu of paid vacations received a corresponding wage supplement. Even in agriculture overtime and vacation pay for hired labour was required. Summer overtime rates began

[1] I.e. 12 working days, or really 2 weeks.

[2] Cf. Annual Holidays Amendment Act of 20 March 1950, described in I.L.O., *Industry and Labour*, Geneva, vol. III, 1950, p. 268. 'Under the new Act all manual workers in industry, mining, commerce, offices and other branches, as specified in the Act, will be entitled to 12 days' annual leave with pay after 1 year of continuous employment; 15 days after 3 years; and 1 month after 10 years of such employment. It is also provided that the Government may issue Orders granting additional leave to workers in specified laborious or unhealthy occupations.'

after 10 hours and workers were to receive 12 to 20 days of paid vacation a year.[1]

Benefits in kind of many sorts were probably more important than cash. Even in the social insurances the effort was being made to throw more and more of the increases in that direction. In Poland the addition of children's allowances in 1948 and their increase in 1949 had for the time being greatly increased the proportion of cash benefits in the social insurances as versus benefits in kind. They had risen to over 70 per cent. But with the expansion of the national health service in succeeding years it was obvious that the current would flow the other way. In Czechoslovakia even under the 1948 insurance law, the greatest expansion had been planned for the benefits in kind, and these already amounted to 60 per cent of the total. Such increases were said to help all the working population and to be of especial benefit to children. Outside the social insurances came a great variety of agencies for mother and child welfare, known in Poland as Social Action. These included mother- and child-care stations, crèches, nursery schools, out-of-school care, children's preventoriums, and so-called rest homes. Parents able to pay paid from 10 to 20 per cent of the costs for the child's food, etc., but not for staff and overhead.[2] And from a fifth to a half of the parents benefited in any given workplace might be excused from fees altogether. The works' council in each establishment was assigned the task of setting the fees and exonerating the lowest-income families. Funds for Social Action were provided in part by industry and in part by one or another agency of the State, but all were planned for as part of the National Economic Plan.

Works' Councils in Administration

The extent to which administration of social benefits was brought close to participating workers was also difficult to assess, but there seemed to be participation at many levels. The women's and young workers' committees of whom mention has been made

[1] Originally this law was framed to apply to hired workers on larger private farms (50 acres for grain, 8 for truck) as well as on State farms. But in 1951 the private farm clause was dropped.

[2] In a neighbourhood nursery school in Warsaw the children were receiving 1,800-calories-a-day meals of excellent quality for which the mother paid from 10 to 15 per cent of the cost wholesale—her only expense. The children could be left for 9 hours. Teachers were provided by the Ministry of Education.

earlier, appeared to be active in asserting the rights of their members not only in matters of wages and working conditions but in social benefits also. There were also workers on so-called 'social commissions' whose duty it was to supervise the justice of claims and allocations. And the direct distribution of the major part of insurance benefits had for some time been under the local works committees at the place of work itself.

In Poland the process had begun with family allowances. From their inception in 1948, all allowances in establishments of over four had been distributed by the local works' committees. The method proving successful, and following the example of the Soviet Union, in 1950 and 1951 the works' councils, first in large plants, then in all medium-sized and a portion of small plants as well, were given the more difficult task of adjudging and distributing sickness benefits. It was to them that the physician reported and the worker appealed. Only pensions for the aged and for long-time invalids were still being handled outside the place of work. In Czechoslovakia the process had been brought to a conclusion earlier: by 1951 the trade unions had become sole operators of the insurance system, and the local works' councils administered the benefits.

At the same time the complementary feature of 'social insurance delegates', also first developed in the Soviet Union, was introduced in both countries. The size of this latter movement was intended to be very great, with all subdivisions of the work place having delegates.[1]

[1] In early 1951 elections in Poland, well over one hundred thousand social insurance delegates had been elected.

In addition to social insurance delegates, both countries had introduced 'social factory inspectors'. Thus the Polish Social Factory Inspection Act of 4 February 1950 provided for elective inspectors operating under the management of the trade unions. They were to check on management's adherence to the terms of collective agreements and to industrial safety, pay and hours of work regulations. They were also to supervise the labour protection aspects of the establishment's technical set-up. 'The inspectors are appointed for a term of 1 year, on [*sic*] the result of an election by the general meeting of the personnel. . . . Any person belonging to the trade union, who is employed in the establishment in a non-managerial capacity and is not responsible for any inspection duty on behalf of management, may be elected as inspector. . . .' (I.L.O., *Industry and Labour*, Geneva, vol. III, 1950, p. 453.) Inspectors were to be paid at normal wages for time spent, from 10 to 30 hours a month. They were empowered to make written recommendations to management for the remedying of abuses, after submitting them to the works' council for approval. 'If the

Writers on social administration in these countries make a great deal of the de-bureaucratizing effect of work place activity. Thus a Polish student of the problem maintains that combining the previous small funds and insurance centrals into a single system would have had the danger of removing it still further from the working masses, unless there was a very distinct organization of workers' direct administration. This would be the only way to prevent bureaucratization of the system. And this direct administration he saw beginning.

'If we are speaking of the direction of development of social insurance (this was written in 1950), we must take account not only of the changes in structure of the legal organs (the beginnings of centralization) but also of such facts as the creation of social insurance committees in each work place, the payment of sick benefits in each work place, and the entrusting to each work place of the distribution of family allowances. . . . It is a fact that the executive functions of social insurance are more and more coming together in the area of the work place itself, although as yet they are carried out through three separate agencies: the trade unions, the industry, and the insurance institution.' He goes on to say that future development will undoubtedly concentrate upon the unions the entire task of administration 'in this same place of work.'[1]

Further Services in Kind

In both countries expenditures for health facilities by the employed individual had become negligible, and even convalescent treatment, in so far as it was available, was virtually free. In Czechoslovakia the fine health resorts of the country, spas as well as sanatoriums and preventoriums, had been nationalized after February 1948; in both countries their number was being added to by the taking over of former estates.

action necessary to remedy an unsatisfactory situation requires the transformation of existing work places . . . and it is impossible . . . to take action within the limits of current expenditure, the inspector must submit . . . a recommendation that provision for the necessary capital expenditure should be included in the financial plan for the coming year.' Major recommendations approved by the trade union concerned could go up to the district labour inspector for hearings, orders, and, if necessary, prosecution for enforcement. (Ibid., p. 454.)

[1] Roman Garlicki, 'Foundations and Significance of the Present Reform in the Structure of Social Insurance', *Prace i Opieka Spoleczna* (*Labour and Social Welfare*), July–August 1950, p. 87.

Vacations could also be spent cheaply at nationalized resorts, in so far as places were open. Boarding-houses and hotels now bore the signs of trade unions and Government agencies over their doors, and the streets of resorts were crowded with workers and their families. The division of vacation costs in Poland in 1950 was said to be: workers, 30 per cent; industry and Government each 35 per cent. The railroads also granted greatly reduced fares. By 1950 the Central Council of Trade Unions had set up a special body to develop further holiday facilities, the Workers' Vacation Fund. That year over half a million workers had spent their holidays at resorts.[1]

Also forming a part of the standard of living outside of wages were the numerous free cultural facilities provided for workers. In Poland a grant equalling ½ per cent of payroll of State undertakings was transmitted periodically from the industries to the unions for cultural purposes, and a smaller amount for sports. Poland had also set up in 1948 a general assessment equalling 5 per cent of payroll for social services. In Czechoslovakia at this time all concerns contributed 10 per cent of profits for both social services and cultural facilities. By 1950 Poland also instituted a profits plan, adding the incentive, developed earlier in the Soviet Union, of distinguishing between 'planned' and 'above-plan' profits. 'In the Soviet Union a socialist enterprise allots a certain part of the yearly profit for social requirements of the staff of the enterprise. Following this example, the Law of 4 February 1950, provides for an Establishment Fund in Industrial State enterprises. The fund . . . is composed of 1 to 4 per cent of the previous year's planned profit and 10 to 30 per cent of the beyond-the-plan profit . . . unless the latter profit was obtained by reasons outside the competency of the enterprise.'[2]

[1] Outstanding workers in both countries received priority in places at rest homes and resorts. They also often received first chance at new housing.

[2] *Review of Polish Law*, Quarterly, Year IV, Nos. 3–4, Warsaw 1950. These sums were to go for above-plan investments in cultural facilities and above-plan housing, as well as for current social expenditure and rewards for outstanding workers.

In July 1950 Czechoslovakia also revised its profits law. The Unified Workers' Fund that it had set up in 1948 under the united trade union organization was now to distribute up to 10 per cent of net (planned) profits and up to 50 per cent of above-plan profits to individual establishment funds. The amounts to be assigned were to vary in accordance with the productivity and also the importance of the branch concerned. (Cf. I.L.O., *Industry and Labour*, Geneva, vol. V, 1951, pp. 414–16.)

In addition, standard collective agreements in Poland required the concern to furnish suitable space for a recreation room, and in undertakings of over 200 workers, a paid full-time director chosen in agreement with the trade union. Workers' club-houses adjacent to factories were a common sight in both countries, often housed in the premises of former managerial personnel. They were heavily patronized. In various of the larger cities there were also full-sized 'Houses of Culture' run by the unions. The workers' theatre movement was highly developed. By contrast library facilities in these houses, as also in the *internats* referred to earlier, appeared to the writer relatively poor.

Provision for children in both countries and at all levels was very considerable and of higher quality than for adults. It was also expanding more rapidly, from clinics and preventoriums to children's theatres. Not only the children of working mothers but those of working fathers could, in so far as there was room, be admitted to all sorts of activities available near the work place. Crèches and nursery schools, because of the large amount of service per child, could as yet accommodate only a fraction of applicants. In Poland by the end of the Six-Year Plan in 1955, nursery school accommodation was to increase from about a third of a million to nearly two-thirds. In Czechoslovakia regular kindergarten service was to be available to all children between the ages of three and six so early as the end of the Five-Year Plan in 1953. Provisions for the school-age child were easier and took care earlier of a larger proportion of the total. There were clubrooms for after school and a very great number of 'colonies' and 'half-colonies', i.e. day and boarding vacation homes for the children's long summer holidays.

Especial efforts were made for the quality of care for the youngest children. Some of the all-day nursery schools and crèches were now housed immediately adjacent to factories in the dwellings once occupied by the former owners or managers of the plants. Others had been newly built. Great pride was shown by neighbourhoods with model institutions of this sort. Thus in the Czech mining centre of Ostrava in 1948 was to be seen a large and particularly well-equipped nursery school that had been recently built by the miners themselves on an empty plot. They had done the work in their spare time, after hours and on Sundays; they had then ordered all the furnishings they could not themselves construct; and they apparently still supervised the operation of the place. Again, in a textile centre in Poland that year the writer recalls a dark and dilapidated factory. Antiquated even before the war and now needing nothing so much as to be torn down, it was still running full blast. Beside it was an elaborate glass-fronted modern dwelling surrounded by gardens, the home of the former owner. Workers in the factory had been eating their midday soup as best they could, some of them by their machines, for there was no proper canteen. But in the former owner's house with the sun pouring in, their children with neat bibs on were eating fruit and milk at excellently appointed little tables, four children to each, with flowers on each table. The intended political lesson of such a scene was, of course, obvious. But the outgoing care given the children, here as elsewhere, was equally obvious and obviously in consonance with the workers' wishes.

Looking back upon the various services in kind provided in the two countries, one is struck by the discrepancy all along the line between the level attained by workers in that part of their consumption which had to come out of wages, and the high level built into the services in kind. The whole unmistakably suggested a building for the future. The idea seemed to be that while wages in cash would have to wait upon increases in production, income in kind must lay a pattern for the future that would not have to be done over again because of poor quality.

CHAPTER XIII

THE REORGANIZATION OF AGRICULTURE

Post-Reform Patterns

Land reform had very considerably modified for both Poland and Czechoslovakia the basic European pattern of rural economy. By 1948 landlords, large and small, were gone or were on the way out: only the man who worked on his place himself could supposedly continue to hold it. The large estate as a private institution, with all the prestige and authority attaching to it, was no more. Agricultural wage labour was still freely permitted, but its numbers were on the decline, since many landless labourers had now received land and since the industrialization programme was beginning to draw them to the towns.

What remained in the country-side was a small number of older holdings ranging up to the permitted 125-acre maximums in the central territories of both countries and 250 in the border or western regions, and an enormous number of small holdings, a large block of them new, averaging around 12 to 15 acres for most of Poland, 15 to 20 acres for most of Czechoslovakia. These latter comprised the vast majority of all farms, and there was little hope of increasing their size yet further in the near future: the limits of enlargement had now been reached. (In the case of Poland, it was the boast of the Government immediately after the Reform that the average holding per head of agricultural population had gone up from under 2½ acres to about 3¾.)

In terms of agricultural output, such a land-holding pattern inevitably means perpetuation of a régime of low productivity per man-hour, combined though it may be, under favourable circumstances, with a relatively high productivity per acre. However, actual post-war conditions were far from favourable, and the inherited internal organization of the small farms bade fair to be a long-time hindrance.

The strip system, with the average farm in twenty to thirty narrow slices, some near, some far away, scattered about among other farmers' holdings, covered a substantial part of agricultural land in both countries. In Czechoslovakia tractors were used on such strips, but at great disadvantage. Scientific crop rotation was most difficult. So-called consolidation of strips was urgently called for, but with good land scarce, the exchange of strips was a difficult legal and economic process: it meant expensive surveying and much haggling.

1948 Views

The basic remedy urged by Czech and Polish planners in 1948 was industrialization.[1] This would, in the case of Poland, drain off surplus agricultural population from the land, and in both countries it would provide native agricultural machinery and chemical fertilizers. Within agriculture itself, more emphasis should be laid upon animal husbandry, fodder, and industrial crops. (It was pointed out that the small farmer raised more cattle per acre than the large, hence that increased cattle production under small farming was rational; however, it was not always pointed out how much smaller and lighter these cattle were.) In general, the handicaps of small-scale farming appeared to be accepted for the present as inevitable,[2] and even consolidation of strips was regarded philosophically as something absolutely necessary for the future, but that would have to be undertaken slowly as yet because of its great expense.

The view of State Farms at this time was that they were important, but that the land under them should be held to a minimum. Only where farm buildings or manor houses required a certain amount of land for proper use, or where there was an important stock farm or other forms of specialty production, where selected

[1] An illustration of the need of industrialization is recalled by the writer. In the summer of 1948 she visited the agricultural regions near Cracow. These were among the most poverty stricken in Poland, with great rural overcrowding and dwarf farms. At the time of the Reform, after giving tiny farms to three thousand odd landless labourers from the estates and to nearly six thousand landless peasants from the villages, only about one and a half acres apiece were left to enlarge existing holdings of poor farmers. Subsequently, in 1949, a giant steel combine was purposely planted in this region.

[2] 'Our social objective is the family-sized farm, not worked by hired labour, except perhaps for a little harvest help—and much of that can be secured by co-operative exchange of labour between farmers (so-called "neighbourly help"). Of course legally our limit of 125 and even 250 acres holds.' (Polish agricultural economist, July 1948.)

seed could be grown under optimum conditions, or again where the ground was unfit for tillage and should be retired to pasture, were State farms to be created and kept.

State Machine Stations were operating for the benefit of the farmer in Czechoslovakia, but in Poland only Co-operative Machine Stations served him and were subsidized. (The few State Stations serviced only the State Farms.) The perspective was one of helping the individual small producer in a myriad of small ways.

Co-operative farms for the present were sternly frowned upon. Absolutely no form of permanently organized producers' collective in agriculture was to be tolerated. The few so-called 'parcellizing' or 'land-distribution' co-operatives that had been permitted temporarily to occupy estate buildings and grounds in the Western Territories were still under strict orders to dissolve within the stipulated three to five years.

Some difficulties were still being experienced with carrying out the terms of the recent Reform. In Czechoslovakia, near Plzen, the writer well remembers visiting an estate of some 1,400 acres at the end of April 1948, where the original owner was still in possession. He did no work himself, but had a superintendent. He had at the time some twenty to thirty convicts ('war criminals', i.e. collaborationists) working on the place under guard, in addition to another dozen or two of regular resident agricultural labourers, paid partly in cash, partly in kind. (The estate owner spoke of the merits of payment in kind.) Thirty very sleek cows were in the stalls, tended by the convicts. Horses were said to number twenty, and there were pigs and chickens in abundance. The fields appeared rich and there was considerable woodland. This owner had been overlooked in the original 1945 Reform (owing, it was said now, to his friendship with the then Chairman of the Agricultural Committee in Parliament), but the 1948 Reform was about to catch up with him. He stated to the writer that he expected to manage all right, as he could pick his residual 125 acres where he wanted to on the estate, and that he would keep his manor house and stables and still make a good thing on stock-raising. His optimism was contradicted by the agronomist with whom the trip was made. He predicted to the writer that the owner would lose all. 'Firstly, he won't work on the land himself—look at his hands. Secondly, he would only be left a few rooms in his manor house in any case, and only part of his cattle. Of course, such a man could be very valuable if he wanted to be a Government agronomist—but he obviously won't. He'll take his "pension" (land payment) and go to the city.'[1]

Another type of difficulty with Land Reform enforcement was described to the writer that summer in Poland. An Agricultural Bank economist was speaking of what he considered the three recent stages in the Reform. 'The first phase, that of general decrees, was in 1945. The second stage, that of realization, was in the period of 1946, when Mikolajczyk was Minister of Agriculture. During this time the original decrees were not carried out in the spirit in which they were intended.' The third phase, the post-parcellation phase of the present (1948) was when a whole reorganization of the agricultural structure needed to be carried through on the basis of 'solid peasant proprietorship'.

'During the second phase it was the particularly crucial division of the land in the Western Territories that was in the hands of the Ministry of Agriculture', much of the land division in the older regions having already been carried through before 1946. 'So when period three came along, a serious difficulty with big farms was inherited by us. For instance, you might have a man who had been assigned a 50-acre farm of the very best land right on the outskirts of a big city where small truck-gardening would be in order and would require only, say, 8 acres. You also had these big owners beginning to pre-empt the best agricultural machinery, get their small neighbours to work for hire for them, and so on.

'In the middle of 1947 we were compelled to put a stop to this process of unduly big new farms being maintained and gobbling the small, and pass implementing legislation to the original land decrees.'[2]

[1] Actually, the agronomist added, this particular individual would probably be indicted as a collaborationist himself, on good evidence, 'and maybe some of the convicts there will be free'. Cases of collaborationism in this region were to be reopened shortly, he stated, on grounds of laxity by the previous Minister of Justice.

[2] The limits now set were: 18, 23, and 30 acres respectively in the western territories, depending on the quality of the land, with sizes near the big cities of 8–12 acres per truck garden. The original Land Decree (6 September 1944) had set much smaller limits because it referred to the more thickly settled areas in the east and centre of the country.

'*Article 13*. (1) The area of newly created farms as well as the area up to which dwarf farms shall be increased shall depend on the quality of the soil and on the relation of local needs to the available land supply. . . .

'(2) This area shall not exceed 12½ acres of land of average quality in the

In addition to juggling with sizes, the Ministry, according to this economist, had held up the final securing of the new farmers' land deeds. 'Under Mikolajczyk there were long drawn-out court proceedings to get your land certificates: meanwhile the farmer would be sitting on what he thought was his newly acquired piece of land, maybe much larger than he should have had, and thinking it his own.' This was very demoralizing to him and also to his envious neighbours.

The immediate need now, according to this economist, was stabilization. The farmer must know precisely where he stood. 'We have to correct the mistakes of the recent past at once and get them over with.' The settling of title deeds was to be finished by the end of that year, 1948. 'In the second phase, the Mikolajczyk period, they actually held back stabilization. Our farmer must know where he stands once and for all and be able to settle down to improve his agriculture. Questions such as collective farms we can leave to the future to worry about.'

Not all new settlers, apparently, conformed to this particular type of stabilization. A visit the writer made at just this time to a 'parcelling' co-operative suggested doubts. The co-operative in question was near Wroclaw. It had been formed only eight months previously by a group of ten Polish families newly arrived together from France, and it was more than evident that when their term was up they had every intention of getting around the law and staying together. They were building for a long future—in the words of a large silk-embroidered banner they had brought with them from France, 'THROUGH KNOWLEDGE AND WORK TO A PROSPEROUS LIFE'.

The place they had selected was in a strategic location for dairy farming, which was what they wanted, and had fertile land, a little river of its own, and woods, some 500-odd acres in all. When asked what the optimum number of families was for its cultivation, the leader answered promptly, eighteen. They were expecting four more families from France that autumn and two from Poland.

The estate owner, a German named Hoess, had lived in Switzerland and farmed through a superintendent. He had owned a number of such properties. Before leaving, the Germans had destroyed everything they could. All ten families when they first arrived the previous December had huddled together in part of one building, with the roof off the rest. They had repaired their houses first, put

case of crop farms, 5 acres in case of orchards, . . . and $\frac{2}{3}$ acre in case of workmen's plots.' (Measurements given in hectares in the original.)

in windows, doors, roofs, then repaired barns for the stock, negotiated with Farmers' Self-Help and apparently two other State sources for inventory—and so to ploughing. At the time of the visit the interiors of the houses were nicely finished, family pictures all over the walls, crucifixes over the doors. The estate house had been too thoroughly wrecked to work on as yet; later they planned to restore part of it as a 'cultural centre'. When they had arrived, 'no cows were here, no horses, no equipment'. What the Germans could not destroy or carry off they had dumped in the river, and the thrifty Poles were still busy salvaging it. At the time of the visit a reaper was being put together, in unusable condition, one would have thought. (The Germans had also taken away key parts.) The group did all their own repairs. They had one tractor, on credit, and were shortly expecting another. They now had 19 cows and 7 horses. They were going to buy 18 more cows the following week, again on credit, and would pay off on them in a year. In a year they hoped to have a hundred altogether, including natural increase, and would then concentrate on dairying. Already their milk was in great demand by housewives.

The big money-making crop for them thus far had been beets, 75 acres of them, all cultivated by their tractor. The ground had been in rough pasture when they arrived. Eleven women and three girls had done the hoeing to thin the young plants. The neighbours, single farm families, had not thought this possible. With the profit of these beet fields they were going to cover all their payments due for the year for everything—all other income from the farm would be clear.

Relations with the outside world were on a strictly business basis, even to the selling of milk direct to customers rather than through any co-operative marketing organization. They also paid current day wages to some building artisans who helped them with their houses. And within the group, the labour of wives and of children over fifteen was treated as an extra and paid at something above the current rate for agricultural day labour. (The younger children were not allowed to work, and at the time of the visit many of them were away at a school vacation resort.) But the male heads of families were strictly co-operative partners, and their reward was on a share basis, in proportion to the time put in by them at the common tasks. Absolutely no property in this collective was kept for private use except the dwelling houses and the families' personal possessions. Unlike, for example, Soviet collective farms, there were no private kitchen gardens and small stock. All productive labour was hence in common. Interestingly enough, all kinds of work were accounted alike, save for some small bonuses for extra arduous work. The unit of reckoning was the normal 8-hour day. An absentee of course had his time docked. But if anyone was ill, he was paid just the same. Men with larger families were paid more.

It would have been extraordinarily interesting to revisit this farm and see what changes a year and a half's time might have wrought. The later pattern of co-operative farming, once the Government had come around to the idea, gave far more play to individual gain motivation, and the groups encouraged were much larger than this one. But in any case, it is safe to predict that this stubborn set of friends would have won out in their original intention to stick together.

Changes After 1948

Once the policy changes of the late summer and autumn of 1948 had got fully under way, emphasis upon rationalization was given free rein. The advantages of large-scale agricultural operations were now to be demonstrated by all possible agencies. The State Farms, instead of being in part parcelled out, were to be increased and made into models of 'socialist management'. State Machine Stations were to be greatly expanded in size and number, and were to work specifically at the task of inducing their customers to operate according to a rational field plan. National industrial plans meanwhile were radically overhauled to provide new stations with new machinery. Local and regional agencies of government were to be reorganized to effectuate the carrying out of a general agricultural production-and-deliveries plan in the villages.

As to class relationships, the power of the larger farmer in the villages was to be definitively broken. He could be expected to oppose the necessary agricultural changes. The small farmer was always and everywhere to be helped specifically against him. Discriminatory State measures were to be exercised against him, and he was to be excluded from predominance in organs of local self-government.

The method of co-operative farming was to be advocated as the only possible long-run solution of the large-scale agriculture problem. The foundations for a mass solution along these lines were to be laid very gradually. Widespread adoption of group sowing and crop rotation practices were to be the most important first step, since they would obliterate, for practical purposes, the evils of the strip system. The various existing village co-operatives were to be unified under one flexible all-purpose co-operative per village, with production rationalization as a chief purpose. The national farmers' unions were to aid them. Actual production co-operatives would be few in number at first and would be substantially helped only if they gave serious promise of success. A national centre for farm production co-operatives was established in each country.

State Farms

Originally, owing to the importance of Poland's western territories, the proportion of land in State Farms was several times as large in Poland as in Czechoslovakia. But in both countries early expectations were that the State-held areas should decrease. 'We still have about 4,000,000 acres in State Farms,' an official of the State Planning Office of Poland told the writer in June 1948. 'We shall subdivide about a third of this and leave the other two-thirds intact. The purpose in keeping State Farms is (1) so that we can regulate price, (2) in order to raise production on peasant farms by providing selected seed, stock, etc.' Similar sentiments were expressed in Czechoslovakia. But by 1949 a quite different emphasis was being given. The stress now was on the need to increase State Farms as productive institutions, especially for meat, and the need to convince the small farmer of the superiority of large-scale methods by direct observation.

In Czechoslovakia 1949, saw a several-fold growth in the area of State Farms. The February events, occurring just before the general changes in agricultural policy of the following summer, had thrown on the public lap, so to say, a good deal of additional agricultural land. Under the new view this land now, apparently, did not have to go through the uneconomical stage of peasant proprietorship. At any rate it is true that a new law concerning State Farms was passed in Czechoslovakia in January 1949. It provided that the land to be forcibly sold under the 125-acre, no-tenancy provisions adopted as a consequence of the February events, was to be purchased at 80 per cent of its market value and that as much of it as lay in large enough lots was to be turned into State Farms. By 1950, consequently, the proportion of State Farm area in Czechoslovakia was almost equal to that of Poland, something under 8 per cent of agricultural land.

The condition of much of this land had at first been deplorable. 'The State Farms often started farming exhausted land, covered with weeds, parcelled out into dispersed fields, with an inadequate supply of manpower.'[1] The bad condition of the land was said to have been increased by the former owners' knowledge that they were about to lose it.[2] 'Poor, even feudal buildings, both houses and barns' were also complained of. 'There were no proper herds, swine, machinery, or workers.'[3]

If this was the way the Czechoslovaks felt about their State Farms, conditions in Poland had been incomparably more difficult. When the writer visited the Wrocław region in the summer of 1948, Polish State Farms administrators pointed proudly to their nearly 5,000 horses and 20,000 cows dispersed over an area of more than 300,000 acres. In 1946–7 they had had only 1,200 horses, 'and as to cows, only a couple of hundred; in plenty of estates, none at all.' There were now about 1,000 tractors of different types, the American ones, however, suffering for lack of spare parts, which at that time were already unobtainable in trade. Only about three or four estates out of 300 had had any sheds for machinery.

Even at this time serious attempts had been made by the Polish administrators to establish rational production and pay schedules. Jobs were being 'normed' and premium systems of pay for extra work established. By late 1949 the writer found systems of 'socialist competition' being boasted of in a number of State Farms. The amount of labour per acre was still very high by British standards, but was said to be considerably less than that employed on individual peasant farms.[4]

Under the Six-Year Plan 'the expanded output of the Polish State Farms will have to supply the *major part* of the farm products needed by . . . the city population', as well as to supply farmers

[1] J. Smirkovsky, *International Agricultural Institute Bulletin*, Prague, Jan. 1950.

[2] Interview material, November 1949.

[3] Ibid.

[4] Norms for the labour force in the Wrocław region in the summer of 1948 were 17 workers and 1·1 of administrative personnel for every 250 acres. Similarly in late 1949 the writer found an average production of 2,000 to 2,500 litres of milk per cow per year claimed for State farms as compared with a 1,600 average for private farms. (In the Six-Year Plan 1,900 litres per year was looked for from the country as a whole for 1955.)

with selected seed and livestock.[1] In the course of the six years a great increase in efficiency was demanded: output per employee was to go up 90 per cent and production costs to go down 30 per cent.

In Czechoslovakia the State Farms, beginning with 1949, had become a National Enterprise, on a par with other State corporations in the nationalized industry and trade fields, and it was evident that analogous standards of business practice were to be expected of the new organization. 'Each State Farm will have to have its own financial and production plan, must make out its own balance sheet . . . they must adopt a daily check of the results of their activities.'[2] 'Socialist estate management' was said to include having norms for each farm and each total estate (i.e. group of farms with a central management) covering (1) materials, supplies, and equipment costs; (2) labour output and pay, in addition to (3) an investment plan.[3]

A mass pig-fattening project was started on Czech State Farms in 1949, accompanied by tremendous publicity. It was soon copied on a smaller scale in Poland. The leading Czech station for this purpose, named 'Gigant', began construction in September, chiefly by volunteer labour outside the Five-Year Plan. Short-cut processes had been used in the construction of the sties. By November there were five such stations in the Czech lands and two in Slovakia. A single station was to put on the market 30,000 pigs a year, in three lots of 10,000 each, and the stations were to employ rationalization to the utmost degree. Models of the buildings were widely advertised. The rationalization, it was pointed out to the writer, consisted of mechanization, plus an appreciation of pig psychology. It appeared that pigs liked to sleep on a warm, dry place and to defecate on a cool, wet one. Accordingly the sties were built on three levels, without any use of straw for bedding. 'The pig feeds on one shelf, the middle one, leaves his excrement on the

[1] *I.A.I. Bulletin*, July–August 1950 (italics mine). For 1950, it was subsequently reported, State Farms had increased their fodder production by a third, whereas agriculture as a whole had fallen short of the fodder Plan by 5 per cent, (I.A.I., *Interagra*, Prague, 1951, Nos. 1-2, p. 30.)

[2] Speech by Prime Minister Zápatocký, quoted in *I. A. I. Bulletin*, January 1950.

[3] *I.A.I. Bulletin*, October 1949. Also beginning with 1949 selected seed production had been made a monopoly of the Czech State Farms. Milk production per cow on the State Farms for the following year was to go up some 15 to 20 per cent, and so on.

cool, low shelf where a stream of water flushes it directly into ponds,[1] and has a higher, warm, wood-floored space to sleep on.' All the manure could thus be automatically saved and utilized. Fish, ducks, and fur-bearing animals as well as a large vegetable farm were to accompany each pig 'combine'; utilizing, in addition to the manure, the by-products of a stockyard attached to each station. Feeding and watering, needless to say, were by a continuous belt process.

The enthusiasm expressed for this rationalization was comparable to what the writer had found expressed in Poland a few weeks earlier for the new rationalization in Warsaw building processes.[2]

[1] 'The manured pond grows plancton, which feeds insects, which feed fish.'

[2] The difficulties inhering in agricultural rationalization and production changes, especially in the absence of a whole economy of large scale units capable of planning is, however, also well illustrated in the pig-raising campaigns, this time in Poland. During 1950 very great successes had been reported for pig production in Poland. The autumn census showed over ten million pigs whereas before the war, it was stated, with a much larger population and more land, the number had never exceeded 7 million. Not only group stations but individual farmers in large numbers had raised output, for State purchase prices were high. Meanwhile an adequate forage base was apparently being neglected. The situation, it seemed, had been building up for some time. '. . . in 1949–50 . . . in all the eastern European countries . . . pig prices were fixed at very high levels in relation to prices of feeding stuffs. . . . Similar price relations . . . may be observed in western Germany and the Netherlands. . . .' (U.N., E.C.E., *Economic Survey . . . for 1951*, Geneva 1952, pp. 27–8.) For the succeeding year we read, '. . . The exceptionally high ratios of pig to fodder prices were carried forward with little change into the new harvest year 1950–1, but the supply of feeding stuffs was far from adequate . . . following the increases of the previous year. . . . In Poland . . . [there were] 13 per cent more cattle and 70 per cent more pigs to be fed by a somewhat lower grain harvest and only 20 per cent more potatoes.' (Ibid., p. 29.)

One explanation subsequently given was that many farmers in any case had long been accustomed to trusting to the purchase of fodder from others rather than raising their own, and now did so more than ever in spite of warnings. In any case, by the first half of 1951 a serious fodder shortage had developed and pigs were slaughtered, many of them now being consumed on the home farm. (Rural pork consumption was reported at 17 kg. per capita in 1950, 22 in 1951. Before the war it had not been over 12.) Similar difficulties on a lesser scale appeared with cattle. Later in the year the situation was made acute by an unusually bad drought which ruined the potato crop. However, just why the fodder-livestock ratio could not be modified in time by changes in price and marketing policies, was not clear. Certainly much publicity in Poland as in all the planned economies had been going on for the past several years on the necessity for more forage crops.

By early 1951 the Czechoslovak large-scale stations were reported to be supplying over a third of the pork market.

Agricultural education was in process of being reorganized during 1950, and the State Farms were scheduled to play an important part in it. On the one hand, ever since the Land Reform measures, one type of old-time agricultural manager was no longer needed: the generalized farm superintendent for the medium-sized estate. His place was now taken by the more specialized manager, to be trained intensively in a particular branch of production. For this, specialized higher educational institutions were necessary. There was also, however, immensely increased need for lesser levels of trained personnel, again preferably with some degree of specialization. It was here that the State Farms were called upon. In February 1950 apprenticeship requirements for farm youth were laid down in an Order of the Ministry of Labour, comparable to the requirements already enacted for city youth. Young farmers aged 15–17 who had finished school were now to be required to attend apprenticeship courses, to be offered by the State Farms. There was to be a year's Basic Agricultural Course and a series of speciality courses lasting one, two, or more years. Girls as well as boys were to be accepted.

State Machine Stations

In Poland, prior to 1949, the spreading out of such machinery as was available for farmers was undertaken exclusively by Co-operative Machine Stations. State Machine Stations in Poland at this time numbered only a handful and served only the State Farms. The machinery co-operatives were described to the writer in 1948 as of three types, all relatively small: (1) with tractors, (2) with smaller agricultural machines, (3) very primitive ones with very little equipment. 'A man may have practically nothing but his piece of land and his two hands—these co-operatives can help him.' The Agricultural Bank at this time was giving the co-operative stations what credit it could to purchase tractors.

'The question was, State or Co-operative?' an agricultural writer said to the author in the late summer of 1948. 'We chose the co-operative form, because it is the best form for activization of the peasants, the best form for social control against exploitation by the rich peasants. The rich peasant has been known to rent his horse to the poor peasant while he himself hires a tractor!'

By 1949 this view had radically changed. In connection with

plans for the development of co-operative farms, large-scale State Machine Stations had come to be regarded as absolutely necessary, to furnish heavy machinery. On the other hand, to put scarce heavy machinery in the hands of small machine co-operatives was considered wasteful; hence future agricultural credits for that purpose were not to be extended to them. 'A tractor gets out of order and stands still, or has to move from one plot to another. Hence to-day we treat the village co-operative stations as machine (i.e. light horse-drawn machine) stations only, not as tractor stations. Those machine co-operatives which already have tractors, we let them be—there are nearly a thousand of these—we help them; but this is not the line of further development.'[1]

By late 1949, 30 State tractor stations were operating, and by 1950 the number was to be raised to over 100. By the end of the Six-Year Plan in 1955 their total was to reach 850. As to tractors, beginning with some 200 in 1949, the stations' tractors by 1955 should number 35,000. State stations were to be established in the first instance in districts where agricultural production was already on a relatively high level, so as to be able to make the most effective use of heavy equipment. In the places where they are set up, they take over tractors, threshing machines, sowing machines, etc., from the co-operative stations. Every station to have 15 to 30 tractors and also a great number of other agricultural machines.[2]

Conditions at first had been hard. 'At first we had no buildings, the machines had to be kept under tents!' Results, however, were said to be rewarding. 'With our larger machines we are handling 8 to 10 acres a day. Smaller tractors used to average 6.' The question was one of heavy investment for the larger machines, and, even more crucial for Poland, the question of trained personnel, 'cadres'. 'We need tractor drivers, mechanics, assistant managers, agronomists. The bottle-neck to-day is personnel, not machines.'[3]

In Czechoslovakia the question of State Machine Stations had been decided much earlier, but even here there was great increase in the scale and objective of their operations after the beginning of 1949.

State stations with a Central Office in Prague had been established in Czechoslovakia so early as 1947. In that year 'forty stations took part in spring ploughing and autumn sowing. Before

[1] Interview material, October 1949.
[2] *I.A.I. Bulletin*, November 1949.
[3] Interview material, October 1949.

15 April 1948 the entire network of 189 farm machinery stations (projected under the Two-Year Plan) in Bohemia and Moravia was organized. . . . The stations have been divided into 61 districts. . . . At the head of each district is a principal station while the others function as branches. . . . Slovakia possesses 44 stations organized along similar lines.'

'The stations are new, non-profit, bodies, created to help in the task of mechanizing Czech agriculture and to lower the cost of farm production. . . . (Their duties are):

'1. To perform with their personnel and machines all farm and forest work on a salary basis;

'2. To do all the repair work on farm machines, their own or those owned by third parties;

'3. To supervise, from the technical standpoint, the activities of the local farm machinery co-operative unions in their districts.'[1] It was added that, 'during the lull in farm work the stations shift to log transportation so as to make full use of their working capacity'.

Early in 1949 machine station organization was considerably tightened up. A new law on the Mechanization of Agriculture raised the central body in Prague to the status of a National Corporation. This Mechanization Centre was not only to establish State Machine Stations and repair shops and train their personnel, but was also to assist in the standardization and simplification of agricultural equipment.

'The central task in the mechanization of agriculture (for 1950) is to restrict the number of types and sub-types, to introduce standardization, and also to distribute the machinery evenly over the whole territory of the Republic. . . .'

The newer types of machines 'will be supplied quickly to State Machine Stations which are speedily becoming the main pillar of mechanization. These stations . . . will extend their activities to repairs . . . and the supply of spare parts. . . .'[2]

It was now also stated to be part of the Mechanization Centre's duties to help the Co-operative Machine Stations in 'legal matters', and to help them and the Farmers' Union to plan field work 'and control (i.e. supervise, check on) its fulfilment'. The Machine Stations were also to conclude agreements with local craftsmen regarding priority in repairs.

[1] *I.A.I. Bulletin*, January 1949.
[2] *I.A.I. Bulletin*, February 1950.

By early 1950 the picture of the State stations' functions had grown further, to include the persuasion of farmers to conclude rationally worked-out crop rotation agreements, and so forth, with the Machine Stations when hiring them to do work. A 'First National Conference of State Machine Station Employees', held in Prague in January 1950, was addressed by the Minister of Agriculture: 'State Machine Stations are not expected to be merely places loaning farm machinery for work in the fields . . . they will be able to carry out their purpose of aiding the small and middle farmers to expand their output only if they take part in the making out of production contracts and plans of Unified Agricultural Co-operatives, if the contracts between the Stations and the U.A.C.'s cease to be merely agreements determining the volume of work to be executed [by the Stations], and contain detailed obligations of both parties to improve the quality of their work. . . . All State Machine Stations must, therefore, primarily discuss the production plans, must know what crop yields are to be reached in different communities. . . . [They should seek to] have the correct crop rotations, common sowing, use of improved seed . . . included in the contracts.'[1]

The very conception of helping the small farmer and yet leaving him in his restricted fields was declared to be contradictory: adequate utilization of large-scale equipment was only possible on large, consolidated fields.[2]

'It is impossible to aid the small and middle farmers and at the same time to leave intact the régime of farm holdings composed of scattered pieces of land . . . which makes a full utilization of machines of the latest type impossible. The Stations should help the small and middle farmers to advance the level of agricultural output through common tilling of the soil and through adoption of higher forms of production carried out with the help of the U.A.C's.

'The State Machine Stations are expected to convince small and middle farmers of the advantages of mechanization . . . and . . . a more perfect organization of labour. . . .'[3]

[1] *I.A.I. Bulletin*, February 1950.

[2] In winter ploughing the average acreage per tractor on individual private farms was stated to have been only 22; by village machine co-operatives 50, while on State Farms it had been 125. Even though a quarter of Czechoslovakia's farm area in 1949 had been tractor ploughed by State Machine Station equipment, full advantage could not be derived from the bigger machines until they had bigger areas to work on.

[3] Ibid.

While in Czechoslovakia State Stations were thus increasing their functions, the number of small co-operative machine stations was also being multiplied. 'Last Spring [1949] . . . farmers in more distant villages, who needed them [co-operative machines] most, could not obtain them.' Now branches of the machine co-operative were to be opened especially in isolated communities. During 1949 the equipment used by machine co-operatives was said to have increased tenfold.

Five- and Six-Year Plan Objectives

The rate of agricultural increase in both countries under their respective Plans was to be only about half that scheduled for industry, but was still very great. Whereas industry in six years in Poland was to go up by 95 per cent agricultural output was to increase by 45 per cent. However, even this, as the Poles pointed out, amounted to no less than 6 per cent each year, a rate, they claimed, unheard of hitherto save in the Soviet Union. In Czechoslovakia the respective figures for five years were 75 per cent for industry and 37 per cent for agriculture.

The added production in both countries was not to be achieved by increase of arable acreage, but exclusively by increased yields.

Crop production was to go up very slightly (in Poland only 3 per cent altogether), while animal production was to increase radically (in Poland 66 per cent). This was not only because of war and drought losses,[1] but because animal production was regarded as much more profitable. Cattle breeding in Poland was to go up 50 per cent and Polish milk production was to double, with an increased yield per cow of nearly 20 per cent. In both countries the shortage of beef cattle was partly to be made good by the mass production of pork, since pigs could be bred quickly (see the 'Gigant' projects just referred to).

In both countries, within the field of crop production there was to be some shift away from cereals and to forage and industrial crops. Both countries were also to increase vegetable and fruit production, Poland by 50 per cent. Great emphasis was laid upon a proper fodder base, to be derived both from natural and artificial pastures. In the case of Poland, farmers were to be encouraged to sow somewhat more wheat and less rye.

'Polish agriculture will move from the extensive grain and

[1] In 1949 herds in both countries had been only about 70 per cent of pre-war, whereas harvests were up to pre-war and beyond.

potato economy of to-day to the large-scale cultivation of industrial crops, root crops, fodder, etc.' 'The problem of fodder is likely to prove a bottle-neck . . . increased yields must be obtained from meadows and pastures.'[1] In Czechoslovakia, it was pointed out, wheat production could in any case never begin to compete with the production of countries more favourably situated for a mass mechanization of the wheat harvest.

The key to successful change throughout was declared to be scientific crop rotation, with regularized increase of forage and leguminous crops. Elaborate rotation plans, six and eight years in length, were called for in Czechoslovakia.

Regional specialization was demanded in both countries. In Czechoslovakia much was already being made of detailed agricultural planning maps at the time of the writer's first visit in 1948. By 1949–50 this had gone much further. A nation-wide new 'geonomic survey' was declared to be one of the chief research tasks of the Five-Year Plan. Under it suitable crop rotations could be worked out for similar groups of regions. And machinery, fertilizers, and agricultural enterprises, such as sugar factories, distilleries, refrigerating plants, could be scientifically distributed.

Similarly, at the end of 1949 in Czechoslovakia one heard of a 'Livestock Transfer Plan' for 1950. This was to secure an optimum distribution of herds in the regions of the Republic. Livestock increases were to be channeled particularly to the Border Regions where surplus stabling still existed. However, cattle were also to be transferred within individual regions. A 'maximum of expansion of herds' was to be 'secured in the Socialist sector of agriculture'. After this sector had been served, new cattle supplies were also to be extended to 'efficient private farmers in the frontier and central districts in which the stable facilities are not being properly utilized'.[2]

State artificial insemination stations meanwhile were to be provided in greater numbers, and State and co-operative fattening stations to be encouraged and subsidized, to prevent cattle and hogs from being brought on the market too early.

At the centre of the technical transformation, of course, was mechanization, and after that, the production of sufficient chemical fertilizers—both dependent upon the high rate of industrializa-

[1] Report of the Polish Minister of Agriculture, abstracted in *Życie Gospodarcze*, Warsaw, 1–15 January 1950.

[2] *I.A.I. Bulletin*, November 1949.

tion called for. The distance to be traversed was viewed with open eyes. In Poland even by 1955, only about a third of the total agricultural operations were expected to be mechanized; sowing, two-thirds. (On State Farms, however, sowing was to be mechanized 100 per cent. In 1949 it had been mechanized on them about 60 per cent.)

Tractor production—and also the furnishing of spare parts[1]—was a major problem. Czechoslovakia in 1949 was already producing at the rate of about 1,000 a month, but some 40 per cent of this output was being exported to pay for needed imports. Poland was to reach a comparable figure only by 1955. Meanwhile the consumption of machines in both countries was to go up tremendously. In 1949 Czechoslovakia was employing tractors variously estimated at between 16,000 and 22,000 all told.[2] By 1953 the number was to be 44,000. In Poland by 1955 the total of tractors in use was to be 60,000.

Plan Enforcement: the Contracts System and Local Government Authorities

Forward contracting by farmers, to stabilize prices and assure supply in the case of certain crops, was already a familiar policy of pre-war governments in the two countries, particularly in the case of Poland. Polish pre-war contracts, pre-empting all or a part of some crops, were applied especially to sugar beets and tobacco. In the post-war, however, the system was increased tenfold, to cover by 1949 nearly a million farmers, and included not only oats, potatoes, and many speciality crops, but also hog-breeding. An important function of Farmers' Self-Help was now declared to be the increase of 'Speciality Production Groups' of small farmers who engaged themselves ahead for stated production in exchange for credit and various forms of government aid. Thus, in May 1950 we read: '(The organization of) groups of rural livestock breeders and grain producers . . . make easier the signing of production and delivery contracts, and the planned supply of farmers with fertilizers, feed, credit, etc. The Union (Farmers' Self-Help) aims at raising the number of these groups from 66,000 to 150,000 and at

[1] By this time American export licensing provisions forbade shipment to eastern Europe of spare parts for the old U.N.R.R.A. machines.

[2] The pre-war figure had been about 3,600. An agricultural statistician told the writer that out of total agricultural costs before the war about 50 per cent had been labour costs, and that now (November 1949) about 35 per cent were labour costs.

increasing their membership to at least 2,000,000.'[1] This form of organization was also spoken of to the writer by an Agricultural Bank official in 1949 as a means of 'activization of the village from below'. 'Such groups have their leaders. There will be one or maybe several such speciality groups per village. We talk with a given group: "Can *you* produce 30 hectares this year? What do *you* need in order to do this?" This extends the influence of planning in the village. Of course, out of 60,000 groups some are good, some bad. We undertake contracts through these groups.'

In Czechoslovakia by 1949 the contracts system was in process of being compulsorily applied to all major crops.[2] 'Each year', we read, 'the State will now conclude contracts with the individual farmers on the production of agricultural products, with the exception of forestry products. These contracts are concluded by the local National Committees or other bodies authorized by the Ministry of Agriculture as its agents. . . .' Under the Two-Year Plan, it was stated, plan details had not got 'to each parish and each single farm. The contracts put the whole planning into a different light. It would otherwise never be possible to discover those who neglect or sabotage, nor would it be possible to give the appropriate assistance and well-earned advantages to honest and careful farmers. . . . Everywhere figures will speak which will be binding for both sides: the farmer and the State.'[3]

Early in 1950 it was stated that immediately after Christmas, local National Committees had begun discussions with the individual farmers in their areas concerning the drawing up of the 1950 production and delivery contracts in accordance with the year's Plan. The contracts were to be signed about 15 January. Rewards for contract fulfilment, i.e. for delivery of the stipulated amounts of produce, were referred to later in connection with the potato harvest. Differential price reductions were being granted for selected seed and chemical fertilizers and also for work done for the individual farmers by the State Machine Stations. After a given date in July complying farmers received a minimum 10 per cent discount. Farmers breaking their contracts, on the other hand,

[1] *I.A.I. Bulletin*, May 1950.

[2] The Five-Year Plan Law, passed late in 1948, had authorized the issuance of Cabinet decrees having the force of law, and it was such a decree issued in January 1949, that set up officially the general contracts system for the purchase and delivery of agricultural products.

[3] *I.A.I. Bulletin*, March 1949.

at least in the case of seed potatoes, of which there had been a shortage, had been liable the previous spring to have their storage pits opened and any surpluses forcibly sold.

Control for Local Planning Illustrated: the Drive for Rationalization of Spring Farm Work

A description of the planning process as applied to spring work on an elementary level was given in one of the Czech agricultural journals in 1950. 'The basic planning unit', it was stated, 'is the village.' Either the village Unified Agricultural Co-operative, or, if there was none, the local branch of the Farmers' Union, was to prepare and supervise the whole. 'A well worked out plan must include an exact list of all areas which must be ploughed, tilled, and sown. . . . Only with an exact list of all fields will it be possible to ascertain whether the prescribed areas . . . for various crops have been adhered to.

'For each village there must also be an exact inventory of machines, draft animals, implements. . . . The principle is that during the period of spring work all of these must be concentrated for a rapid carrying out of all work.' However, the farmer was warned, 'Care should be taken that cows should not be used at all as draught animals'.[1]

Finally, 'a further ingredient of each plan must be an exact time-table stating the time during which a certain job must be completed. This entails the planning of necessary labour. Full use must be made of aid by neighbours.'[2]

Forms of Discrimination against the Larger Farmer

When the United Nations' F.A.O. Mission to Poland made its report in early 1948 it recommended that 50 acres be made the upper limit for farms in that country.[3] This was in view of the lack of equipment for the single farmer to handle a larger acreage efficiently, and also because of the inefficiently small size of the bulk of dwarf farms that needed the extra land.

[1] The writer well remembers the attempts of local agronomists in Poland to persuade farmers that they should use cows thus, during the severe shortages of 1948; and the resistance of the progressive little 'parcelling co-operative' near Wroclaw, referred to earlier, to such proposals.

[2] *I.A.I. Bulletin*, February 1950.

[3] United Nations, Food and Agriculture Organization, *Report of the F.A.O. Mission for Poland*, May 1948, Part III.

Actual legal limits, however, at this time in Poland were 125 acres and remained so. In the case of Czechoslovakia, as we know, the land surface was less crowded, and the 125-acre legal limit was set only after the events of February 1948—before that it had been twice as large and but little enforced.

The terms in which the legal assurances to the larger farmer in both countries were couched were unmistakable. In Czechoslovakia they were embodied in the Constitution.[1] So long as a man worked on the land himself he had the right to keep his acres up to 125 and to pass them on to his heirs.

Technically, these rights continued to be scrupulously observed. But when once, after 1948, social policy against the larger farmer had sharpened, administrative measures began to be taken against the farmers of the over-50-acre group.[2] It amounted to a class-war orientation in the country-side, and the farmers on the wrong side of the ledger represented the whole range of from roughly 50- all the way up to 125-acre ownership, although in total numbers they comprised not more than about 8 per cent of the agricultural population.[3]

In implementation of policy, various modifying conditions were supposed to be taken account of when classifying the individual farmstead and its owner: poorer land and a more than average-sized family would make a 50-acres-plus man only a 'middle' farmer. On the other hand, the employment of much hired labour and engaging in profitable middleman's transactions would be likely to clinch the 'large farmer' definition at precisely the 50-acre mark.

In addition, the whole range of classifications tended to be somewhat lower in Poland than in Czechoslovakia, corresponding to the perforce smaller size of Polish land allotments. The 'poor' farmer in social parlance in Poland meant a man with less than about 12 acres; in Czechoslovakia, of less than 20. In turn, the 'true' Polish middle farmer was held to be the man of, say, not

[1] 'The private ownership of land, in respect to farmers who till the land in person, shall be guaranteed up to the limit of 50 hectares (125 acres). Details shall be prescribed by Act.' (Constitution of the Czechoslovak Republic, 9 May 1948, Art. XII, Section 15.)

[2] Needless to say, the coincidence of this figure with that of the F.A.O. Mission did not indicate any cause and effect. The writer never heard of the F.A.O. Mission's report in this connection.

[3] In Czechoslovakia this meant only 35,000 men.

over 35 or 40 acres normally, even though administratively the 50-acre definition held here as in Czechoslovakia.

In any case, once the class-war orientation had been well adopted, the significant distinction in treatment was that between the poor and middle farmers on the one hand and the larger farmer on the other. The usual advantages and privileges attaching to a 50- to 125-acre status in Europe were being, to put it mildly, whittled away.

The original Land Reforms had given considerable temporary opportunity to the 50–125-acre owners to profit by the existing scarcity of equipment among the new smaller farmers, the beneficiaries of the Reform. For a time advantageous terms of hire could be exacted against them, chiefly in the form of a labour rent or the advance pledging of crops. However, the Reform itself had cut down the number of landless labourers, depriving the 50-plus-acre man of his easiest access to a labour force. Presently stringent legislation was passed in both countries raising the pay requirements for hired labour. The standards granted State Farm labourers were applicable to private employers as well. Thus, in Poland by the summer of 1948, the writer was told: 'Our pay is being made more expensive by the terms of the Collective Agreement between the Agricultural Trade Union and the State—to which private employers also are subject.' Social insurance requirements, paid altogether by the employer under this agreement, amounted to a 28 per cent net addition to wages. By Government decree all agricultural workers had to belong to trade unions and hence became a party to the benefits granted under the Agreement.[1] Overtime pay under the Agreement, at double the basic rates, was granted after 10 hours. (In Czechoslovakia by 1949 agricultural workers were stated to be becoming restive over the question of a basic 8-hour day.) Czech agricultural wages in late 1949 were said to be averaging about 8 to 11 kroner per hour as compared to industry's 12 to 14 kroner—a greatly decreased differential as compared to pre-war.

Further losses to the larger farmer were the cutting down of profitable middleman's activities. The purchase and sale of the smaller farmers' produce as well as profitable sale of his own produce on 'black' markets, was being reduced by the various State and co-operative purchase agencies described in the previous

[1] By 1951, with the decrease in hired labour, benefits were made applicable only to State Farm employees.

chapter. Particularly lucrative transactions, now being lost, had been the making of private crop loans and the advance purchase of grain from smaller farmers. All these forms of, so to say, negative discrimination against the larger farmer, took place more or less automatically in the course of seeking to protect and strengthen the poorer farmer and wage labourer and to stabilize prices and maintain supply for the city consumer. But positive forms of discrimination were added, designed to restrict the power of the wealthier farmer as such.

Agricultural taxes were levied on a progressive scale, with complete tax exemption for the smallest farmers.[1] For those who did pay taxes, first in Czechoslovakia, then also in Poland, all the land taxes were presently amalgamated into one sharply progressive Agricultural Income-Tax.

In addition, however, the system of State produce contracts and deliveries was organized in such a way as to amount to a tax upon the larger farmer. Formerly such a farmer could afford to store his crops for the most advantageous season; now he, as well as the small farmer who probably could not have held his over in any case, was required to contract ahead at a fixed price. But the quotas required of the large farmer *per acre* were larger than the small farmer's, on the theory that his means of production should be more efficient.[2] Moreover the type of product required of him differed somewhat in some cases. In animal production in Czechoslovakia, 1949 regulations were to require the large farmer to concentrate on, i.e. to produce a maximum of, hogs under contract, leaving the more profitable raising of cattle primarily to the smaller farmers. Of course, the pig-concentration idea had also, and probably predominantly, a technological base: the more immediately applicable methods of large-scale production in this case; but the class side of the policy was certainly stressed in the press.[3]

[1] In Czechoslovakia the exemptions (Law of 1 April 1948) were: wheat land, up to 20 acres; sugar beet, 12 acres; potato, 30 acres; pasture, 50 acres.

[2] 'The view that big farmers are able to achieve higher crop yields per acre than the small ones is being generally accepted. . . . The entire production of big farms, outside the produce needed by the owner for his . . . family's sustenance, must be used for deliveries to the Government . . . the small farmer will have more produce for sale on the free market.' (*I.A.I. Bulletin*, January 1950.)

[3] 'In the allotment of animal production quotas, the aim is to enable the small and middle farmers to expand their herds of cattle, and, at the same time, to make the big farmers raise mainly pigs.' Ibid.

The farmer himself was responsible, under oath, for furnishing the basic data upon which his correct classification could be based. 'In signing the 1950 production and delivery contracts the farmers also sign an affidavit about the size and the number of their livestock.'[1] Other, individual conditions were also to be taken into account by the assigning agency, such as the quality of the land and the equipment at the farmer's disposal.

In this connection an all-important administrative distinction should be noted. Formerly the larger farmers had exercised much of their authority through local government, credit association, etc., posts. (In the case of co-operatives this matter has already been noted in the previous chapter.) Now major efforts were made to dislodge and displace them altogether: administration in crucial economic matters was shifted in so far as possible into the hands of organizations specifically designated as composed of small and middle farmers only. Thus in the matter of assignment of delivery quotas we read: 'Quotas are allotted by committees composed of members of the Local National Committee, of the Czech or Slovak Farmers' Union, the National Front Action Committee, and the Unified Agricultural Co-operative.'[2] All of these organizations were either altogether closed to the over-50-acre farmer, or the proportion of such farmers who could serve on their boards was sharply limited. Throughout the range of regulations discriminating against the larger farmer it was this type of organization in whose hands the measures restricting him were placed.

It has already been pointed out that in the matter of labour-power the larger farmer was becoming progressively less privileged, hired hands were becoming dearer, scarcer, and their use opened up the employing farmer to more certain inclusion in the category of large-farmer-to-be-discriminated-against. Now, however, the possession of machinery on a privileged scale was also being made difficult. In Czechoslovakia, under 1949 regulations, the Ministry of Agriculture was given the right to buy up compulsorily agricultural machinery 'from individual farmers who either do not fulfil the agricultural target or who do not fully utilize their machinery.' By mid-April 1950, almost 10,000 tractors were said to have been thus purchased by the Ministry, with the implication that many of them came under this regulation.[3]

The class aspect of this technological move was expressly emphasized by the Minister of Agriculture. 'The Mechanization of

[1] Ibid. [2] Ibid. [3] See *I.A.I. Bulletin*, May 1950.

Agriculture Act directs the entire activity of the State Machine Stations towards serving the interests of the small and middle farmers. The stations, accordingly, purchase farm machines from the village rich for the benefit of small and middle farmers.'[1]

The Minister added, 'They (the Stations) are also expected to see to it that all machines and draught animals in the community are fully utilized in the interest of these groups of farmers.' This was a reference to yet earlier regulations, operative in both Poland and Czechoslovakia, providing for the compulsory loaning (renting) of private equipment during rush seasons. Quite obviously, the differential advantages of amassing more and better private equipment were up against heavy odds.

Finally, the terms under which increasingly important forms of Government aid were rendered to the individual farmers were sharply discriminatory against the larger farmer. He had to pay more for his selected seed and chemical fertilizer than the smaller man. The terms upon which he could secure farm credit were much harder.[2] The State Machine Station was to charge him higher rentals for its servicing of his fields. And wherever there was a shortage, he would come last.

'*Unified Agricultural Co-operatives*' *and Preparatory Committees*

The 90-odd per cent of Polish and Czechoslovak farmers who were not classed as large farmers were being drawn by every means available toward common enterprises. The fulcrum of the matter, operationally, was joint field work based on common sowing and the abolition of strips. Organizationally speaking, the fulcrum was one common co-operative per village, taking over all the specialized functions of previous co-operatives and adding thereto production features. This type of co-operative was fostered in all the newer planned economies. Its holding-company nature was clearly expressed in the phrase 'universal succession without liquidation'.[3]

In the case of Czechoslovakia, after a number of localities had

[1] *I.A.I. Bulletin*, January 1950.

[2] See Chapter VIII.

[3] To be concentrated in it were: 'All activities connected with mechanization, land consolidation (i.e. elimination of the strip system), reclamation, electrification, breeding, purchase and sale of agricultural products, and implements, erection of rural laundries and nurseries, etc.' (*I.A.I. Bulletin*, February 1949.)

established unified co-operatives, legal form was given to the movement by the Consolidated Co-operatives Act of 1949.[1] Significantly enough, membership in the new organizations was supposed to be restricted to farmers of 50 acres or less—at any rate, the obverse was specifically stated, that all farmers of less than 50 acres and working members of their families over 16 years of age were eligible. Membership shares were modest, 100 to 500 crowns (15s. to £3 10s.), payable over a period of time. Membership was to be wholly voluntary and members could withdraw at any time. Membership meetings were to be held monthly, members were to have an active share in all negotiations of the organization, officers were to be elected by universal secret ballot and were to be continuously accountable to the membership. Income of the organization, from membership shares, rental of equipment and so forth, was to remain in the local unit for its use.

National standardization of the organization was, however, assured by yet other provisions. The locals became an integral part of the Central Council of Co-operatives, of which they were to form a separate division. This division in turn was to be administered by an executive body elected by the entire Co-operative Council and approved by the Minister of Agriculture. The statutes of the Co-operatives similarly had to be centrally approved. Within the local, any breaches of statute or procedure by its officers could be brought up by its members to their District Council for action. Moreover, in the event of voluntary dissolution of the organization, its assets would go over to the national organization for the use of other co-operatives.

The setting up of unified co-operatives was made easy by provision for so-called 'preparatory committees'. A group of 5 to 10 persons in a village could petition to set up such a committee,[2] and, if approved as adequately representative by the Central Co-operative Council, it would be authorized to begin organizing

[1] Cabinet Decree No. 75 and Act No. 69, 23 February 1949, *Collected Laws* (Sbiřka Zakonu), Prague, 1949. The object of the law was declared to be 'to remedy the dispersion and overlapping which have characterized co-operative activities in the past'. 'If there is only one agricultural co-operative in a municipality, this becomes transformed into a unified co-operative; when there are a number of organizations, these are merged. . . . The unified agricultural co-operative societies form a specialized group under the administration of a board of nine members within the Central Co-operative Council.' (Act of 23 February 1949, cited in I.L.O., *Industry and Labour*, vol. II, 1949, pp. 211–12.)

[2] However the actual number was said to be usually about twenty.

for a full-fledged U.A.C. (The objective was to have a U.A.C. in every borough-community, i.e. group of village hamlets, in the country.) Apparently preparatory committees were especially effective in localities having as yet none or very few co-operative features. Once a U.A.C. had been formally established in a locality, previous co-operatives automatically became a part of it as branches and subject to its regulations. Where only a preparatory committee existed, it would begin planning for elementary forms of rationalization of the next season's farm work.

In 1950 universal emphasis was being placed on the widest possible adoption of large-scale sowing as the first task of the co-operatives. Again and again points like the following were reiterated in the Czech press: 'The arable land in Czechoslovakia is divided into 33,000,000 lots. The average size of each farm holding equals 13·5 acres divided into 33 separate parcels of ½ acre each. . . .'[1] In May, President Gottwald was quoted as saying that the 'mass adoption of collective sowing' by the U.A.C.'s was 'the principal task at the present time'.[2] 'Collective planting based on land consolidation will enable the farmers to avail themselves of all the advantages of large-scale farming.'[3] Rearrangement of land for collective sowing was said to save 3·5 per cent of arable surface. Simultaneous sowing of adjacent plots was essential for rational land use generally. Selected seed could not be properly used on strips. And so forth.

Arguments against the strip system and in favour of 'consolidated' land for each farmer had long been familiar in the Czech and Polish country-side. The writer well remembers the hesitant views of the future in this respect expressed by agricultural administrators in both countries in the first half of 1948. The need for consolidation was regarded as absolute, and the process was indeed proceeding a little, but the time and costs involved were enormous, a measure of the desperate importance attached by each farmer to the value of each strip he might have to exchange. Now, under the prospect of common sowing, even without legal abolition of the strips, their importance declined greatly and the next step, of actual 'consolidation' and exchange of strips, could

[1] *I.A.I. Bulletin*, July-August, 1950.

[2] Ibid., June 1950.

[3] Ibid., July–Agust 1950. 'Tractors are no argument for our farmers. In Bulgaria you can argue this, but not here. But *how to use them rationally* is.' (Agricultural economist to the writer, November 1949.)

be undertaken on an altogether different basis. As an agricultural economist put it to the writer in late 1949, 'To-day we are not working specifically on consolidation. We expect it to come "automatically" with co-operation.'

The U.A.C.'s were to be helped in every way possible to make the consolidation process easy. 'As soon as a Unified Agricultural Co-operative decides to adopt collective sowing and gains the adherence of the overwhelming majority of small and middle farmers in the community to this idea, it will request the Regional National Committee . . . to carry out the rearrangement of its lands. The Regional Committee keeps field squads for this purpose, composed of a land survey specialist and an agronomist. . . .' These were to advise the farmers 'on the fastest and least expensive method of sowing their fields after their rearrangement'. It was optimistically added that the only cost to the farmers would be 'the few hours of labour involved in the survey of the terrain' and in the time consumed 'in the meetings at which the plan for collective sowing is adopted and the mutual exchanges of pieces of land belonging to members and also non-members of the Co-operative agreed upon'.[1] Obviously, however, even a protracted haggling process should have paid if it reached its desired conclusion.

No individual either inside or outside the Co-operative could be forced to join the collective sowing scheme.[2] However, substantial differential advantages were held out to those who would join. 'On the basis of past experience it is expected that small and middle farmers who are not members of the Co-operative will become parties to the collective sowing scheme because their participation will secure them the same advantages as those enjoyed before only by the . . . U.A.C.'[3] Among these were mentioned 'preferential allotment of selected seeds and larger allotments of fertilizers at substantially lower prices. The State Machine Stations also charge . . . less for labour executed on their fields.'[4]

[1] *I.A.I. Bulletin*, June 1950.

[2] 'No member of a United Agricultural Co-operative nor individual farmer can be forced by any method to join the system of collective planting; the decision of each farmer must be entirely voluntary, based on consideration of the fact that the system of collective planting serves his interests and brings him material advantages.' (Ibid., July–August 1950.)

[3] Ibid.

[4] Ibid.

Some degree of these advantages could be secured even if only a portion of the lands owned by U.A.C. members were sown in common. Various tables of rates were cited at different times. It was apparently common practice in some U.A.C.'s, especially new ones just starting, to organize, not 'unified' sowing operations including the entire membership, but only partial or 'group' sowing operations. In that case partially reduced rates would be offered by the Machine Stations, etc., to the farmers participating in the group scheme, provided the common area exceeded certain minima.[1]

In addition to advantages in servicing and a generous loan policy, land co-operatively sown received tax reductions, and farmers all of whose land was in U.A.C.'s paid only 3·5 per cent tax altogether. Moreover, where lands obtained through the Land Reform were still being held in reserve by the Government, these might be turned over to the Co-operatives.

Farmers wishing to remain outside the scheme were to be allotted parcels equivalent to those in the centre of fields that were now being collectively worked. 'Collective planting makes it possible to allot to farmers who are not yet convinced of the advantages of collective effort and who desire to farm individually, new parcels in exchange for those placed under collective cultivation, equal in size to the ones they held before. . . . On these they may grow all the crops which they must produce if they are to deliver to the Government the prescribed quantities of various products.'[2]

The consolidated land meanwhile would be split into divisions of approximately 60 acres each and planted with crops in 5- to 8-year rotations.

A booklet published in February 1950, called *The Czech and Slovak Village is Taking the Road to Socialism*, rehearses the arguments being addressed to farmers.

'The small and middle farmers know that all this (the supply of machinery by the Government for their use) is not sufficient to bring a basic solution to the problem of the productivity of farm labour. Machines work more slowly on small plots of land scat-

[1] E.g. 'The State Machine Stations afford the U.A.C.'s which want to introduce a unified rotation system on an area of at least 125 acres in pieces of at least 12½ acres, a 45 per cent reduction in the price of ploughing.' (*I.A.I. Bulletin*, October 1949.)

[2] Ibid.

tered over a vast area than on large contiguous fields. Their work is also more expensive because much fuel is used in driving the machines from one plot to another. . . . The farmers will inevitably reach the conclusion that collective tilling, sowing, and harvesting are indispensable if the output is to be expanded. The same applies to livestock economy. . . .'[1]

The booklet then turns to the recent history of common sowing. 'During the autumn sowing period (i.e. of 1949) the so-called collective sowing movement made its appearance. This movement is without doubt an important milestone in the development of the United Agricultural Co-operatives, because by it the farmers are passing from the collective organization of labour to the collective tilling of land. The first who came forward with this plan were the members of the United Agricultural Co-operative in Bohatice. . . . In order to utilize better their farm machinery, save time, manpower, and money, and increase their crop yields, these farmers decided to plant a single crop on land owned by a whole group of them whose fields bordered on each other. They used, at the same time, the same strain of seed. In this way, out of the former 376 plots, 32 large field complexes only, measuring 25 to 30 acres each, were formed, each planted with a single crop. The advantages of this arrangement became immediately evident. It became possible to use machines on large fields on which the crop ripens at one and the same time.'

Strictly similar arguments and methods of persuasion were being used in Poland. But here the discussion of the transition stages of Preparatory Committees and U.A.C.'s was not so precise. In both countries it was very evident that various functions formerly exercised by the Farmers' Union and Farmers' Self-Help respectively were now in process of transfer to the Co-operatives. In the case of Poland's Farmers' Self-Help, much the more active of the two national organizations, it was expressly stated at its 1949 Congress that one of its prime tasks now would be to help the Co-operatives directly, and, secondly, to 'cement' individual farmers with co-operatives by founding common cultural organizations. (Such cultural organizations were said to have tripled during the year.) However, the important thing was that the Co-operatives themselves, under their new lease of life, were no longer to be as before under the aegis of Farmers' Self-Help as such. Instead, a new Central Office for Farm Production Co-operatives was to direct

[1] Quoted in *I.A.I. Bulletin*, March 1950.

their affairs, co-ordinate rather than subordinate to F.S.H. nationally.[1]

By May 1950, Czechoslovakia claimed 3,000 U.A.C.'s and 1,500 Preparatory Committees; while by July 1950, Poland claimed 1,000 Producers' Co-operatives.

Co-operative Farms

Like much else in organizational forms, types of actual co-operative farms in the two countries appeared as yet to be highly fluid. In all the newer planned economies one heard of three and four types[2] or stages of co-operative farming, in a hierarchy of closeness of association and/or emphasis upon labour and de-emphasis upon original property in the distribution of earnings. But the forms were complex.

In Poland the classification in use was:

(1) 'Associations for Joint Tillage'.

(2) 'Farm Production Co-operatives'.

(3) 'Producers' Unions' or 'Collective Co-operatives'.

Of these three, the last form represented really pure collectives, with that portion of the property that was to be used in common merged indistinguishably and with income divided exclusively in proportion to labour used for service. Sometimes this form was used for only a part of the farmer's production, as in livestock breeding, leaving the rest of his property under other arrangements. The only valid distinction between Type III and a modern Soviet collective farm was that here the land remained technically private property. (In addition, in all the 'people's democracies' as well as in the Soviet farms, a small area for kitchen-gardens, surrounding his home was kept intact for each farmholder and he was to keep privately, if he wished, one or two cows and unlimited pigs, poultry, etc.)

Type I was said to resemble some of the earlier Soviet collective

[1] 'It has long remained undecided whether this system of co-operatives should be put under the direction of the (Self-Help) Union or whether the rural co-operatives should form their own central office. The rapid development of the movement . . . has resulted in the *severance of the ties* between the co-operatives and the Union for Farmers' Self-Help and in the organization of a special centre of these co-operatives, which received the name "Central Office of Farm Production Co-operatives Farmers' Self-Help".' (*I.A.I. Bulletin*, May 1950. Italics mine.)

[2] By means of subdivision, the Czechoslovak types were soon accounted as four or even five.

farms and also the 'cultivators' co-operatives' formed in Denmark after World War I. In them, while fields were worked in common, final crop income was distributed in proportion to the size of the members' property, and joint expenses were met in the same proportion.

Under the second type, a considerable range of division of income between property and labour service was possible, but in Poland the national statutes of the Farm Production Co-operatives stipulated that approximately a fifth should be retained for improvement of the common enterprise and the remainder distributed among members as follows: a fourth to a fifth in proportion to the land brought in by the individual members, 10 or more per cent in proportion to the inventory brought in by them, and about two-thirds in proportion to the number of 'man-days' of labour. (As in the case of Soviet collective farms, the 'man-day' of labour represents a norm of accomplishment for different kinds of ordinary work. Work of extra skill or difficulty rates more than a single 'man-day' per diem, and so does excess accomplishment at ordinary work.[1])

Strikingly enough, in Poland throughout 1950 and even in 1951, the great majority of co-operatives were of Type III, where produce is divided only according to the number of man-days of labour. At the same time a large proportion of co-operative members were reported to be 'middle' rather than 'poor' farmers. The explanation subsequently accepted for both features was that a large part of these ventures were started in the Western Territories where holdings were less crowded but more even, so that sizes of individual holdings would more or less cancel each other out, leaving labour as the differential feature.[2] Another factor emphasized was that these men, being re-settlers, had themselves but recently been poor or even landless peasants, with less conservative attachment to their particular acres and ways of work. Later this was recognized as a danger signal, for similar motivation could certainly not be expected to actuate the peasants of the interior.

In both Poland and Czechoslovakia, but especially of course in Poland, a technical bottle-neck in more widespread setting up of

[1] For instance: cutting $\frac{3}{4}$ acre rye = 1 man-day, therefore cutting 1 acre in 1 day = $1\frac{1}{2}$ man-days.

[2] As an agricultural writer had said to the author late in 1949, 'Peasants who received 5 or 6 or 7 hectares in the Land Reform realize that rent means little to them and work means much'.

Type II or III co-operatives was early recognized to be the question of administrative personnel. 'A lack of organizing and managing workers who could carry on agricultural work on greater areas,' was the complaint in Poland.[1] And in Czechoslovakia the writer was told enthusiastically by an agricultural writer, 'It has gone quicker than we wanted. Administratively we can't keep up with it.'

For the mass of farmers, however, as the Six Year Plan of Poland ambitiously but soberly put it, the basic task was held to lie in 'creating the *prerequisites*, material and technical, for a voluntary grouping of a large part of farm holdings in Poland into [Type II] Farm Production Co-operatives'.[2]

[1] Speech by the United People's Party Secretary at the Unity Congress of Peasant Parties, Warsaw, December 1949; cited in *I.A.I. Bulletin*, January 1950.

[2] Italics mine. Further discussion of co-operative farms will be found in Chapter XV.

CHAPTER XIV

INTER-STATE ECONOMIC RELATIONS

Under a planned economy, Poles and Czechoslovaks frequently pointed out, foreign trade must itself be planned. Exports must be secured on a planned basis to cover scheduled imports necessary for the fulfilment of the domestic plan.[1] And imports themselves need to be such as can be counted upon, in quantities and in so far as possible in price, for a long enough period ahead to cover not only current production but investment planning. The need had been particularly felt in the most recent period when all the planned economies were trying to industrialize at the same time. In the absence of stable trade conditions the most serious dislocations of domestic plan would be possible.

The desirable form of international trade for a planned economy therefore was held to be one by long or at least middle-term trade agreements specifying the goods to be exchanged over a period of years. And the desirable trade partner—if only he had the goods—was one willing and able to make such agreements binding and to carry them through without interruption. Finally, the most desirable form of trade agreement itself would be one that allowed for the varying credit needs of the two sides during the period of the agreement, since investment goods especially are slow in maturing.

All these considerations were cited by Czechs and Poles in discussing their countries' foreign trade policy in the past few years.

It was frequently stated by the Poles and Czechs that capitalist economies are too much at the mercy of business cycles to be ideal trade partners[2] and that their governments held, or at least exer-

[1] Cf. *Five-Year Plan Act of Czechoslovakia*, 27 October 1948, Art. 26, section 1: 'Foreign trade shall be so organized and directed that by means of essential imports the implementation of the targets set by the Five-Year Plan be ensured, and that by means of exports the expenditure incurred through imports be defrayed and the national budget balanced.'

[2] Cf. *Five-Year Plan Act of Czechoslovakia*, Art. 26, section 2: '. . . by means of long-term economic agreements—in particular with the countries with planned

cised, insufficient control to make private traders live up to governmental undertakings. Dealing with a trade partner on the other hand that had control of its own major economic resources and operated its own foreign trade apparatus 'ensures speed, directness, and certainty in the execution of mutually accepted engagements'.[1] Foreign trade planning, therefore, should include if possible having enough of one's trade anchored within the orbit of the other planned economies to save one from the worst effects of business fluctuations and economic irresponsibility.

The intention of Czech and Polish planners originally was to move gradually from the existing proportions of predominance of Western trade to a greater proportion of trade with the other planned economies, while continuing to increase the absolute amount of their trade with the capitalist countries. So late as the time of the formulation of the Five- and Six-Year Plans respectively, the perspective was for approximately a half-and-half proportion by the end of the period.[2] The added motivation of wishing

economies—the constancy of our economic progress and the resistance of our economy against crises shall be assured.'

[1] Dr. Stanislaw Raczkowski, 'Planned Economy and International Economic Co-operation', Polish Institute of International Affairs, International Studies Conference, XIV Session, Warsaw, August 1949 (multigraphed), p. 10.

[2] In the case of Czechoslovakia, western trade had been 80 per cent of her total in 1947, 63 per cent in 1948, and only 55 per cent in 1949, although total foreign trade turnover had gone up. The original Five-Year Plan had aimed to get down to a 50 to 55 per cent proportion of western trade only by 1953. By that time there was to be a total growth in foreign trade turnover of about 40 per cent, with western trade increasing 10 per cent in absolute figures and eastern trade nearly doubling. The net result of these changes was to show a proportion for Czechoslovakia not so very different from her pre-war pattern except for the very important removal of Germany as her chief trade partner and middleman and the taking of first place in her trade by the Soviet Union instead. With these exceptions, '. . . trade with the East and the West is planned at roughly the same relative share that it held historically.' (K. V. Rivet, U.S. Department of Commerce, *Foreign Commerce Weekly*, 9 May 1949.)

In the case of Poland, western trade had been nearly 60 per cent in 1948 and 56 per cent in 1949. But as her total trade turnover had increased nearly 20 per cent, her absolute trade with the West had gone up. Czechoslovakia's total trade, however, both with West and East, remained considerably larger than Poland's.

For 1952, President Gottwald announced in his New Year's Day speech, 'Trade with the U.S.S.R. and the people's democracies will make up 70·6 per cent of Czechoslovakia's imports and 68·1 per cent of her exports.' (I.L.O., *Industry and Labour*, vol. VII, Geneva, 1952, p. 255.)

to help one another was also mentioned. But the characteristic emphasis was that of the inscription placed over the door of the Foreign Trade Building in Prague, in 1949, by the Ministry's employees: 'Trade With Five Continents Under the Five-Year Plan.'

Both countries had inherited a difficult foreign trade pattern from before the war. Both had suffered from the economic domination of Germany. Now the Poles stated that Poland had 'given up for good its old role of semi-colonial bread-basket nation'. As for Czechoslovakia, that country had originally had a particular incentive for replacing Germany as the centre of east European trade. 'It was inevitable that Czechoslovakia, a highly industrialized country, situated deep in the heart of Europe, should seek, within the limits of its capacity, to take Germany's place as the supplier of heavy goods . . . for central Europe. . . . The social upheaval in post-war Europe served to emphasize the opportunity for Czechoslovak trade in the products of heavy industry.'[1]

The intention for future foreign trade was that both countries would be diversifying and shifting gradually to more heavy industry exports. Poland would export less coal and more foundry products and rolling stock; Czechoslovakia fewer textiles and more heavy machinery, precisely the goods needed by their fellow-planned economies. However, products saleable in western Europe would be built up also if only suitable long-term agreements could be reached. Thus, in 1949, when Poland was still conducting some 56 per cent of her trade with the West, she managed to conclude on top of it a five-year trade agreement with Britain which was very optimistically spoken of at the time. 'Of major importance for the expansion of East-West trade', the United Nations Economic Commission for Europe wrote.[2] Almost £150,000,000 worth of products were to be exchanged, with Poland sending increasing quantities of bacon, eggs and timber, and the United Kingdom raw materials and manufactured goods including considerable amounts of capital equipment.

By early 1952, the Czechoslovak State Planning Commission reported the following changes in the direction of Czech trade since 1949. Trade with the Soviet Union and the other planned economies: 1949, 45·5 per cent; 1950, 55·0 per cent; 1951, 60·5 per cent. (*New York Herald Tribune*, 29 January 1952.)

[1] William Diamond, *Czechoslovakia Between East and West*, London, 1947, p. 137. President Beneš had emphasized this point in a speech at the heavy industry centre of Ostrava in May 1946.

[2] *Economic Survey of Europe for 1948*, Geneva, 1949, p. 155.

Wherever it was possible, trade agreements were concluded on the basis of several years' duration[1] and with some form of credit provision payable in goods. The content of the agreements differed from the usual agreements of, say, the United Kingdom, in specifying not merely global sums but the specific goods to be exchanged, going into detail on the export as well as the import side. The Poles and Czechs claimed that this constituted 'a far more advanced stage of our foreign economic arrangements'.[2]

In the view of the Czechs and Poles, 'The type of bilateral agreement concluded nowadays between different Western countries is very loose. For example, generally speaking, the United Kingdom when concluding a bilateral agreement establishes a limited agreement on the financial side and does not restrict on the export side different classes of exportable commodities. The dimension of the bilateral trade is limited by a certain amount of pounds, and on the commodity side there are only restrictions on the import half of the ledger.

'In our bilateral quota agreements there are provisions concening (*a*) financial terms; (*b*) import and export quotas of different goods; and (*c*) in several such agreements, even provisions concerning prices—selling prices and purchasing prices. This is possible only with the degree of internal planning that we have in our country. Given a more or less liberal economy, you cannot have this kind of trade agreement.'[3]

In both countries foreign trade has been, for all practical purposes, nationalized. In Czechoslovakia since 1948 there has been a legal foreign trade monopoly. In Poland the same result was achieved more gradually by operating import and export prohibitions and exchange restrictions. So early as 1948 over 98 per cent of Polish foreign trade was in public hands, and by 1950 all of it was.

Various new developments took place in the structure of the foreign trade apparatus. Neither country followed the Soviet pattern of a single trade agency for each foreign country, but neither did they maintain the checker-board patterns of private agencies.

[1] Cf. Czechoslovak Five-Year Plan Act, Art. 26, section 2: '. . . by means of long-term economic agreements—in particular with the countries with planned economies—the constancy of our economic progress and the resistance of our economy against crises shall be ensured.'

[2] Interview material, July 1948.

[3] Ibid.

In Czechoslovakia where the need for trade was most acute and former structures were highly developed, the rationalization process could be seen most clearly. The major changes were made during 1949. Each industry thereafter had its own central Trading Corporation with branches in the various foreign countries. This Trading Corporation was quite separate, legally and financially, from the National (producing) Corporation of its industry. It had its own separate price and accounting system. Cost discrepancies of establishments of varying technical level within the industry could have no effect upon the Trading Corporation's books—it was the National (producing) Corporation that evened these out. And, conversely, it was the business of the Trading Corporation to absorb the shock of price fluctuations coming from the outside. However, these individual trade centrals, it was pointed out, did not have to compare the movement of trade with the year's plan for the mass of goods. The Ministry of Trade attended to that, working out co-ordinated plans.[1]

The director of the Trading Corporation now carried a parallel responsibility to that of the director of the industry itself. Under him were an import and an export division with their separate staffs, again divided, particularly on the export side, according to the specialty product that was being handled.

Trade agencies in various foreign cities were maintained in the usual neighbourhoods; the Czech agent for a particular line of goods sought to deal on equal terms with the sales agents of foreign private enterprises, and much trade was conducted through nationals of the country concerned. The difference between this and the usual private form of trade organization lay thus not in any lessening of specialization but merely in the size and attempted simplification of the structure.[2] With the elimination of competing trade agencies, great efforts were made at rationalizing the entire export and import services, and large savings in manpower and costs were claimed. In the case of the Czechoslovak textile industry, overhead costs in 1949, it was stated, amounted to only 2·5 per cent of the goods turnover for the export division and 1 per cent

[1] Cf. J. Krinicki, 'Planning Goods Turnover in Foreign Trade', *Gospodarka Planowa* (*Planned Economy*), Warsaw, December 1950, p. 136.

[2] According to the Czechs, an overall trade monopoly, such as the Soviet Union's Amtorg, dealing in all types of goods, might do for a country that exported only 2 per cent of its textiles, but hardly for one like Czechoslovakia that exported 30 per cent.

for the import division. Global quotas for exports were assigned—so much to the sterling area, so much to the dollar area, so much to the soft currency area—and within these, detail assignments were given to the various branch offices so that the individual agent should know what his part was.

Methods of import regulation have differed in the two countries. To all intents and purposes Poland early threw overboard her protective tariff. As a Polish official put it in 1948, 'Since we have very strict quantity and quality import controls,[1] we have no interest whatever in making our imports more expensive by putting on top of them a sum to go to the Ministry of Finance.' In Czechoslovakia, alongside of import permits, tariffs continued during the early years. This was probably because the process of nationalization there had been gradual, and with a part of their industry still in private hands the Czechs had use for a tariff.[2]

Obstacles to East–West Trade

The total figure for East-West trade in 1949 was cited at Geneva as having been only 42 per cent of 1938.[3] In the words of the Chairman of the United Nations' Economic Commission for Europe, 'The continued stagnation of East-West trade is costing the people of Europe and the United States too much.'[4] He was referring, of course, to the Marshall Aid countries' need to trade outside the dollar area and to the eastern countries' need for equipment.

Certain obvious technical difficulties were stressed by the Poles

[1] The controls referred to consisted of the system of permits issued at that time by the Ministry of Commerce either on the basis of national need or on the basis of bilateral agreement.

[2] Both countries continued to use a tariff in a very minor way, to protect small so-called 'free' import of gifts, etc., against speculation. A single pair of silk stockings, for instance, might carry a very low duty; a dozen pairs, a prohibitively heavy one.

[3] *New York Times*, 26 March 1950.

[4] *New York Herald Tribune*, 13 February 1950. Subsequently the stagnation was increased much further. In 1952 the Commission stated: '. . . trade between eastern and western Europe in 1951 declined further from the already abnormally low level it had reached by 1950, and, judging from present trends, there are prospects of still greater difficulties in the near future . . . in the first 9 months of 1951, exports to eastern Europe (not including eastern Germany and Czechoslovakia) amounted to only 2·4 per cent of the total exports of western European countries, against 3 per cent in 1950 and 5 per cent in 1949.' (U.N., E.C.E., *Economic Survey . . . for 1951*, Geneva 1952, pp. 88–9.)

and Czechs as tending to hamper East-West trade in Europe unless countered by positive measures. A country like Poland, one of its trade experts pointed out,[1] however great its need for investment goods, was yet not like a South American country from which large quantities of extractive products may be pumped at once. Her population was much too great, her effective domestic needs too pressing. Surpluses had to be created before they could be exported. Hence the great importance for a country like Poland for permission to buy its equipment freely and for forms of medium term credit, tied in to current trade, to finance it.

In 1948 and early 1949 the representatives of the Eastern countries at the sessions of the Economic Commission for Europe were proposing various forms of middle-term credit that would enable them to expand their exports in this way. 'Eastern Europeans', we read, 'are arguing that increased production must precede increased trade. . . . Eastern Europe cannot rapidly increase output without imports of equipment.'[2] For example, it was urged, if the United Kingdom would furnish Poland on credit with cooling chambers for her pork products, Poland could pay off in the course of three or four years in bacon and could thereafter assure a greatly increased and steady supply of this and kindred foodstuffs to the British.

Actually the final British-Polish four-year trade pact of January 1949, large though it was in size of turnover, provided only an insignificant revolving fund for credit purposes and hence did not help specifically in this type of development. The earlier Polish-Swedish agreement of 1947 had been far more generous in its credit terms.

Originally the connection between production and trade had appeared so clear that a 'Committee for Industrial Development and Trade' had been set up within the Economic Commission for Europe; but by 1949, as East-West relations worsened, the majority on the Commission had the offending words 'Industrial Development' stricken from its title and agenda.[3]

At its meeting in September 1948 the Economic Commission for Europe had worked out a project, subsequently approved in principle by the World Bank, whereby the western European coun-

[1] Interview material, October 1949.

[2] Vera M. Dean, *Foreign Policy Bulletin*, New York, 27 May 1949.

[3] Cf. *Foreign Policy Bulletin*, loc. cit. The earlier Committee had been *ad hoc*; in its truncated form it was now made a standing committee.

tries would underwrite a loan enabling the east European countries to purchase machinery for their timber industries. This loan was to be repaid in due course with the foreign exchange proceeds of the eastern countries' increased timber exports. However, nothing came of it. Nothing came either from repeated applications by Poland to the World Bank for credit as a member nation. Finally, in March 1950, Poland withdrew from the World Bank, citing as a reason her inability to obtain loans in spite of conformity with Bank requirements. She was the last of the planned economies to have maintained membership in the Bank.

Another technical difficulty, as put by one expert, was the relatively small role played in any case by East-West trade from the point of view of the major west European economies. A trade turnover, even in the most popular articles, of 7 or 8 or 10 per cent of their total intake was not going to be looked at by them as crucial. Even the chance of doubling such trade would not weigh heavily in the face of political considerations. 'They are too occupied by immediate necessities and immediate difficulties.'

The Export Licence System

Early in 1948 the United States established a system of special export licences applicable to the east European countries. The object of the licences was declared to be to prevent shipment to those countries of goods of 'potential military value'.

A brief list, open to the public, named articles that could be shipped to eastern countries without a licence. This list was very short and contained for the most part either food and forestry products or else finished consumer goods of a minor character. Omitted from it were all major chemical products, industrial raw materials, and industrial and agricultural equipment.[1] No list of

[1] As published on 30 April 1948, by the Department of Commerce the permitted list included chiefly: poultry, horse meat, vegetables and fruits, tea and coffee, confectionery, chewing gum; beverages, except malt; seeds except oilseed; nursery and greenhouse stock; tobacco and its products; logs, firewood, sawmill products, except various hardwoods; wood furniture; paper stock, etc., except filter paper and heavy cartons; glass, except opthalmic; of iron and steel manufactures, cutlery only; of aluminum, table and hospital ware; of electrical machinery, flashlights, electric flat-irons, coffee percolators, electric razors; of office equipment, typewriters, etc.; of agricultural machinery, bee-keeping equipment; dairy equipment except milk-shipping cans; incubators, lawnmowers; no harvesting machinery, seed separators, tractors or parts; 'other vehicles and parts: wheelbarrows'; 'medicinal preparations: white mineral oil. . .'

forbidden articles was made public.[1] Strict secrecy was maintained concerning it, for security reasons, it was stated.[2]

There was no way for shipper or recipient to ascertain in advance whether a proposed shipment would or would not fall under the ban. Inquiries to this effect were not answered. In order to find out, an order had already to be placed and presumably paid for and shipment requested. Moreover the licence system was made retroactive. Orders placed earlier, before the regulations were established, could now neither be cancelled nor filled. Particularly hard hit were major investment orders of the more expensive type which had taken some years for American firms to execute. Heavy machinery began to accumulate at docksides. Sometimes it could be sold for scrap or otherwise. But often the contracting country held on to it, paying storage charges for years in the hope that the policy might be changed. Thus the Czechs, in 1950, were still paying storage charges in New York on a $25,000,000 hot strip rolling mill ordered four years previously.[3]

Connected with this retroactive feature was the impossibility of securing parts for machinery previously purchased or received as a gift from U.N.R.R.A. Thus the Poles were unable to secure parts for their U.N.R.R.A. farm tractors. Lack of all types of automotive spare parts and ball-bearings were a continuing difficulty.

Similarly with machinery for manufacturing penicillin. U.N.R.R.A. had originally supplied both Poland and Czechoslovakia with some older type machinery, but neither parts for it nor machinery of the newer type producing a purer product and

[1] 'The list of goods rated as war potentials has been secret. . . . It does not deal in weapons and other direct war materials.' (*New York Times*, 13 May 1948.)

[2] Certain broad categories of goods, however, were known to be forbidden, and the Department of Commerce subsequently verified this. These included: machine tools and all metalworking machines; electrical, construction, petroleum, mining, and conveying machinery, as well as automotive parts. Beyond this, one could not tell: an individual licence had to be secured for each shipment. 'Except for a small list of relatively unimportant merchandise, all shipments . . . required an individual licence as of 1 March.' (United States Department of Commerce, Office of International Trade, February 1949, 'United States Trade with the Soviet Union, 1948'.)

[3] 'The shipment was to have begun in the spring of 1949 under a contract concluded with the United Engineering Company of Pittsburgh and the Westinghouse Electric Corporation in 1946.' (*New York Times*, 14 April 1949.)

on a larger scale (crystalline penicillin) could now be shipped.[1] Nor could the drug itself be exported to the eastern countries. Poland claimed urgent need of penicillin for its post-war venereal disease campaign and appealed to the World Health Organization for aid. The W.H.O. attempted procurement, but failed.[2] In July 1949 the first native Polish penicillin plant was opened, making penicillin by the more cumbersome older method. Whether spare parts had been obtained elsewhere or whether old type machinery had been made at home in Poland the writer does not know.

During the period when the export licence pressure was being increased in the United States it was also being spread from there to western Europe. The instrument here was Marshall Plan Aid. Under Section 117(d) of the Foreign Assistance Act of 1948, participating countries were in effect forbidden to ship eastward banned products made in any part from American supplies. Non-conforming countries were 'in so far as practicable' to be refused supplies.[3] For example, under this policy Italy was not to ship tractors to Poland in exchange for coal.[4]

[1] 'Poland and Czechoslovakia have plants installed by the United Nations Relief and Rehabilitation Administration for making amorphous penicillin, but large scale production of even this form, which is less easy to handle and store, is held up by the refusal of the United States to sell spare parts, the eastern delegates assert.' (*New York Times*, 2 March 1949.)

[2] In March 1949 it was reported from Geneva that 'the organization's secretariat has initiated the procurement action despite the contention of the United States representative on the executive board that such activities are not appropriate to the World Health Organization.' (*New York Times*, 2 March 1949. A summary account of the problems is contained in the *Chronicle of the World Health Organization*, vol. 3, no. 2, March 1949.) However, in May 1950, the general embargo still stood. A dispatch from Geneva stated: 'A discussion arose (in the W.H.O.) on the report of the committee of experts which had expressed firm disagreement with the United States official view that the export of Podbielnak extractors used in bulk manufacture of penicillin must be restricted because of the potential military value of such machines.' United States and British delegates 'objected to publication of the committee's report'. (*New York Times*, 19 May 1950.)

[3] Section 117 (d) directed the American Marshall Aid Administrator: 'To refuse delivery, in so far as practicable, to participating countries, of commodities which go into the production of any commodity for delivery to any non-participating European country which would be refused export licences to those countries by the United States in the interests of national security.'

[4] 'Under a policy of preventing exports of "strategic items" to eastern Europe the United States Government has discouraged Italy from developing a market for tractors in eastern Europe where the demand is enormous. The East would be Italy's normal outlet under the bilateral trade system prevailing

How far the ban went was questioned by some of the participating countries. French manufacturers, for example, were contending early in 1949 that 85 per cent of certain automotive parts and ball bearings which they wished to ship were to service machines built previously with their own materials.

The question became acute at the time of the signing of the British-Polish five-year trade pact in January 1949. Soon thereafter the United States sent Britain and France a general list of non-licensable articles, irrespective of the entry of American materials into their composition, 'with the request that the goods listed be not exported to Communist countries'.[1] The key, non-military list was still to be kept secret.

The President of the British Board of Trade thereupon announced that Britain was setting up an export licensing system of her own. The British list of forbidden products was however open.[2] The Economic Commission for Europe commented that even the British list was severely restrictive in effect since it included 'products which, while having a potential military value, are also indispensable to ordinary economic life and growth'.[3]

in Europe because Italy could use coal and timber that the eastern countries have to exchange.' (*New York Times*, 11 March 1949.) However, in the June 1950 issue of *Poland of Today* it was stated: 'The new Polish-Italian three-year agreement, reached in June 1949, provides for three times the volume of trade covered by a previous agreement. In exchange for Polish coal and other items, Italy is to deliver machines, electro-mechanical equipment, and ships.'

[1] *New York Herald Tribune*, 1 April 1949.

[2] A week before the news of the American request the President of the Board of Trade had stated that: 'His Majesty's Government are guided in their trade relations with these countries by considerations of economic advantage and cannot make a rule that trade agreements with these countries shall be subject to the settlement of political questions.' He now issued a new order withholding goods of 'potential military value'. 'Mr. Harold Wilson announced in the Commons to-day that an order to this effect was signed to-day and would be enforced as of April 8. The new order follows United States Senate criticism of Mr. Harold Wilson's statement last Thursday.' (*New York Herald Tribune*, 1 April 1949.) However, 'There was considerable dismay in some United States delegation circles (i.e. at Geneva) that Mr. Mayhew made a big point of the fact that Britain's so-called blacklist of products unsaleable to eastern Europe was public. It was felt that Britain invited comparisons with the United States which does not publish any such lists.' (*New York Times*, 14 May 1949.)

[3] United Nations, Economic Comission for Europe, *Economic Survey of Europe in 1948*, Geneva, 1949, p. 164. Cf. M. Dewar, *Soviet Trade with Eastern Europe, 1945–1949*, London, Royal Institute of International Affairs, 1951, p. 99: 'The chief requirements of the Eastern European countries are machinery,

Meanwhile, at successive sessions of the Commission, continued plans for expansion of East-West trade were being presented by the eastern countries. The most developed form of these plans was for an East-West multilateral trade system, to be worked out by the Commission's secretariat. The western European countries would present 'shopping lists' of commodities needed by them.

'Each eastern Government would then draw up its own shopping list, consisting of goods it would have to import to step up its output of commodities demanded by the West. Poland, for example, would be able to say with fair certainty that she could meet a demand for 1,000,000 tons of meat over three years if she could increase her imports of fertilizers, transport equipment, and refrigeration machinery by such and such amounts. . . .'[1] As indicated earlier, however, nothing came of these plans.

In the matter of multilateral trade with the West, some successes had been obtained by the planned economies prior to 1949. The Economic Commission for Europe's *Survey* for 1948 called attention to several such items. Usually the deals had been triangular, with the Soviet Union acting as intermediary.[2] The *Survey* also called attention to Czechoslovakia's achievement of East-West multilateral trade through sterling balances.[3]

In 1949, following the formation of the Council for Mutual

electrical and other equipment, machine tools, raw materials; in agriculture, tractors, implements. . . .'

A matter especially exercising the Poles in 1951 was the case of the two tankers taken over that summer by Britain. Constructed in British shipyards under a 1948 contract, almost entirely paid for in advance, and apparently assured of clearance after Britain's export licensing systems had gone into effect, by a special undertaking at the time of the Polish-British Trade Agreement of 1949, the tankers were nevertheless taken over a few days before their sailing dates, for security reasons.

[1] *New York Times*, 16 February 1949: '. . . It is a system that might produce results, in the opinion of both western and eastern European delegates . . . tying western exports up to specific undertakings of eastern countries to meet western import demands.'

[2] 'For instance, the U.S.S.R. has imported cotton from Egypt and wool from the Sterling Area, a part of which was for the use of other eastern European countries.' (Op. cit., p. 147.)

[3] During 1947 and 1948 Czechoslovakia accumulated sterling credits through one-sided trade with the United Kingdom, and apparently used most of them in subsequent trade, conducted via England once more, with the Sterling Area overseas.

Economic Assistance, a series of interlocking one-year triangular trade agreements, including three members of the planned economies and one outside the circle, were concluded between the Soviet Union, Finland, Poland, and Czechoslovakia. Under them Finland shipped 100,000,000 roubles worth of prefabricated houses, timber, and ships to the Soviet Union, the Soviet Union shipped food products to Poland and Czechoslovakia totalling the same amount, and Poland and Czechoslovakia shipped, respectively, coal, and sugar and machinery to Finland.

Dealings Between the Smaller Planned Economies

Trade among the various Eastern countries managed to expand greatly, *pari passu* with the difficulties experienced in securing Western products.[7] Trade with the Soviet Union was naturally by far the greatest single factor in that expansion, but trade between the smaller economies also became increasingly important, and an analysis of its forms is revealing. At the outset Czechoslovakia furnished the minor economies chiefly machinery, and Poland, coal, and both received various raw materials in return. Subsequently Poland began to furnish more rolling stock, and still later, chemicals, and in general trade among the smaller economies became more diversified.

Czechs as well as Poles emphasized the increasingly industrialized nature of Poland's exports to Czechoslovakia, and for that matter to the rest of the planned economies, 'under collaboration in industry'. Instead of Czechoslovakia's receiving, as before the war, first, live hogs, and second, coal, imports from Poland now included, it was pointed out, industrial raw materials and even textile machinery. In the case of Bulgaria, under Poland's first trade treaty with that country the Bulgarians 'did not want coal —so we sold them steel and locomotives'. Also, as eastern Germany became an important trade partner with the group, exchanges became still more industrialized. Under a four-year agreement concluded in late 1951, to run from 1952 through 1955, Poland was to ship eastern Germany coal and coal derivatives, zinc and chemicals, and some manufactured products, and was to receive from Germany installations for the power, machine-building and chemical industries, as well as chemical fertilizers. This agreement

[1] For 1950 the Economic Commission for Europe estimated the general growth of inter-eastern trade as 25 per cent over the preceding year.

was said to be 'among the largest' trade agreements concluded by Poland.[1]

Meanwhile the Soviet Union's placing of the rouble on a gold parity basis, not tied to the dollar, in January 1950, had affected the smaller planned economies. These now began to use the rouble in calculating their terms of foreign trade, and several presently revalued their own currency to raise it to a similar basis. This was the case with Poland's currency reform in late 1950. The claim of the Soviet Union in initiating the change had been that dollars were at present over-valued and that the new gold rouble would be less subject to fluctuations.

Bilateral Development Pacts: The Polish-Czech Prototype

Many of the characteristic features of the planned economies' collaboration were shown early in an important series of agreements and a covering Convention between Poland and Czechoslovakia concluded in 1947. It has seemed worth while to describe this particular arrangement in detail, since it was widely discussed and analysed at the time in a way that subsequent pacts were not. However, it should be remembered that it was presently followed by similar bilateral dealings with various of the other of the smaller economies, and that in ultimate importance it was overshadowed by the size and character of subsequent investment aids from the Soviet Union.

The Polish-Czech Economic Collaboration Convention, as it was called, was signed in 1947. It was good for five years and then renewable. At the time it represented by far the most advanced

[1] The importance of eastern Germany's trade was first emphasized in the Economic Commission for Europe's *Survey . . . for 1950*. Under the heading 'Trade Expansion in Eastern Europe', the *Survey* noted: 'Trade among the eastern European countries appears to have continued a rapid increase in 1950. . . . The increase would appear to have been in the order of 25 per cent above the 1949 level. . . . A considerable part of the expansion in 1950', it added, 'appeared to have been in the trade of eastern Germany with the eastern European countries. . . . This development, together with the substantial increase of trade among the other smaller countries of eastern Europe, contrasts to some extent with the growth of trade in the earlier years which had been centred mainly in the trade of each of these other countries with the Soviet Union.' For 1951 the Commission stated: 'Eastern Germany's trade with other countries within the region began to expand already in 1950, when it rose 43 per cent . . . (above 1949). In the second and third quarter of 1951, the increase over the previous year was, however, of the order of 80 to 90 per cent.' (U.N., E.C.E., *Survey . . . for 1951*, Geneva, 1952, p. 89.)

form of co-operation between the planned economies, and it was hailed accordingly. What was universally stressed was the inter-relatedness of its various parts and the focusing of the whole upon further industrial development. 'The various agreements signed simultaneously here form a harmonious economic system.'[1] Previously only cartels, it was maintained, had had mutual adaptation of resources in comparable fashion across national boundaries, and then only for restricted lines of products.

In contrast to 'normal' trade treaties, it was stated, one had here 'not a co-operation based on mere exchange of surpluses, but one taking into consideration the actual structural peculiarities of each country and aiming *to build up both*'. Therefore the Convention presented unlimited possibilities for further co-operation. The Convention, it was stressed, was one between equals. 'And both are on the way to Socialism: neither partner fears the further industrialization of the other. Each tries to help the other industrialize.'[2]

The same note was struck in the preamble to the Convention itself. 'Close co-operation in every field' would help increase the 'creative power' of the two countries and their people's prosperity. And it would help the two to develop economic relations with other countries. To achieve permanent co-operation 'legal standards and properly organized machinery' were necessary.

The machinery was to consist of a permanent joint Council and its subordinate bodies. The Council was made up of five members from each country, appointed by their respective Governments. It was to hold sessions twice a year. Under it were to be a set of speciality Commissions meeting every three or four months. It was the duty of each such Commission actively to seek out and exploit areas of collaboration with the partner country in its field. The number of Commissions was subsequently enlarged, but the original eight were Planning and Statistics, Investments, Finance, Transport, Exchange of Goods, Industry, Agriculture, Scientific-Technical. Of the eight fields, it will be seen, the exchange of goods was only one. Each of the major speciality Commissions in turn was authorized to set up committees and sub-committees at various levels, with the subordinate bodies ranging from the narrowly technical to those involving broad policy-making decisions.

[1] Interview material, July 1948.

[2] Ibid. Cf. also Waclaw Jastrzebowski, 'Polish-Czechoslovak Economic Co-operation', *Mysl Wspolczesna*, (Contemporary Thought), January, 1948.

By 1949 some 150 committees and sub-committees were reported to be functioning, with a total membership of over 3,000 persons.

Much was made initially of the complete equality and independence of the partners. No recommendations were to be made without the full assent of both national sections, and all questions of importance, unless previously delegated to the Commissions, had to be referred back to the respective Governments. As one of the administrators of the scheme put it to the writer early during the planning experience:[1] 'There is no common "dispositions centre": sovereignty remains unimpaired, each country retains its own national Plan.' What the Council was to do was to seek at all levels points of fruitful collaboration, 'areas of overlap' in their countries' respective Plans.[2] Later such matters as the maintenance of sovereignty would have been taken for granted, and co-operation in planning would have been viewed at a deeper level.

In the case of Poland and Czechoslovakia the potential areas of overlap of interests were said to be particularly broad since the two were physical neighbours, relatively complementary in their economies yet both on the march toward further industrialization, and geographically with a heavily industrialized area at both sides of a strategic portion of their common border.[3] However, even with all these advantages, it was stated, it sometimes happened that in a particular case the looked-for overlap could not be found. In that case the subject could be passed on to a higher committee. The process was one of continually looking for, seeking out, and, when found, making the most of fruitful opportunities for co-operation.[4]

[1] July 1948.

[2] Theoretically, it was said, there was no reason why any two countries sufficiently interested in economic collaboration could not set up such machinery. 'But for us to set up all-around collaboration with, say, Costa Rica, would hardly be realistic.' There must be a reasonable amount of geographic proximity and common interests. Moreover among capitalist countries, the Poles and Czechs maintained, such depth of collaboration was not going to be feasible: there were too many conflicting ownerships and not enough stability of plan.

[3] This last was of course a post-war gain. The pre-war Polish-Czech frontiers ran through very weakly industrialized areas, chiefly farming areas, very primitive. The industrial centres of the two countries, the Poles and Czechs pointed out, were divided by a highly industrialized section belonging to Germany, Silesia. Previously this Silesian territory had served to hamper the industrial development of its neighbours.

[4] The proceedings were uniformly conducted, the writer was told, in an atmosphere of shirt-sleeve intimacy. 'I looked around at the people working

Trade between the two countries was small at the time the agreements were signed. It amounted to no more than 10 per cent of Poland's total exports and 5 per cent of Czechoslovakia's. Even at the end of several years it was not half so large as that of either country with the Soviet Union. But at the time the development features of the collaboration were considered a model for others. Subsequently the forms of investment aid from the Soviet Union overshadowed the Polish-Czech ones also.

At the outset it was obviously Poland whose new economic construction had been the most pressing. Hence investment goods secured by trade were necessarily on her side of the ledger. But needed construction for Czechoslovakia was also presently to be installed under the same mechanism. The method was said to avoid long-term unilateral credit by adjusting trade balances over a period of years.

The network of treaties covering these points was elaborate.[1] The significant point was that the two sets of arrangements interlocked: the investment deliveries were to be equated gradually by trade.

The total exchange ran to about £125,000,000 over the five years; a balance between imports and exports was to be achieved only at the end of that time. During the course of the five years there were to be three alternating periods of imbalance running roughly as follows: In the first period, Polish coal was to be exported beyond the return of goods from Czechoslovakia; in the second, the investment goods ordered from Czechoslovakia would begin coming in in quantities exceeding current coal shipments; in the third, coal and some of the products of the new equipment would exceed Czech shipments. At the end a balance would be struck.

The principle of trade-investment balances extended also to the

there with their coats off and I could not believe we were at an international conference.'

[1] Thus the Treaty on Exchange of Goods provided for the time of shipments and the quantity of goods to be exchanged. The Commission in charge of this sector was annually to define the list of goods needed. A special protocol on the purchase and sale of coal, zinc, and electric energy from Poland to Czechoslovakia defined quantities and conditions of these deliveries for five years. A separate treaty on Czechoslovak investment deliveries to Poland provided for essential capital goods, chiefly machinery, to be shipped in to Poland by Czechoslovakia.

field of construction. Various industrial facilities were to be constructed jointly on the territory of one or the other partner, in the first instance, Poland. The facilities were to remain the property of the country on whose soil they were constructed, but they were to be made large enough for part of the output to go to the assisting country. The first major undertaking of the kind was a great electric power station at Oswiecim, the former Nazi concentration camp site in Poland near the Czechoslovak border. It was to operate in major part with Czech machinery but Polish fuel. Half the output would be transmitted to Czechoslovakia through high-tension lines. At first the power would be transmitted free in payment for the machinery. Once Poland had paid for the machinery, the deliveries would be credited against normal payments to Czechoslovakia, again in goods.

There was also a transport agreement under which, among other things, Czechoslovakia subsequently negotiated for and received the right to use some two miles of the port of Szczecin (Stettin) as a 'free zone', constructing there her own harbour facilities and using shipping on the Oder.

In industry there were present the beginnings of some important joint planning, but the details of this were not made public. At first the Industry Committee apparently chiefly worked out various arrangements for joint or alternative use of materials. For example, as a Polish engineer pointed out to the writer early in its career, 'Czechoslovakia is using up good coking coal—which we could use.' Cheaper Polish coal was now to be used instead. More important, there was a beginning of common standardization and specialization of equipment and products. Large savings were claimed. The Economic Commission for Europe had spoken of the 'agreement for allocation of production in a number of branches of the engineering industry'.[1] This had apparently developed considerably. In some cases semi-finished products by one or another partner were even sent for completion to the other's plants. There was also talk of a general joint electrical power production industry of the two countries.

The prototype nature of the agreements was soon widely stressed and the subject of the principles of socialist co-operation between economies pursued further in various publications. There was much reference to the geographic division of labour aspect of the relationships. But the development aspect was singled out even

[1] U.N., E.C.E., *Survey . . . for 1948*, Geneva, 1949, p. 202.

more. And after a year or two a great deal was said about the integral planning aspect. '. . . In the two co-operating countries', stated a paper read before the Polish Institute of International Affairs in 1949, 'the raw materials and existing capital equipment are better utilized. Thanks to that and to wider markets, specializing in production is made easier, as well as mass production in the country which possesses most suitable natural conditions.[1] . . . Apart from these immediate advantages, owing to the gearing in of complementary elements in two economic organs, there is a more rapid increase in economic development and productive forces in the two countries. *This increase may also be planned for*. . . .'[2]

In April 1951 a new five-year agreement was signed between Czechoslovakia and Poland, under which annual goods turnover was to increase some 50 per cent. Investment goods were to be sent by both countries. For the first time, it was stated, Poland was to export to Czechoslovakia industrial and transport equipment 'in considerable quantities'. Czechoslovakia in return was to export machine tools, machines, and equipment for a number of industries. This was in addition to the usual variety of manufactured goods from Czechoslovakia and coal, zinc, chemical, and agricultural products from Poland.

Trade and Investment Agreements with the Soviet Union

For each of the planned economies the Soviet Union was the largest trade partner. For Czechoslovakia and Poland Soviet trade during 1948–52 ranged in the order of 25 per cent of their global trade, and represented over half of their planned economy trade, even though toward the end of this period the share of the other planned economies was growing faster.

In total amount Soviet trade increased quickly from year to

[1] Cf. U.N., E.C.E., *Economic Survey of Europe for 1948*, Geneva, 1949, p. 228: '. . . In Europe, the size of the national economies is such that, in most cases, full advantage could be taken of the economies of large-scale production only through international specialization in industrial development.'

[2] Raczkowski, op. cit., 1949, p. 17 (italics mine). 'In certain cases they (the 'Popular Democracies') establish in common the volume of production for given products according to the accessibility of raw materials sources, and unite for the "typing" of production as well as for serial and mass production.' (M. Parmov, 'Economic Co-operation of the U.S.S.R. with the Countries of People's Democracy', *Neue Welt*, Berlin, 1 June 1951, p. 58.)

year.[1] But it was its composition and accompanying credit arrangements that made it crucial for industrial development. For 1948 the Economic Commission for Europe noted: 'The Soviet Union has not only supplied capital equipment such as tractors and machinery, but also raw materials such as cotton, iron ore, manganese and chemicals. . . . Apart from its agreements for the reciprocal exchange of commodities . . . (it) has granted . . . credits for long-term deliveries of specific products. Thus, under the 1948 agreement, Poland was granted a credit of $450,000,000 to finance the supply of a complete steel plant and other industrial equipment in future years.'[2]

Czechoslovakia in 1948 and 1949 was receiving ball bearings as well as iron ore and other metals, in addition to grains and textile raw materials. For a country like Czechoslovakia the Soviet Union also offered an important market for some of the products of her light industry, particularly textiles and shoes. 'Another important element in trade between the U.S.S.R. and some of the other eastern European countries has been the exchange of textile raw materials from the U.S.S.R. against finished textiles manufactured from these raw materials in the other countries.'[3]

[1] Thus, for 1949, the original plans for an increase of 35 per cent and 45 per cent respectively for Poland and Czechoslovakia were stated to have been substantially exceeded, and by 1950 still further long-term agreements running for 1951–5 and 1951–8 were to increase the 1948–50 averages by 50 and 60 per cent.

[2] U.N., E.C.E., *Economic Survey . . . for 1948*, Geneva, 1949, pp. 146, 147.

[3] Ibid. However, it was subsequently stressed by Czech sources that a major part of the country's textile exports was still available to the West: Soviet purchases had taken 18 per cent only. (Cf. *Foreign Policy Bulletin*, New York, 27 May 1949.)

Czechoslovak and Polish trade personnel in 1949 had much to say concerning charges of exploitative Soviet trade relations, made by Western officials at Geneva and elsewhere. For example, the charge that emergency grain shipments to Czechoslovakia after the 1947 drought had been at interest rates 1 per cent higher than Export-Import Bank rates, was met by assertions that this was a rush order requiring altogether exceptional shipping and handling. Similarly with the charge that Poland had agreed to ship several million tons of coal to the Soviet Union for $1.20 a ton when the world price was $14 to $20. Poles commented that the $1.20 covered transportation charges only. The coal had been reparations coal from Germany, due to the Soviet Union from Silesia. Cf. M. Dewar, Royal Institute of International Affairs, op. cit., pp. 39–40: 'A frontier and reparations agreement . . . on 16 August 1945. According to this Poland was to receive 15 per cent of all reparations obtained by the U.S.S.R. from her zone of occupation, and 15 per cent of the reparations

The Polish-Soviet Trade and Investment Agreement of January 1948 referred to above by the Economic Commission for Europe, was stressed in after years by the Poles as a landmark in their industrial history. Besides providing for the exchange of goods, it extended to Poland credits for great amounts of industrial equipment to be sent during 1948–56. Payment was to be over a period of ten years, chiefly in goods, at 3 per cent interest. This credit, the Poles later stressed, was the largest that Poland had ever received. The investment credit amounted to some £112,000,000, and enabled Poland to start carrying out her Six-Year Plan in more than thirty industrial branches. The investment goods were destined for plants of both heavy and light industry. In heavy industry the Poles made much of the new steel plant of Nowa Huta that, when completed, was to double the country's existing steel capacity: they pointed out that it was wholly Soviet financed and was built mainly on Soviet deliveries. The next most important items were several large chemical factories. Pre-war Poland had had no chemical industry. In light industry the Poles made a dramatic showing of the Soviet Union's contribution in 1951 by having a series of plants in different parts of the country start production within a few days of each other close to 7 November. These included a factory producing the first passenger motor-car in Poland, a new lorry factory, a new textile factory, and a large transporter for the mechanical loading of ships. All of these, the press emphasized at the time, had been not only Soviet financed, but had been erected on the basis of Soviet plans and machines and with the aid of Soviet specialists.

In 1950 Poland received further increase of credit from the Soviet Union. By the close of 1951 not all of this had as yet been used. The new agreement to run from 1953–8 provided that nearly 40 per cent of all Soviet exports to Poland would be capital goods.

The Council for Mutual Economic Assistance

For the smaller planned economies plainly a double process had been at work. From the Soviet Union came major investment credits, technical equipment and industrial raw materials, as well

due to the U.S.S.R. from the western zone. In return for this industrial equipment, the U.S.S.R. demanded delivery, at a special price, of certain quantities of coal, namely, 8 million tons in 1946, 13 million tons in each of the years 1947–50, and 12 million tons per annum thereafter throughout the occupation of Germany. (In March 1947 these quantities were reduced by 50 per cent.).'

as, especially in times of stress, grains and feeding stuffs. Accompanying the technical equipment came a mass of specialist information which will be referred to more fully in Chapter XVI. In return, Czechoslovakia and Poland sent for the present a good deal of light industry products, light machinery and, in the case of Poland, rolling stock. Between the smaller economies, in pairs, there was growing up a series of bilateral dealings, also on a long-term basis, allowing for increasing technical adaptation of one economy to another.

But there was yet a third relationship whose importance over the years might grow, serving as a framework or 'hat' for both major processes. This was the Council for Mutual Economic Assistance, the common organization formed in early 1949 to include both the Soviet Union and all the lesser economies at once.

Even before this, it was clear, the foreign trade apparatus of so central a country as the Soviet Union must have had planning functions over against all the planned economies at once.[1] Now both this relation and the separate relations and mutual adaptations of all the lesser economies were brought together in a joint association.

The Council originally included as members the U.S.S.R., Poland, Czechoslovakia, Hungary, Rumania, and Bulgaria. Later Albania and eastern Germany were added. It was also provided that any European country that 'adheres to the principles of the plan' could join it. The various countries were to be equally represented on the Council and sessions were to be held successively at different capitals, the host country in each case presiding for that session. No permanent headquarters and no secretariat were provided. The object of the organization, expressed in very general terms, was declared to be, on the one hand, to foster multilateral trade between the member states and to facilitate their clearing arrangements, and on the other hand, to help them to develop further their respective economies. Later it was made

[1] Cf. B. H. Kerblay, 'The Economic Relations of the U.S.S.R. with Foreign Countries During the War and in the Post-War Period', *Bulletins on Soviet Economic Development*, Bulletin 5, Department of Economics and Institutions of the U.S.S.R., University of Birmingham, March 1951, p. 22. 'Finally, where such extensive economic co-operation exists, the very functions of the foreign trade monopoly become transformed. Instead of being simply an instrument of the protection *of a single economic system*, it becomes an instrument for the integral *planning of foreign trade of several related economies*.' (Italics in the original.)

clear that planned mutual adaptation of the member countries and further technical advance were looked for especially by further bilateral agreements, covering the topics already familiar from the original Polish-Czech Convention: mutual economic co-operation in general, exchange of goods and payments, credit and the delivery of equipment on credit, scientific and technical aid, the setting up of mixed commissions to effectuate these policies, and so on. But it was obvious that the systematic meeting together of all the planned economies at once, on a basis of mutual adjustment of their several economic plans, might be very important indeed, even though concrete embodiments of policy had all to be worked out in separate conventions.[1]

Viewing the international economic policies of Poland and Czechoslovakia as a whole, it is easy to see the interrelations between their several portions.

The trade pattern has been obvious. Trade with other planned economies was from the outset looked upon as good in itself. These other economies were said to be stable, free from economic crises. They were said to be in a position to carry through their trade commitments, since they owned their own instruments of production and foreign trade apparatus. They were looked upon as reliable friends whose intentions would not change, who desired to build up, not tear down the Polish and Czechoslovak economies. Consequently a great absolute and relative growth in trade with them was on all accounts desirable.

On the other hand, increased trade with the West was to be worked for also. In so far as possible, stable long-term agreements should be concluded with the capitalist countries, specifying precisely the types of goods to be exchanged and tying in production with delivery arrangements. No effort should be spared to consolidate one or another arrangement, whether through bilateral trade agreements individually concluded, through United Nations

[1] In its *Survey* for 1951 the Economic Commission for Europe points out that 'Eastern Germany is to share with Czechoslovakia the main responsibility for supplying the whole area with heavy electrical equipment, mining and foundry equipment, chemical machinery and heavy railway machine tools. In the field of railway wagons, Poland provides a particularly interesting example of specialization; Polish targets for the production of wagons were considerably stepped up and those for eastern Germany reduced. In fact, it seems that Poland manufactured in 1951 a quantity of wagons little smaller than did the United Kingdom.' (Pp. 61–2.)

agency via the Economic Commission for Europe and its various subcommittees, or through clearing balances and multilateral pacts. If one arrangement was refused, another must be sought. This process in 1950–1 was still going on.

The original perspective, however, had had to be changed radically. Restrictions, starting in the United States and spreading to Europe, had perforce speeded up and sharpened the process of trade reorientation. Developments planned to occupy five or six years had been compressed into two years or less, and further were in sight. It was at this point that the rapid recovery of the Soviet Union from its war losses had played a major role. The acceleration of Soviet recovery to a point some 40 per cent beyond pre-war output came just at the time that Western trade barriers began to be most seriously applied. And by the close of 1951 a 100 per cent output gain had been claimed by the Soviet Union. As it was, a very large amount of compensatory trade was developed and the blow to the smaller economies was greatly cushioned. Figures of total Czechoslovak and Polish trade and of further industrialization continued to rise.

Whether a further development of the newer type of trade patterns desired by the planned economies with the West was going to be possible, and if so when, would apparently depend, not upon the efficacy of the new forms but upon East-West tensions generally. So far as Poland, Czechoslovakia, and the others were themselves concerned, what was envisaged was apparently a middle ground of trade; relations with capitalist economies would be incomparably looser than those with planned economies, yet they would be considerably firmer and longer lived than the classical trade pattern. If the case of Finland, where, as we saw, a close quadrilateral trade arrangement had been achieved between three planned economies and one unplanned one, be considered as a special case, yet in several other cases, including Sweden, Switzerland, Denmark, and Holland, new types of bilateral trade agreement had been concluded guaranteeing a long cycle of investment goods on credit. The 1948–50 attempts at negotiations via the Economic Commission for Europe were a further extension of the trade-investment tie-in principle. It will be recalled that they proposed to tie in timber with timber-cutting machinery, food with fertilizers and refrigeration equipment, and so on. It appeared abundantly evident that rather than any form of economic autarchy, the planned economies were looking towards a new type of geographic division of labour along exceedingly complex lines.

Meanwhile the most structurally significant part of the planned economies' interstate economic relations were obviously those between one another. The patterns first seen in detail between Poland and Czechoslovakia were applied increasingly between the whole circle of sister nations. And in the case of the Soviet Union, the stream of technical and material influence in their industrialization programmes was patently greatest of all. Although the rate of growth of trade between the smaller nations was greater than theirs with the U.S.S.R., the total size of Soviet trade and investment dealing with them and its concentration upon key development projects could not be matched elsewhere.

IV

'TRANSITION TO . . . SOCIALISM'

CHAPTER XV

DISSOLVING THE PRIVATE SECTOR

Some of the characteristics of the 'People's Democracy' type of pattern for a transition economy should by now have become evident. In these countries' discussions it was not only a question of the rate of change from private to public ownership, but of the basic means whereby change was to be carried out. The 'People's Democracies' had always laid prime emphasis upon the absence of major centres of opposition economic strength to thwart their policies. Even in Stage 1 of their régimes they claimed that it was only the circumstances of war-time capital destruction and early land reform that had made partial nationalization schemes and planning effective. Under Stage 2 they made clear that they considered the danger of a re-coalescence of hostile economic and hence political power centres much more threatening than the relatively smooth picture drawn by the Gomułka school would suggest. Strong political domination against these groups, they now held, would always be needed in a transition period, and active economic measures must be taken to break down their power. In effect, there was now considered to be no one critical economic point after which all would be smooth sailing: the process of building a socialist structure, whether slow or fast, would have to be continuous and militant right up to the end. Moreover, in view of the situation in the European variant of a 'People's Democracy', it was a relatively fast pace that was decided upon.

The present chapter tries to draw together the many different types of economic and administrative means used to make the private sector dwindle.

Early Relations

In Poland and Czechoslovakia in the early post-war period, once the initial land reform and nationalization measures had taken effect, the status of private property had been approximately as follows.

On the land, well over 90 per cent of the farms remained in private hands. State Farms did not account for more than 6 or 7 per cent of arable surface in Poland and much less in Czechoslovakia, and co-operative farming was as yet statistically non-existent. Small landed property had multiplied with the land reform, many previously landless peasants and hired hands now having small farms of their own. Conversely, with the break-up of larger estates the scale of operations was reduced and the number of agricultural employees fell sharply. Capitalist operations in the country-side were on the way out. The dominant economic force in the country-side now became the wealthier working peasant, with a few hired hands under him. The problem of his relation to the smaller working peasantry, particularly the new recipients of land, had not yet been worked out.

In trade, no legal changes had taken place, the overwhelming mass of retail traders, large and small, remained untouched. Co-operative stores had multiplied since the war but had not yet made a decisive change in town or country-side. Wholesale trade was also for the most part private, particularly in Czechoslovakia where war-time destruction had not been great, and gave rise to considerable profits. Complaints of speculation were rife, especially in foodstuffs. Foreign trade was almost entirely in State hands in Poland, because private capital was not available. But in Czechoslovakia private capital in considerable concentration continued to do business in foreign trade and handled a large share of the country's total. In Czechoslovakia also at first considerable sums of lucrative investment were held in the hotel and restaurant business, health resort premises, and so on. In Poland, neither premises nor capital on a large scale were available for such purposes.

It was in industry in both countries that the really sharp changes had taken place. It was here that nationalization, entire in some basic industries, partial and applying to all larger establishments in others, had sharply altered the balance of economic forces. The absence of decisive aggregations of industrial capital obviously meant the absence of command points for a rallying of such capitalist forces in the economy as did remain. And, obversely, the major economic forces were now in State hands. What existed was a relatively dwarf capitalism in size and concentration compared to the size and prevalence of the State units.

Changing Theory

The original conception, not only of the moderate but of the Communist parties in both Poland and Czechoslovakia, was that the small employer must be protected and encouraged. This was not only because of the emergency transitional need for him, but because he was considered relatively safe. Hemmed in as he was, economically and politically, by larger State aggregates of labour, capital, and prestige, he could be brought to play out his role in his lifetime constructively, within the limits open to him. This was the early picture.

In Czechoslovakia the February 1948 crisis and the experiences leading up to it modified this picture considerably. Elements of class struggle were now stressed and the reliance of Czechoslovak capitalists and their parties upon help from the West was emphasized. Attention was called to the previous 'sabotage' of national Plan fulfilment by those very industries which had predominantly been manned by private enterprise. The subsequent reduction of the legal limits of private ownership, it will be recalled, brought the Czech maxima to a level even somewhat lower than the Polish. In Poland, however, no appreciable change occurred at this time. The Czechoslovak events were ascribed to the special and more privileged position of Czech capital previously. The general perspective for the peaceful and relatively co-operative absorption of private by public enterprise under the conditions of 'People's Democracy' remained. It was not until the Tito-Cominform split of the summer of 1948 that a general recasting of views among the planned economies began to take place.

In Poland, so late as June 1948, the writer found the following a typical and coherent statement of the current doctrine.

In answer to the question, How about the desire of the small businessman to become a large one? one Polish answer was that there was not now the objective opportunity. While there was now no legal limit to the size a business enterprise could grow to, there were no large enough commercial and financial opportunities for the small business man out of his profits in five or ten years to amass a fortune and become a big one. As to the question of the small business man's probable discontent with such a limited horizon, and hence his probable hostility to the régime, it was pointed out that central European capitalism had always been rather rigidly stratified. The little man wanted to keep his place, not be pushed down from it. 'He knows here, too, he can keep his place.'

The old cartels had very narrowly circumscribed his field of action in any case.

'However, there is a very sharp social question.' At present the business man was at the top of the economic scale. 'But the workers are putting on terrific pressure to lower this. . . . It is very difficult to explain to them that under the leadership of a working-class State these others should have such a big economic differential.' In the Soviet Union the working class had had 'social priority'. In Poland this was true politically, but not economically.

It rather looked, the writer was told, as if questions regarding taxation were going to be 'a permanent difficulty so long as you have any private enterprise'. The feelings of the workers was bound to be strong, yet 'private enterprise is a delicate thing'. At first the size of private profits in such a war-ravaged country had not been a primary question: the basic problem had been to get production going. But now it was prominent. 'The complaint can be made, ironically enough, that the whole burden of the reconstruction here has been borne by the working class.' The peasants on the one hand, and business men on the other, were treated much better. 'The working class has had the doubtful privilege of paying economically for its political power.' However, it had to be conceded that any other Road to Socialism would have been yet more costly to the working class—'but this is hard to explain to the housewife'! Explanation, it was pointed out, was one of the functions of the working-class party, 'to assure the full understanding by the working class of its own position'.

What was considered the full perspective of the current period was described to the writer in approximately these terms.

People's Democracy is a political-sociological form. It consists of workers, peasants, intelligentsia, plus some lower middle class. Politically this coalition differs from both socialist and capitalist societies. It is not like a socialist society, for it still has these three social classes. It is not like a capitalist society, for there is no longer political power of large capitalists or landlords. Correspondingly it is considered that in these class structures the antagonistic interests of these classes are reduced to a minimum, and that the people's democracies give the basis for co-operation of these classes, including even the small capitalist.

Undoubtedly in this coalition the leadership is exercised by the workers' parties. This is both because of better organization and, more important, because they have a clear-cut programme. 'In capitalism, leadership as toward the middle class and peasants was exercised by capitalists—to-day this attraction and influence is exercised by workers.'

It should be noted that this whole revolution was accomplished without bloodshed. Usually much smaller social changes (for example, the English Revolution, the French Revolution, the abolition of slavery in the United States) have cost more.

But there have been negative costs: most of this cost had already been exacted by the Germans! The old capitalist and semi-feudal State, this the Germans destroyed—there was no State—political power was, so to say, on the streets, for anyone to organize.

Note here the contrasting condition in Czechoslovakia. The Czechoslovak middle class was preserved, it was not destroyed by the Germans. Hence there came a second instalment of the revolution in February. (Usually revolutions which happen later are more radical than those which happen earlier.)

In Poland there has been no dictatorship of the proletariat—there has been no capitalist state machine to be destroyed—the Germans had done it. The remnants of the old ruling classes could be integrated into the national effort.

There were elements of civil war, of course. During 1945–6 there was even an armed underground—2,000 government officials were killed by them. An amnesty was granted at the last session of Parliament, and a whole social action was developed by the trade unions to integrate these amnestied men into normal life.

However, one factor must not be forgotten. Undoubtedly the fact that Poland and the other People's Democracies were able to institute such far-reaching changes without civil war was due to the fact of having been liberated by the Red Army—so that the pre-war machinery of the pre-war State from London could not re-establish itself here. They found a new government already there, to which they had to adapt themselves.

What are the expected developments? Undoubtedly the present structure of the People's Democracy is being considered as a transitional stage to a socialist society. This means: (1) Politically, it does not require any political revolution, because the basic power is already in the hands of the workers. Therefore no dictatorship of the proletariat is needed, since there is no old State machine that needs to be smashed. Therefore there is a chance for a gradual and peaceful transition to a socialist society. (2) The economic transition will not be automatic but planned, and planned under the leadership of the working class.

What are the ways and means of this transition? It does not require the destruction of either simple commodity production (i.e. peasant and artisan production) or even of capitalist enterprise. The question is one of fully integrating them and changing the weight of the different factors. As to changing the weight, an increase of the relative weight of the socialized sector will do this. Planned industrialization of the country will change the balance in course of time automatically. The process may take a generation or more. Simple commodity production will be partly socialized by the co-operative movement. The productive processes and the contact with the market will be increasingly socialized without socializing of the means of production themselves. The capitalist sector is starting, for the past year or more, to be integrated into the national economy by a combination of economic measures (e.g. taxation) and administrative controls (e.g. price fixing). Through both of these the policy of the State Planning Commission will be carried out. The private business man will be absorbed into the national economy rather than destroyed. Enterprises increasingly work on a fixed margin; they bear a satellite character to the big nationalized enterprises. (This is comparable to garages and repair shops as satellites to big private enterprises under capitalism.) The private capitalist turns into a kind of public official. An effort is being made to give this private sector of the economy a less speculative and more productive character; we are trying to encourage long-term investment. Much of the speculative character was due to political uncertainty. As the system gets stabilized, the private business men get accustomed to their place.

This whole perspective we call 'the Polish Road to Socialism'.

By the end of 1948 the Polish perspective, as well as the Czechoslovak would no longer have been described in these terms. In the case of Poland the change culminated at the time of the Unification Congress of the Polish Socialist and Communist parties in December 1948.

Radicalization of both these Left parties had preceded their merger. Henceforth they formed the United Workers' Party, with a programme well to the left of the former stand of either. All of this had occurred just at the time the original version of the Six-Year Plan was being drawn. Thereafter the remaining political parties of Poland also underwent changes and amalgamations. Within the year the two Peasant Parties had combined to form one, again on a more radicalized programme than either had held originally. And in the middle of 1950 the Catholic (Christian Labour) Party went over in a body to join the Democratic Party, the latter representing, as it itself declared in a welcoming resolution, the 'progressive middle class'. There were thus three neatly delimited groupings: the large and leading working-class party; a smaller and clearly ancillary peasant party; and a very small middle-class party.

It is noteworthy that in Poland, during the period of the beginnings of co-operative farming as well as previously, the portfolio of agriculture continued to be held by a representative of the Peasant Party. Quite obviously, fundamental policy-making concerning agriculture was not in the hands of the Peasant Party but of the United Workers' Party, and the Peasant Party accepted this. Similarly, in the case of the Democratic Party: while it represented the 'progressive middle class', it could in no sense expect to legislate for small business and the professions. The function of each of the minority parties apparently was to see that the laws adopted under the 'dictatorship of the proletariat' were administered as fairly as possible for their members, to mediate their members' attitudes to the dominant United Workers' Party, and, conversely, to reconcile their members to the carrying out of policy which was fundamentally not peasant and certainly not middle class but working class.

In both countries the new views were thoroughly formulated and made into a programme. To the observer it would seem that the earlier picture of a long-drawn-out, relatively harmonious transition period had been based upon the implicit companion picture of a friendly western Europe, itself, in the eyes of eastern Europe, perhaps soon to begin first steps towards socialism. However, the later statements of Government and Party were in absolutes: such and such attitudes had been wrong and they were now to be righted.

In any case such sentences as, 'The People's Democracies give the basis for co-operation of these classes, including even the small capitalist,' would no longer have been used. The capitalist was now to be regarded as a naturally hostile element, not to be trusted. Where, as in industry, he formed an inconsiderable element of the whole, his elimination could proceed gradually as means were found to replace him. Where, as in trade, his role was still preponderant, his hold must be broken by State and co-operative competition. And where, as in agriculture, the capitalist elements, though small in absolute size, had yet no rival in power in the country-side, the small farmers must be arrayed actively against them and must finally overcome them by co-operative farming. The question was one of relative danger, not of size of income or establishment.

I. INDUSTRY AND HANDICRAFT

The Small Employer

By western standards, as aforesaid, even in the early post-war period such private capital as remained in the industry of the two countries had been reduced to exceedingly small proportions. This was obviously the result, not only of the actual nationalization decrees, but of the general economic and social atmosphere of the times, as well as the effects of war-time destruction. The predominating business units were indeed far smaller than the legal limits would have permitted (50 employees per shift in Poland, 300 to 500 at first in Czechoslovakia). Thus, in Poland in early 1948, the average number of employees per industrial establishment was 17·5. Even in Czechoslovakia before February 1948, private industrial concerns were employing only about 20 per cent of the country's industrial workers, and after that the figure fell to something over 5 per cent. In Poland the proportion from the outset was only about 8 per cent.

Moreover, an increasing proportion of such small capital as remained was now invested in making semi-finished products.[1] These so-called semi-products industries were increasingly ancillary to and dependent upon larger State industry for their raw materials and markets. They were not in an independent position.

Organically small industry was also connected, albeit at first loosely, to national planning via its local Chambers of Industry. These were supposed to help especially the newer and more ignorant small employers in procurement of necessary materials and in marketing.[2]

[1] In this respect small capitalist industry was to be distinguished in the main from handicraft: handicraft for the most part turned out finished articles.

[2] Subsequently, in Poland, early in 1950, by a decree of the State Planning Commission, local organizations of private industry were ordered to organize into a series of nineteen central branch agencies.

In Poland, by a 1949 regulation, the small employer with up to 15 employees, provided he worked in his establishment himself, was classified not as an employer but as an artisan. This gave him favourable tax standing, but it also made him subject to compulsory membership in the Artisans' Guild of his trade, with strong co-operative features of which we shall speak later.

In both countries one heard much of attempts to get small remaining industry away from speculative and into productive channels. Late in 1949 the private sector was described to the writer as occupying 'empty places', where co-operatives and Government enterprise had not reached, and complaints were still being made of finished goods turned out from 'black', i.e. pilfered or diverted materials. For example, tricycles were being made from needed bicycle parts, toilet soap from 'black' oils. Petty local industry, on the other hand, was said to be operating increasingly under local government hands. By early 1950 only some 80,000 workers in Poland were listed as working on the premises of private industry proper (as contrasted with crafts). In addition, private industrial employers gave out work to some 170,000 industrial home workers. That was all.

The Handicraftsman

The role played in much non-agricultural production by the small artisan working alone or with a few assistants has been large in central Europe. Even in so advanced a state as Czechoslovakia handicraft production continued to fill an important need after the war, while in Poland the need was crucial. Before the war some 1,300,000 craftsmen, largely Jews, had carried on the tailoring trade, much of shoemaking and other leather production, watchmaking, and a multitude of other vital crafts. With the extermination of the Jews and the scattering of craftsmen generally, this number was reduced by 1946 to under 600,000, and many artisans subsequently left the craft field altogether. The Government was hard put to it accordingly to seek to revive artisan production and to increase its output. Various methods of financial subsidy, provision of materials, assistance to apprentices entering the crafts, were tried in the early years. Larger co-operative workshops were set up in considerable numbers for the surviving Jews whose plight was especially desperate. But the general scale and level of efficiency of the bulk of small craftsmen's shops remained extremely low. So late as the end of 1947 Polish figures gave some

327,000 craft workers in almost 146,000 separate 'establishments'.

Typically, of course, handicraft production is not only exceedingly wasteful of labour and chaotic in its use of raw materials. It also offers a fertile field for middlemen upon whom the craftsman depends for his supplies. In times of shortages this may greatly squeeze the craftsman and raise the cost of his product. On the sales side moreover it proved difficult for the authorities to enmesh the small craftsman in the connections of nationalized industry, since, unlike the typical small manufacturer, he ordinarily made, not a semi-finished but a complete article. However, from the outset efforts were made not only to increase handicraft personnel and output, but to introduce some degree of rationalization into the craftsman's business methods. These efforts were considerably sharpened after the summer of 1948, together with efforts to bring the smaller craftsman to the top.

Early steps in Poland consisted largely in improving the supply side of the picture. A 1947 report speaks of 'a well-developing co-operation' between handicraft and local (i.e. local government) industry. 'Nearly all managements of the local industry are to a greater or less extent supplying the artisan's shops with supplementary articles, raw materials, half-products, and accessories indispensable for handicraft production.'[1]

By early 1948 we read of greatly increased credits to be allocated to the handicrafts, and a lowering, for a five years' period, of some of the regulations of the industrial law concerning apprenticeship training. Mention is made of the increasing role played by the Central Handicraft Establishment for Supply and Sale, and of a project for fostering so-called 'linked transactions', whereby this organization would receive special allocations of raw materials 'on condition that the respective articles . . . will be delivered at suitably calculated prices to Universal (i.e. State) Department Stores, as well as to trade unions for sale to their members'.[2]

The largest changes however came in the autumn of 1948, following the general changes of perspective already spoken of concening private industry. The chief subject and instrumentality of change was the old craft guild itself, a carry-over from pre-war. (Guild membership had remained strong, and individual craftsmen still carried their old craft certificates—when they could find them.) The guilds were organized on both an occupational and a

[1] National Economic Bank, *Quarterly Review*, Warsaw, December 1947.

[2] Ibid., March 1948.

territorial basis, culminating in a national Handicraft Chambers' Union. The project was to establish a direct pipe-line from nationalized industry to the individual craftsmen, cutting out the middleman, by increasing the supply functions of the guilds. (Gradually further co-operative features could be added.) A new Central Handicraft Agency, a State Co-operative affair, was accordingly formed on 1 September 1948. It took the place of a much smaller and narrower Central Board of Handicraft Supply. Membership in branch guilds was made compulsory, to enable the guilds to calculate overall handicraft needs. Purchasing co-operatives were to be set up. A National Craftsmen's Congress held that month in Wrocław listed the possibilities of the change. 'The new organization is in the craftsmen's own interest, since it gives them a firm financial basis, the possibility of real production planning, better conditions for raw material supply and better conditions for co-operating with State industry.'[1]

The handicraft branches were to begin drawing up their own economic plans, to indicate their global raw materials requirements from nationalized industry. This, it was said significantly, would lower the individual craftsmen's production costs 'since they will not be forced to acquire the necessary raw materials at higher free market prices'.[2]

In drawing up requirements lists, the handicraft chambers were to classify their members by size of establishment, and the smaller establishments were to receive priority in allocation of scarce materials. 'One of the principles of the new system of distributing raw materials from State sources is the granting of preferences to the smallest craftsmen's establishments, as to the economically weakest.'[3] Here, as also presently in agriculture, a class principle was plainly at work, favouring those members of the occupational group whose natural interests would lead them most readily in the direction of co-operation. (Or, to put it in another way, giving them priority over the 'capitalist elements'.) Within the organizations also it was the initiative of the smaller craftsmen that was now encouraged. They were urged to run for office, to displace previous, larger incumbents.

Meanwhile, at the other end of the scale, the ranks of craftsmen —and of their organizations—were being added to by the acces-

[1] *National Bank Bulletin*, Warsaw, December 1948.
[2] Ibid.
[3] Ibid.

sion of what had previously been considered small manufacturers. As indicated earlier, a new legal provision declared that henceforth working employers with less than fifteen hands would be classified, not as manufacturers, but as artisans. Such a classification gave these men priority as over against their previous 'capitalist' confrères in matters of taxes, credits, and raw materials allocations. However, as new members of the compulsory Guild organization of their craft, they would be outnumbered and outprivileged by the smaller craftsmen. In course of time presumably they would find themselves involved in far closer forms of co-operation than they would themselves have chosen.

Obviously, taking handicraft as a whole, the individual enterprise character of these occupations was being undermined, without alteration of property rights as such. The craftsman could still own his business and employ others under him. But through regulation of purchase and sale his guild organization was becoming a full-fledged marketing co-operative, with unusually strong credit and supply features. In addition, as we shall see later, the reorganization of the Central Supply Board promised to multiply actual producers' co-operatives in this field.

2. GROWTH OF SOCIALIZED TRADE

Foreign and Wholesale Trade

In the early post-war period private foreign trade was encouraged in both Czechoslovakia and Poland, although in Poland there was but little that could be revived. In Czechoslovakia following the February 1948 events all foreign and all wholesale trade were included under the nationalization laws. Within a few weeks National Administrators were appointed for the private foreign trade enterprises, and by the end of the year they were grouped under monopoly trading companies. These concerns were very large. For textiles and glass their turnover was said to be the largest in the world.[1] During the early part of 1949 further amalgamation had been undertaken. The various industrial National Enterprises had their commercial and foreign trade departments taken from them, and these were added to the National Trading Corporations of their respective fields. The latter now included separate foreign trade and domestic trade branches.

In Poland no foreign trade monopoly at the time was attempted.

[1] Interview material, November 1949.

However, for all practical purposes foreign trade was in government hands. Already in December 1948, it was reported that the share of private trade was only 0·6 per cent of Polish imports and 1·5 per cent of exports.[1] Private foreign traders operated on a very small scale indeed and were for the most part grouped together on a voluntary basis in the Federation of Polish Importers and Exporters. By late 1950 at the time of the currency reform all foreign trade was carried on by the State Trading Corporations.

Private wholesale trade on the other hand had revived much more rapidly and early became a problem. This was particularly true in the field of foodstuffs. For some time the Government attempted to meet price and supply difficulties by subsidizing the setting up of grain purchasing agencies under the consumers' co-operative wholesale societies. When this proved unsatisfactory, two new forms of purchasing and processing agencies were developed. There was a State enterprise type, employed in the flour-milling and slaughtering industries. The other and more widely used type was that of a mixed State co-operative enterprise, employed particularly in the grain trade. Here the organization at its purchasing end was an agency manned in major part by members of farmers' marketing co-operatives; but at the wholesale distribution end it was manned entirely by State representatives. The idea obviously was to narrow the gap between produce-market and wholesale prices. The means used to enforce patronage varied. So far as the wholesale trader himself was concerned, he was at no point ruled off the market but rather crowded out, or, as it was put to the writer, 'drowned out'.[2] The individual farmer was brought to desert the trader by price and credit advantages. He was still free to sell to whom he would, and he did sell direct to the consumer to some extent. But for general trading he was, through his marketing co-operatives, offered better terms by the State purchasing agencies. Particularly he was offered advance contracts, usually ahead of the growing season, at more favourable prices than the private trader could, or would, offer.

Retail Trade

In Czechoslovakia the private retailer and also the private

[1] Ministry of Foreign Affairs, Warsaw, *Information on Poland*, HX 31.

[2] 'We didn't legally nationalize wholesale trade, we just set up a series of State trading institutions which drowned the others (which were poorly organized) out.' (Interview material, November 1949.)

restaurateur and hotel owner with more than 50 employees had been included under the nationalization laws following February 1948. In Poland no such legal limitations were set—nor were they necessary. However, the country swarmed with tiny stores and not so tiny restaurants and it was inevitable that sooner or later a government travelling toward socialism would try to do something about them. By 1949 the traveller in Warsaw could see a few State department stores, some co-operatives, and a number of co-operative and State food outlets as well as restaurants.[1] By and large, however, the multiplicity of small private shops still struck the eye. It was a surprise to read the greatly shrinking figures on private trade. By late 1949 half of retail trade was said to be out of private hands. Thereafter the proportion rapidly increased. By 1950 it was four-fifths and for 1951 it was planned to be nine-tenths. Co-operatives alone by 1951 controlled about 55 per cent of urban retail turnover. In answer to questions concerning the relative merits of State and co-operative forms for retail trade, the Poles stated that in cities the aim was to achieve competition between them. In the villages the co-operative store would be the only form. In any case, however, they believed trade should be kept separate from industry, 'so that the consumer may be king'.[2] They did not wish to perpetuate the previously popular form of retail outlets by big industry.

In Czechoslovakia striking forms of State and co-operative competition with the private retailer had developed by 1949, and were visibly and rapidly proceeding to take over the field. In addition to larger department stores, two new types of chain store were in evidence. One, 'Braterstvy', as its name indicates, was a co-operative. It dealt in food products. The other, 'Pramen', was a National Enterprise. It dealt in a great variety of manufactured goods, but especially textiles. These two chains had penetrated deeply into the private field, not by expropriation and not by prohibition, but

[1] In the interval of a year the writer found three newly opened restaurants within two blocks of where she was staying: a fashionable restaurant operated by a war invalids' co-operative, a sea-food restaurant of the Fisheries Industry, and a branch cafeteria of a State dairy products chain.

[2] Interview material, October 1949. The following month a very large chain, Municipal Retail Trade, was founded. Two years later it was reported that this chain ran 8,000 shops in 500 towns. In the country-side by 1951 99 per cent of all retail supply was reported co-operative. (*Polish Co-operative News Service*, Warsaw, September 1951.)

by economic pressure.[1] The little independent dealer found it difficult to get supplies: once started, the co-operative and State stores had priority over him. (In the country, it was said, he could hold on longer, because there he had a direct line to the goods.) He also found himself less able to raise his prices in times of special demand, to make up for losses at other times, since the State stores and co-operatives kept their prices stable.[2] At this time if the dealer did capitulate and join a co-operative, he was commonly offered the management of his former store on a salary, plus a percentage of the turnover, and for the use of the premises he was paid a rent. The great majority of stores in late 1949 that bore the State or co-operative signs appeared to be under the same management as before.

From the point of view of rationalization these procedures were obviously only a first step. Physical amalgamation of many of these small stores into more economical units would have to come sooner or later. However, the great expense of erecting suitable premises and the need for neighbourhood stores bade fair to make the process a gradual one.

[1] 'A big organizational effort, a big persuading effort, and a big coercing effort, all three,' a Czech official called it. (Interview material, November 1949.) He acknowledged various failures at the outset; for example, in the handling of perishable fruit.

[2] The writer was told of what had happened to the florist trade on All Saints' Day, just passed. Private florists had trebled their prices, the co-operatives had made no change. Customers had switched. The net effect upon the private florist trade in Warsaw was said to have been disastrous. (Cf. *Polish Facts and Figures*, London, 27 January 1951.)

Administrative discriminations were also sometimes used. Differential regulations for closing hours of socialized as versus private shops had been instituted in Warsaw in late 1949, and were to be extended to other large urban centres. State and co-operative stores were permitted to stay open evenings and during certain hours on Sunday. 'Private commerce must continue to conform to the previous shop-closing hours.' (*Tribuna Ludu*, 28 December 1949, quoted in I.L.O., *Industry and Labour*, Geneva, 1950, vol. III, p. 436.)

In some cases more drastic measures were used to secure change. By early 1951 the Polish press was speaking of a complete nationalization of the pharmaceutical trade. Apparently this had been carried out by a process quite different from that of competition. 'Social commissions' had been sent to take over the shops and they were henceforth to operate under the Ministry of Health. The previous managers had been for the most part retained, but there was to be more even apportionment of personnel. 'During the taking-over period, none of the 1,500 pharmacies stopped work. . . . The first objective of the Ministry of Health will be the planned supply of medical drugs to chemists' shops and a proper location of the shops.' (*Polish Facts and Figures*, loc. cit.)

3. THE CO-OPERATIVE MOVEMENT IN TRANSITION

New Role of the Co-operative Movement

It will have been noted how large a part co-operatives of various kinds have played in the displacing of private enterprise. In the course of this process in both Poland and Czechoslovakia the co-operative movement itself has undergone striking changes, not without elements of internal conflict.

Early leaders of the co-operative movement in central Europe, as elsewhere, had tended often to be anti-State as much as anti-capitalist. The picture of co-operation as a possible 'third form', permanently intermediate between public and private enterprise and independent of both, was a popular one among them. The idea of a State-on-the-way-to-socialism, with strong central planning features, to which co-operatives as well as other social forms would be ancillary, was actively opposed by considerable circles of co-operators. Moreover, once the war and its aftermath had discredited more flatly conservative positions, it was through a co-operative programme along classic lines that a maximum of private property interest might legitimately continue to be voiced and preserved. Hence the conceptions of co-operative 'autonomy' and 'neutrality' acquired fresh emotional force.

Early formulations along classic lines may be seen in the theses published by the Polish Right-wing co-operative leaders in the early days of liberation. They called for restriction of State enterprise to heavy industry, with medium-sized industry in the hands of the co-operatives. Later these views were elaborated, by champions of the so-called 'intermediate' conception of co-operation, to call for the return from State hands of all manufacturing industry proper, whatever its size, leaving only heavy and raw materials enterprises under the State and subject to State planning. 'Such a widening of the field of co-operative production would automatically extend the limits of co-operative trading activity, and in consequence the tasks of its central government apparatus. The co-operative movement would be based upon important industry and trade, *leaving its auxiliary role in national economy*, and would become a serious partner of the State economic governing apparatus. . . .'[1]

[1] *Polish Co-operative News Service*, vol. I, No. 1 (multigraphed), Warsaw, May 1948, p. 39 (italics mine).

Obviously such theses never prevailed. But the general conception of co-operative autonomy for a time did. Polish co-operators prided themselves upon having formulated the famous 'three-sectoral' definition of the national economy—Public, Private, and Co-operative—(even though the co-operative sector at this time represented less than 4 per cent of the total) and getting it incorporated in the Three-Year Plan. By the time of the Six-Year Plan this formulation had been dropped. But in the earlier period its proponents had succeeded in having national income calculation and even the banking structure based upon it. Planning itself under the Three-Year Plan was to be adapted to the requirements of maximum autonomy for the co-operatives. They were to draw up their own plans for expansion and weigh them in their own central organizations. Apparently Government affected them but indirectly by granting them sums for investment and credit that were global. It was not until 1949 that co-operative activity was included as an integral part of the State Economic Plan.

The structure of the co-operatives also was a source of struggle. In both Poland and Czechoslovakia the pre-war pattern had been one of extreme diversity and overlapping comparable to that of the trade unions. In the underground during the Occupation attempts at unification increased but did not have the driving force of those of the trade unions. In Czechoslovakia final unification was not achieved until after February 1948. In Poland nominal unification came almost at once, but the forms of organization kept changing. At first the leading consumers' organization, Spolem, itself a combination of four previous consumers' centrals, was declared the receptacle for all types of co-operatives. Later, citing the rapid growth and vitality of a rural organization, Peasants' Self-Help, that had started to function as a land-distributing and rehabilitation agency during the land reform, Spolem's jurisdiction over village co-operative stores was turned over to it. Presently the smaller producers' co-operatives were given their own line organization. And so on. A general reorganization of co-operatives in the middle of 1948 followed what amounted to a self-denying ordinance on the part of Spolem at its congress the previous December. There were now to be no less than nine separate groupings, of which Spolem and Peasants' Self-Help were the chief. They were all to be federated together at the top by a Central Co-operative Council, not an administrative but a supervisory and policy-making body. During 1949 this structure was further modified. Some of the smaller groupings of co-operatives had merged or were disappearing. By early 1950 three main functional groups of co-operatives were spoken of as of prime importance: town consumers' co-operatives under Spolem, with a membership of slightly under 2,000,000; rural co-operatives of all types under Farmers' Self-Help, with a membership of slightly over 2,000,000; and labour and artisan co-operatives, with a membership of something over 100,000. In addition there were numerous building co-operatives, credit co-operatives, etc., bringing the apparent total up to some 5,000,000; but these memberships were considered largely overlapping, leaving a net of not over 4,000,000 members. The optimum aimed at for the future was 8,000,000.

Of this total, some 800,000 or about a tenth would, it was hoped, be made up of various forms of industrial and artisan co-operatives. That would still leave the bulk of members to the two big centrals, the consumers' for the cities and the all-purpose rural co-operatives for the country. Further new proliferations in the country-side we shall speak of in the next chapter.

The philosophy of co-operation meanwhile had squarely shifted to a socialized basis. Co-operatives were now officially classified as part of the 'Socialist' part of the national economy. Their function was to act as transforming agencies of small production and trade. Hence the relative unimportance of precise demarcation lines between different types of co-operatives and the ease of their shifting from one central to another. Established interests in one or another form or agency of co-operation had given way. The whole picture had become fluid.

Industrial and Handicraft Co-operatives

The shifting and interplay of co-operative forms was quite clear in the handicraft field. We have already seen the successive taking over of supply functions by the Polish guilds, enmeshing the individual artisan in marketing co-operative functions. But there were also transitional forms to straight producers' co-operatives here.

Besides the general servicing of its individual members, the guild organization since the war had come to include some struggling so-called 'auxiliary production' co-operatives. These produced some of the raw and semi-finished materials for the individual craftsmen. Beginning in late 1948, as the central feature of the general reorganization of guild structure, these auxiliary co-operatives were assiduously fostered to turn to major production. A report in early 1950 speaks of the changes.

'Heretofore the production of craftsmen's co-operatives was effected almost exclusively by individual artisans supplied with raw materials by the co-operatives which purchased all or part of the goods manufactured from those raw materials. Now the Craftsmen's Central Board has started organizing common co-operative manufacturing workshops with a planned production.' Great progress was reported as having been made in two important craft lines, clothing and leather goods.[1] Altogether during 1949 'nearly 20,000 new members have amalgamated their craft workshops into craftsmen's co-operatives'. However, 'about half a million craftsmen and home workers still remain outside the co-operative movement'.[2]

For the following year, while very considerable expansion of handicraft co-operatives into additional fields was looked for, and in point of fact achieved, more emphasis was laid upon economy of operations. It appeared obvious that the whole field of small production was beginning to be looked upon as a unit, and that the co-operatives, where these were established, were by no means operating as ends in themselves. The aim was to be, not co-operative expansion *per se*, but expansion into vacant places and/or places where group production could be most economical. The fields listed for successful co-operatives were: ancillary production

[1] 'A very high percentage' of the output in these two lines was now said to be co-operatively produced. However, the making up of goods from customers' own materials, very common in the tailoring trade, was apparently still in the hands of individual craftsmen. (*Polish Co-operative News Service*, Warsaw, May 1950 (multigraphed), pp. 17–18, 7, 9.)

[2] By mid-1951 it was reported that total employment in producer co-operatives was now over 245,000. There were 400 auxiliary co-operatives, 700 craftsmen's labour co-operatives, and large numbers of rural home-workers and some shop workers organized under the Central Board of Folk Art Industry. (Ibid., September 1951.) There were also a number of invalid co-operatives. All these groups, including the homeworkers, had their own committees of management. The home-workers 'execute their work either individually or in teams'. Regulations governing the Folk Art co-operatives were typical:

'If a member of a co-operative has his own workshop he must sign a declaration that he will not execute in his workshop any work for his own account.' Paid work by non-members might be used only for auxiliary work processes, not for the co-operative's basic processes. The number of non-members employed might not exceed 20 per cent of the co-operative's total. (Multigraphed material issued by Central Co-operative Union, 1951.)

for key industry ('supplementary articles and finishing work'); fashion and speciality goods; so-called regional articles, and finally, articles 'of simple technique, designed for local needs'.[1]

More extensive use of surplus local materials was called for, and also the use of otherwise unutilized by-products of large industry, 'industrial left-overs'. In general the picture was one of filling in the chinks of national production and raising to a maximum the value added by manufacture to inexpensive materials.

In the middle of 1949 still another handwork centre had been established, to foster co-operatives of home-workers, the Co-operative-State Central Board of Peasant and Artistic Industries. Arts production, it was pointed out, had especially low investment costs, it could use local and left-over materials, it could give employment to local reserves of manpower (widows, elderly people, and so on) and it could turn out high-value articles, some of them for export.

The major establishments in the co-operative small production field had always been the so-called Labour Co-operatives, some of them formed as early as 1945 and 1946. These covered a great range of occupations, most of them much less skilled and individualized than those of the craftsmen. Many of the Labour Co-operatives operated in good-sized business units, amounting to small factories in size and equipment. Averages here are unimportant, for the range is very great, but the average number of workers in such co-operative establishments in 1949 was fifty-two. A 1950 report noted that the Labour Co-operatives 'have been largely availing themselves of their own distribution machinery', in the form of retail shops.[2] Altogether 'the production of the Labour Co-operatives constituted about 15 per cent of the total of manufactured goods destined for home consumption', thus 'supplementing to an important degree the mass production of State-owned industries'.

Labour productivity in these co-operatives was stated to have risen rapidly during the preceding year: employment had risen by half in them, whereas output had doubled.[3]

[1] *Polish Co-operative News Service*, Warsaw, May 1950, p. 9.

[2] In the preceding year these had handled virtually half their products. 'The remainder was distributed by the consumers' co-operatives, by the village co-operatives, and by the State-owned stores.' (Ibid.)

[3] 'A 44 per cent growth in employment in the producers' co-operative organizations produced a 98·9 per cent increase in the value of the output.' (Ibid., pp. 16–17, 21.)

Until 1950 the Labour Co-operatives had been organized into two centrals, one of them Jewish and the other general. The general one had included under its jurisdiction the co-operatives for the unemployed, more particularly those for women founded by the powerful Women's League. By the beginning of 1950, following a unity congress, these two centrals had merged to form the Union of Producers' Co-operatives. Still another, smaller centre, newly formed in 1949, was the Central Board of Invalids' Co-operatives. Taking all these together, it is easy to see how strong a framework was being set up for rationalization of hitherto scattered petty production.

A further organizational step was envisaged early in 1950. It had been estimated at this time that there were some 170,000 industrial home-workers still working for private industry, besides some 80,000 in private industrial plants, or about a quarter of a million in all still working under private employers. Besides this there were estimated to be some 350,000 workers in handicraft, of whom 80,000 were organized owners of handicraft establishments. In addition there were the 70,000 or so workers in outright production co-operatives. The State Planning Commission already had a special section, the Department for Small Industry and Handicraft, embracing all these types of small production. State local industry meanwhile was supervised by the Department of Local Industry of the Ministry of Light Industry. Now it was planned to form a single Central Office for Small Production. Its task would be 'to ensure development of local industry and co-operative industry; to settle the mutual relations of small industry and the basic branches of national industry; to plan supplying of materials; to plan production; to plan *turnover of goods*, *finances*, *and investments*; to supervise local industry producers' co-operatives and auxiliary handicraft co-operatives, and to supervise handicraft self-government.'[1]

The small production field was itself to grow. Rationalization was to increase output, not reduce the total of persons employed in small production. Indeed there would be some further accessions to their ranks from the under-employed in rural areas. The new Centre would thus have a task of very considerable magnitude on its hands. By the end of the Six-Year Plan it was hoped order would have been brought to the production of some 800,000 people.

[1] Kazimierz Godowski, 'Handicraft Co-operatives in the 1950 Plan', *Gospodarka Planowa*, No. 2, Warsaw, 1950 (italics mine).

Consumers' Co-operation

For consumers' co-operatives size of membership figures obviously means less than it does for producers'. (In Poland membership for mid-1951 was reported at nearly 2,000,000.) Number of employees and size and growth of trade turnover are more significant. In 1950 it was stated flatly that the Polish consumers' societies had employed over 116,000 people in 1949, a growth of over a third over the preceding year, and by 1951 there had apparently been a growth of another third. Furthermore, this '36 per cent growth in employment in 1949 resulted in a 63·3 per cent increase in the value of goods handled'.[1] Obviously, rationalization had been at work here.

The network of urban co-operative stores under Spolem at this time was undergoing changes in two directions. The individual stores were being consolidated into larger units, and their supply system was taking new channels.

To take the less important change first, Spolem's original function had been first of all that of a co-operative wholesale. It also operated a number of large food-processing co-operatives, the greater part of whose output went into the co-operative retail trade. Now it appeared that an increasing proportion of the retail stores' supplies were coming in outside of Spolem's jurisdiction, in the shape of direct trade with State wholesale undertakings and provisions from local co-operative butcheries, bakeries, and so forth, founded by the retail societies themselves.[2] This latter venture shows once more the extreme fluidity of co-operative forms.

Rationalization among the multitude of little stores was being begun systematically. A consolidation process among the stores was proceeding by stages. The first step had already been completed, namely the grouping of the individual store units under common direction. Hitherto a separate co-operative membership society had often managed a single store. With the readiness to cut across vested interests of which we spoke earlier, these memberships now merged to form larger groups, each of which directed a

[1] *Polish Co-operative News Service*, Warsaw, May 1950, p. 21. By 1951, in spite of amalgamations, the network of consumers' co-operative shops had increased another third over 1949, so that their employees must have numbered well over 150,000. Total employees of the co-operative movement by this time were reported as numbering over 613,000. (Ibid., September 1951.)

[2] Ibid., May 1950, p. 13. Spolem's turnover during 1949 had grown 11 per cent, that of the retail stores 40 per cent.

series of stores. 'One town, one membership society' was the rule. A small town co-operative society therefore might have two or three stores, a large city co-operative society, hundreds. In the latter case operation obviously approached the chain-store principle. Thus the Warsaw Co-operative Society had some 500 branch stores, that of Lodz, 400, that of Katowice, 300.[1]

It is easy to see that with the focus of ownership shifted from the single store to the chain, co-operative members would be readier to amalgamate small units, closing down unnecessary premises. This process had already begun, although it was hampered by physical scarcities. Meanwhile uniform methods of book-keeping were being introduced, as even with common direction only, the small stores' overhead could be cut. Better purchasing and saving in management costs were claimed. The opening of further branch stores in those quarters where there was need for them, and in no others, was also facilitated.[2] The whole process was of peculiar importance at a time when large numbers of private stores were being taken over. The chain store principle, as we saw earlier, was the fulcrum of change here.

Size of co-operative membership units necessarily brought its own problems. How maintain control by the membership? With tens of thousands of members scattered over an entire city, opportunities for bureaucracy, it was said, were great: it was easy to lose track of the members' specific wishes for goods. There were also opportunities for groups with more business know-how than the rank and file to insert themselves into control of the societies to their own advantage. To combat these tendencies, during 1949 the societies set up so-called 'members' committees', elected bodies comprising perhaps 10 per cent of the membership. These had power over the selection of goods. There were also enlarged 'control', i.e. auditing committees to check on finances. Also, general members' meetings were made more frequent. They now had to be held quarterly instead of annually. Much emphasis was given in co-operative reports to the percentage of attendance at these meetings.

[1] At the time these changes were first recorded, there were almost five hundred town co-operatives in Poland with over eight thousand stores; by the end of 1949 there were over twelve thousand stores.

[2] Already in 1948, however, Polish co-operators were boasting, 'Now we open a store only if we have one or two hundred members signed up for it.' This was supposed to be an example of 'planned economy without crises'. (Interview material, July 1948.)

Rural All-Purpose Co-operatives

Over the various forms of rural organization in Poland was the Farmers' Self-Help Association, which supposedly had branches in every village. It was itself not a co-operative but a broad farmers' union, not all of whose members necessarily belonged to co-operatives. However, in 1949 there was a mass drive to urge the Self-Help members to join the co-operatives. (In the towns a similar drive was going on among the members of trade unions, not more than half of whom belonged to consumers' co-operatives, and among the members of the Women's League and the National Youth organizations.)

The basic unit of organization among rural co-operatives, not only in Poland but in Czechoslovakia and the other new planned economies, had come to be the single all-purpose local. It had its roots either in the single village or in the 'commune' (group of village hamlets), and was then federated into larger, also initially undifferentiated units. These larger units subsequently began to have branches with different functions. The object of the single line organization was apparently to maintain mass membership control and encourage fluidity of forms. At any rate, in 1948 it was unmistakable how fluid local forms were. In one village the chief interest might centre about a store, in another around a community welfare project—a co-operative kindergarten, crèche, laundry, bakery, clubhouse—in another around a co-operative machine station or other common production project. The stores at this time had been newly awakened to life, the group welfare projects appeared to be very strong organizing mediums, the common production projects were just beginning. By 1949, organization was undoubtedly much more general and the centre of gravity had shifted unmistakably to the projects of production.

By 1949 also mass membership control of the co-operatives, over against any 'capitalist' elements, was being implemented more than ever before. The village Members' Committees and Control (financial) Committees referred to above were in operation.

Rural Trade Functions

The process of unification in rural trade at this time seemed to be going on chiefly by the tying together as much as possible of supply and marketing functions. Older specialized forms of farmers' marketing co-operatives were tending to be absorbed into the new pattern, either at the original village or the district level. (However, in Poland the Dairy and Egg Co-operative, a purely marketing organization, was still strong in 1950.)

Co-operative supply functions were at first centred in the village stores, themselves supposedly under the original consumers' (Spolem's) district wholesale establishments. But with the setting up of many new and stronger stores by the all-purpose village co-operatives, and with the growth of district marketing associations as well, Spolem in 1947 had withdrawn from this field. The Farmers' Self-Help co-operatives now had jurisdiction over all the stores and district wholesales. At the district level they also co-ordinated, supposedly, the various farmers' speciality marketing organizations. Actually, by 1950 several of these, as national organizations, had gone out of existence.

Rationalization of rural distribution was beginning. It was taking place at two levels, the village store for actual sales, and, in Poland, the County Associations of Village Co-operatives for wholesaling and planning. At the local level the unit for initial change, here as in the city, was not the store itself but the membership society operating it. Reorganization was to involve having one and only one society for the rural borough (commune or *gmine* in Poland), comprising on an average four villages. In the borough centre it could then operate one really effective store, closing down if necessary one or more of the outlying ones and operating the remainder as branches.

At the district level, comprising a number of *gmines*, County Associations of Village Co-operatives were formally established in 1949.[1] These continued regular wholesaling operations and also served as agencies for their villages in the purchase of manufactured goods from State Central Boards. They were to register local requirements and organize proper deliveries.

In the farmers' marketing field, in several basic commodities the village co-operatives had absorbed most of the middleman's function at the retail purchase end. This was true, as we saw earlier, almost 100 per cent in the grain trade and increasingly so in meat. The co-operatives bought from the individual farmer. However,

[1] The relative size of the different units may be seen by the following figures: In 1949 there were almost 30,000 rural co-operative stores in Poland, something over 3,000 co-operatives on the *gmine* level, and 266 County Co-operative Associations.

at this point a new, mixed form began. The village co-operatives passed on the commodity either to a State or to a State-co-operative processing and wholesaling enterprise. The whole was a belt line rather than a linked process: the Mixed State-co-operative organizations were entirely farmer-owned and operated at one end and entirely or predominantly State-owned and operated at the other.

Rural Production Functions: the Co-operative Farm

With the new perspective on co-operative farming beginning at the end of 1948, all the previous small beginnings of common production functions were treated with new enthusiasm. Co-operative use of scarce machinery, of draught animals, co-operative raising of pigs or other livestock as a sideline to private farming, all these were now favoured and helped more than ever before. However, in one respect co-operative effort was not so much favoured and subsidized as earlier. Co-operative tractor stations, where they had been already established, would continue to be helped, the writer was told in Poland in late 1949, but no new ones would be founded: for tractors and other heavy machinery, State stations were more efficient. New co-operative machinery stations would be helped to secure light machines only.[1]

Formerly, attempts by farmers to merge small holdings into co-operative farms had been held sternly in check. In Czechoslovakia, early so-called mountain pasture co-operatives had been permitted in border regions where settlement was inadequate and soil poor. Small farmers, while maintaining their own home farms, were allowed to use these pastures in common as a sideline. But other, more complete, co-operatives were permitted only on a temporary basis, in certain of the border regions of Czechoslovakia and in the western territories of Poland, in special cases. Such co-operatives were very few in number. In the Western Territories of Poland altogether in 1948 there were only 103. They were set up by groups of settlers who were allowed temporarily to occupy existing estate buildings for themselves and their livestock and to cultivate

[1] By 1951 it was stated that it was now impossible for the individual farmer to purchase tractors at all; hence saving for this purpose was useless. However, all the equipment of the co-operative stations, such as it was, was now reserved for the individual farmer exclusively; the State stations with their heavy equipment would also service him in addition to the co-operative farms, and co-operative as well as State stations received government subsidy.

in common. Within three to five years, however, these settlers were bound by law to build themselves individual houses and barns and divide up the land.

So late as the summer of 1948 in Poland the writer had the opportunity to talk with the heads of such a small co-operative, recently launched, which was still under orders to dissolve within the five-year limit but had every intention to circumvent the law.

Once policy had changed, the aim was, here as elsewhere, to have operation take rational forms. There was an added motive in this case, since failure by ill-planned groups would retard the whole movement upon which great political emphasis was now laid. Moreover, here the field was virgin: there was no need to start with obvious mistakes. The writer found, accordingly, in Poland at the end of 1949 that local preparations for co-operatives were being definitely discouraged under certain conditions, more particularly if the manpower involved and the area to be cultivated in common were not considered to be sufficiently large or if the fields were too scattered. Hence the rule: no co-operative to be helped in a locality unless the majority of a village has voted for it. A whole village, or the major part of it in any case, was considered necessary for success. Careful advance planning by the farmers' organization concerned was also required. And the total number of co-operatives seeking formation must not be larger than could be supplied adequately with the necessary machinery and materials for large-scale production. Conversely, certain general regions, giving advance promise of success, were marked out for receiving priority in State aid if, as, and when co-operatives should be started there.

Thoroughness and gradualness of advance preparations by the end of 1949 were particularly marked in Czechoslovakia. Here about a quarter of the villages had formed so-called Preparatory Committees, to undertake advance planning and preparations for one or more agricultural operations in common in the ensuing year.[1] And about 3,000 had formed units of the United Agricultural Co-operatives themselves.

This brings up a point of interest. In both Poland and Czechoslovakia not only was the all-purpose village co-operative now markedly centreing its attention upon features of co-operative production. It looked as if shortly it would be indeed revolving around them. In Poland, a consequence was that the erstwhile national

[1] Detailed discussion of this work will be found in the chapter on agriculture.

centre for all agricultural activity, Farmers' Self-Help, was now apparently about to be replaced in the field of this particular activity. A special Centre for Co-operative Farms was to be established.[1]

The actual number of co-operative farms was much smaller in Poland than in Czechoslovakia and their rate of growth was less rapid. In March 1950 their number was reported at 1,000, and by the latter part of 1951 as something over 3,000. In terms of area, about 3 per cent of Polish grain land was now co-operative and about 10 per cent lay in State Farms. In Czechoslovakia meanwhile, not counting loose forms of quasi-co-operatives of which there were a great many in that country, the solid production co-operatives by 1 November 1951 numbered over 4,300. And this, of course, was from a much smaller country with a much smaller proportion of its population living on the land.[2] All told, about 17 per cent or one-sixth of Czechoslovakia's agricultural land by this time was being worked co-operatively, with the old field barriers obliterated. Adding the 9 per cent of land that was by this time in State farms, a full quarter of Czechoslovak land was now operated outside the sphere of private enterprise. By January 1952 the State Planning Commission announced that the figure had risen to 30 per cent.

Types of Co-operative Farms

The different types and gradations of farm co-operatives attempted in one and another of the 'People's Democracies' would be a most interesting study for the future social historian. The classic formulation of three basic types, graded in a progression toward fuller socialization of means of production, has already been referred to in the chapter on agriculture, and at first sight it looks very simple.[3] However, in practice the differences within any one

[1] By 1951 not only was this true, but all the former agro-technical activities of Farmers' Self-Help were in process of being taken over by the Ministry of Agriculture and greatly enlarged. Self-Help was now coming to confine itself to social and cultural activities, plus supervision of the rural stores.

[2] The looser and preparatory type co-operatives in Czechoslovakia at this time numbered over 3,450. If one were to include them, there would be nearly 7,800 farming co-operatives of one sort or another, or one for every second one of Czechoslovakia's 15,000 villages.

[3] An early version of the distinctions in their simplest form is given below. 'First Conference of Agricultural Instructors (County Agents), regarding Productive Agricultural Co-operatives.

country as well as between countries become very complex indeed.

The first type was really only a highly developed form of mutual aid. It had been found helpful in the Soviet Union at the close of the 1920's.[1] Individual farm holdings were kept intact and all net proceeds were divided according to the land held. Only labour was pooled, and usually only for the given season. Often only a specified portion of the fields was set aside for common cultivation. Use of a man's equipment and draught animals was of course paid for. This very elementary type of co-operative was very scarce in Poland but extremely common, with a good many more sophisticated variations, in Czechoslovakia. It was said to have two marked technological advantages over individual farming: it provided for an organized and common plan of work, and it made for a more all-round use of equipment. In addition, of course, and this was how it had come to be fostered so much in Czechoslovakia, it appealed to the more conservative type of medium farmer. Once he had tried this, he was said to be far more ready to go on to still more efficient forms.

The second type, it will be recalled, was where fields were permanently consolidated and only a portion of the joint income went for land rent. Major equipment and work animals were permanently pooled, and paid for in instalments. Members entering this type of co-operative commonly bound themselves for several years. In any case, a member leaving such a co-operative would have to be satisfied with the nearest thing to equivalent land on the outskirts, for his own original acres would remain merged. All

'This conference, which took place in April 1949, . . . worked out rules for the co-operatives, as well as principles of their organization and economy. . . .

'The conference analyzed the three main classes of rules. The first one concerns the so-called cultivation co-operatives where all the means of production and the crop remain the private property of individual members who only cultivate, in a collective way, the fields assigned for this purpose and for a determined period of time. The second class of rules deals with collective work on a common farm; in such co-operatives the income is shared among members according to the amount of land, cattle, pigs, machines and work contributed by each member. The third class relates to co-operatives where all the members work together on a common farm, and the income is shared exclusively in accordance with the amount of work done by each member.' (*Co-operative Scientific Review*, Warsaw, April–June 1949, p. 86.)

[1] 'Such forms of distribution were not accidental. . . . They made it possible for the peasant without equipment to associate himself with the peasant who had equipment.' (V. Ovchinnikova, 'The Kolkhoz Work-Day Unit during Twenty Years', *Voprosi Ekonomiki*, Moscow, 1951, No. 8, p. 63.)

Bulgarian co-operatives were said to be of this type, and by late 1951 they were reported as occupying half the arable land of that country.

In the third type, no land rent was paid at all. All the net proceeds went to labour alone, once the contributed draught animals, equipment, seed, etc., had been paid for.[1] Virtually all the Romanian and Hungarian co-operatives were of this type, for they had been established in the first instance on State lands taken over from the former large estates. There were far fewer co-operatives here than in Bulgaria.

In both Types II and III, houses remained private and, as in the Soviet collective farms, each family was entitled to keep a large kitchen garden (in Poland and Czechoslovakia about 2½ acres) and one or two cows and calves, together with an unlimited number of pigs, goats, poultry, and so on. Horses, however, had to be turned in (and paid for) and so did surplus cattle.[2]

Analysis of the types and their prevalence, shows up interesting technical and social problems. There is no doubt that once production co-operation is attempted at all, the basic condition for really big technological change is consolidation, permanent merging of little fields into big continuous areas. And there is no doubt in addition that the more there remains to the erstwhile farmer of his erstwhile property, the less effectively is he going to join in the new division of labour.

However, social factors enter in as well. The one place apparently in both Poland and Czechoslovakia where the middle farmer was willing to come in rapidly without a continuing income for his land (i.e. without demanding ground rent) was in the border regions. Here there were hardly any small peasants or peasants working in industry, and everyone had about the same sized medium holding, usually a little over 30 acres, which had been assigned to him in the land reform. Here potential rents would

[1] Technically, however, in the land registry offices, a man's land remained his own. In this respect only did the Type III co-operatives appear to differ from the Soviet Union's collective farms. Of course, as Soviet writers point out, the 'People's Democracies' have never had land nationalization. In Russia after the Revolution peasants had had a claim to the land they tilled, but no actual ownership title.

[2] This distinction was a direct result of early experience in the Soviet Union. In the opening days of collectivization there, uncertainty about how much a man might retain and how much, if anything, he would be paid for what he turned in, had led to large-scale advance slaughtering of livestock.

pretty well cancel each other out. In Poland, with 70 per cent of the co-operatives in 1951 of the no-rent type, the great majority lay in the western territories; in Czechoslovakia about half of all co-operatives lay in the border regions. Equally important perhaps, the settlers in such regions, recently themselves agricultural labourers or poor peasants from the interior, were often also radical-minded to begin with.[1]

With the poorest peasants, of course, it was different: they would come in on the whole more readily, wherever they were situated. In Czechoslovakia in 1951 two-thirds of the membership of co-operative farms of the consolidated type consisted as yet of men who had formerly held less than 12½ acres or none at all. Such men obviously were not going to put up a strong demand for land rent, although they might be willing to pay a rent in order to be able to associate themselves with those who did have land and equipment. But the poorest peasants formed only a minority of all farmers, and the total acreage they controlled was even smaller. The decisive figure in all agriculture remained the middle farmer.

The problem then was how to attract the middle farmer in the bulk of the country. In Czechoslovakia apparently the solution had been twofold. First, there had been the very careful preparatory work alluded to earlier, together with widespread propagation of the most elementary trial forms of mutual-aid cultivation of specified fields,[2] each member paying for the work done on his fields and receiving payment for work executed on other members' fields by himself, his family, his machinery or draught animals. Even in 1951 nearly half the Czech co-operatives were of so loose a type that in Poland and most of the other planned economies they would not have been listed as producer co-operatives at all.

Then there had also been wide and successful propagation of an intermediate form between this and the classic Type II. In the intermediate form, unlike Type II, the whole of net income continued to be divided exclusively in accordance with the size of the original acreage but, unlike Type I, *the boundary lines were ploughed up*. Hence the beginnings of truly large-scale cultivation could be

[1] The author well remembers a visit to the Marianske Lazne (Marienbad) region of Czechoslovakia in the spring of 1948. Here the new settlers had early voted themselves into the Communist Party and let the old parties die out, at a period when in the rest of the country equality of parties was strictly observed.

[2] 'Several adjoining fields, separated by boundary lines, are planted to one and the same crop.' ('Types of United Agricultural Co-operatives in Czechoslovakia' (multigraphed), International Agricultural Institute, Prague, 1951.)

seen. 'Large consolidated fields enable the co-operative to make a more efficient use of heavy farm machinery. . . . The collective labour can also be better organized and specialized because the farmers are not diverted from collective work by care of their own private land.'[1]

In Poland, where the entire first stage had to all intents and purposes been skipped,[2] effort in 1951 was apparently being concentrated on popularizing a softened variant of Type II, known generally as the 'Fourth' or 'New' Type. In this, while fields remained finally consolidated, more leeway was given in the matter of property; more particularly there was to be unlimited private cattle-owning.[3]

[1] Ibid.

[2] In late 1951 it was estimated that no more than 300 to 400 Type I farms were in existence.

[3] In practice more allowance was apparently also made for income from the use of formerly private horses, for one heard of horses being paid for at 'day's work' rates comparable to those of a man.

The complexity of the matters to be decided by an individual Type II co-operative, or for that matter by any co-operative, can be seen in a description given of the statutes of the first co-operative of this type to be established in Czechoslovakia. 'Members of the Co-operative adopted the statutes at their General Assembly held on 7 March 1950.

' "We the members of the United Agricultural Co-operative in Velen, District Prague-North, having weighed the favourable results . . . have decided . . . to put our land and other means of production together and to farm henceforth in a collective manner. The lands will remain the private property of each member."

'The statutes designate, first of all the lands which are going to be collectively tilled. The latter include lands owned by the members of the Co-operative, those owned directly by the United Agricultural Co-operative, and those owned by non-members which have been leased to the Co-operative.

'The right of ownership to lands brought into the Co-operative by individual members remains intact in the form in which it appears on the public land register. However, the limits and boundaries between individual plots will be removed and the individual plots merged into one economic unit which will be tilled by the members . . . following a uniform sowing plan. At the same time, each family will keep for itself $2\frac{1}{2}$ acres of land for its own private use.

'The next chapter of the statutes deals with the way in which the previously individually tilled lands will be put under the régime of collective farming. This chapter contains the interesting rule entitling the members to a special payment for [improvements] by them on their land before it was taken over by the Co-operative. A similar rule applies when an orchard is turned over. . . .

'Membership in the Co-operative lasts at least three years. If a member retires from the Co-operative, his land is returned to him, naturally in a manner safeguarding the vital interests of the Co-operative, which means that he may,

Rationalization: Problems of Optimum Size

Very naturally, in the opening days of co-operative farming in

eventually, receive other pieces of land than those originally owned by him, but of the same quality and area.

'The next chapter . . . deals with chattel and farm buildings. Members of the Co-operative turn over to it . . . their livestock and equipment needed for collective farming. . . .

'Each member keeps for his private use as much equipment as he needs for his own household, together with one cow (eventually with one calf) and an unlimited number of pigs, sheep, goats and poultry. The amount of the indemnity for the stock taken over by the Co-operative is calculated on the basis of the current market prices; it is, however, not paid in cash but credited to the former owner and paid off without interest in several instalments. . . .

'. . . Seeds, plants, seedlings, and forage taken over by the Co-operative are paid for not later than at the end of the first harvest. . . . Dwelling houses remain the private property of each member. . . .

'The next chapter . . . deals with organization of work, payment for labour, and distribution of profits. . . .

'Each member of the Co-operative, as well as the working members of his family, have the duty to participate in person in the common farm work. The daily amount of work performed by each member is entered into his work check book. The general meeting of the members of the Co-operative fixes the minimum number of man-days of labour required from each member.

'The Co-operative has the right to hire outside workers whenever necesseary (e.g. agronomists, accountants). . . .

'The work in the Co-operative is, as far as possible, to be put on a piece-work basis, with norms approved by the General Meeting. . . .

'For every norm fulfilled, each individual is credited with a number of "labour units" corresponding to the amount of units fixed by the General Meeting for the respective class and type of work.

'The total number of "labour units" earned by each member in the course of the year forms the basis for the determination of the size of his share in the common output. . . .

'All work in the Co-operative is carried out according to a plan and is managed by the Chairman of the Co-operative or his assistant.

'The work is done by labour groups [brigades] formed, on the one hand, for the various kinds of field work, and, on the other, for work in the stables and cowsheds. The members are expected to stay with their respective group throughout the whole year, and each group has a definite piece of land assigned to it for the duration of at least one season. Each group is headed by a foreman appointed by the General Meeting. . . .

'In the course of the year, each member is entitled to receive produce or money as an advance on his reward. . . .

'The amounts paid for use of land brought into the Co-operative by each member are fixed by the General Meeting in the form of a share in the net income from the common work. These payments must not constitute together more than 10 to 20 per cent of the net income.'

(*International Agricultural Institute Bulletin*, Prague, September 1950.)

any country the groups formed tended to be small and to vary very much one from the other. In the Soviet Union collective farms had originally started up haphazard, often several to a village, and of course the villages themselves had varied in size. As technology improved, the question of optimum extent became important. There was also the question, increasingly pressing in all industrializing countries, as Poland soon found, of manpower conservation, particularly of specialist and higher managerial personnel. The Soviet Union had attacked this problem in a very large-scale way after the war, by a campaign to amalgamate its smaller co-operative farms into very large affairs indeed.[1]

At a long remove, the smaller planned economies were taking note of this experience and attempting to copy its more elementary features. They were urging the advantages of co-operatives of at least several hundred members rather than a hundred or less. This required accretion when possible of new membership to existing farms rather than the setting up of new small adjacent units. And it involved more careful planning and preparatory work for initial farms in localities where none as yet existed. Both conditions, of course, could successfully be met only where adhesions to the co-operative form came in a rather large stream.[2]

Internal Structure: 'Brigades'

From the outset the smaller economies urged upon their co-operatives the importance of a stable division of labour in groups

[1] Often the number of members was 1,000 or more, furnishing a total population of, say, 5,000. Such an aggregation could have a 'collective farm town', fully equipped with its own health and cultural features. Any such move would naturally be possible only if the collective areas in a country were contiguous and continuous. In the Soviet Union during 1950, amalgamations among the country's 252,000 collective farms had reduced their numbers to 123,000.

[2] Thus, in Bulgaria, a country of especially small holdings to begin with, it was stated in early 1951 that during the previous year the average co-operative farm had increased in size from a membership of less than 100 to well over 200. At the same time 1,000 new co-operatives had been formed and total co-operative acreage had increased from 13 per cent of agricultural land to 43 per cent. In other words, along with increase in members per farm had gone a more than proportional increase in acreage.

Again, the fact was advertised that in Hungary five out of seven co-operatives of a given region had coalesced to form one over-500 member super-farm, enabling them to hire a professional accountant and an agronomist. (International Agricultural Institute, *Interagra*, Prague, 1951, Nos. 1–2, pp. 34–5.)

large enough to function effectively. Such groups in the Soviet Union had been called 'brigades'. Brigades of not less than twenty to thirty were recommended, with the members working continuously together at one kind of work for at least a season, preferably longer. In the larger farms there would be several brigades for each form of production, the most basic being the field brigades.[1] Brigades, in addition to maintenance advances, were paid their share of the farm total in a lump sum at the end of the season, and carried their own book-keeping of the work turned in by each member and the consequent individual share due him. The brigade head ordinarily worked alongside his fellows and was paid something extra for his administration and accounting labours. There were also team leaders with five to ten members under them.[2] They received about half as much extra as the brigadier. Brigade leaders were appointed by the executive committee of the co-operative, which in turn was to be elected at an annual members' meeting. (There were also monthly or other meetings of the membership to deal with ordinary farm affairs.)

Earnings and Output Standards: the Work-Day Unit

Attempts to individualize earnings and to set up rational scales of farm operations on the basis of their difficulty and importance had come early in the Soviet Union, along with the brigade system just referred to.[3] Beginning with a narrow range, the

[1] 'The field brigade is fundamental . . . and upon its proper functioning depends the outcome of the labours of the whole farm. . . .

'The field brigade should be a self-sufficient production unit, able to carry out all manual and draught-animal operations. . . . Hence it may include in its ranks from thirty to fifty workers, men, women, and young people. . . . A brigade of more than fifty is hard to direct.' [Livestock brigades could be smaller.] (Ministry of Agriculture, Institute of Agricultural Economics, 'Standard Norms of Work and Principles for Reckoning Work-Days', Part I, Warsaw, July 1951, p. 12, in Polish.)

[2] In recent years in the Soviet Union much had been made of concentrating all major work responsibility upon the brigades, as over against the teams. The latter had become over-prominent, it was said, owing to their functioning during the war, when larger operations had perforce been disrupted from lack of equipment and skilled personnel. Now, with fresh mechanization, the more rational, larger structure was to be emphasized more than ever.

[3] In elementary fashion, in January 1931, the first all-union assembly of *kolkhozes* had recommended that all work processes be divided into light, medium, heavy, and skilled, and that these be rated on a scale of ·75, 1·00, 1·25, and 1·50, i.e. with 'skilled' work rating twice as much as 'light'. The same assembly had recommended that a system of permanent brigades be instituted.

Soviet rating-scale of operations had latterly become very wide, with the top category rating five times the bottom.[1]

In the 'Popular Democracies' the ranges were smaller, more like the original Soviet one. In Poland in 1951, following research by its Institute of Agricultural Economics, the recommended scale was even reduced slightly, until its range was only half as great as that now used in the Soviet Union.[2] A Polish writer explains that they could not possibly adopt the Soviet nine-class system, because 'This would be too hard for us, and too rapid a step from the kind of criteria used up to now. We . . . are only building Socialism. . . . They are on a higher stage of collective farms.'[3]

The new Polish tables were much more elaborate than previous attempts. They now covered several hundred job classifications, with new types of rating for administrative work and animal husbandry. In this connection it was emphasized that while the contents of a normal day's work would change with improved technology, the relative ratings of occupations in the occupational hierarchy could remain constant over a much longer time.

Directly connected with occupational ratings and overshadowing them in importance was the basic question of labour income. Patently a prerequisite to joining a co-operative was to work in it oneself. Even in a Type I farm, the member could not get income from his lands otherwise. Commonly the minimum amount of work in the elementary co-operatives was 100 days a year for the member and his family combined; in the more consolidated types, 100 days for each adult not otherwise occupied, taken separately.

But this was only a prerequisite. The serious question was, how secure the necessary differentiation of reward for individual effort? For needless to say, the lesser planned economies no less than the Soviet Union eschewed equalitarianism for the co-operatives, as they had long ago for industry. In Poland in the opening year of co-operatives, 1949, it is said, the unit of reckoning as a rule simply equalled the physical day. 'Such a system dominated the year 1949.' It was condemned as amounting merely to a *per capita*

[1] There were nine ratings running from ·50 to 2·50, with a 25 per cent step-up between each.

[2] Poland had only seven classes with 20 per cent step-ups. The top category rated 2·2 times the bottom.

[3] W. Schmidt, 'Work-Day Units in Producers' Co-operatives', *Gospodarka Planowa*, Warsaw, September 1951, p. 23.

dividing of the income of the co-operative. 'Now we meet such faults only in the new, inexperienced co-operatives.'[1]

The system finally propagated, apparently with success, was the one long since worked out in the Soviet Union, the 'work-day unit' system.[2] It took as standard the amount of accomplishment normal to a given operation under given local conditions per man-day, and then applied to this the job rating-scale already referred to. Thus if a job because of its difficulty rated 1:50 on the rating-scale, a man finishing it in a day would have earned 1½ 'work-day units'; if he finished it in less than a day, he would earn proportionately more. The system obviously differed from a piece-rate wage system in that the unit was elastic instead of fixed: its value could not be known until after the harvest, at which time the total of units earned on the farm would be divided into the net proceeds. However, it exerted a similar pressure for accomplishment upon the individual worker.[3]

It was claimed that institution of the work-day unit and a proper organization of work in brigades went hand in hand. The unit system 'enables the worker to compare his work with that of others . . . scores are set up, emulation begins . . . brigades are set up, and such people (i.e. those with high output) become their leaders and thus have added incentives. The work-day unit system also itself makes it necessary to have a proper organization of work: the two are interdependent.'[4]

[1] Ibid., p. 21.

[2] This sytem, in rough version, had begun in 1930–1, spreading first in the basic grain regions. Then it was taken up by the Communist Party and propagated. (V. Ovchinnikova, 'The Kolkhoz Work-Day Unit during Twenty Years', *Voprosi Ekonomiki*, Moscow, 1951, p. 64.)

[3] Czechoslovak and Polish norms fell far short of being so elaborate as the Soviet ones. In 1947–8 'The Ministry of Agriculture of the U.S.S.R. in collaboration with the "Council for Kolkhoz Affairs" worked out a new system of model production norms and piece rates, expressed in working days, *for 350 most common types of agricultural work, and of 1,130 norms and rates for other types of work*. . . . All kolkhozes were asked to revise norms practised by them on the basis of the model ones, and—while taking into consideration the conditions of particular kolkhozes—to bring their norms to approximate more closely to those achieved in the more progressive kolkhozes. . . . In M.T.S.'s [Machine Tractor Stations] especially high qualitative and quantitative production norms were introduced. . . .' (Alexander Baykov, 'Agricultural Development in the U.S.S.R.', University of Birmingham, *Bulletins on Soviet Economic Development*, Bulletin 2, December 1949, p. 24 (italics mine).)

[4] W. Schmidt, op. cit., p. 20. Even in livestock production, norms had been established, although these were 'difficult to fix because of uncontrolled fac-

In Czechoslovakia it had been found possible to introduce careful work-day unit reckoning even for the types of co-operative where a large share of the proceeds still went for the originally contributed land and stock. This was a very different sequence of social-technical changes from what had originally taken place in the Soviet Union. But there was no doubt that the end results looked to here as in the other planned economies, were the same: a wholly collective, large-scale agriculture, with no income save for labour.

Summing up the policies pursued toward all forms of private enterprise in the two countries, it is evident that by the beginning of the longer-term Plans, i.e. from 1949–50 on, their elimination had become a clear and consistent goal. Capitalist forms, wherever found and however small in scale, were to be actively replaced by co-operative and public ones. There was no longer any question of leaving them to fall of their own weight, still less of encouraging them to grow temporarily. In the words of the opening section of the Czechoslovak Five-Year Plan, 'Capitalist elements . . . will be progressively restricted and eliminated from all sections of the national economy'.

The Polish Six-Year Plan, coming a year later, had been even more emphatic, '. . . The curbing and restriction of capitalist elements, their further gradual elimination, and finally their liquidation as a class.' To this Mr. Minc added concerning the richer farmers: 'The conditions for the liquidation of the rural capitalists as a class will grow and mature.'[1]

Annual production and income figures underscored the rapidity of the changes that had already taken place. The rapporteur for the Polish Parliament's Economic Plan and Budget Committee summed them up in 1951.[2]

tors'. The solution attempted was to have pay consist of two parts: a low fixed portion on a time basis graded according to the number of head of livestock under a man's care, and a series of premium payments for offspring. The large total premiums possible for the successful stock-raiser would, it was hoped, attract competent people into this branch.

[1] 'The Six-Year Plan', Warsaw, 1950, p. 49.

[2] Oskar Lange, 'Polish National Economy in the Second Year of the Six-Year Plan' (being the substance of Dr. Lange's report to Parliament, 21 March 1951, on behalf of the Parliamentary Commission on Economic Planning and the Budget. In Polish), Warsaw, 1951, p. 12.

From some 45 per cent of the national income in 1946, the share of socialist economy had risen to 70 per cent in 1950. In employment the increase had been from 2,600,000 persons in 1946 to 4,700,000 in 1950.[1] Industrial production of course had shown a major proportion of socialized economy from the outset: even in industry and crafts combined the socialist output was already almost 80 per cent in 1946 and rose to 94 per cent by 1950. In construction the change had been dramatic: from 32 per cent in 1946 to 99 per cent in 1950.[2] Retail trade had also shown very rapid change, which was still in progress, from something over 20 per cent in 1946 to 80 per cent in 1950, and with a plan for over 90 per cent for 1951.[3]

The contrast between these proportions and those for agriculture was very great. Here progress had only been from something under 8 per cent of total agricultural production in 1947, to something over 10 per cent in 1950. For 1951 the plan was to reach 15 per cent, of which State Farms' production was still to furnish much the greater part, leaving to co-operatives only about 4 per cent of the national total. Even this figure was not quite reached.[4] And no Plan figure in this realm was set for 1955.

[1] Counting non-agricultural employment only, the change had been from something over 70 per cent in 1946 to well over 90 per cent in 1950.

[2] 'The process of taking over the construction industry was very, very simple. We simply gave the contracts for public building to public contractors. So the private architects, and so on, came swarming over to us. Now only small repairs and such things, remain in private hands.' (Interview material, October 1949.)

[3] As for wholesale trade, not to mention foreign trade, by the end of 1950 President Bierut had stated that 'in wholesale turn-over private capitalist establishments have been completely removed'. (*Polish Facts and Figures*, London, 16 December 1950.)

[4] In detail the changes listed were as follows:

Share of Socialist (State and Co-operative) Economy in Poland, 1946–50

	1946	*1949*	*1950*	*1951* (Plan)	*1955* (Plan)
National Income	45·5	64·0	70·0	75·0	—
Employment (non-agricultural)	72·0	79·1	86·5	90·4	93·6
Industry and Crafts Output	79·0	89·0	94·0	96·0	99·0
Building Output	32·0	92·5	99·1	99·2	99·6
Retail Trade Turnover	22·0	52·0	80·0	92·0	97·0
Agricultural Output	7·7 (1947)	8·4	10·5	15·2	—

State Farms=11·1. Co-operatives=4·1.

(From O. Lange, op. cit., pp. 12–13. Compiled.)

However, everyone concerned with State policy on co-operatives warned against seeking to force farmers to come in. Speaking at a time of great agricultural difficulty in the autumn of 1951, Vice-Premier Minc re-emphasized the point.

'The question arises, if individual farming cannot keep pace with the tempo of development of industrialization of the country . . . should the tempo of agricultural development . . . be forced by intensifying artificially producer-co-operative farming? It is clear that such a solution would . . . be erroneous and harmful.

'The change-over from an agriculture based on individual holdings to an agriculture based on collective economy is a long process based on the growth of material forces of the State and its reserves, on the increase of industrial production . . . on the growth of the financial strength of the State, on a radical change in peasant psychology, on the necessity of understanding this process, on complete free will, on the adequate growth of peasant cadres [key personnel] for managing the future collectives, and finally on the strengthening and development of the existing producer-co-operative farms which would serve as examples for the peasant masses. Any artificial forcing, any skipping of stages, would be harmful and would undermine the change-over to producer-co-operative farming.'[1]

By 1951, then, it was clear that in Poland as well as Czechoslovakia capitalist elements in everything but agriculture had already become purely vestigial. Evidently the only thing left uncertain now was precise dates and final forms of clearance. The successive stages up to the final ones were already clearly marked and pursued with success. Very probably, in the writer's opinion, the concept, 'final liquidation as a class', would entail an actual change in the law of property. Hitherto, it will be remembered, the legal size of business and agricultural units had remained unchanged in spite of sharpening policy. But ultimately, if the writer's interpretation is correct, once the hold of vestigial capitalist elements had been thoroughly broken, especially in the country-side, the laws themselves would be altered as in the Soviet Union, to recognize and codify the new relations. If so, there might be complete legal prohibition, as in the Soviet Union, against hiring others for profit and against trading for profit in the produce of

[1] Paper read by Deputy Prime Minister Hilary Minc, at National Conference of Workers' Party, 9 October, 1951, *Information Bulletin of the Polish Press Agency*, Warsaw, 13 October 1951.

others' labour. In that case the last vestiges of the merchant as such, in all his forms, however petty, would go, along with all traces of the capitalist employer. Even the collective farmer would no longer be allowed to sell for a profit his neighbour's produce, only his own. Here and there the very small private farm would continue, spotted in in the back country beyond the great grain and meat collectives. Similarly with the occasional individual handicraft workshop. But in both cases they would perforce be limited in size to what one family could work without outside labour.

CHAPTER XVI

'SOCIALIST INDUSTRIALIZATION'

By the time the planned economies had entered the final, 'building of Socialism' stage of their transition, their attempts to follow Soviet economic methods had reached a new level. They looked back along their own past and forward to its end results in terms of detailed likenesses and differences to Soviet experience. They shared the same ideology. And they sought to absorb Soviet methods and Soviet technology in their most recent form in order to speed their own economic programmes.

The note of Communist ideology and the sense of forward pressure to still more rapid economic change was very evident in their latest Plans. 'The people have taken power', read the preface to the final version of Poland's Six-Year Plan, 'in a country devastated by war and Hitler's occupation. . . . The Polish masses led by the working class . . . have taken over the government in Poland, establishing and consolidating the State of People's Democracy, which is carrying out the basic function of the dictatorship of the proletariat.' On the economic side, '. . . Our country has been able to . . . burst the capitalist fetters which were hindering the development of productive forces. . . . The results achieved in the reconstruction period make possible the transition to a new stage: the building of Socialism. . . .' And a year later it was stated, 'The characteristic feature of our economic system is the steady and systematic general offensive of Socialism.'[1]

Soviet aid in speeding these countries' development plans was marked. Long-term trade and investment agreements in rising amounts bore directly upon a heightened technology. In the case of Poland,[2] an important part of the technical aid furnished con-

[1] Oskar Lange, 'Polish National Economy in the Second Year of the Six-Year Plan', Warsaw, 1951, p. 12 (in Polish). Dr. Lange at the time was rapporteur for the Parliamentary Commission on Economic Planning.

[2] As was noted in Chapter XIV, the second Soviet-Polish loan and trade agreement, entered into in 1950, had provided for a sharp rise in heavy investment goods for the next four years, with the same arrangement for payment in

sisted, as we saw earlier, in key portions, and in some cases wholes, of basic plants and processes. For example, the whole of the new Polish chemical industry, projected under the Six-Year Plan, was to be equipped with Soviet installations. So was the entire new iron and steel combine at Nowa Huta, near Cracow. 'Complete documentation' was said to accompany these installations, including a full setting forth of all patented processes.

Assistance from Soviet specialists was used. And technical delegations of all sorts from the two countries visited the Soviet Union. The Polish Government, stated President Bierut at the end of 1950, in discussing innovations under the Six-Year Plan, had asked for and received the services for several months of groups of Soviet specialists. 'The Soviet specialists made an analysis of our Plan in those branches which are of foremost importance to us: coal, metallurgy, machinery, chemicals, and power; they gave exceptionally valuable advice to our engineers and industrial managers; they corrected individual mistakes and made important suggestions. . . .' He added, significantly enough, a note on personal contacts: 'In the course of exchange of professional views and experience. . . . Polish engineers and industrial managers . . . were thus able to become acquainted with the talents, science, and style of work of a new intelligentsia. . . .'[1]

Several different notes were struck in regard to the interdependent progress of the planned economies. Emphasis was laid, as above, upon Soviet aid. At the same time emphasis was laid upon the 'flowering' of Czechoslovakia's and Poland's own tech-

the future products of those industries that Poland had already had chiefly with Czechoslovakia.

In the case of Czechoslovakia, raw industrial materials rather than development goods *per se* formed a major portion of her imports from the Soviet. In turn Czechoslovakia found in the Soviet a market for finished products of light industry, while her own heavy production chiefly went to build up her own industry and that of her smaller neighbours.

It was to be noted, however, that so far as Poland and Czechoslovakia's total pattern of east European trade went, it had become less centred upon the Soviet Union in the latest period: trade with eastern Germany and with the smaller planned economies had grown even faster. (Cf. United Nations, Economic Commission for Europe, *Economic Survey of Europe in 1950*, Geneva, 1951, p. 41.)

[1] 'Poland on the Path of Socialist Building', *Tribuna Ludu*, Warsaw, 2 December 1950; quoted in *Polish Facts and Figures*, London, 16 December 1950.

niques.[1] And emphasis was laid upon the importance of being able to count on current investment supplies from all the planned economies on a planned basis no different from that used for domestic manufacture: 'Now the supplies coming from the Soviet Union and the People's Democracies are planned on the same basis as those produced at home.'[2]

In seeking to follow Soviet methods and techniques, it was frequently urged that the newest of Soviet methods be the ones followed. There was no need to recapitulate successive stages of Soviet experience. 'We have the advantage of being able to take the experience of the Soviet Union for the latest period, that of the building of Communism,[3] with its "tempestuous" development of technique on the basis of a wide development of heavy industry.'[4]

Soviet achievements in post-war production were looked to for copying,[5] and so were *per capita* productivity rates, although at a remove.[6] Comparable figures could not be expected, but the

[1] Thus in opening the new Częstochowa steel works the manager boasted that 'every motor, every installation, even the most complicated . . . is the work of Polish workers'. (*Polish Facts and Figures*, London, 23 June 1951.)

[2] K. Sekominiski, 'Changes in the Methodology of Investment Planning', *Gospodarka Planowa*, July 1950, p. 541.

[3] Under future Communism, reward was to be on the basis, 'To each according to his need,' instead of '. . . to his work'; for this a very abundant prior creation of wealth was held to be necessary.

[4] Bronislaw Minc, 'Changes in the Methodology of Planning for the Year 1952', *Gospodarka Planowa*, Warsaw, July 1951, p. 9.

[5] In 1950 the Soviet Union had shown the highest production increase of any of the planned economies, 23 per cent over the previous year. The level reached was 17 per cent higher than planned for under the 1945–50 Plan. (Cf. United Nations, Economic Commission for Europe, *Economic Survey of Europe in 1950*, Geneva, 1951, pp. 39–41.)

[6] Soviet methods of avoiding inflation under increased productivity were also looked to for guidance. 'The question remains whether the benefits from increased productivity should be reaped in the form of lower prices . . . or higher money incomes. . . . The first alternative, which is that postulated by classical economic theory, has become the regular practice in the Soviet Union, where a series of price reductions have been decreed at the beginning of each year since 1948.' (Ibid., pp. 139–40.) The following year the statement was generalized: 'It is the declared policy of eastern European Governments to pass on the fruits of higher productivity in the form of price reductions rather than of adjustments of money wages. . . .' (U.N., E.C.E., *Economic Survey . . . for 1951*, Geneva, 1952, p. 111.)

The Economic Commission for Europe pointed out that the widespread adoption of incentive ('output') wages does not necessarily avoid the threat of inflation, if the increase in output comes largely in the capital goods field. 'Al-

methods of standard-setting ('norming') of work processes and machine loads could be followed.[1]

Even for agriculture the process could be begun.[2] The whole organization of incipient co-operative farming, on its technical side, could look to the 'brigade' and 'work-day-unit' methods of organizing and paying the labour of members on Soviet collective farms; the degree of admixture of private with co-operative economy in the more advanced types of co-operatives could copy the Soviet model; and even recent Soviet experience in amalgamating uneconomically small collective farms into larger ones could be followed, on a much more modest scale, in their own co-operatives. Soviet emphasis upon animal husbandry and upon ley farming, as also Soviet 'agrobiology' generally, were given wide publicity.

To be followed at a long remove were the very wide sweep of Soviet mechanization of agriculture, possible only to very large units, and the large Soviet programme of 'transforming nature' through drought control, and so on, undertaken in the most recent years.

In industry, much was heard of individual accountability, *khozraschot*, of economic enterprises, on the Soviet pattern, and of the reorganization of enterprises to make the working unit compact and strictly localized. And as part of the planning system also there was much more vigorous application of the combined techni-

though any increase in money earnings under this system is automatically matched by an increase in output, this may not avoid inflationary consequences if the increase in productivity is concentrated in the capital goods industries rather than in the consumers' goods industries.' (U.N., E.C.E., *Economic Bulletin*, Third Quarter, 1950, Geneva, 1950, p. 60.)

But this is precisely what the widespread drive in handicraft and distribution was calculated to prevent. 'Increases in productivity (in eastern Europe) were highest in the engineering and chemical industries, and in the light industries, where factory production took the place of the handicraft trades.' (U.N., E.C.E., *Economic Survey . . . for 1950*, Geneva, 1951, p. 38.)

In Poland for 1950 the year's increase in output of heavy industry had been 19 per cent and in light industry no less than 27 per cent. In Czechoslovakia the two figures had been 16 per cent and 11 per cent respectively. (Ibid., pp. 37–8.) Poland had of course started at a much lower level and worse organization of consumers' goods output to begin with.

[1] Cf. Chapter XI, pp. 218–9, and Chapter VII, pp. 134–5. Much was made during 1951 of the Soviet 'Kovalov method' of job analysis, a combination of worker and engineering analysis.

[2] Cf. Chapter XV, pp. 351–2.

cal-industrial-financial plan first developed in the Soviet Union, with its provisions for continuous financial check and multiform tie-ins between technical research and its applications to industry.

In labour relations there was much publicity of the latest forms of the labour emulation movement in the Soviet Union, particularly of its connections between ordinary workers and scientists. 'Rationalizers' clubs' multiplied in the smaller planned economies as well as in the Soviet Union. And emphasis was laid, comparable to that in the Soviet Union, upon the personal qualities of the star worker, his readiness and ability to analyse his new methods and transmit them to others.

The 'Law of Socialist Industrialization'

The planned economies followed Soviet formulation in treating of the industrialization process during the building of socialism as a 'law' of their development.[1] It was, of course, industrialization with a difference. The conception had been formulated in the Soviet Union during the early stages of its planning. A simple later expression of it is to be found in a well-known post-war speech of Stalin's to a meeting of voters in Moscow in 1946, in which he was describing what he called the 'leap' in industrialization that had taken place during the thirteen years prior to Germany's attack in 1941.[2]

Capitalist industrialization, said Stalin, had usually started with light industry, where initial investments could be small and returns relatively quick. It was only after the lapse of a considerable time, during which the profits from light industry could be accumulated and seek further investment outlets, that the large long-term financing necessary for heavy industry development had been attempted. Such a delay, he stated, had been impossible for the Soviet Union: it had therefore tackled the hard end first and with great sacrifice had constructed heavy industry.[3] At the same time, with the pressure for a more modern agriculture, and because

[1] Cf. Y. Yakovleva, 'The Socialist Industrialization of Poland', *Neue Welt*, Berlin, 1 June 1951, p. 106: 'Socialist industrialization is a law of development of the historical period of the transition from capitalism to a higher social order, to socialism.'

[2] Speech delivered by J. V. Stalin . . . 9 February 1946', *Information Bulletin*, Embassy of the U.S.S.R., Washington, D.C., March 1946.

[3] 'It was very difficult, but not impossible. A valuable aid in this work was the nationalization of industry and banking which made possible the rapid accumulation and transfer of funds to heavy industry.' (P. 11.)

the path of large-scale capitalist farming would in any case have been closed to it, collectivization and mechanization of agriculture had been undertaken. The fruits of the all round industrialization programme had proved themselves in the test of war. The country was now highly productive, after the shortest development period in history.

Such a theory of industrialization, militantly operative and centrally applied in each country, has undoubtedly been a major factor in the development of all the planned economies at the present time.

Industrialization on this model differs in its impact not only from the classic type of industrial revolution described by Stalin in the speech referred to, but from the projects undertaken in more recent times in undeveloped countries elsewhere. It has been noted repeatedly that even very large-scale imported development projects have a way of sealing themselves off from the rest of the economy of such a country, leaving the major, domestic portion of it in a backwater outside the currents of change.[1]

Projects intended meanwhile for the domestic portions of such economies have tended to remain small in scale and relatively unrelated to any powerful centres of development in the country.

The process of 'Socialist industrialization' has used both the forms of small local industry such as one hears of in connection with the domestic projects just referred to, and, most decidedly, some of the forms of very large single concentrations such as have been often operated by foreign capital. But its most characteristic feature is a third one, the distributing of industry in general throughout the territory of the industrializing nation. The idea has been, as was pointed out in Chapter VII, that no sizable region whatsoever should remain hinterland; none, however agricultural to begin with, should remain deprived of some good-sized industry of its own. The effectiveness of this policy in helping to bring forward the economies of such formerly backward territories as the Central Asian republics of the U.S.S.R. has apparently been very

[1] A recent writer speaks of the 'dualistic economic structure' of such countries, 'a high productivity sector producing for export co-existing with a low productivity sector producing for the domestic market. . . . The more productive export sectors have not become a real part of the economies . . . the process of traditional investment taken by itself has not been sufficient to initiate domestic development.' (H. W. Singer, 'The Distribution of Gains between Investing and Borrowing Countries', *American Economic Review, Supplement*, March 1950, pp. 474, 475, 477.)

great. On a smaller scale, and starting at an altogether higher level, a similar regional policy has been begun for Slovakia in Czechoslovakia and for some of the older central provinces of Poland.

Looking at this sort of industrialization geographically, one might picture the process as going on in triple form: many small growing points of local and light industry, in the interstices of the bigger ones; larger growing centres of large industry very broadly distributed indeed; and heavy concentrations of basic industry growing up to form solid stretches in a few major industrial regions. None of these, of course, certainly not the larger ones, and least of all those purposely planted in the previously undesired regions, would grow with the speed demanded unless there were powerful central planning to begin with, centrally organized investment funds ready to hand and unafraid of immediate consequences; and unless the connection between planning and operations were close. Given these conditions, however, the results could apparently be formidable.

Complementary to the 'Law of Socialist industrialization', as might well be expected, was another conception referred to in the planned economies as the 'Law of Socialist accumulation'. In order to provide for the great investment needs of industry, not only must productivity be increased but consumption must be kept below it. Stress on the latter point had begun earlier in Czechoslovakia than in Poland,[1] since wages there had not been so low to begin with. But by the end of the Three-Year Plan living standards in Poland had improved, and by 1950 we find Mr. Minc referring to 'the erroneous view that a growth of labour productivity must always be accompanied by an equal or greater rise in earnings'. 'We cannot . . . and will not apply this type of policy', he declared, 'during the period of the Six-Year Plan. It runs counter to the basic laws of socialist accumulation. These laws state that the increase of wages must progress more slowly than the increase of labour productivity, for only in this way can we obtain a lowering of prime costs and an increased accumulation for investment needs.'[2]

By late 1951 it was announced that for the first nine months of that year, investments had increased by over 50 per cent over the

[1] During the Three-Year Plan period, according to Mr. Minc, Polish productivity in industry had gone up 60 per cent while real wages had doubled.

[2] Vice-Premier Hilary Minc, 'The Six-Year Plan', Warsaw, 1950, p. 61.

year before,[1] and some months earlier it was stated that 'the turning point' had at last been reached in the relation between labour productivity and wages: productivity was now going up the faster of the two.[2]

It now looked accordingly as if the total proportion of the Polish national income devoted to investment would be able to approximate that of the Soviet Union. Czechoslovakia's had already reached that point. For 1951 Soviet investments had been at the level of 24 per cent, those of Czechoslovakia at 24·7.[3]

How much of the difficulties of this latest period of industrialization and investment had been enhanced by the economic policy of the Western powers, it would be difficult to estimate. Certainly strategic cutting off of trade had gone very far.[4] Possibly the net effect was rather to speed the processes of change than otherwise, in spite of the hardships involved. Certainly it speeded the two countries' efforts to achieve change.

By January 1952 the State Planning Commission of Czechoslovakia announced that 60 per cent of that country's trade was now with the other planned economies. Poland had already passed that figure the year before.

Meanwhile the combination of rapid 'Socialist industrialization', 'Socialist accumulation', the adoption of new techniques, and the organizational and social changes incident to the squeezing out of the remaining capitalist elements in small industry and trade, were going on as a more or less unified process.

The large production increases recorded in the period, however, had all been in the non-agricultural field. In agriculture the production-accumulation picture was very different. Output increases in agriculture for both countries under the Five- and Six-Year Plans were only expected to be at about half the rate of industrial,

[1] State Commission on Economic Planning, *Communiqué*, Warsaw, 23 October 1951. The figure cited was 54 per cent. By 1955 Polish investments were scheduled to more than treble in actual amount over 1949, and almost to double in terms of percentage of the national income.

[2] Bronislaw Minc, op. cit., *Gospodarka Planowa*, July 1951, p. 9. At the same time it was announced that while industrial production had gone up 20 per cent in the past year, retail trade turnover had increased only 8 per cent.

[3] Cf. U.N., E.C.E., *Economic Survey of Europe in 1951*, Geneva, 1952, and I.L.O., *Industry and Labour*, vol. VII, Geneva, 1 April 1952, p. 256.

[4] It extended to 'products which, while having a potential military value, are also indispensable to ordinary economic life and growth'. (U.N., E.C.E., *Economic Survey of Europe in 1948*, Geneva, 1949.)

and the faster industry's current rate of progress, the more striking the disproportions appeared.

People were being absorbed rapidly from agriculture into industry,[1] and on the whole their labour was not missed. But the industrial influx meant a heightened demand for marketable farm products, hence a further strain on the rural supply mechanism and the structure of rural prices, just at a time when the governments concerned were trying to get a strong grip on both. Patently, with the aid of a solicitous State purchasing apparatus, it was much easier to keep prices up for the farmer at periods when supply was over-abundant than to keep them down for the townsman when supply was scarce.[2] Systems of sale on contract, in process of being instituted, gave way periodically to 'the wind of speculation' in times of short supply.[3]

The answer of the planned economies' leaders to these difficulties was, more or less, that they must be lived through. 'Our agriculture is based at present and for a certain time will continue to be based predominantly upon small commodity economy.' 'It is necessary to understand . . . that the disproportions between the pace of industrial development and agricultural development are unavoidable and that they will for a long time accompany our agricultural development.'[4] 'In the preponderant part of agriculture we do not as yet have direct planning, and the influence of the State on its development takes place solely by means of planned regulation. The stronger the position of the State in the field of socialist industry, in the finance system, and in trade, the more

[1] In Poland a total of over a million was added to an existing industrial force of under 4 million in the two years 1949–51.

[2] As part of its agricultural programme, government price policy in all the transition economies had consistently favoured the farmer. Not only were farm produce prices supported, but the prices of farm equipment and fertilizer were kept low in relation to them. Much publicity was accorded these ratios. In effect, the city worker with his own wages strictly controlled, was thereby subsidizing the farmer.

[3] 'But, as it is known, the middle holder, who is the central figure of our agriculture, just as in other countries, has two souls: the soul of a working man and the soul of a small owner. It is a known fact that the middle holder oscillates between these two souls, and when the wind of market fluctuations and speculation is blowing . . . the oscillations . . . become more pronounced.' (Speech by Hilary Minc, Polish Press Agency, *Information Bulletin*, Warsaw, 23 October 1951.)

[4] Ibid.

effective does this planned regulation become.'[1] Only by yet further development of 'Socialist industrialization', the leaders held, could agriculture itself be 'saturated' with mechanical equipment and thus be prepared effectively to change its form, take the Socialist path, and become adequately productive.

Looking back upon the seven post-war years comprised in this account of the two transition economies, it is clear how sharply and increasingly the second half of the period differs from the first, with the year 1948 forming its watershed. Once the Communist parties of the two countries had sharpened their own ideology and had moved over into the forefront of the countries' political realignments, the whole pace of social transformation altered.

Starting with the prospect of a long and, in important fields, more or less static pause at a half-way stage of social change, the régimes moved over in the course of 1948 to the prospect of a quite different rate of change, with a very full, Soviet Union type of socialization as its next goal. The change was one from a perspective of several generations to a period of years; and from a process of hoped-for slav attrition if not indeed very gradual absorption of the private sector into socialism, to a process of active class struggle by the advocates of socialism and their State against all remaining forms of capitalist economy. Most of all, there was change from a picture of a long future for the private farmer, larger as well as small, to a picture of energetic preparations for the introduction of socialism here too, by the fostering of co-operative farms and by systematic discrimination against the economy of the larger farmer.

As compared with the history of the Soviet Union, the economic changes of the 'Popular Democracies' have been relatively simple. Here has been no single initial revolution, followed by long civil war, by the economic-retreat period of an N.E.P., by the gradual restoration of a shattered economy during many years, and finally by the dramatic and at the time untried attempts at heavy industrialization and the collectivization of agriculture. During all this period, it must be remembered, the initial political revolution in the Soviet Union already lay in the past: it was economic reorganization that was still to be made. In the 'Popular Democracies', on the other hand, a considerable body of important economic change had preceded the definitive period of new political orientation; and certainly in the case of Poland, at least, there was no one

[1] Hilary Minc, 'The Six-Year Plan', Warsaw, 1950, pp. 62–3.

moment of time when one could speak of 'the' political revolution being accomplished there. Finally, in its formative years every step actually taken in the Soviet Union in the economic field in pursuance of its picture of socialism, had been subject to the most violent disputes. Could industrialization beginning with heavy industry be accomplished at all? Could it be accomplished without foreign aid? How could farming possibly be brought into a socialist form, and if so, what one? And so on endlessly. In the case of the 'Popular Democracies', all these questions, in their opinion, had already been answered, broadly speaking and in terms of organization, by the theory and practice of the Soviet Union. Given political agreement, therefore, there was but little economic ground for basic doubts as to the feasibility of the countries' programmes and for prolonged searchings after new method. Matters of historical difference and special conditions could be thrashed out without pulling the whole subject of a new institution or even a technical means up by the roots to question it all over again. Whether in the process a number of potential new fruits of initiative were buried forever, and if so which ones, can of course never be known. In any case, many even of the most difficult of the practical economic problems of the smaller economies were now foreseen and discussed as having been handled before.

The 'Popular Democracies', finally, unfavourable as their economic situation was in many ways in a divided world, had the Soviet Union and the other planned economies to lean upon and deal with. The problem of 'socialism in one country' was never one confronting them.

It is perhaps no wonder then that the economic processes working in these countries were able on the whole to develop very rapidly, and that the latest stage of their transition away from capitalism had in it so much of technological transformation.

INDEX

Absenteeism, 96, 223; Polish law on, 228–9
Action Committees, 87, 124–5, 189, 280
Agriculture, 15–17, 28, 35–9, 49–53, 67, 72–4, 83–5, 98, 103–5, 120, 133, 192–4, Chap. XIII (257–89) *passim*, 340–57, 365–6; agricultural credit (*see* Banking, agriculture; Credit policy); agricultural labourers, 38, 50, 84, 90, 97, 210, 244 n, 250–1, 257, 258 n(1), 259, 262, 277–8, 280, 318; contracts system, 271, 274–6, 279–80, 329; machinery stations, co-operative, 268–72, 342; Machinery Stations, State, 259, 263, 268–72, 275; place in the economy, 66–7, 71–3, 128–9, 133, 133 n, 134, 244, 365–6, 366 n(2); Plans (*see also* Planning, indirect), 67, 127, 128, 193, 266, 272–6; strip system, consolidation of strips (commassation), 16, 193, 257–8, 263–4, 271, 283–6, 348. *See also:* Co-operative farms; Farmer, larger; Farmer, small and middle; Landed estates; Land reform; Manpower problems; Planning, agriculture; Private enterprise; Rationalization, agriculture; State Farms
Apprenticeship and vocational education, 75, 97, 97 n, 159–60, 177, 185, 268, 326. *See also* Workers, juvenile

Banking, 141–2, Chap. VIII (143–53) *passim. See also* Credit policy; Investments and investment planning
Bat'a-Svit concern, Chap. IX (176–96)
Bat'a, Thomas, 176–80
Beneš, Edvard, 79, 81, 86–7
Bierut, Bolesław, 359
Business cycles, crises, depressions, 16–17, 19, 20–1, 108, 161, 178, 193, 200, 237, 243, 290 n(2), 291, 303

Capital goods, 59–61, 67–8, 103, 310
Capitalist employer, 119, 209, 318–21, 324–5, 328; in agriculture, 210. *See also* Private enterprise
Children's allowances, 249–52
Child care, 187, 191–2, 251, 255–6
Classes, Working class; *see* Ideology; February events; Private enterprise, Capitalist employer; Nationalization; Farmer, larger; Farmer, small and middle; Agricultural labourers; Trade unions
Coal industry, 15, 19, 60, 102, 107–8, 110, 115, 132, 161–2, 164, 166–7, 169, 204, 208, 213, 213 n(5), 216, 218, 231, 226, 246, 249–50, 302, 306–7
Collective agreements, 206, 208–12, 216–17
Collective farms, 48–9, 244, 262–3, 287, 346 n(1), 351, 356. *See also* Co-operative farms
Cominform; *see* Tito-Cominform split
Committee of National Liberation (Lublin Committee), 5, 44–5, 50–1, 242
Communism, 'building of Communism', 137, 137 n(7), 138 n
Communists, Communist Party; *see* Political parties; Ideology; Popular Democracies

Compulsory labour, court restrictions on right to give notice, 229; legislation on, 211–12; under German Occupation, 24–5, 29, 33
Consumption goods, 59, 62–3, 66, 68, 103, 115, 338
Construction industry, 61–2, 64, 105–6, 108–9, 135, 157–8, 170, 223–4. *See also* Housing; Investments; War losses
Co-operative farms, 57, 88, 261–4, 286–9, 323–4, 342–57; establishment of, 261–4, 342–3; rates of growth, 287–9, 344; types of, 287–8, 344–8; work and pay (brigades; work-day system), 280, 288, 349 n, 350–4, 351 n(1), 351 n(2). *See also* Co-operatives, rural-all-purpose
Co-operative machinery stations; *see* Agriculture, machinery stations, co-operative
Co-operatives, 325–42; conceptions of, the 'Co-operative Sector' (*see also* Ideology), 8, 49–50, 56–7, 118, 119, 145 n(2), 148 n(2), 322–4, 332–4; consumers, co-operatives, 333, 338–9; industrial and handicraft, 127, 151–2, 325–8, 334–7; rural all-purpose ('unified agricultural'), 240 n, 264, 271, 276, 280, 281–7, 340, 343–4; State-co-operative wholesale, 329, 341–2; structure, and relation to governmental units, 282, 332–4, 337, 339, 341. *See also* Agriculture; Co-operative farms; Farmer, small; Trade, retail; Trade, wholesale
Council for Mutual Economic Assistance, 301–2, 310–12. *See also* Foreign trade, inter-eastern
Credit policy, 21, 52, 78, 98, 143–52, 269, 279–81, 285, 290, 296–7, 301 n(3), 309–10, 309 n(3), 312. 325, 328, 329. *See also* Banking
Currency reforms, 153 n(2), 303

Decapitalization; *see* Investment; War losses
Directed labour, 226–9
East–West trade; *see* Foreign trade, East–West; Economic Commission for Europe; Bilateral trade agreements; Multilateral trade
Economic Commission for Europe, U.N.E.C.E., 292, 295–7, 300, 301, 308 n(1), 309, 313
Education, technical and professional, 24, 26, 97 n, 186–7, 227–8, 234, 249–50, 268. *See also* Apprenticeship and vocational training; Manpower problems; Vocational guidance
Employment; *see* Manpower problems and policy
Equal pay principle, 8, 207–8
Estates; *see* Landed estates
Export problem, 60, 66, 72, 102–3, 104, 107–9, 110, 120, 123, 190, 194, 215. *See also* Foreign trade

Farmer, larger, 2, 51, 72–3, 88, 119, 128, 153 n, 241, 257, 258 n, 260, 263, 276–81, 318, 324
Farmer, small and 'middle', 2, 16, 51–3, 88, 97–8, 119, 128, 145, 153 n, 193, 241, 257–8, 258 n(2), 260, 260–1 n, 263, 271, 276–82, 288, 318, 324, 345–7, 357, 366 n(3)
Farmers' Self-Help Union, 274–5, 286, 333–4, 341. *See also* Agriculture; Farmer, small and middle
February events, 85–9, 106, 110, 124, 189, 239–40, 264, 319, 321
Finance; *see* Banking; Investments; Credit policy; Planning, financial; Taxation
Foreign trade, 18, 66, 67, 75, 102–5, 107–8, 110, Chap. XIV (290–314) *passim*, 318; apparatus of, 293–5; bilateral agreements, 290–1, 292–3, 301–2, 312–13; bilateral development pacts, 290, 303–8; concepts of planned trade, 290–3, 303–4, 307–8, 308 n(1), 308 n(2), 311 n, 312–14; Council of Mutual Economic Assistance, 310–12; East-West trade, 63, 107, 110, 194, 265, 274 n(2), 291–2, 295–302, 312–14; export

Foreign trade—contd.
licence system, 274 n(2), 297–300; inter-eastern trade, 302–3, 308–12, 365; trade and investment agreements with U.S.S.R., 308–10, 314. *See also* Export problem; Trade, State trading corporations

Germany, Eastern, Post-War relations with, 302–3, 303 n, 311–12, 312 n
Germany, Occupation policies, 23–33, 53, 78–80, 162, 164, 199; pre-war relations with, 17–18, 74, 78, 292; territorial losses, expulsion of Germans, 33–40, 82, 101, 305 n(3)
Gomułka, Władisław, 46–9
Gottwald, Klement, 126

Handicrafts; *see* Co-operatives, handicraft; Industry, local and small; Jews
Health service, 75, 115, 241, 242–3, 253, 331 n(2)
Holidays, paid, 246, 250–1, 254
Hours of work, 19, 75, 153, 179–80, 185, 210, 232–3, 250–1, 278
Housing, 62, 99, 103, 105, 106, 109, 178–9, 191–2, 215, 249. *See also* Construction industry; Living standards

Ideology, 1–3, 44–9, 49 n(1), 49 n (2), 80–2, 85–9, 90–3, 110, 119, 124–6, 132, 136 n, 137–8, 137 n(7), 197, 199, 202, 207, 317, 319–24, 332–3, 356–9, 367–8. *See also* Political parties
Income; *see* National income, National product, shares of
Industrialization, 48, 94, 100, 107, 129–32, 235, 257–8, 273–4, 302, 304, 306–10, 313–14, 359–60, 365–7; pre-war, Czechoslovakia, 71–2, 73–4, 92–3; and Poland, 17–21; Slovakia, 92–5; 'Socialist industrialization', 362–4. *See also* Ideology; Industry; Investments and Investment Planning; Plans; Plan fulfilment; Regional planning
Industry, coal (*see* Coal industry); construction (*see* Construction industry); heavy, 99, 103, 104, 106, 107–8, 109–10, 121–2, 130–3, 159 n, 226, 292, 312 n, 332, 364; leather (*see* Leather industry); light, 102–3, 107–8, 309, 311, local and small, 17, 74, 99, 104, 130, 170, 174–5, 324–5, 327–8, 337; machinery and metals (*see* Machinery and metals industry); Ministry of, Ministries of, 157–60, 170, 172, 337; textiles (*see* Textile industry). *See also* Co-operatives, industrial and handicraft; Industrialization; Nationalized industry; National income, national product; Plans, national, Plan fulfilment
Internats; *see* Apprenticeship; Juvenile workers
Inventions and innovations, 224–5, 225 n. *See also* Rationalization movement
Investments and investment planning, 58–62, 59 n(2), 62 n, 64, 74, 66–8, 99, 130–5, 138–46, 143–8, 163, 235, 290, 306, 310, 314, 322, 360, 364–5; investment-and-construction planning, 138–40, 139 n(2). *See also* Financial planning and accounting

Jews, 28, 29–32, 97–8, 325, 337. *See also* Minority populations; Population losses
Juvenile workers, 75, 96, 159–60, 177, 185, 208, 232. *See also* Apprenticeship; Vocational guidance; Social security

Košice Programme, 79, 81–4, 91

Labour emulation; *see* Output competition movement
Labour, juveniles, *see* Juvenile workers
Labour legislation; *see* Absenteeism; Agricultural labourers; Coal mining; Compulsory labour; Holidays, paid; Hours of work; Social insurance; Trades unions and works councils; Wages; Juvenile workers; Women workers

Labour market; *see* Manpower problems
Labour, Ministry of, 209–12, 226, 241–2, 243
Labour organization; *see* Trades unions and works councils
Labour productivity; *see* Productivity, labour
Labour, women; *see* Women workers
Land consolidation; *see* Agriculture, strip system
Landed estates, estate owners, 15, 16, 35, 51–2, 55, 73, 84–5, 90, 92, 97–8, 161, 253, 257, 259, 261, 318, 320
Landholding; *see* Co-operative farms; Farmer, larger; Farmer, small and middle; Landed estates; Land reform; Private enterprise
Landholdings, consolidation of; *see* Agriculture, strip system
Land reform, Czechoslovak, 82, 83–5, 88, 90, 92, 97–8, 257, 259–60; and Polish, 45, 50–3, 257, 260–1; pre-war, Czechoslovak, 72–3; and Polish, 15–17; land committees in, 51, 84; residual estates, 16, 73, 84–5; Slovakia, German policy, 78, 97–8
Land rent, 52, 288, 345–7, 348 n(3)–349 n
Leather industry, 59, 167, 176–90 309
Living standards, 129, 131, 207; Czechoslovakia, 74, 77, 83–4, 93–4, 96–101, 103, 105, 109–11, 115, 177, 183–4, 191–3, 213–16; Poland, 15–16, 19, 28, 29, 39, 52, 59, 61–4, 66, 67, 132, 138, 213, 213 n(5), 217, 244
Local planning, 118 n(2), 139 n(3), 140–1, 337
Lublin Committee; *see* Committee of National Liberation

Machinery and metals industry, 99, 127, 162–4, 270, 292, 302, 308
Manpower problems and planning, 63, 82, 94–5, 98–9, 101–3, 104, 109, 122, 135, 138, 162, 165–6, 208, 221, 225–34, 350, 366 n
Marshall Plan, 7, 11, 299
Mikołajcyk, Stanisław, 45, 260–1
Minc, Hilary, 54–5, 58–9, 119, 127–8, 354, 356, 364
Minority populations, 6, 15, 21, 22, 25, 28–32, 33, 34 n, 36–7, 39, 39 n–40 n, 71–2, 74, 77–9, 81–2, 84, 85, 91–8, 101, 109, 121, 162, 181, 193, 200, 261. *See also* Germans; Jews; Slovakia, problems of; Western territories

National committees, People's committees, 81–2, 87, 123, 140 n, 174–5, 183, 229, 275–6, 280, 284
National enterprises, forms of and relations between, 155–6, 165, 171–3, 195, 328
National Front, 80–3, 87, 91, 125–6, 202, 239
National income, national product, shares of, 65–6, 68, 109, 119, 136 n, 241, 355, 355 n(4)
National minorities; *see* Minority populations
Nationalized industry, Chap. VIII (154–75) *passim*, 183–90; Bat'a-Svit concern, Chap. IX (179–96) *passim*; internal structure and relation to Ministries and governmental units, 154–60, 167–8, 170–5, 195–6; labour relations, 168–9, 187–9; personnel and salaries, 162, 165–7; 'profits' and prices, 121, 155, 157, 158–9, 247, 254, 254 n(2), 294; relations to national planning, 160–1. *See also* Banking; Industrialization; Investments; Nationalization; Planning; Rationalization, industry
Nationalization, nationalization laws, 54–5, 80, 82–3, 89–90, 92, 94–5, 106, 123, 156, 160, 161, 162, 317, 318

Occupational rating scales, 217–219, 218. n(2); agricultural, 351–4, 351 n(3), 352 n(1), n(2)
Old age pensions, 241–2, 245–6. *See also* Coal mining; Social insurance
Output competition movement, 'socialist competition', 99, 221–4, 265, 362. *See also* Productivity, labour

Outrata, V., 120–2, 125–6

Piece wages; *see* Wages policy; Wages, premium pay

Planned economies, 66, 159 n, 161, 175, 237, 290–2, 301–3, 308, 310–14, 319, 352, 354, 358, 359–60, 362–4, 368. *See also* Popular democracies

Planning, local; *see* Local planning

Planning, national economic, 1, 7, 57–8, 102–4, Chap. VII (115–42) *passim*, 290–2, 311–12, 311 n, 312 n, 322, 332–3, 337, 360; agriculture (*see also* Planning, indirect), 116, 120, 128, 133–4, 192–4, 275–6; annual ('operative'), 68, 116, 138–41; beginnings of, Poland, 57–8, 60–1, 115–19; and Czechoslovakia, 119–26; check-ups on fulfilment, 116–19, 120–1, 135–6, 141–2, 144, 150; conceptions of (*see also* Ideology; Co-operatives, conceptions of), 118–19, 317; enterprise planning, 122, 135–7, 141, 153; financial planning and accounting, 58, 121, 123, 137, 141, 143–4, 241; indirect (*see also* Planning, agriculture; co-operatives), 104, 118, 118 n(2), 119, 120, 123, 128, 274–6, 324, 366–7; international, 139 n(3), 307–8, 310–12, 311 n, 312 n; multi-annual ('perspective'), 68, 116, 122; organs of, 117, 120, 121, 125, 134, 139 n(3), 140–2; regional (*see* Regional planning); sectional, 57–8, 115, 121; system of balances, 138–9, 138 n(2), techniques of, 134–42. *See also* Foreign trade, concepts of planned trade; Investments and investment planning; Manpower problems and planning; Plans; Planned economies; Regional planning; Urban planning

Plans, National, Czechoslovakia, Two Year Plan (1947–8), 85, 94, 100–6, 111, 121, 123, 125, 134–6, 174; and Five-Year Plan (1949–53), 94, 106–11, 124, 126, 255, 272–7, 291, 292, 393 n(1), 354, 365–6; Poland, Three-Year Plan (1947–9), 57–68, 115, 118, 136, 333; and Six-Year Plan (1950–5), 127–33, 137, 255, 265–6, 268, 272–7, 291, 322, 333, 354, 358–9, 364, 365–6. *See also* Planning, national economic

Political parties, Czechoslovakia, 1–2, 7–8, 75–9, 81–2, 85–9, 91–2, 100, 123, 125–6, 135, 190, 198–9, 202, 214, 239, 347 n(1), 367; Poland, 1–2, 7–8, 19–20, 44–9, 119, 200, 319, 322–3, 367

Popular Democracies, People's Democracies, 1–3, 7, 49, 88, 110, 124, 291n, 317, 319–24, 344, 346n, 352, 358–60, 367–8. *See also* Ideology; Planned economies; Socialism; Building of Socialism

Population losses and transfers, Czechoslovakia, 71, 78, 101, 162, 181; Poland, 6, 22–3, 26, 28–32, 37–40, 39 n–42 n

Price policy, 16, 18–19, 27, 51–2, 54, 56, 73, 83, 84, 150, 150n(3), 158–9, 159n, 177–8, 180, 190, 247–8, 275–6, 279, 281, 284, 290, 293–5, 309 n(3), 322, 326–7, 329, 331, 331 n(2), 360 n(6), 366, 366 n(2)

Private enterprise, private property, 49–50, 53–7, 65–6, 72, 82–3, 88, 90, 94–5, 106, 123, 124, 127–8, 151, 160–1, 206, 209, 247, 317–32, 337, 354–7, 365–7. *See also* Capitalist employer; Farmer, larger; Farmer, smaller; Ideology

Producers' goods; *see* Capital goods; Investments; Industry, heavy; National income, national product shares of

Productive forces, 59, 108, 127, 128, 308

Productivity, labour, 98, 102, 104, 110, 135, 177, 183–4, 197, 206, 223–5, 257, 265, 265 n(4), 266, 336. *See also* Output competition; Rationalization, agriculture; Rationalization, industry

'Profits' in nationalized enterprises; *see* Nationalized industry, 'profits' and prices

Rationalization, in agriculture, 133–4, 249–50, 257, 263–7, 267 n(2), 271, 273–4, 276, 283, 286, 345, 349–50, 351 n(2); in banking, 152–3; in foreign trade, 294; geographic division of labour, 307; in handicrafts, 335–7; in industry, 134–5, 155–65, 177, 183–4, 194, 230 n, 270; of labour (*see also* Output competition; Productivity, labour; Wages), 208, 223–5, 225 n; means of spreading, 224–5; in retail trade, 331, 338–9, 341. *See also* Inventions and innovations; Occupational rating scales; Output competition; Planning, financial and accounting; Productivity, labour

Rationing, 97, 123, 210, 210 n, 215–17, 216 n(1), 217 n(1). *See also* Living standards; Wages

Recruitment of labour, 226–8, 229, 234. *See also* Apprenticeship; Vocational guidance

Regional planning, 103, 109, 121–3, 122 n(3), 126, 128–34, 363–4

Rural trade, 57, 329, 340–2

Slovakia, problems of, 71–2, 77–9, 81–2, 84–6, 91–9, 100–1, 109, 111

'Small commodity production', 'simple commodity production', 119, 322, 366. *See also* Ideology

Socialism, 'building of Socialism', 5, 44, 46, 49, 110, 124, 137 n(7), 138 n, 143, 197, 304, 317, 320–3, 332, 358, 362, 367–8

Socialists, Socialist Party; *see* Political parties; Ideology; Popular Democracies

Social security (social insurance and allied benefits), Chap. XII (235–56), *passim*; administration, 237–8, 241–4, 251–3; benefit rates and qualifications, 244–6; conceptions of, 235–8, 247–8; costs and contribution rates, 240–1, 241 n(2), 244, 246–8; Czechoslovak system, 75, 198, 238–42, 244–6; and for farmers, 240, 240 n(1); Polish system, 19, 242–4, 244–6; social benefit, other forms of, 249–51, 253–6

Stalin, J.V., on industrialization, 362–3

State Farms, 67, 210, 258–9, 263, 264–8, 274, 278, 281, 284, 318, 344

State Machinery Stations; *see* Agriculture, Machinery Stations, State

State and mixed enterprises, pre-war, 19–21, 74, 154

State trading corporations; *see* Trade

Taxation, 123, 179, 190, 223, 236–7, 240, 247–8, 254, 279, 279 n(2), 285, 320, 322, 325, 328

Territorial changes, 6. *See also* Western territories

Textile industry, 59, 67, 95, 98–9, 102, 105, 107–8, 123, 164–6, 195, 292, 294, 309

Tiso régime, 78, 91

Tito-Cominform split, 2, 88, 106, 319

Trade, retail, 56, 127–8, 318, 329–31

Trade, State trading corporations, foreign and wholesale, 195, 294, 328–9

Trade, wholesale, 318, 329. *See also* State trading corporations

Trade unions and works councils, history and structure, 46, 74–5, 123, 125, 179, 182–3, 187–9, 197–202, 203–6, 210, 222, 223, 240, 250–3, 278; production emphasis, 106, 189, 197, 207; relation to nationalization, 89–90, 205

Transport, 58, 60, 61, 63–7, 63 n, 93, 103, 131

Unemployment and full employment, 8, 19, 75, 97, 102, 134 n(1), 169, 179–80, 198, 225–6, 235–6, 236 n(2), 237, 245

U.N.R.R.A. assistance, 15 n, 63, 162, 298–9

Urban planning, 115, 129–31, 129 n(1), 175, 195–6
U.S.S.R. influences, Chap. I (5–12), *passim*; 44, 64, 115, 129, 129 n(2), 130, 137, 143, 173, 237, 243, 246–7, 252, 254, 288, 293, 301–3, 301 n(2), 306–10, 314, 345–6, 346 n(1), n (2), 350–4, 358–64, 367–8
Vacations, *see* Holidays, paid
Vocational guidance and placement, 105, 230–2, 245. *See also* Apprenticeship; Directed labour; Manpower problems

Wages, 19, 178, 180, 184, 207–21, 292; premium pay, types of (*see also* Occupational rating scales), 219–21, 265; wages funds, wages planning, 139 n(1), 142 n(1), 209, 246 n(2); wages in kind, 210 n(3), 216–17; wage levels, comparative, 213–15, 213 n(5), 215 n(1), 278; wage policy, 97, 207–8; wage rate structure, rationalization of, 159, 183–4, 208–12, 216–17; wage setting, process of 188, 208–12
War losses, Czechoslovakia, 8, 78–9; Poland, 22–33, 35–7, 58–61
Western territories and border districts, 8, 33–43, 66–7, 101, 120, 131–2, 260, 347
Women workers, 8, 75, 183–4, 186–7, 246, 251–2
Work brigades, 102, 189, 192, 221–2
Works councils; *see* Trade unions and works councils

Founded by KARL MANNHEIM
Late Professor of Education in the University of London

Edited by W. J. H. SPROTT
Professor of Philosophy in the University of Nottingham

The International Library of Sociology and Social Reconstruction

ROUTLEDGE & KEGAN PAUL
BROADWAY HOUSE, CARTER LANE, LONDON, E.C.4

SOCIOLOGY OF EDUCATION

Mission of the University

JOSÉ ORTEGA Y GASSET. Translated and introduced by Howard Lee Nostrand *Second Impression.* 12*s.* 6*d.*

Total Education

A Plea for Synthesis

M. L. JACKS, *Director of the Institute of Education, Oxford*

Third Impression. 15*s.*

Education in Transition

A Sociological Analysis of the Impact of the War on English Education

H. C. DENT, *Late Editor of the "Times Educational Supplement"*

Fifth Impression. 14*s.*

The Social Psychology of Education

An Introduction and Guide to its Study

C. M. FLEMING, *Reader in Education, Institute of Education, London*

Seventh Impression. 9*s.* 6*d.*

Education and Society in Modern Germany

R. H. SAMUEL, *Professor of Germanic Languages, Melbourne,* and

R. HINTON THOMAS, *Lecturer in German, Birmingham* 14*s.*

The Museum

Its History and Its Tasks in Education

ALMA S. WITTLIN *Illustrated.* 25*s.*

Educational Thought and Influence of Matthew Arnold

W. F. CONNELL, *Senior Lecturer in Education, Sydney.* With an Introduction by Sir Fred Clarke 21*s.*

Comparative Education

A Study of Educational Factors and Traditions

NICHOLAS HANS, *Reader in Education, Institute of Education, London*

Third Impression. 21*s.*

New Trends in Education in the 18th Century
NICHOLAS HANS 18*s.*

From School to University
A Study, with special reference to University Entrance
R. R. DALE, *Lecturer in Education, University College, Swansea* 21*s.*

Education and Society
An Introduction to the Sociology of Education
A. K. C. OTTAWAY, *Lecturer in Education, Leeds.* With an Introduction by W. O. Lester Smith 18*s.*

German Youth: Bond or Free
HOWARD BECKER, *Associate Professor in Primary Education, Akron* 18*s.*

SOCIOLOGY OF RELIGION

Sociology of Religion
JOACHIM WACH, *Professor of the History of Religions, Chicago* 30*s.*

The Economic Order and Religion
FRANK KNIGHT, *Professor of Social Science, Chicago*, and THORNTON W. MERRIAM 16*s.*

SOCIOLOGY OF ART AND LITERATURE

Sociology of the Renaissance
ALFRED VON MARTIN, translated by W. L. Luetkens
Second Impression. 8*s.* 6*d.*

Chekhov and His Russia: A Sociological Study

W. H. BRUFORD, *Schröder Professor of German, Cambridge* 16*s*.

The Sociology of Literary Taste

LEVIN L. SCHÜCKING *Third Impression.* 8*s*. 6*d*.

Men of Letters and the English Public in the 18th Century, 1660-1744, Dryden, Addison, Pope

ALEXANDRE BELJAME, Edited with an Introduction and Notes by Bonamy Dobrée. Translated by E. O. Lorimer 25*s*.

SOCIOLOGICAL APPROACH TO THE STUDY OF HISTORY

The Aftermath of the Napoleonic Wars

The Concert of Europe—An Experiment

H. G. SCHENK, *Lecturer in Political Economics, Oxford* *Illustrated.* 16*s*.

Military Organization and Society

STANISLAW ANDRZEJEWSKI, *Lecturer in Sociology, Rhodes University*. Foreword by A. Radcliffe-Brown 21*s*.

SOCIOLOGY OF LAW

Sociology of Law

GEORGES GURVITCH, *Professor of Sociology, Sorbonne*. With an Intrduction by Roscoe Pound 21*s*.

The Institutions of Private Law and their Social Functions

KARL RENNER. Edited with an Introduction and Notes by O. Kahn-Freund 25*s*.

Legal Aid

ROBERT EGERTON, With an Introduction by D. L. Goodhart

Second Impression. 12*s*. 6*d*.

Soviet Legal Theory: Its Social Background and Development

RUDOLF SCHLESINGER, *Lecturer in Soviet Social and Economic Institutions, Glasgow* *Second Edition.* 25*s*.

CRIMINOLOGY AND THE SOCIAL SERVICES

Juvenile Delinquency in an English Middletown

HERMANN MANNHEIM, *Reader in Criminology, London School of Economics* 12*s*. 6*d*.

Criminal Justice and Social Reconstruction

HERMANN MANNHEIM *Second Impression.* 18*s*.

The Psycho-Analytical Approach to Juvenile Delinquency: Theory, Case Studies, Treatment

KATE FRIEDLANDER, *Late Hon. Psychiatrist, Institute Scientific Treatment of Delinquency* *Fourth Impression.* 21*s*.

The English Prison and Borstal Systems

LIONEL FOX, K.C.B., M.C., *Chairman of the Prison Commission for England and Wales* 30*s*.

Social Service and Mental Health

An Essay on Psychiatric Social Workers

M. ASHDOWN and S. C. BROWN 16*s*.

Voluntary Social Services since 1918

HENRY A. MESS, in collaboration with Constance Braithwaite, Violet Creech-Jones, Hilda Jennings, Pearl Jephcott, Harold King, Nora Milnes, John Morgan, Gertrude Williams and W. E. Williams

Edited by GERTRUDE WILLIAMS 21*s*.

The Social Services of Modern England
M. PENELOPE HALL, *Lecturer in Social Science, Liverpool*
Second Edition (*Revised*). 25*s*.

Crime and the Services
JOHN SPENCER, *Research Fellow in the Social Sciences, Bristol University*
28*s*.

SOCIOLOGY AND POLITICS

Social-Economic Movements
An Historical and Comparative Survey of Socialism, Communism, Co-operation, Utopianism; and Other Systems of Reform and Reconstruction
H. W. LAIDLER, *Executive Director, League for Industrial Democracy*
Second Impression. Illustrated. 35*s*.

The Analysis of Political Behaviour: An Empirical Approach
HAROLD D. LASSWELL, *Professor of Law, Yale* *Third Impression* 21*s*.

Dictatorship and Political Police
The Technique of Control by Fear
E. K. BRAMSTEDT 18*s*.

Nationality in History and Politics
A Psychology and Sociology of National Sentiment and Nationalism
FRIEDRICH HERTZ *Third Impression.* 28*s*.

The Logic of Liberty: Reflections and Rejoinders
MICHAEL POLANYI, F.R.S., *Professor of Social Studies, Manchester*
15*s*.

Power and Society

A Framework for Political Inquiry

HAROLD D. LASSWELL, *Professor of Law, Yale*, and A. KAPLAN, *Professor of Liberal Studies, Indiana* 23*s.*

The Political Element in the Development of Economic Theory

GUNNAR MYRDAL, *Professor of Economics, Stockholm, Executive Secretary, United Nations Economic Commission for Europe.* Translated from the German by Paul Streeten 25*s.*

FOREIGN AFFAIRS, THEIR SOCIAL, POLITICAL AND ECONOMIC FOUNDATIONS

Patterns of Peacemaking

DAVID THOMSON, *Research Fellow, Sidney Sussex College, Cambridge,* E. MEYER and ASA BRIGGS, *Fellow of Worcester College, Oxford* 21*s.*

French Canada in Transition

EVERETT C. HUGHES, *Professor of Sociology, Chicago* 15*s.*

State and Economics in the Middle East

A Society in Transition

A. BONNÉ, *Director of the Institute of Economic Research, Jerusalem*

Revised Edition in preparation

Economic Development of the Middle East

An Outline of Planned Reconstruction

A. BONNÉ *Third Impression.* 15*s.*

The Danube Basin and the German Economic Sphere

ANTONIN BASCH 18*s.*

Peasant Renaissance in Yugoslavia, 1900-1950

A Study of the Development of Yugoslav Peasant Society as Affected by Education

RUTH TROUTON 28*s.*

Transitional Economic Systems

The Polish-Czech Example

DOROTHY W. DOUGLAS 25*s.*

The Regions of Germany

R. E. DICKINSON, *Professor of Geography, Syracuse*

Second Impression. 12*s.* 6*d.*

Political Thought in France from the Revolution to the Fourth Republic

J. P. MAYER 14*s.*

Central European Democracy and its Background

Economic and Political Group Organization

RUDOLF SCHLESINGER 30*s.*

ECONOMIC PLANNING

Retail Trade Associations

A New Form of Monopolist Organization in Britain

HERMANN LEVY *Second Impression.* 18*s.*

The Shops of Britain

A Study of Retail Distribution

HERMANN LEVY *Second Impression.* 21*s.*

Private Corporations and their Control

A. B. LEVY *Two volumes. 70s. the set*

Plan for Reconstruction

A Project for Victory in War and Peace

W. H. HUTT, *Professor of Commerce, Cape Town* 21*s.*

SOCIOLOGY OF THE FAMILY AND ALLIED TOPICS

The Family and Democratic Society

J. K. FOLSOM, *Professor of Economics, Vassar College* 30*s.*

Nation and Family

The Swedish Experiment in Democratic Family and Population Policy

ALVA MYRDAL, *Director of the Dept. of Social Sciences, UNESCO*

Second Impression. 25*s.*

Adolescence

Its Social Psychology: With an Introduction to recent findings from the fields of Anthropology, Physiology, Medicine, Psychometrics and Sociometry

C. M. FLEMING, *Reader in Education, Institute of Education, London*

Third Impression. 18*s.*

Studies in the Social Psychology of Adolescence

J. E. RICHARDSON, J. F. FORRESTER, J. K. SHUKLA and P. J. HIGGINBOTHAM

Edited by C. M. FLEMING 21*s.*

The Deprived and the Privileged

Personality Development in English Society

B. M. SPINLEY, *Educational Psychologist, Sheffield Child Guidance Clinic* 18*s.*

Prosperity and Parenthood
J. A. BANKS, *Assistant Lecturer in Sociology, Leicester* 21*s.*

TOWN AND COUNTRY PLANNING. HUMAN ECOLOGY

The Social Background of a Plan: A Study of Middlesbrough
Edited by RUTH GLASS. With Maps and Plans 42*s.*

City Region and Regionalism
A Geographical Contribution to Human Ecology
ROBERT E. DICKINSON. With Maps and Plans
Second Impression. 25*s.*

The West European City: A Study in Urban Geography
ROBERT E. DICKINSON. With Maps and Plans 42*s.*

Revolution of Environment
E. A. GUTKIND *Illustrated.* 30*s.*

The Journey to Work
Its Significance for Industrial and Community Life
K. LIEPMANN, *Research Fellow in Economics, Bristol.* With a Foreword by Sir Alexander Carr-Saunders *Second Impression.* 15*s.*

Stevenage: A Sociological Study of a New Town
HAROLD ORLANS 30*s.*

The Genesis of Modern British Town Planning
A Study in Economic and Social History of the Nineteenth and Twentieth Centuries
W. ASHWORTH, *Lecturer in Economic History, London School of Economics*
21*s.*

SOCIOLOGICAL STUDIES OF MODERN COMMUNITIES

Negroes in Britain

A Study of Racial Relations in English Society
K. L. LITTLE, *Reader in Anthropology, Edinburgh* 25*s.*

Co-operative Living in Palestine

HENRIK F. INFIELD. With a Foreword by General Sir Arthur Wauchope *Illustrated.* 10*s.* 6*d.*

Co-operative Communities at Work

HENRIK F. INFIELD 18*s.*

Colour Prejudice in Britain

A Study of West Indian Workers in Liverpool, 1941-1951
ANTHONY H. RICHMOND, *Lecturer in Social Theory, Edinburgh* 18*s.*

Social Mobility in Britain

Edited by DAVID V. GLASS, *Professor of Sociology, London School of Economics* *In preparation*

Mobility in the Labour Market

MARGOT JEFFERYS, *Lecturer, London School of Hygiene and Tropical Medicine* 15*s.*

The Adsorption of Immigrants

S. N. EISENSTADT, *Head of the Department of Sociology, Hebrew University, Jerusalem* *In preparation*

ANTHROPOLOGY AND COLONIAL POLICY

The Sociology of Colonies: An Introduction to the Study of Race Contact

RENÉ MAUNIER, *Member of the French Academy of Colonial Sciences.* Translated from the French by E. O. Lorimer *Two volumes.* 63*s. the set*

A Chinese Village: Taitou, Shantung Province
MARTIN C. YANG 21*s*.

A Japanese Village: Suye Mura
JOHN F. EMBREE, *Associate Professor of Anthropology, California*. With an Introduction by A. R. Radcliffe-Brown *Illustrated*. 21*s*.

The Golden Wing: A Sociological Study of Chinese Familism
YUEH-HWA LIN, *Professor of Social Anthropology, Yenching*. Introduction by Raymond Firth 16*s*.

Earthbound China: A Study of Rural Economy in Yunnan
HSIAO-TUNG FEI, *Professor of Sociology, National Yunnan*, and CHIH-I CHANG, *Lecturer in Sociology, National Yunnan* *Illustrated*. 18*s*.

Under the Ancestors' Shadow: Chinese Culture and Personality
FRANCIS L. K. HSU, *Professor of Anthropology, College of Liberal Arts, North Western University* *Illustrated*. 21*s*.

The Mende of Sierra Leone
A West African People in Transition
K. L. LITTLE 28*s*.

Transformation Scene: The Changing Culture of a New Guinea Village
H. IAN HOGBIN, *Reader in Anthropology, Sydney* *Illustrated*. 30*s*.

Indians of the Andes: Aymaras and Quechuas
HAROLD OSBORNE *Illustrated*. 25*s*.

Religion, Science and Human Crises
A Study of China in Transition and Its Implications for the West
FRANCIS L. K. HSU 14*s*.

Colour and Culture in South Africa
A Study of the Status of the Cape Coloured People within the Social Structure of the Union of South Africa
SHEILA PATTERSON 30*s*.

The Family Herds

P. M. GULLIVER, *Government Sociologist, Tanganyika* *In preparation*

Growing Up in an Egyptian Village

HAMED AMMAR, *Lecturer in the Sociology of Education, Heliopolis University, Cairo* 28*s.*

SOCIOLOGY AND PSYCHOLOGY OF THE PRESENT CRISIS

Diagnosis of Our Time

Wartime Essays of a Sociologist

KARL MANNHEIM *Sixth Impression.* 18*s.*

Farewell to European History or the Conquest of Nihilism

ALFRED WEBER 16*s.*

The Fear of Freedom

ERICH FROMM *Sixth Impression.* 21*s.*

Freedom, Power, and Democratic Planning

KARL MANNHEIM. Edited by Hans Gerth and E. K. Bramstedt 25*s.*

Essays on Sociology and Social Psychology

KARL MANNHEIM. Edited by Paul Kecskemeti 25*s.*

SOCIAL PSYCHOLOGY AND PSYCHO-ANALYSIS

Psychology and the Social Pattern

JULIAN BLACKBURN, *Associate Professor of Psychology, McGill University, Canada* *Fifth Impression.* 14*s.*

The Framework of Human Behaviour

JULIAN BLACKBURN *Second Impression.* 15*s.*

A Handbook of Social Psychology

KIMBALL YOUNG, *Professor of Sociology, Northwestern University*
Fourth Impression. 28*s.*

Solitude and Privacy

A Study of Social Isolation, Its Causes and Therapy

PAUL HALMOS, *Lecturer in Social Psychology, Social Studies Dept., South West Essex Technical College* 21*s.*

The Human Group

GEORGE C. HOMANS, *Associate Professor of Sociology, Harvard* 25*s.*

Sigmund Freud: An Introduction

A Presentation of his Theories and a Discussion of the Relationship between Psycho-analysis and Sociology

WALTER HOLLITSCHER, *Professor of Philosophy and Sociology, Humboldt University, Berlin* *Second Impression.* 10*s.* 6*d.*

The Social Problems of an Industrial Civilization

ELTON MAYO, *Late Professor of Industrial Research, Harvard Business School* *Second Impression.* 15*s.*

Oppression

A Study in Social and Criminal Psychology

TADEUSZ GRYGIER. Foreword by Hermann Mannheim 28*s.*

APPROACHES TO THE PROBLEM OF PERSONALITY

The Cultural Background of Personality

RALPH LINTON, *Professor of Anthropology, Yale*
Third Impression. 12*s.* 6*d.*

The Feminine Character: History of an Ideology

VIOLA KLEIN. With an Introduction by Karl Mannheim 14*s.*

A History of Autobiography in Antiquity

GEORG MISCH, *Professor of Philosophy, Göttingen*. Translated by E. W. Dickes. *Two volumes.* 42*s. the set*

Personality and Problems of Adjustment
KIMBALL YOUNG *Second Edition* (*Revised*). 35*s.*

PHILOSOPHICAL AND SOCIAL FOUNDATIONS OF THOUGHT

Homo Ludens: A Study of the Play Element in Culture
J. HUIZINGA 18*s.*

The Ideal Foundations of Economic Thought
Three Essays on the Philosophy of Economics
WERNER STARK, *Reader in Economics, Manchester*
Third Impression. 15*s.*

The History of Economics in its Relation to Social Development
WERNER STARK *Third Impression.* 10*s.* 6*d.*

America: Ideal and Reality
The United States of 1776 in Contemporary European Philosophy
WERNER STARK 10*s.* 6*d.*

The Decline of Liberalism as an Ideology
With Particular Reference to German Politico-Legal Thought
J. H. HALLOWELL 12*s.* 6*d.*

Society and Nature: A Sociological Inquiry
HANS KELSEN, *Department of Political Science, California* 25*s.*

Marx: His Time and Ours
R. SCHLESINGER *Second Impression.* 30*s.*

The Philosophy of Wilhelm Dilthey
H. A. HODGES, *Professor of Philosophy, Reading* 28*s.*

Essays on the Sociology of Knowledge
KARL MANNHEIM 25*s.*

GENERAL SOCIOLOGY

A Handbook of Sociology

W. F. OGBURN, *Professor of Sociology, Chicago*, and
M. F. NIMKOFF, *Professor of Sociology, Bricknell*

Third Edition (*Revised*). 28*s*.

Social Organization

ROBERT H. LOWIE, *Professor of Anthropology, Chicago* 25*s*.

FOREIGN CLASSICS OF SOCIOLOGY

Wilhelm Dilthey: An Introduction

A comprehensive account of his sociological and philosophical work, with translations of selected passages.

H. A. HODGES *Second Impression.* 12*s*. 6*d*.

From Max Weber: Essays in Sociology

Translated, Edited, and with an Introduction by H. H. GERTH and C. W. MILLS *Second Impression.* 25*s*.

Suicide: A Study in Sociology

EMILE DURKHEIM. Translated by J. A. Spaulding and George Simpson 25*s*.

DOCUMENTARY

Changing Attitudes in Soviet Russia

The Family in the U.S.S.R.

Documents and Readings, Edited with an Introduction
RUDOLF SCHLESINGER 28*s*.

All prices are net

28454 THE WESTMINSTER PRESS, LONDON W.9